THE FIGHT FOR CHINA'S FUTURE

The Fight for China's Future throws light on the quintessence of 21st century Chinese politics through the prism of the struggle between the Chinese Communist Party (CCP) and China's vibrant intelligentsia and civil society.

This book examines Xi Jinping's 24-hour, multidimensional, AI-enabled police-state apparatus and explores the CCP's policy towards civil society. Through exclusive interviews with activists from different provinces, it analyzes the experiences and aspirations of key stakeholders in Chinese society, especially intellectuals, human rights attorneys and Christian worshippers. Providing an examination of recent global trends in relation to CCP policies, including China's relationship with the U.S., it also goes on to explore the possible trajectories of future change.

Featuring an assessment of Xi Jinping's leadership style and the opportunities this has given certain groups to promote the rule of law, media freedom and other global norms, this book will be invaluable to students of Chinese politics, society and culture.

Willy Wo-Lap Lam is Adjunct Professor at the Center for China Studies and the Department of History, Chinese University of Hong Kong, Hong Kong. He is the author of *Chinese Politics in the Era of Xi Jinping* (Routledge, 2015) and the editor of *Routledge Handbook of the Chinese Communist Party* (2018).

THE FIGHT FOR CHINA'S FUTURE

Civil Society vs. the Chinese Communist Party

Willy Wo-Lap Lam

Routledge
Taylor & Francis Group

LONDON AND NEW YORK

First published 2020
by Routledge
2 Park Square, Milton Park, Abingdon, Oxon OX14 4RN

and by Routledge
52 Vanderbilt Avenue, New York, NY 10017

Routledge is an imprint of the Taylor & Francis Group, an informa business

British Library Cataloguing-in-Publication Data
A catalogue record for this book is available from the British Library

Library of Congress Cataloging-in-Publication Data
A catalog record has been requested for this book

ISBN: 978-0-367-18866-5 (hbk)
ISBN: 978-0-367-18869-6 (pbk)
ISBN: 978-0-429-19891-5 (ebk)

Typeset in Bembo
by Taylor & Francis Books

For Grace, Ching-Wen, Wen-Chung and James

CONTENTS

ACKNOWLEDGMENT

History has its coincidences. No sooner had Xi Jinping amended the Chinese Constitution in March 2018 to enable him to rule for life than Donald Trump unleashed upon the People's Republic of China multiple salvoes in areas including trade, technology and geopolitical contention. The years 2018 and 2019 would be remembered as the beginning of a ferocious "new Cold War" between the status quo superpower that largely supports global norms, and a quasi-superpower that thrives on hard authoritarianism, a party-controlled economy, and an unprecedentedly tight control over the civil society and such of its components as dissidents, intellectuals, rights attorneys, house church followers and labor activists.

History, however, also has ironclad rules that punish those who have refused to draw the proper lessons from past fiascos. China's topsy-turvy history has been dramatized the past two years by a series of anniversaries. The year 2018 marked the 120th anniversary of the short-lived 100 Days Reform of the Qing Dynasty and the 40th anniversary of Deng Xiaoping's Era of Reform and the Open Door. The year 2019 marked the centenary of the May Fourth Movement, the 125th anniversary of the beginning of the First Sino-Japanese War, and, of course, the 70th birthday of the People's Republic of China. While trying to fend off constant surveillance and harassment by Xi's AI-enabled police state apparatus, intellectuals and NGO pioneers are wrestling with some overwhelming questions. For example, although CCP leaders ranging from Jiang Zemin to Xi Jinping have insisted that "Western" values such as rule of law and civil rights are not suitable for China's *guoqing* ("national conditions"), Marxism not only hails from the West but is widely regarded as a failed creed by European and American intellectuals. (In May 2018, Xi lavishly celebrated Marx's 200th birthday and even sent a five-meter statue of the thinker to his birthplace Trier. But most Germans were lukewarm toward the controversial founder of Marxism and Communism.) Many of the mistakes made by the CCP during the Mao era were partly due to the Great

Helmsman's self-serving misinterpretations of the teachings of Marx and Lenin; yet Mao disciple Xi seems destined to perpetuate blunders such as erecting a personality cult around himself, upholding the party's monopoly on power, tightening the "dictatorship of the proletariat" and squashing the breathing space of intellectuals and other activists in the country's fast-growing civil society. Despite the pranks that history seems to have played on China, civil society pacesetters are adamant that the Cultural Revolution (1966–1976) and related mistakes must never be allowed to recur.

While pondering such weighty issues, I have benefited from much-needed encouragement, expert advice and timely tips, tea and sympathy from the following friends and colleagues: Robert Barnett, Jean-Philippe Béja, Bo Zhiyue, Keith Bradsher, Anne-Marie Brady, Kerry Brown, Jean-Pierre Cabestan, Anson Chan, Jane Chan, Chan Kin-man, Priscilla Chan, Gordon Chang, Nicholas V. Chen, Helen Cheng, Joseph Y.S. Cheng, Pearl Chih, Ching Cheong, Linda Choy, David Faure, Edward Friedman, Chloé Froissart, Brad Glosserman, Ryoichi Hamamoto, Harry Harding, Chiew-Siang Bryan Ho, Russell Hsiao, Bertel Heurlin, Hung Ching-tin, Peter Jennings, Jan Kiely, Amy King, Timmy Kwai, Patricia Kolb, Carol Lai, Jimmy Lai, Lai Ming Chiu, Diana Lary, Emily Lau, Franky F.L. Leung, Theresa Leung, Angela Li, Linda Li, Joe Lian Yi-Zheng, Lee Yee, Albert Lim, Delia Lin, Perry Link, Dimon Liu, Sonny Lo, Paul Loong, Bruce Lui, Michelle Ng, Mak Yin-ting, Norihito Mizuno, Jeanne Moore, Ng Ka Po, Joyce Nip, Minxin Pei, Eva Pils, David Shambaugh, Simon Shen, Victor Shih, Claude Smadja, Masaru Soma, Volker Stanzel, Robert Suettinger, Norihiko Suzuki, Carina Szeto, Akio Takahara, Marina Thorborg, Luigi Tomba, Kristof van den Troost, Steve Tsang, King Tsao, Jonathan Unger, Sebastian Veg, Arthur Waldron, Kan-Tai Wong, Pak Nung Wong, Alfred Wu, Guoguang Wu, Wu Lik-hon, Ray Yep, Chris Yeung, Yukiko Yokono, Fong-ying Yu, Maochun Yu, Ricky Yue and Zhang Baohui.

I would like to express my gratitude to the Smith Richardson Foundation, whose generous support has been crucial to the success of this project. Thanks are particularly due to the Foundation's Senior Program Officer Allan Song for his advice and counsel. The Jamestown Foundation, of which I've been a nonresident Senior Fellow since the early 2000s, has been an unfailing source of encouragement and support. I salute, in particular, President Glen Howard for many years of unfailing help.

Special thanks are due to the editorial, production and marketing staff of Routledge for taking very good care of this manuscript. I am particularly indebted to the generous help of Publisher, East Asia Stephanie Rogers and Senior Editorial Assistant Georgina Bishop. I would like to record my gratitude to the Notre Dame University Press for permission to reuse tidbits of my chapter on the Chinese intellectual in *Public Intellectuals in the Global Arena: Professors or Pundits?* (2016). Two good friends, C.W. Li and Verna Yu, have helped me with research, particularly regarding Chapter 5.

Since 2007, I have been associated with the Chinese University of Hong Kong (CUHK) as an Adjunct Professor in its History Department, the Center for China

Studies, and the Master's Program in Global Political Economy. I am much indebted to my CUHK colleagues for their unfailing guidance and support. While researching this book, I have also benefitted from the help of the following institutions: the China Human Rights Lawyers Concern Group (especially Albert Ho); the China Labor Bulletin (Geoffrey Crothall and Han Dongfang); and the Divinity School of Chung Chi College, Chinese University of Hong Kong, and its Director Professor Ying Fuk-tsang.

I must also salute my siblings for several decades of warm support and close camaraderie: my sisters Pansy, Kin-Hung, Miranda and Leslie, and brothers Wo Hei and Justin. Above all, I must express my gratitude for the spiritual and other support that my dear, sweet wife, Grace, has given me for so many years. We are very thankful to have two loving, smart, and kind-hearted children, Ching-Wen and Wen-Chung. I am somewhat optimistic that my grandson James will see a China that is more in tune with universal values such as rule of law, freedom of expression and democratic elections.

LIST OF ABBREVIATIONS

ACFTU	All-China Federation of Trade Unions
AIIB	Asia Infrastructure Investment Bank
ASEAN	Association of Southeast Asian Nations
BRI	Belt and Road Initiative
CAC	Cyberspace Administration of China
CAS	Chinese Academy of Sciences
CASS	Chinese Academy of Social Sciences
CCAC	Central Cyberspace Affairs Commission
CCCDR	Central Commission for Comprehensively Deepening Reforms
CCDI	Central Commission for Discipline Inspection
CCFA	Central Commission for Foreign Affairs
CCFE	Central Commission for Finance and Economics
CCP	Chinese Communist Party
CCPIW	Central Commission for Propaganda and Ideology Work
CCTV	China Central Television
CDP	China Democracy Party
CGF	China Gospel Fellowship
CHRLG	China Human Rights Lawyers Group
CICIR	China Institutes of Contemporary International Relations
CLB	China Labor Bulletin
CMC	Central Military Commission
CNSC	Central National Security Commission
COD	Central Organization Department
CPLC	Central Political-Legal Commission
CPPCC	Chinese People's Political Consultative Conference
CSL	Cybersecurity Law
CUFWD	Central United Front Work Department

CYL	Communist Youth League
CYLF	Communist Youth League Faction
ERAO	Ethnic and Religious Affairs Office
FYP	Five-Year Plan
GDP	Gross Domestic Product
LGBT	Lesbian, gay, bisexual and transgender
MCA	Ministry of Civil Affairs
MOC	Ministry of Commerce
MOF	Ministry of Finance
MOFA	Ministry of Foreign Affairs
MPS	Ministry of Public Security
MSS	Ministry of State Security
NCM	New Citizens' Movement
NDRC	National Development and Reform Commission
NPC	National People's Congress
OBOR	One Belt One Road
PAP	People's Armed Police
PBoC	People's Bank of China
PBSC	Politburo Standing Committee
PHSA	Protect the Harbor Seal Association
PLA	People's Liberation Army
PRC	People's Republic of China
RMB	Renminbi
SAR	Special Administration Region
SARA	State Administration of Religious Affairs
SASAC	State Assets Supervision and Administration Commission
SEAC	State Ethnic Affairs Commission
SOE	State-owned Enterprise
SPC	Supreme People's Court
TAR	Tibet Autonomous Region
VPN	Virtual Private Network
WTO	World Trade Organization
XUAR	Xinjiang Uyghur Autonomous Region

1

INTRODUCTION

The civil society versus Xi Jinping's police-state apparatus

Introduction:
how a hard-authoritarian state squeezes freedom of thought and the public sphere

In its late 2017 report on the global development of the public sphere in more than 100 countries, the World Alliance for Citizen Participation (CIVICUS) downgraded China's rating from "repressed" to "closed." CIVICUS deplored the "continued escalation of the assault on basic civil freedoms under Xi Jinping." The Johannesburg-based watchdog noted that "China has since 2015 relentlessly pursued its critics through mass arrests of lawyers and activists, the shutdown of websites promoting peaceful dialogue and the deployment of security forces [against dissidents and NGO groups]." It suggested that the already besieged civil society in China would be further circumscribed by new laws on NGOs and on state security.[1]

Although the CCP administration's suppression of intellectuals, rights attorneys, house church worshippers and other civil-society participants has been widely commented upon, this chapter attempts to elucidate the peculiarly Chinese characteristics of the battle between hard authoritarianism on the one hand and civil-society crusaders on the other. Up until the early 2010s, the leadership under ex-President Hu and President Xi had won plaudits for its economic success from opinion makers, even in democracies such as the United States. Yet economic problems including massive debt, poor industrial performance, lackluster consumer spending and over-dependence on government input to stimulate growth have come to the fore. Hong Kong-based labor NGOs reckon that the number of reported strikes – probably just a portion of the total figure – surged from fewer than 200 in 2011 to 1,256 in 2017. The estimated annual cases of "mass incidents," or protests and demonstrations, were 180,000 in 2010, the last year when figures were available.[2] In an apparent effort to preempt disturbances that could come in the wake of an economic downturn, the party-state apparatus has put together a high-tech police-state apparatus that has left little room for maneuver for intellectuals and other civil-society affiliates.

However, the unexpected events of 2018 have not only further exposed weak links in Xi Jinping's bid to attain the proverbial "long reign and perennial stability" for the party and for himself, they have also given an opening to intellectuals, human rights attorneys, house church campaigners and the NGO community in general. Xi, who has changed the Constitution to enable himself to rule for life, has failed to tackle the challenges posed by President Donald Trump on both the economic and geopolitical fronts. While the Xi leadership has repeatedly succumbed to American pressure on the trade front – such as agreeing to buy more American products while curtailing tariffs on U.S.-made autos – it has failed to prevent the bilateral fracas from deteriorating into a full-fledged Cold War. More significantly, the fervent disciple of Chairman Mao has refused to pick up on the threads of Deng Xiaoping's market reforms despite strong support for liberalization coming from the great majority of Chinese who are beneficiaries of Deng's dispensations. Moreover, the bulk of Trump's complaints about Beijing's economic policy are precisely targeted at the Xi leadership's insistence on the Maoist credo of strict party control over the economy.

The paramount leader is in no danger of losing his power. However, his perceived failure to rectify the economy – and in particular his inability to avert a head-on collision with the U.S. – has resulted in criticisms emanating from different sectors of the party and the populace. They include princelings (kin of party elders) close to the Deng Xiaoping clan; pro-market cadres, particularly in the central government; private entrepreneurs; and members of China's estimated 400 million middle class who are nervous about a decline in their standard of living.[3] Members of the civil society, particularly intellectuals, journalists, professors, jurists and rights attorneys, have piggybacked on these anti-Xi sentiments to press their case for universal values such as rule of law and respect for human rights (see Chapter 5).

Increasingly bold calls for reform in the public sphere, however, are being ruthlessly crushed by the CCP regime. The chapter argues that an integral goal – and signature policy – of the party since the days of Mao Zedong has been to emasculate the freedom of individuals and to crush non-party-affiliated social groupings. Explanations will be given as to why it is second nature for party leaders to nip potentially destabilizing forces in the bud. As "core leader" Xi gets ready to mark the centenary of the founding of the CCP in 2021, he is following time-honored tradition by denying anti-establishment forces any platform to operate anywhere in China. Both Mao and Xi consider society – especially arenas having to do with ideology and thought – as a front or combat zone over which the party must have total control.[4] Despite the fact that, after 70 years, the rule of the People's Republic seems well entrenched, the party leadership is obsessed with taking out perceived rebels, saboteurs and myriad enemies through never-ending skirmishes on the Chinese battlefield.

Herein lies perhaps the biggest paradox of Xi's China. On the one hand, the Xi administration waxes eloquent about the fact that party members and citizens alike boast a "fourfold self-confidence" – self-confidence in the path, theory, system and culture of socialism with Chinese characteristics. Xi exudes confidence that the CCP will remain China's "perennial ruling party."[5] At the same time, Xi, who became what his critics call "Emperor for Life" at the 19th Party Congress of 2017, is paranoid about the most infinitesimal challenge to CCP authority. As the Chinese proverb goes, the supreme leader seems to see "an enemy soldier behind every tree and every stalk of grass." The most convincing explanation seems to be that the party – which portrays itself as always "great, brilliant and correct" – has too many things to hide. Intellectuals, as well as NGO activists, have laid bare the core causes behind party-initiated disasters ranging from the Great Leap Forward to the Tiananmen Square massacre: the top leadership's total refusal to share power with disparate sectors of society. Also exposed to all Chinese are the glaring imperfections of the "China model," or what Xi called at the 19th Party Congress "Chinese wisdom and the Chinese blueprint." Moreover, the CCP is paranoid about the possibility that social or religious groupings could metamorphose into alternate centers of power that are comparable to the Solidarity Movement and the Catholic Church in Poland.

The sections below delineate the CCP's multidimensional measures geared toward subjugating the individual and compressing the breathing space of the civil society and public sphere. The brutal and despotic policies of *zuigaotongshuai* ("Supreme Commander") Xi will be compared with the relatively tolerant approaches of ex-Presidents Jiang Zemin and Hu Jintao. The party's post-Orwellian, artificial intelligence (AI)-enabled police-state apparatus will be examined. This chapter ends by looking at how civil-society groupings are fighting back. An assessment will be made as to whether NGO pace-setters are poised to make contributions toward political liberalization despite Beijing's relentlessly escalating repression.

The subjugation of the individual

How the party crushes individualism

A widely circulated 2015 article entitled "How many people with conscience has God left in China?" has summed up the plight of Chinese who don't want to become a cog in the machinery of "socialism with Chinese characteristics." Not since the late Qing Dynasty – when Chinese intellectuals started their "self-strengthening movement" as well as a quixotic quest toward democracy – have the Chinese been so disappointed by their dictatorial rulers. The anonymous article, which is a collection of quotations from famous personages, cited intellectuals as telling how the party-state machinery had tried to reduce them to minions and serfs of the "dictatorship of the proletariat."[6] For Zhou Ruijin, a prominent member of the Chinese Academy of Social Sciences, the social contract between officials and ordinary folks has been sundered. "Officials think their mission is to rule and manage people – and there is no concept of service," he noted. "They think that if you are disobedient and do not follow instructions, they can lock you up."[7]

Well-known novelist Zhang Kangkang went further regarding the party-state apparatus's determination to brainwash citizens into submission. Zhang argued that the party "could, if need be, transform everybody into the same type [of people]. They are a highly efficient machinery and they have for the past few decades been churning out a product called slave."[8] Zi Zhongyun, a ranking expert on America studies who was once Mao Zedong's interpreter, agrees. Zi was convinced that the mission of China's most prestigious institutes of learning was to "to recruit the most talented students and then to destroy them [...] This is a heinous crime against heaven and earth." Zi expressed fears about the "degeneration of the [qualities] of the Chinese race."[9]

For several years before the Tiananmen Square crackdown, Deng Xiaoping and such of his liberal disciples as former Party Secretaries Hu Yaobang and Zhao Ziyang tried to liberate the minds of not only officials and intellectuals, but also ordinary Chinese from the yoke of stultifying Maoism. The very notion of "thought liberation," which was the rallying call of then-General Secretary Hu Yaobang (1915–1989) and such of his colleagues as President Xi's father, party elder Xi Zhongxun (1913–2002), presupposed that all citizens were entitled to their own way of thinking – and that they should be free to absorb whatever is best in both the Eastern and the Western traditions.[10] Hu and Deng – at least before the latter turned conservative by the mid-1980s – supported the slogan of liberal intellectuals: "Practice is the sole criteria of truth." Hu, who was sacked from his position of general secretary after the first wave of the student movement in December 1986, even went so far as to say that "Marxism cannot solve all the problems of today."[11] For President Xi, however, truth is what the *zhongyang*, or the central party leadership symbolized by himself, says. And party members, and by extension well-educated professors and professionals, cannot *wangyi* ("make groundless criticism of") the *zhongyang*. [12]

Dangxing versus individualism: intellectuals as cogs in the socialist machinery

Much of the CCP's dogma about the relationship between intellectuals and ordinary citizens on the one hand and the party-state apparatus on the other is encapsulated in Mao Zedong's idea that individuals are no more than humble servants and serfs of the party machinery. Following Marx and Lenin, Mao indicated that every person has a "class nature" and a *dangxing* ("party nature"). The goal of the party-state authorities is to ensure that citizens – particularly those who belong to "black categories," such as capitalists and bourgeois-liberal intellectuals – should undergo self-transformation and thought reform until they have totally subsumed their individuality under a bona fide "proletariat class nature." Mao also noted that not only CCP members, but all Chinese, should acquire the requisite *dangxing* ("party nature"), meaning that their thoughts, goals and aspirations should all dovetail with the party's requirements.[13]

In his "Talk at the Yan'an Forum on Literature and Art" of May 1942, the Great Helmsman argued that the triumph of *dangxing* would "curtail [the phenomena of] 'individualism,' 'heroism' or 'anarchy' among less committed party members." The corollary of this insistence on "pure upon pure *dangxing*" is that every party cadre and member should be transmuted – through brainwashing and other means – into a figure like Lei Feng, the altruistic proletariat hero lionized by Mao in the 1950s.[14]

Moreover, Mao's interpretation of Marxism-Leninism not only consigns every Chinese to the role of a slave of the party machinery, but also insists that all knowledge must be politically correct and at the service of the regime. Thus, the Great Helmsman underscored the fact that the *dangxing* theory applied to all kinds of knowledge. He admonished proletariat writers and artists to "take the stand of the party, take the stand of *dangxing* and the party's policies."[15] According to Mao, art – together with other forms of knowledge and expertise – has no innate self-sufficiency of its own: it must subserve the higher cause of the revolution. "There is in fact no such thing as art for art's sake, art that stands above classes, or art that is detached from or independent of politics," Mao said. "Proletarian literature and art are part of the whole proletarian revolutionary cause." Citing Lenin, Mao argued that intellectuals and citizens were but "cogs and wheels in the whole revolutionary machine."[16] As knowledge – and what goes through people's minds – must totally dovetail with *dangxing*, it is not surprising that Mao devised all sorts of thought control techniques to help CCP members and even ordinary citizens get rid of politically suspect ideas. As Mao put it in another speech during the Yan'an era, there are many fully registered CCP members "who in their thoughts have not fully joined the party – or who have not joined the party at all." He pointed out that the brains of these unqualified members were full of *zangdongxi* ("dirty things") like those of the exploitative classes.[17]

Mao's fans included President Xi, who has endorsed many of the tyrant's most insidious proclivities. The fifth-generation leader gave a strong reaffirmation of the *dangxing* theory in his August 19, 2013 talk to cadres in charge of ideology and propaganda, when Xi pointed out unequivocally that,

> *dangxing* and *renminxing* ["the nature of the people"] have always been uniform and unified [...] Upholding *dangxing* means upholding the nature of the people ... There is no *dangxing* that is alienated from the nature of the people, and similarly there is no nature of the people that has forsaken *dangxing*. [18]

In other words, ideas and aspirations of the people that are prejudicial to the party's interests must be banished (see Chapter 2). Marxist theorist Yang Faxiang even claimed that *dangxing* is the amelioration and sublimation of *renxing* ("human nature"). "*Dangxing* serves as guidance to social development and is acquired and followed by advanced members of society," Yang claimed. "People with high-quality *renxing* may not qualify to be a superior party member, yet those with high-quality *dangxing* must necessarily evince *renxing*."[19]

Despite Xi's claims that he is a disciple of Great Architect of Reform Deng Xiaoping, there is a fundamental difference between the epistemology and world-view of the two leaders. It is true that Deng was adamant about party members heeding the "Four Cardinal Principles" of socialism and CCP leadership. Yet, at least before the Tiananmen Square crackdown, Deng adopted an open-minded – and near-heretical – approach to orthodox theories and doctrines, including ways and means of running the economy and society. Unlike Xi, who stresses that everything must be conceived and executed using *dangxing* as a yardstick, Deng advocated the famous "doctrine of the non-insistence of surnames."[20] This variation of the "two cats theory" meant that, when the party evaluates goals and policies, it should not be bogged down by arguments as to whether they are "surnamed socialist or surnamed capitalist." All that matters is whether the goals and policies in question are capable of producing beneficial results. Using Deng's figure of speech, Xi would have serious objections to economic and social theories and policies that are "surnamed capitalist."[21]

Xi Jinping's talk on literature and the arts

President Xi has revived theories about literature and the arts that are a throwback to the strictures of Maoism, which militate against not only global norms, but also former Chinese leader Deng Xiaoping's ethos about the open-door policy. In October 2014, Xi presided over a seminar on literature and the arts for several dozen exemplary "engineers of the soul," or writers, artists, musicians and performers who had received official plaudits for singing the praises of orthodox values. The unusual conclave was modeled upon Chairman Mao Zedong's Yan'an Talks on Arts and Literature, held in the Shaanxi revolutionary base in 1942.[22]

The CCP general secretary admonished these top intellectuals to "take patriotism as the leitmotif for artistic creation [...] We must provide guidance for people to establish and uphold correct views about history and the state ... so that their integrity and backbone as [model] Chinese will be enhanced," said the party boss. At first, Xi went through the motions of reiterating the Maoist ideals of "letting a hundred flowers bloom, a hundred schools of thought contend." It was clear, however, that Mao – and Xi – was using these nice-sounding words to, in his words, "coax the snakes to come out of their pits."[23]

"We must develop academic democracy, cultural democracy ... and advocate the full discussion of different viewpoints and schools of thought," Xi said at the meeting. Yet the speech was a stern embodiment of Maoist orthodoxy, beginning with the late chairman's innocuous-sounding slogan of "serving the masses." "Literature and the arts should reflect well the people's voices," the supreme leader said, and added:

> They must uphold the fundamental direction of serving the people and serving socialism [...] This is a fundamental demand that the party has made ... and whether [the serve-the-people credo] can be fulfilled will determine the future and fate of our literature and the arts.

Reverting to the crass rhetoric of the commissars, the general secretary urged cultural workers to "use light to dissipate darkness, use beauty and goodness to win over ugliness … and let the people see that goodness, hope and dreams lie right in front of them."[24] The obvious corollary is that works that cast doubt on the greatness of Chinese-style socialism and the glorious achievements of the party should be eliminated.

Although Xi cited the importance of "the fusion of Chinese and Western [traditions]," he repeated Mao's dictum that "things from abroad should subserve Chinese needs."[25] Xi saluted the works of ultra-nationalist blogger Zhou Xiaoping as an example of lofty patriotism. The 33-year-old writer is famous for articles that eulogize the "Chinese Dream" and that criticize the U.S. government for trying to subvert China's socialist regime. "China's oriental culture will ultimately defeat Western hegemony," Zhou wrote in a recent article. He outlined in another article the nine strategies with which "the United States is waging a cultural Cold War against China." "We must uphold our own cultural values," he told the *People's Daily*. Xi's decision to heap praise on Zhou, combined with earlier *People's Daily* commentaries, seems to indicate that the general secretary is asking artists and men of letters to emulate party sycophants.[26]

Xi's war against the "new black categories" and new efforts to brainwash Chinese

The year 2016 being the 50th anniversary of the start of the Cultural Revolution, many commentators have wondered whether the hard-line Xi administration would start a mini cultural revolution. What is indisputable, however, is that the CCP has made it clear that people belonging to the *xinheiwulei*, or "five new black categories," would be subject to the dictatorship of the proletariat. These five sectors of the population deemed destabilizing by the regime are: human rights lawyers, underground religious practitioners, dissidents, opinion-leaders on the Internet, and disadvantaged social groupings. Even before the Cultural Revolution, Mao had fingered "landlords, rich peasants, counter-revolutionaries, evil elements and 'rightists'" as the enemies of the people who should be done away with.[27]

The logic of targeting these "black categories" was cogently explained by Yuan Peng, a senior researcher at the China Institutes of Contemporary International Relations (CICIR), a think tank affiliated with the Ministry of State Security (MSS). The veteran America expert claimed in an article titled "Where do China's real challenges lie?" that the U.S. was trying to turn members of these five categories into "core groups through which they will infiltrate different strata of China in 'bottom up' fashion, so as to create conditions for the 'transformation' of China [into a capitalistic country]."[28]

As we shall see in the following sections, police and state security departments and networks have put together a labyrinthine, all-weather, 24-hour quasi-police-state apparatus to keep even ordinary citizens under control. The anxiety to control the minds and actions of citizens is second nature to the CCP leadership – and not necessarily tied to particular national or international conditions. For example, spying on the people and trying to thwart "collusion" between destabilizing elements and "anti-China Western forces" are as ferociously pursued today as they were in the days of Mao. This is despite the fact that Maoist China was poor and despised by Western countries, whereas China under Xi has become a quasi-superpower that is diligently projecting its hard and soft power around the world.[29]

One of the secrets of the longevity of CCP rule is its ability to control and tame people, especially intellectuals and NGO organizers who could pose a threat to the regime. Many of the CCP's cruelest political campaigns, such as the Anti-Right Movement (1957–1959) and the Cultural Revolution (1966–1976) were designed to emasculate intellectuals. Indeed *guanren*, which can be translated as "controlling people" or "keeping people on a tight leash," is a central tenet of the CCP's human-resources strategy. Even relatively liberal leaders such as the late state president Liu Shaoqi, who was hounded to death by Mao during the Cultural Revolution, contributed to the party tradition of nurturing robot-like cadres who unthinkingly toe the party line. Liu's most famous work, *On the Cultivation of a Communist Party Member*, is a primer on how to turn cadres into model proletariats who profess undying loyalty to the party.[30] For Xi Jinping, ideological and political work must be geared toward changing the worldview of people. "Political work consists of doing work regarding the people," Xi liked to say. "We must pay close attention to individuals when we do [people-oriented] work. We must never look at things and concepts alone while forgetting [that we are dealing with] people."[31]

Whereas the Chinese were forced to recite Mao's Little Red Book during the Cultural Revolution, Xi's recipe for building up "people's beliefs" seemed at first sight less doctrinaire and more rounded. In 2014, Xi put forward an array of "socialist core values" to which all party members and citizens should subscribe. The authorities have laid down a 24-character definition of "core values." At the national level, these norms consist of "prosperity and strength, democracy, civilization and harmony." At the social level, emphasis is put on "freedom, equality, justice and rule by law." And at the level of individuals, the relevant values are "patriotism, respect for work, honesty and friendliness."[32] These benchmarks, however, are geared toward the ideological mission of boosting "self-confidence in the path, theory, system and culture" of socialism with Chinese characteristics. As Xi put it repeatedly, the whole party and society must "lift high the leitmotif [of patriotism and socialism] and sing the song of righteousness. [...] Only if the people have [the right set of] beliefs can there be hope for the Chinese people and strength for the nation," he warned.[33]

Socialist core values and the *shidai zhuxuanlv* ("leitmotifs of the times") are taught in schools and universities as well as propagated in factories and workplaces. As Xi reiterated,

> we must pay attention to rendering the core values of socialism a matter of routine, tangible, easy to visualize and close to life so that everybody can feel and understand the values and internalize them as spiritual pursuit and externalize them as practical action.[34]

The corollary of this stringent instruction seems to be that party members and citizens who do not agree with these values will be ostracized and heavily penalized. At the very least, intellectuals and NGO pathfinders who want to propagate other values would be denied any platforms.

Xi's views on the control of the vehicles of news dissemination – including the Internet and social media (see the following section) – do not depart from the classic CCP notion that information is a weapon that must be wielded by the state.[35] Xi has repeatedly called on party and government units handling the media to "deeply push forward propaganda and education on socialism with Chinese characteristics, so that people of all nationalities can unify themselves under the great flag of Chinese-style socialism." "We must strengthen [public education] on socialist core values," he noted in late 2013. "We must inculcate a superior atmosphere of positive values that sets store by devotion [to the party] and fostering harmony."[36] *Seeking Truth*, a well-known CCP mouthpiece, was even more straightforward. It said in a commentary at about the same time that, "at this stage, China cannot sustain the consequence of the loss of control of public opinion."[37]

The party's subjugation of the civil society

Reasons behind Beijing's negative attitude toward NGOs

The civil society movement in the 1980s

From numbers alone, it would seem that the growth of the civil society is relatively fast in China. The concept and practice of civil society or the public sphere did not gain currency even among men and women of letters until several years after Deng Xiaoping kicked off the Era of Reform and Open Door in the late 1970s. According to the Ministry of Civil Affairs (MCA), the number of legally registered NGOs had reached 460,000 in 2012 – the year when Xi came to power – up from 354,000 in 2007.[38]

A big gap, however, exists between the definitions of NGOs given by party and government cadres on the one hand, and liberal professors and civil-society pioneers on the other. Whereas official English media such as *China Daily* or the English editions of Xinhua and *People's Daily* usually use NGOs (or, less frequently, NPOs) to denote civil society organizations, the Chinese versions vary significantly.[39] Peking University political scientist and one-time government adviser Yu Keping has identified more than ten types of civil society organizations (CSOs). They include NGOs, NPOs, *minjian* (people's or "people-level") organizations, *gongmin tuanti* or citizens' groups, "intermediary organizations," *qunzhong tuanti* or groups of the masses, *renmin tuanti* or people's groups, *shehui zuzhi* or social organizations, "Third-Department organizations," and volunteer groups. "Generally speaking, these different names do not point to substantial differences," Yu wrote. "Yet a strict examination of their connotations shows that unmistakable differences exist among [these concepts]."[40] The major difference seems to be the degree to which the party-state exercises control over these units. Most cadres do not approve of the existence of organizations that are outside the control or purview of the party-state apparatus. What they support are rightly called government-organized NGOs (GONGOs). President Hu Jintao would only recognize government-controlled *shehui tuanti* ("social groups") and *shehui zuzhi* ("social organizations") that are geared toward providing charity and other social services. Xi has followed a similar tack except that he has put significantly more pressure on pretty much all social groupings; the conservative leader has also tried to boost the "decision-making" powers of party cells within these *shehui zuzhi*. [41]

Beijing's basic attitude toward nongovernmental units is a lot more understandable if we examine Deng Xiaoping's paranoia about civil-society groups wreaking havoc on authoritarian regimes. During the first wave of the student movement in China in December 1986, Deng was immediately alerted to the dangers of Chinese intellectuals taking a leaf out of the book of the anti-communist movement in Poland, which had flourished partly owing to the growth of the civil society. From the early 1980s, non-party and nongovernment groups – mainly the Catholic Church and the independent Solidarity labor movement, as well as disparate organizations of intellectuals and students – were delivering death knells to the Polish Communist Party. In an internal speech in late 1986, Deng told party cadres that "we must beware the Polish disease." Part of the late patriarch's meaning was that civil society organizations must never be allowed to sprout in China. [42]

Then came the student democracy movement of 1989 – which led to the Tiananmen Square incident on June 4 the same year. Although the pro-democracy movement of 1989 was mostly spearheaded by academics and students, there was for the first time sizeable participation by private businessmen as well as labor groups not affiliated with the All-China Federation of Trade Unions (a party-run organization that is the only legal labor association in China). After the Tiananmen Square movement was crushed, then-Party General Secretary Jiang Zemin warned that "he would bankrupt all the private entrepreneurs." [43] This harsh statement – which was never carried out – was motivated partly by non-state-sector business-people's overall sympathy with and support for the students. The Tiananmen Square incident served to delay the development of the Chinese civil society by almost a decade.

Values of the civil society are incompatible with party dominance

Wang Ming, vice-director of Tsinghua University's School of Public Policy, hit the nail on the head when he said that "those who think that the civil society will negate party leadership have not only misunderstood what a civil society is, they have also manifested a lack of political confidence and confidence in the system and institutions [of Chinese-style socialism]." [44] Wang was, of course, poking fun at one of President Xi's most often quoted axioms, that cadres and ordinary citizens must have "self-confidence in the path, theory, system and culture" of socialism with Chinese characteristics. As Professor Wang pointed out in a paper in *People's*

Forum in 2013, the idea of a civil society presupposes the recognition of certain civil liberties and norms. "The values of civil societies consist of commonly accepted social values expressed in the course of citizens taking their own initiatives in participating in different social activities," he wrote. "They include a civil spirit based on [the ideas of] freedom, independence and sense of entitlement … as well as social equality and justice."[45]

For a political party that is so determined about eliminating real and potential threats, the CCP's objections to NGOs consists of one word: organization. The party-state apparatus cannot tolerate a well-organized sociopolitical or religious organization that is beyond its control and is capable of at least potentially mounting a challenge to its authority owing to its intricate networking. Li Fan, the well-known head of The World and China Institute, which is an NGO involved with grassroots election issues, pointed out that the most salient feature of Chinese NGOs was their determination to form a network. In a speech given in Beijing in 2014, Li noted that the first goal of NGOs is "to get organized": "As the CCP often puts it, we must get organized first before we can do anything," Li said. "When elements in society put together organizations, their major goal is to defend the rights [of disparate sectors]."[46] Professor Xia Ming of New York City University argued that it would not be possible for the Xi administration to allow civil-society groups to develop further. "The further development of the civil society will result in the formation of political parties," he wrote. "That's why I feel that Xi Jinping is wary of the maturation of the civil society."[47]

Most scholars of the civil society envisage inevitable conflict between NGOs and the party-state apparatus. Li Fan noted that, at least in the initial phase of the development of the public sphere, conflict between individual groups and regional governments – especially grassroots administrations at the level of counties, town-ships and rural townships – would be most vehement. "The relations between NGOs and provincial-level governments are better, and [the former] do not have direct contradictions with the central leadership," Li said. "While it is true that regional policies often come from the top, conflicts between the civil society and government mostly take place at the grassroots level."[48] Since Xi ascended the pinnacle of power, however, he has taken initiatives to snuff out even mild, apparently non-politicized, units of the public sphere.

From the perspective of Xi Jinping – and social sciences specialists aligned with the party – NGOs as a whole constitute a direct threat to national security. This is particularly so given the apparently close association between a good number of social- and political-oriented NGOs and their counterparts in Western countries. According to deputy director of the government-funded China Charity Informa-tion Centre, Liu Youping, the 1,000-odd American NGOs active in China have donated some 20 billion yuan to the country in the past three decades. The bulk of this funding has gone into colleges, think thanks and government organs. Yet, even though only an estimated 17 percent of the funds has been donated to Chinese NGOs, Liu asserted that financing from American NGOs "has had an impact [on China's sociopolitical development] that is bigger than the 2 trillion yuan invested by American companies in the PRC." Liu cited institutions such as the Carnegie Foundation, the Open Society Fund, the Asia Foundation and the Ford Foundation as having a significant impact on "the research and dissemination of [ideas related to] political reform, human rights, democracy and the rule of law."[49]

Beijing's fear of collusion between politically active domestic NGOs and their foreign patrons is the reason behind the promulgation of a stringent law applied to overseas NGOs in 2016 (see the following section). It is significant that the CCP administration is also nervous about the activities of Hong Kong-based foreign NGOs, which range from missionary organizations to democracy-fostering American foundations, spreading their influence into the mainland. However, with the imminent promulgation in Hong Kong of the so-called Article 23 National Security Legislation, Beijing and Hong Kong authorities might secure the legal basis for banning or strictly constricting the activities of foreign NGOs and even foreign human rights watchdogs based in the special administration region.[50]

The civil society under Hu Jintao

Hu's ambivalent attitude toward mianjian zuzhi

One year after Hu Jintao came to power at the 16th Party Congress of late 2002, there were 142,000 social, unofficial and non-party-affiliated organizations in China, up 6.8 percent from the year before. However, only 1,736 of such units had national or cross-provincial networks, and most of these organizations were GONGOs. All of them needed to be registered by – and to accept the supervision of – the MCA. It should also be noted that the MCA and other party cadres usually use the terms *minjian zuzhi* (non-official or "people's organizations") or *shehui zuzhi* (social organizations) – and not NGOs – to denote these unofficial outfits.[51]

Two of the enduring slogans of the Hu Jintao era (2002–2012) were "putting people first" and "creating a harmonious society." Both teachings would seem to predispose the Hu administration toward showing more tolerance to the fledgling civil society. Being an innately conservative politician, however, Hu was hardly a supporter of non-party-controlled social organizations. In fact, he shared the paranoia of Russian president Vladimir Putin that civil society groupings in Ukraine, Georgia and Kyrgyzstan – which had reportedly secured financial and other kinds of support from the U.S. – were behind the "color revolutions" in these countries. Not long after the change of regime in Kyrgyzstan in 2005, Hu issued internal instructions to counter the fast growth of NGOs in China.[52]

Hu adopted a largely two-pronged approach toward *minjian zuzhi* and social organizations. Those which defy party and government leadership – and which are deemed to be potentially destabilizing – should be tightly controlled by police departments, if not abolished outright. However, Hu also realized that nonpolitical units, especially *shehui zuzhi* or social organizations that provide *gongyi* or "public welfare" services, should be encouraged, particularly if they accept close government supervision. In a number of cases, however, these *shehui zuzhi* were more akin to privately run and financed, government-approved, charity and social-service providers rather than "Western-style" NGOs that are geared toward promoting social justice.[53]

In a speech on "social management and its innovation" given to senior cadres in March 2011, Hu noted that the party and government should "provide guidance to different social organizations to strengthen their self-construction and to boost their ability to provide services." The fourth-generation potentate also highlighted the need to "push forward the healthy and orderly development of social organizations."[54] It is clear, however, that Hu and his colleagues had no intention of propagating NGOs that might boost public consciousness of civil rights. A June 2004 report in the Chinese-controlled *Wen Wei Po* newspaper in Hong Kong quoted Beijing think-tank members as saying that the CCP should boost efforts in "guiding and leading" *minjian zuzhi*. It was even suggested that party cells be established within such unofficial associations.[55]

Hu's views notwithstanding, liberal cadres and scholars within Hu's Communist Youth League Faction demonstrated considerable tolerance toward NGOs. One of them was "Young Marshal" Wang Yang, who was a Politburo member and party secretary of Guangdong from 2007 to 2012. Under the rallying call of "improving social management," Wang argued that more leeway and authority should be given to *shehui zuzhi*. "We should enhance [the extent of] transferring the functions of government [to society]," Wang said in a meeting of Guangdong officials in 2011. "We should not be stingy in 'delegating powers' to social organizations, and allowing social organizations to 'take over the baton' [from the government]." Wang said the Guangdong administration should gradually farm out more work to *shehui zuzhi*, "if social organizations are up to the task of taking over jobs [handed over to them by official units] and if they can manage them well." Guangdong also liberalized registration procedures for NGOs: they no longer needed to be a subsidiary of a body recognized by the party-state apparatus.[56] Unfortunately, Wang's open-mindedness about social organizations not directly controlled by the CCP was not shared by too many other regional party secretaries, governors or mayors. His successor for the period 2012–2017, Hu Chunhua, rolled back a significant number of liberalization measures introduced by Wang, including the lenient treatment of NGOs. For example, several labor-oriented NGOs were disbanded – and their office-bearers arrested – in late 2015 and early 2016.[57]

Prominent scholars' support for Western-style NGOs

Indeed, the atmosphere for the enlargement of the public sphere could not be characterized as negative through the 2000s. Prominent scholars and social planners who were close to the party-state apparatus were giving relatively positive assessments of NGOs and the civil society. This was despite the fact that many academics' definition of NGOs presupposed at least some degree of party-state control, if not acquiescence over such outfits.

Despite his official status, Director of the Institute of International Strategy at the Central Party School Zhou Tianyong was an avid supporter of the civil society, which he called *minjian* organizations. "In countries with a developed market economy, *minjian* organizations, in tandem with a modern government and the system of market economy, constitute the basic structure of modern governance," he wrote in *People's Daily* in 2008. Zhou argued that the function of such *minjian* units was to "act as a bridge among the party, government and society" in addition to "pushing forward the self-regulation and self-government of society and cutting the administrative costs of running a society." Although Zhou underscored the imperative of *minjian* organizations obeying party leadership and government coordination, he at the same time noted that these units "serve to safeguard citizens' rights to form associations and to promote citizens' participation in public affairs."[58]

Many observers considered 2008 – the year of the horrendous earthquake in Sichuan province – as the Year of the Birth of the NGO. As Xu Yongguang, a pioneer in establishing charitable and *gongyi* (public interest) groups in China, put it, the natural disaster precipitated the large-scale flowering of *gongmin yishi* ("citizen consciousness") or "public consciousness under modern rule of law" among ordinary citizens. On the one hand, he said, "citizen consciousness represents people's sense of responsibility to the country and society." At the same time, *gongmin yishi* incorporated ideals such as "democracy and the rule of law, liberty and equality as well as fairness and righteousness." "During the earthquake," Xu concluded, "citizens' rights to know, to participate [in society] and to supervise [the government] received unprecedented respect, and their sense of responsibility as citizens enjoyed tremendous expression." NGOs and allied groups raised more than 30 billion yuan in funds for the reconstruction of devastated northern Sichuan.[59]

Among "establishment intellectuals" or government-affiliated scholars who often serve in the informal think tanks of Politburo members, Yu Keping (born 1959) was the most eloquent supporter of the civil society. Yu defined NGOs as "social and people's organizations that are not run by the government, that are non-profit making, and that manifest voluntarism and are geared toward economic and social service." Yu argued that NGOs could contribute to "social renovation," a term that first gained currency during the Hu regime. "There are similarities and differences between social renovation and government renovation," Yu said in 2010. "Social innovation is innovation in the [*minjian*] field; it is innovation that is being spearheaded by citizens themselves." He argued that citizens' social participation through working in NGOs "can not only lower the government's administrative costs but also materialize the *zhutixing* ['initiative and self-sufficiency'] of citizens by encouraging them to express the popular will and to boost their enthusiasm for [social] participation." The scholar suggested that, in tandem with the development and improvement of the social management system, the government could *fenliu* ("farm out") some of its administrative powers to civil organizations, so that the latter can help the government shoulder part of its administrative and management functions. "This tallies well with the spirit of democracy," Yu concluded.[60]

The early 2000s witnessed the beginning of party-state units funding at least partially government-controlled social organizations to provide public services. In 2010, for example, the Beijing municipal government earmarked 100 million yuan for the "purchase" of 300 items of charitable and social services provided by some 250 *shehui zuzhi*. Each variety of service was eligible to receive 30,000–300,000 yuan. In 2014, the municipal government of Suzhou in Jiangsu Province doled out an unspecified amount of funds to buy social services from five private-sector social-service providers to furnish old-age services to 3,000 local citizens.[61]

The Xi Jinping era: open warfare against the public sphere

From the outset, the Xi Jinping administration has made it clear that it does not recognize NGOs or NPOs as they are universally defined. At most, Xi only tolerates so-called *shehui zuzhi* or social organizations that provide supplementary social and public services to Chinese residents. As in other socio-economic arenas, Xi has placed the utmost emphasis on party leadership of such *shehui zuzhi*, which can be interpreted as GONGOs that are under enhanced control by the party-state apparatus. The imperative of the establishment of party cells in social organizations and similar outfits was spelled out in the "Draft Regulation on the Work of Chinese Communist Party organizations," which was passed in May 2015. The draft regulation empowered "party organizations to be set up within the leadership organs of state departments, mass organizations, economic organizations, cultural organizations, social organizations and other organizations." It was the first time that a party regulation unequivocally stipulated that party cells must be established in civil-society units. According to Professor Zhang Xixian of the Central Party School, this new rule was geared toward "boosting the party's leadership over social organizations at a time when social organizations are going through the stage of vigorous development."[62]

Xi's approach to taming the civil society was further revealed by the dissemination of *Opinion on reforming the management system of social organizations and promoting the healthy and orderly development of social organizations* (hereafter "Opinion"), which was largely drafted by the MCA, the "mother-in-law" unit that regulates civil-society organizations. *Opinion*, which was released in 2016, said that the central authorities were committed to "clarifying the relationship between the government, the market and society" and to "improving the ways in which public services are provided [so as to] strengthen and make innovations regarding *shehui zhili* ['social governance']." The MCA indicated that Beijing was positive about social organizations providing services that the government or the market could not provide – and it noted that the government would continue to provide funds for qualified *shehui zuzhi* to offer public services. However, echoing the imperative that Xi has underscored about party leadership, *Opinion* stressed that all social organizations must establish party cells, which would take charge of decision-making. "The core political role of party organizations must be fulfilled," *Opinion* said. "Party construction must be strengthened in social organizations." Must strikingly, the MCA pointed out that *shehui zuzhi* must not develop hierarchical units, nor must they establish regional branches.[63] The CCP's paranoia about social organizations developing cross-regional networks and becoming a nationwide "base of subversion" seems evident.

Against this background, it is not difficult to understand the scorched-earth policy that the Xi administration has implemented toward NGOs that are not only outside the purview of the party and the police, but are also suspected of harboring destabilizing tendencies. Since 2012, the persecution of civil-society groups such as intellectuals, human rights lawyers and underground church officials has become more pronounced (see Chapters 2–4). Even apparently nonpolitical NGOs campaigning for rights for women as well as environmental causes have not been spared the police's brutal treatment.[64]

Just ahead of International Women's Day in March 2015, Beijing detained five feminists for allegedly "picking quarrels and provoking troubles." Although they were released one month later, international human rights organizations were highly critical of Beijing's action. Then- U.S. ambassador to the United Nations, Samantha Power, lambasted Chinese authorities for arresting the activists apparently using the premise that the planned protests against sexual harassment might cause "disturbances."[65] Also consider the sorry fate of the Protect the Harbor Seal Association (PHSA), which was founded in 2010 by Tian Jiguang. Tian's mission was to protect the harbor seal along the Liao River, a 1,345-km waterway that stretched from the mountains of Hebei Province and poured into Bohai Sea near Liaoning Province. The habitat for the seals, however, was threatened by highway building and oil excavation. In 2013, Tian succeeded in forcing local authorities to reroute a highway so that the seals would not be directly affected. At its height, the PHSA had more than 3,000 volunteers; it also had good relations with environmental protection NGOs in other parts of China. However, PHSA was suppressed by police in 2015, and Tian was arrested for alleged "economic crimes" involving more than 150,000 yuan. In late 2015 he was sentenced to 12 years.[66]

The government is not taking chances even with miniscule NGOs concerned about animal rights. A case in point is Beijing resident Qin Xiao'na, who had run an animal protection organization for more than 20 years. She said in late 2015 that police had warned her against hosting activities to raise public awareness about humane treatment of stray dogs and cats. Given the fact that animal rights had become a serious issue for many middle-class urban families, an NGO in this sector could easily mobilize several thousand participants in either e-platform petitions or street protests.[67] Take, for instance, the campaign against eating dog meat, which is popular in provinces such as Guangdong and Heilongjiang. In mid-2016, animal-rights NGOs such as the Humane Society International and Beijing Mothers Against Animal Cruelty gathered 11 million signatures online demanding the closure of a dog-meat festival in the southern city of Yulin. Although these two organizations had not been harassed by police, the latter were adamant that animal-rights NGOs must not hold public protests, on the grounds that law and order would be threatened.[68]

A 2016 report on the state of the civil society compiled by the New York-based Chinese Human Rights Defenders (CHRD) accused the Xi administration of efforts to choke off the public sphere. Xi and his administration were "really intent on shutting off any avenue for civil society to participate in the improvement of the Chinese nation," said Frances Eve, a CHRD researcher. CHRD noted that groups seeking to fight corruption and to ameliorate the status of women had all been targeted, even though the CCP itself had made at least rhetorical commitments to improving the same sociopolitical ills. "The government is saying, 'you're not allowed to participate … This is something that only we the Communist Party can do,'" Eve said. "And not only are they not letting people participate, but they're criminalizing different forms of public participation in governance and social issues."[69]

Laws and proscriptions against the civil society

NGOs and related organizations have assumed a disturbingly low public profile during the Xi Jinping era. Central Document No. 9 of 2013 forbade college professors and intellectuals in general from talking about seven "taboo areas," one of which was "the civil society." Although the Xi leadership does not frequently make pronouncements on domestic NGOs, its attitude toward the civil society was made clear by the 2016 Law on the Management of the Activities of Overseas Non-Governmental Organizations within Mainland China (hereafter Overseas NGO Law). The statute said that foreign NGOs must neither "damage Chinese national interests" nor "endanger Chinese national unity, security and the solidarity of the people." Most significantly, the 7,000-odd foreign-based NGOs in China must register with the Ministry of Public Security (MPS) or the police, which will check whether these units have given financial or other kinds of support to prodemocracy organizations or "separatist" elements in Xinjiang and Tibet. Foreign NGOs have to file annual reports to the police detailing their activities, profiles of personnel, as well as their finances. Police are authorized to detain NGO staff accused of conducting activities including "spreading rumors," "engaging in defamation" or creating "situations that endanger state security or damage the national or public interest."[70]

Xie Zengyi, a specialist on NGOs at the Peking University Law School, indicated that the police "should act according to the law and pursue the twin tasks of guaranteeing service as well as supervision and management […] The Ministry of Public Security should establish a relationship of mutual trust and benevolent interaction with foreign NGOs."[71] Other academics, however, have expressed worries about the quality of scrutiny and supervision that the police will be exerting over foreign organizations. According to Jia Xijun, a social scientist at Tsinghua University, the new NGO law "may give a lot of discretionary powers to the police in terms of the interpretation of the requirements of national security and national interest." "It is possible that the police could be given leeway to interpret the law stringently or loosely and that political factors could play a role in the interpretations," she argued.[72]

The Overseas NGO Law has raised alarm in the foreign diplomatic and NGO community. In June 2016, 20 leading foreign NGOs and rights watchdogs, including Freedom House, Reporters without Borders, the International Center for Charity Law, Christian Solidarity Worldwide and Chaplain Alliance for Religious Liberty published a joint letter calling on the National People's Congress (NPC) to repeal the law:

> This law constrains opportunities for Chinese citizens, together with overseas NGO partners, to develop new approaches to social problems affecting their country – social problems that, if left unchecked by the civil society, could lead to greater instability and burden on the state ... This law now formalizes many of the problematic bureaucratic tools already in use against Chinese civil society organizations, and legalizes arbitrary police actions against domestic and overseas NGOs.[73]

That this statute is seen as a symbol of China's resistance to international values was evidenced by then-U.S. Secretary of State John Kerry raising the issue with the CCP leadership during the Obama administration's last Strategic and Economic Dialogue with Beijing. Kerry noted that President Xi told him that China would apply the law fairly and that, "China intends to open up even more than it is from today." Xi was also quoted as saying that the new NGO legislation would "not be applied in any way to affect the ability of foreign businesses to feel confident operating there."[74] It seemed clear, however, that Kerry and Xi were talking at cross-purposes. Xi had very little interest in the welfare of the civil society; he was only concerned about the possibility of foreign businesses being turned off by the expansion of hard authoritarianism in Chinese politics.

"The people's society" versus the civil society

Right from the start of the Xi Jinping era, official scholars began to advertise the superiority of the *renmin shehui*, or "people's society," over the civil society. "The substance of the people's society is socialism," said well-known social scientist Hu Angang. "The mainstay of the people's society are the entire people ... and the goal of constructing such a society is the service of all people." Hu, who teaches at Tsinghua University, claimed that, whereas the people's society is based on the principles of public ownership, the public good, equality and justice, the civil society is based on "private profits and private interests." Hu also added that leadership for the people's society is provided by the party, and that it is distinguished by the ideal of a "harmonious society."[75]

A commentary in the overseas edition of the *People's Daily* in 2013 even claimed that, "the people's society is a major theoretical innovation as well as innovation in practice." The commentator pointed out that the people's society was superior to "the civil society of the West" because its "method of construction consists in ceaselessly improving democracy." Citing the Chinese dream mantra laid down by

President Xi in late 2012, the commentator claimed that, "only the people can become the biggest propellant toward 'the Chinese dream.'" The commentary also noted that the people's society "has its origin in Chinese culture and it tallies with the *guoqing* ['national situation'] of China." "The people's society is a socialist society with Chinese characteristics that is established by all the people," the paper added.[76]

For noted political scientist Wang Shaoguang, civil-society, or *minjian*, organizations are a dubious concept because "they have manifested elements of fakeness, evil and ugliness" in their development. For example, wrote Wang, many NGOs depended on commercial activities and other sources for income; even worse, they could be manipulated by overseas donors. "Some NGOs could metamorphose into spokespeople for foreign forces," he argued. "If we were to construct some form of ideal society, 'people's societies' are obviously a goal that is more worthy to go after," he contended. One reason, Wang noted, was that, in China, there were already people's institutions such as "people's government," "people's army," "people's police" and "people's banks." The former Chinese University of Hong Kong professor pointed out that the task of "people's societies" is to realize democracy, as manifested by the ideal of the people *dangjia zuozhu* ("becoming masters of their own affairs").[77] It must be noted, however, that *dangjia zuozhu* is a euphemism used by CCP leaders from Mao to Xi to denote citizens running their affairs under the unrelenting supervision of the party. For example, Xi cited the goal of *dangjia zuozhu* several times in his *Political Report to the 19th Party Congress*. But he was careful to point out that, "there should be an organic unity in upholding party leadership, the people *dangjia zuozhu* and running the country according to law." He further stressed that party leadership was the "fundamental guarantee" for the people running their own affairs.[78]

The control mechanism: Xi Jinping's unparalleled quasi-police state

Although most China observers remember Deng Xiaoping as a fervent economic reformer, it must also be noted that the Great Architect of Reform laid down institutions and mechanisms to substantiate the Four Cardinal Principles of the primacy of Marxism, Leninism and Mao Thought, as well as CCP dictatorship. From the 1980s onwards, internal security – including the suppression of dissent – has been the responsibility of the Central Political-Legal Commission (CPLC), which is usually headed by a member of the Politburo Standing Committee (PBSC). Charged with promoting internal security, the CPLC has direct control over the MPS (police), the MSS, the courts and the procuratorate.[79]

One of Xi Jinping's lasting contributions to CCP-style authoritarianism is his establishment of the Central National Security Commission (CNSC) at the Third Plenum of the Central Committee held in late 2013. The philosophy of the CNSC is that the CCP must embrace the concept of "mega-security." First, the security apparatus must adopt a "holistic" attitude to combating both internal and external threats, particularly given the party's perception that enemies of the state within China often collude with "hostile foreign forces." Moreover, the concept of *zongti guojia'anquan* ("overall national security") has been extended to cover the following 11 arenas: politics, territorial, military, economy, culture, society, science and technology, information, ecology, resources and nuclear.[80] As Xi noted in his speech to the plenum: "China is facing two [kinds of] pressures: internationally, the country needs to safeguard its sovereignty, security and development interests; domestically, political security and social stability should be ensured."[81]

What is new about the concept of "overall national security"? As Xi put it, Beijing would "pay utmost attention to both external and internal security; territorial security as well as citizens' security; traditional and non-traditional security."[82] Chaired by Xi himself, the CNSC has direct control over the CPLC, which is now only headed by an ordinary Politburo member. Top party, state and military units that are given representation on the superagency include the People's Liberation Army (PLA), the People's Armed Police (PAP), the Ministry of Foreign Affairs (MOFA), the MPS, the MSS, the Ministry of Trade, the CCP Department of Propaganda and the CCP International Liaison Department. Cadres responsible for Tibet and Xinjiang are also represented. And, given that the CNSC's interests include Taiwan and Hong Kong, the Taiwan Affairs Office and the Hong Kong and Macau Affairs Office – which are ministerial units within the State Council – also have a presence on the Commission.[83] At the regional level, a member of the Standing Committee of the provincial, municipal or county-level Communist Party Committee is designated a *zhengfa shuji* (secretary in charge of law and order). The *zhengfa shuji* is tasked with tackling the threats in the 11 areas of national security enunciated by Xi.[84]

According to Li Wei, head of the CICIR's Anti-Terrorism Research Center, the CNSC is "geared toward handling the increasing number of major incidents and mishaps that impinge upon our country's security and interests." Li indicated that the CNSC's concerns included non-traditional arenas including economic and financial security, environmental safety, terrorism and piracy.[85] A sizeable number of liberal intellectuals are alarmed by the CNSC's apparent similarity to the all-powerful internal-security apparatus of the former Soviet Union. According to economist Xia Yeliang, a former Peking University professor and noted public intellectual, "the authorities are very worried about stability despite the apparent achievements in economic development." "The CNSC will make better use of the military, the PAP, spies and even anti-corruption agents to promote internal security," he told the foreign media. "There are parallels between the CNSC and the KGB [under the Soviets]."[86]

A labyrinthine security apparatus

As far as its domestic stability agenda is concerned, the CNSC is overseeing – and expanding – a labyrinthine *weiwen* ("stability maintenance") apparatus that was put together by the Hu-Wen administration from 2002 to 2012. In 2011, the *weiwen* budget, at 624.4 billion yuan, exceeded the PLA budget of 601.1 billion yuan for the first time. In 2016, spending on stability maintenance was estimated at 950.4 billion yuan.[87]

From the second half of the Hu Jintao administration (2007–2012), the CPLC has been charged with constructing a *fangkong* ("prevention-and-control") grid that is "multi-dimensional, all-weather, and foolproof." According to Guo Shengkun, who took up the post of CPLC secretary in 2012, more resources would be poured into constructing a "social order *fangkong* system." This 24-hour, multi-faceted law-and-order apparatus would, according to Guo, incorporate the "new line of thinking and new methodology of 'the feet plus the Internet,' tradition and technology, specialist work and the mass line." There will be networks based on vigilante groups in streets and communities; internal security and anti-sabotage units in government offices, colleges and commercial firms; CCTV and surveillance mechanisms especially in big cities; coordination networks among security-related units in each province and region; and Internet and AI-enabled policing facilities.[88]

Indeed, the Xi administration has put together a fully digitalized and all-embracing *tianluo diwang* ("a dragnet that stretches from heaven to earth") to snuff out dissent and to emasculate the civil society. This *weiwen* grid has fulfilled what Xi called "a road map for national security with Chinese characteristics that will meet the challenges of the 21st century."[89] The paramount leader's biggest contribution to thwarting pro-democracy and other "anti-government" movements has been his determination to modernize Beijing's already formidable police-state apparatus through the application of first-class spy and related surveillance software. The state security apparatus has built the world's largest digitalized "big data" bank to keep tabs on "destabilizing elements" ranging from criminals and terrorists to dissidents, underground church personnel and NGO participants. Specialized *weiwen* cadres have the full cooperation of the country's social-media and e-commerce platforms, as well as cloud-computing and related high-tech firms, in establishing a seamless and all-encompassing intelligence network that would do George Orwell's Big Brother proud.[90]

The biggest breakthrough is the successful use of AI to uphold political stability. As the *Anhui Daily* put it in mid-2017, *anfang* – "security protection," which covers police and national-security work – has taken a leap forward owing to AI-enabled security systems that have benefited from big data, cloud computing, "deep learning," and identification and surveillance software. "'AI plus *anfang*' has changed passive defense [against dissent] to active advance-warning," the official daily said. "This has rendered possible management of public safety based on [high] visibility, digitalization and AI-enablement."[91] Indigenously developed facial-recognition software has enabled police and state-security agencies to keep track of all "destabilizing agents" in society. The mugshots of criminals and suspects, as well as dissidents, are stored in police-run facial-recognition data banks. China boasts more than 200 million surveillance cameras and video facilities all over the country, most of which are interfaced with these state-of-the-art, AI-enabled data collections.[92]

Although facial-recognition techniques have been used in recent years for mundane activities such as accessing ATM machines or unlocking mobile phones, more instances of *anfang*-related applications have been reported in the open media. Take, for example, the case of a Wuhan resident surnamed Xiao who was wanted by the police for alleged fraud. In July 2017 he was cycling along the city's famed East Lake when the computer in the local police surveillance center blipped. Xiao's face had appeared on one of several facial-recognition-enabled surveillance cameras installed on the East Lake waterfront. The local media reported that there was a 97.44 percent resemblance between Xiao's facial features as captured by the spy camera and the photo that was stored in the data bank for criminals on the run. Xiao was arrested within 24 hours.[93]

Both Chinese and foreign experts reckon that China has the most advanced – and cheapest – AI-enabled surveillance technology in the world. The reason is simple: China has the fastest-expanding market for facial-recognition and similar know-how. This is coupled with the absence of enforceable laws and regulations protecting citizens' privacy. According to Zhao Yong, the CEO of DeepGlint, a successful AI firm, it takes a mere second for company technology to compare and contrast tens of millions of sets of facial features.[94] Zhong An Wang (literally "China Security Net," or www.CPS.com.cn/), a popular website for *anfang*-related AI start-ups, noted that this sector manufactured products worth 486 billion yuan in 2015. Major funders included not only the MPS, the MSS and other government departments, but also private companies. Multi-billion-dollar firms in the areas of IT, e-commerce, finance, as well as universities, which have made big investments in facial-recognition technology include Alibaba, the CITIC Group, the Pingan Group, Vanke and Tsinghua University. Megvii Technology Inc., a leading facial-recognition software manufacturer, has received hefty investments from multinationals including the Taiwan IT giant Foxconn Technology.[95]

China's formidable clout in big-data engineering has also yielded a bonanza for the crafting of a police-state apparatus chockablock with essential data on its estimated 800 million netizens. The Central Cyberspace Affairs Commission has fostered the establishment of a national "social credit" data bank. With information provided by the social media, e-commerce platforms, as well as banks and e-banking firms, police and state-security departments have since 2015 established a nationwide social credit system to keep tabs on even the apparently mundane activities of citizens.[96]

Social credit data depositories are not unique to China. Banks and credit card companies in Western and Asian countries keep thick files on the income and credit-worthiness of customers. The difference is that, in China, all such information kept by supposedly privacy-conscious banks, e-banking and e-commerce platforms, as well as social-media firms, is fed into the security forces' mass surveillance system. Big Brother has a full picture of citizens' credit ratings, their spending habits and punctuality in paying taxes. Also input into the data pool are citizens' education levels, consumption patterns and records of travel abroad.[97] Although these sensitive data are not necessarily security-related, they form an important part of a comprehensive database that police departments can use to rapidly access important information about every Chinese citizen.

Of course, the crudest form of data collection is happening particularly in restive districts such as the Xinjiang Uyghur Autonomous Region, where the police and the paramilitary PAP are battling what Beijing claims to be separatist and "terrorist" activities perpetrated by radicalized Uighurs. Since 2016, police have been collecting samples of the DNA of Uighurs with the apparent purpose of constructing a national Uighur DNA bank. International human rights watchdogs have reported that Xinjiang authorities had bought equipment worth billions of yuan for the purpose of DNA collection, storage and analysis. HRW China Director Sophie Richardson pointed out that "mass DNA collection by the powerful Chinese police absent effective privacy protections or an independent judicial system is a perfect storm for abuses."[98]

International news agencies and newspapers, throughout 2018, reported in detail about horrendous internment camps set up by the Xinjiang government to apparently brainwash recalcitrant Uighurs. Some estimates say there could be up to 1 million internees. According to the relatives of Uighurs locked up in the concentration camp-like facilities, Uighurs are subjected to both physical and emotional torture in an apparent attempt by the authorities to force them to profess loyalty to Beijing. In a September 2018 report, HRW condemned the Chinese administration's "mass arbitrary detention, torture, and mistreatment of Turkic Muslims in Xinjiang," as well as the "systemic and increasingly pervasive controls on the daily life [of Uighurs]." "These rampant abuses violate fundamental rights to freedom of expression, religion, and privacy, and protections from torture and unfair trials," said the watchdog.[99]

Although Xinjiang authorities claim that the internment camps are "vocational education" centers to train unemployed Uighurs and to stave off terrorism, the Trump administration and various EU leaders have put pressure on China to give a full explanation of what critics call the practice of forced Sinicization, or obliging Uighurs to shed their own culture and to embrace a Han Chinese identity. U.S. congressmen wrote to the State Department and the Treasury Department in September 2018 to ask them to impose sanctions on Xinjiang Party Secretary Chen Quanguo, as well as police officers responsible for imposing a regime in Xinjiang that bears disturbing comparisons to ethnic cleansing practiced by several dictatorial regimes since World War II.[100]

Applying Mao's "People's Warfare" concept to fight destabilizing agents

The emphasis on high-tech surveillance has been complemented by ground-level "human intelligence" gathering based on Chairman Mao's famous "people's warfare" strategy. Mobilizing the masses for the cause of *anfang* and *fangkong* was first used successfully to prevent mishaps during the 2008 Summer Olympics. That year, 850,000 "volunteer-vigilantes" or "law-and-order volunteers" were recruited in the capital. One of their jobs was to provide information to local public-security bureaus upon seeing "suspicious characters" or coming upon "plots" supposedly hatched by terrorist and dissident groups.[101] The same tactics were adopted by Shanghai and Hangzhou authorities to ensure public safety during the 2010 Shanghai Expo and the G20 summit in 2016.[102]

Cai Qi, the newly appointed party secretary of Beijing, has taken things further by pledging to draft significantly more Beijing residents into the capital's *fangkong* network. The *New Beijing Post* reported that different categories of informants and other *weiwen* personnel had breached the 1.4 million mark. Cai heaped particular praise on the *weiwen* contributions of the city's Chaoyang and Xicheng districts. Registered volunteer-vigilantes in Chaoyang numbered more than 130,000, meaning there are 277 such personnel per square kilometer. The party chief vowed to turn volunteer-vigilantes in Chaoyang into "the world's fifth-largest intelligence agency."[103] According to Yan Mancheng, the deputy head of the Political-Legal Department of the Beijing municipal party committee, volunteers in the Chaoyang district provided the police with 210,000 pieces of information in a recent year, which led to the successful prosecution of 483 cases.[104]

Using traditional Communist parlance, a citizen is not only a cog in the machinery: he must also be all eyes and all ears toward real and potential threats to stability so that the party can be alerted in good time. As former Minister of Public Security Guo Shengkun pointed out, public security personnel must "fully exploit and develop the foresightedness and guidance [provided by grassroots] intelligence and to follow their lead."[105] This staggering number of part-time spies and informants has rendered it even more difficult for NGOs and dissident groups to either expand their organization or to stage public events.

The importance of a comprehensive intelligence-gathering network was underscored by Xue Lansuo, who heads a research department under the *zhengfa* apparatus of Hebei Province. Xue noted that, in order to prevent "enemy forces" – including terrorists, religious organizations and foreign NGOs – from wreaking havoc on stability, the police must be able to collect intelligence "from deep inside" the hostile organizations. With the benefit of intelligence that can enable police forces to take preemptive action, Xue said, the authorities "could firmly seize the initiative in the struggle."[106] Human rights organizations were shocked by the ubiquitous network of informants throughout China. In 2010, the police chief of Kailu County, Inner Mongolia, told the official media that he had recruited one in every 33 local residents as a part-time informant. Of the county's 400,000 inhabitants, 12,093 are tasked with providing intelligence to the police if they are aware of suspicious characters – or destabilizing "plots" – that could jeopardize law and order.[107]

Another manifestation of the "people's warfare" approach to promoting stability is the creation of yet another security force: the *cunjing* or village police. Media reports have noted that, in western provinces including Xinjiang, Gansu and Qinghai, at least a few tens of thousands of such police officers have been recruited. Unlike ordinary police, *cunjing* are hired by the Ministry of Human Resources. Top priority is given to recruiting demobilized soldiers and party members. The *cunjing* is attached to individual villages. In addition to policing areas under their jurisdiction at night, they also contribute to farming work in the daytime. Through mixing with ordinary farmers, these village police are also in a position to indoctrinate their charges – and turn them into part-time informants.[108]

China held its first National Security Education Day in April 2016 with the goal of raising public awareness about how political stability and national security could be jeopardized by internal and external enemies. In cosmopolitan cities such as Beijing, police put out posters telling citizens to be wary of solicitations and "entrapment" by foreign spies. A 16-panel cartoon that the Beijing authorities posted in subway stations showed a gullible Ms. Li, a state employee, falling for the gifts and compliments of a handsome Caucasian man, who happened to be a spy recruiter from an unnamed Western country. In Xinjiang in 2016, 300,000 civil servants took part in a "legal knowledge test," which quizzed them on their awareness of statutes such as the National Security Law and the Anti-Espionage Law. In thousands of high schools in the autonomous region, students are assembled to sing the national anthem and to sign a pledge under the national flag to uphold state security. Civil servants and students are told to boost their sense of safeguarding national security in the age of the Internet.[109]

National security awareness has also been promoted in the nation's high schools. Schools nationwide have, since 2016, made available supplementary learning materials on state security, including lessons about the dangers of foreign spies making use of gullible young minds to lay their hands on state secrets. According to Zheng Qian, a commentator for the China Education News Net, although today's youngsters have a strong curiosity and frequent interactions with the Internet, "they have limited experience and inadequate awareness [about state security], meaning that we must prevent young people from being duped." Students are also eligible for rewards of up to 500,000 yuan that various local governments have put up for tips leading to the arrest of spies or the thwarting of plots that would threaten national security.[110]

Intensified clampdown on the Internet – and the success of the CCP's control of information

The Internet has been described as a potent weapon against dictatorial governments. And the social media such as Facebook played a significant role in the series of Arab Spring political upheavals that seized North Africa and the Middle East beginning in 2010.[111] However, the CCP administration has, particularly since the early 2010s, tightened control over China's 800 million netizens' access to the information superhighway. Not only are Facebook, Twitter and other Western social media banned in China, their Chinese equivalents such as WeChat are subject to perhaps the tightest scrutiny among authoritarian countries. Government-controlled service providers have a strict registration system. And an estimated 50,000 Internet police work 24 hours a day to scrub out offensive articles – or just sensitive words and phrases – almost the moment they are posted. Moreover, netizens who are caught putting up "anti-government" or "destabilizing" messages or materials on the net are subject to punishment, including jail terms of at least a few years. This tight control of information has made it difficult for intellectuals or NGO pace-setters to use the net to spread universal values. Equally significant is the fact that it has become easier for the authorities to impose a collective amnesia about events such as the Tiananmen Square massacre of 1989.[112]

Consider what happened to Liu Xiaobo in the run-up to and immediately after his demise in 2017. After his ashes were scattered in the ocean – against the wishes of his wife and close friends – all references to Liu, his wife Liu Xia, or even associated terms such as the Nobel Peace Prize, Charter 08, "sea burial," and the initials RIP were scrubbed from Chinese websites and media. Even a candle-shaped emoji used by some as a memorial was blocked. And, despite Liu's world-wide recognition after he won the Nobel Peace Prize in 2010, relatively few Chinese know who the freedom fighter was. As veteran human rights activist Hu Jia put it days after his burial, "In Beijing, if you ask 100 people and one of them says he has heard of Liu Xiaobo, it is quite something."[113]

The Xi administration has upped the ante in enforcing control on the Internet, which conservatives regard as a potent threat to state security. In his now-famous August 19, 2013 speech on ideology and propaganda, Xi pointed out that, "whether the Internet can be controlled is a matter of life and death for the party."[114] Six months later, Xi established the Central Leading Group for Cyberspace Affairs (later renamed Central Cyberspace Affairs Commission or CCAC) and became its head. The CCAC takes charge of existing organs on internet censorship and development of the IT industry such as the Cyberspace Administration of China (CAC), the State Internet Information Office, the Cyberpolice division within the MPS, and the Ministry of Industry and Information Technology.[115]

"No Internet safety means no national security," Xi pointed out in the inaugural meeting of the CCAC, whose two vice-heads were Premier Li Keqiang and then-PBSC member in charge of ideology and propaganda Wang Huning. "Cyberspace should be made clean," the supremo instructed, adding that, "we should be fully aware of the importance and urgency of Internet security and informatization." China had to balance its needs to develop IT technologies and safeguard Internet security, the president said, describing the two issues as "two wings of a bird and two wheels of an engine."[116]

Xinhua quoted Xi as calling for innovative methods to spread "discipline and mainstream values" and to stimulate positive energy while maintaining proper guidance of online opinions in terms of timing, intensity and impact. Laws and regulations would be drawn up to "perfect Internet information content management," to boost supervision of cyberspace and to protect people's legal rights, he said.[117] The Xi administration had, by 2013, already introduced tougher measures to police the Internet. For example, netizens could be detained and jailed for "spreading rumors" and even "inciting subversion of state power" for circulating politically incorrect articles or materials deemed destabilizing by the Internet police.[118] From the mid-2010s, the CAC also started cracking down on "illegal" providers of virtual private networks (VPNs), which could be used by netizens to circumvent the Great Firewall of China. In December 2017, Guangxi resident Wu Xiangyang was jailed for five and a half years and fined 500,000 yuan for selling VPNs without a proper license from 2013 to mid-2017. During this period, Xu reportedly generated 792,000 yuan in revenue and 500,000 yuan in "illegal profits."[119]

Equally draconian is the policy of targeting so-called "Big Vs," Net-based opinion leaders who boast at least 100,000 registered fans. They include controversial writers, businessmen and professionals whose piquant views on social and political issues are often regarded by CCP censors as destabilizing or outright seditious. According to the 2014 Blue Book on Social Development Trends put out by the Chinese Academy of Social Science, 300 Big Vs dominated microblogging, and these opinion leaders could have an influence on the public that was even bigger than that of official media. In 2013, several Big Vs – Chinese-American investor Charles Biqun Xue (aka Xue Manzi), IT mogul Wang Gongquan, environmentalist Dong Xuejie, and Internet marketing whizzes Yang Xiuyu and Qin Zhihui (Qin Huohuo) – were detained by the police for crimes including "disturbing the public order," "creating disturbances," illegal business activities and spreading rumors.[120]

Apart from enhancing scrutiny to rid the information superhighway of destabilizing elements, the CCAC is expected to roll out new measures against "Internet-based terrorism." The years 2013 and 2014 witnessed flare-ups of alleged terrorist incidents brought about by Uighurs, which culminated in the March 1, 2014 Kunming Railway Station bloodbath in which 29 people were killed. The *Global Times* cited CICIR's expert Li Wei as saying that "the important [role] of the Internet in terrorism activities has risen." "The Internet has become a convenient propaganda tool for extremist ideas," said Li. "It has raised the efficiency of spreading terrorist ideas in both speed and territorial coverage."[121]

The Xi concept of "Internet sovereignty" was reinforced at the Fourth World Internet Conference held in Zhejiang in late 2016. In a written speech, Xi committed China to the goal of promoting separate jurisdictions for cyberspace according to state boundaries, with each "Internet jurisdiction" regulated by the government in question, "without external interference." The newly promoted PBSC member in charge of ideology and propaganda, Wang Huning, pointed out at the meeting that, "China stands ready to develop new rules and systems of Internet governance to serve all parties and counteract current imbalances." He also called for more aggressive online controls to crack down on Internet-based criminal activity and "terrorism." As part of a periodic *weiwen* exercise, in 2018, the social network WeChat reportedly removed more than 300,000 articles and closed more than 200,000 user accounts it deemed to contain violent, pornographic or misleading content.[122]

According to David Bandurski, an expert on the Chinese Internet, apparently successful measures geared toward policing and taming the information superhighway have rendered the CCP "increasingly confident that its control methods and infrastructure at home are not just effective, but have applicability and relevance for the entire world, over and against the Clintonesque view of the Internet as a force of inescapable liberalization."[123] Suffice it to say, however, the battle between 800 million netizens and Internet censors is far from over. At least well-educated netizens in the big cities have ways and means to vault over the Great Firewall. Moreover, intellectuals and NGO crusaders can still get their messages about political openness and liberalization – albeit in coded and otherwise camouflaged IT instruments – across to both their colleagues and a wider public.

Conclusion: how the dissident community and the civil society are fighting back

In a lecture at the Central Party School in January 2019, President Xi Jinping asked ministerial-level cadres to "maintain a high degree of vigilance" against a host of threats to national security and stability. "We must keep our highest alert about 'black swan' [unforeseen] incidents and also take steps to prevent any 'gray rhino' [highly possible yet ignored] threats," the party chief warned. "[We are] confronted with unpredictable international developments and a complicated and sensitive external environment," he added. "Our task at hand is to maintain stability as we continue our reform and development."[124] The instructions given by the "core leader" amounted to a very tall order: "we must fight well the pre-emptive warfare so as to prevent and withstand risks and at the same time fight well the war of strategic initiatives [so as] to render danger into safety and turn threats into opportunities."[125] Xi's stark warning seems an admission that China's apparently growing clout in the world scene – together with its AI-enabled *fangkong* apparatus at home – may not be sufficient to maintain the CCP's perennial ruling party status.

That Xi seems no longer to sing the praises of the "fourfold self-confidence" of socialism with Chinese characteristics is good news for intellectuals, rights attorneys, house church leaders and NGO activists. As a popular Chinese saying goes, "while the priest climbs up one foot, the devil climbs ten." This proverb could be interpreted to mean that, however stringent and foolproof government fiats and strictures may be, members of the opposition can always find ways of circumventing, if not defeating, the draconian measures of the regime, particularly one whose mandate of heaven seems highly jeopardized. Despite the authorities' supposedly ironclad control over the Internet, new technologies have enabled dissidents, intellectuals and other civic organizers to at least send their messages along the information superhighway – even if such messages might be wiped out within 10 hours or so. Moreover, the following chapters in this book illustrate that disparate organizations, ranging from house churches to NGOs fighting for the welfare of migrant laborers and demobilized soldiers, have ways and means of not only staying connected, but also organizing activities on and off the net. The refusal of the resurgent Chinese civil society to retreat before Xi's formidable police-state behemoth has kept the flames of reform, especially political reform, alive.

Crackdown with unprecedented force

As China assumes the status of a quasi-superpower whose goal is to overtake the comprehensive strength of the United States by the middle of the century, elements of the CCP leadership seem confident they can defy world opinion through adopting what critics call a scorched-earth policy toward dissidents, intellectuals,

NGO organizers and other potential enemies of the state. The following chapters of the book will give a detailed treatment of Beijing's policy toward intellectuals, human rights lawyers, as well as the underground church. After nearly seven years in office, it has become apparent that, in terms of both the number of targets and the severity of repressive measures, President Xi's treatment of so-called foes of the regime is much more iron-fisted than that of former Presidents Jiang Zemin and Hu Jintao.

Perhaps the best illustration of the party-state's paranoia is its anxiety to ensure that possible aftereffects of political and social movements would be eradicated. This includes muzzling the voices of members who used to be associated with now-defunct rival political parties, as well as participants in social movements such as the student demonstrations in the spring of 1989.

Despite the fact that underground political parties have virtually disappeared, the authorities have continued to crack down on former adherents of these organized groups of opposition. Take, for example, the China Democracy Party, which was active mostly in the 1990s. Remnant members of the CDP, however, have continued to be rounded up – and penalized with heavy jail terms. Thus, Chen Shuqing and Lu Gensong, who are Zhejiang-based members of the CDP, were sentenced in June 2016 to, respectively, 10 and a half years and 11 years in jail. Given that, to all intents and purposes, the CDP had been wiped out by the new century, it was not surprising that Chen and Lu were charged with subverting state power based on articles they had written for overseas-based Chinese websites. For example, Chen was alleged to have written 20-odd articles for Boxun.com and Canyu.com criticizing the regime. Yet there was no explanation as to how these articles could have any possibility of bringing down the party![126]

The quasi-police-state apparatus has also zeroed in on the supporters and kinfolk of generations of victims of party dictatorship. Police suppression of the Tiananmen Mothers – the parents and relatives of students killed in the capital during the June 4, 1989 crackdown – is well known. In late May every year, prominent members of the Tiananmen Mothers would be barred from talking to foreign reporters; in many instances, they were forced to "take holidays in the provinces" so that they would not be in a position to stage protests in the capital.[127] In May 2016, Sichuan resident Fu Hailu was detained by the police after he had posted on social media pictures of bottles of wine with labels that read "Ming Company *bajiu liusi*," which was a clear reference to what happened on June 4, 1989. (In Chinese, the words "Ming Company" and "deeply remember" sound the same; *bajiu liusi* is the pinyin version of June 4, 1989). The police locked him up on alleged charges of "inciting subversion of state power."[128]

Even more stringent are the measures taken by the police to prevent ordinary citizens from paying their respects to victims of the Cultural Revolution. Take the case of Lin Zhao, a Peking University student who was executed on April 30, 1968 for daring to criticize Chairman Mao. Every year since the early 2010s, more than 100 public security personnel have cordoned off her grave in Lingyan Hill, Suzhou. This prompted Yu Jianrong, a respected sociologist at the Chinese

Academy of Social Sciences, to issue a protest on his blog: "I can't help asking. Where is the self-confidence of the CCP?" Yu was, of course referring to a key slogan of President Xi, that party members should have "self-confidence in the path, theories, system and culture" of socialism with Chinese characteristics.[129]

The police also take drastic steps to ensure that relatives of victims of major disasters will not take vocal measures to fight for their rights. Take, for example, the two most devastating accidents in 2015: the sinking of the tourist boat Eastern Star in the Yangtze River, which resulted in the loss of 442 lives, and explosions at a chemical warehouse in Tianjin, which killed 173 firefighters and workers. Relatives who demanded an official account of the "real causes" behind the two mishaps – or who wanted to get a higher level of compensation than the measly sums offered by the authorities – were beaten by the police. In many cases, leaders of the bereaved relatives were put on 24-hour surveillance for fear that they would organize demonstrations and otherwise disturb stability.[130]

During the Cultural Revolution, not only were the cream of the intelligentsia subjected to the most heinous humiliation, but those who chose to commit suicide were further accused of *zijueyu renmin* ("terminally alienating oneself from the people").[131] This has begged the question of whether the CCP administration's ruthless suppression of dissidents and civil-society activists amounts also to some form of "terminally alienating oneself from the people." Owing to the Xi leadership's apparently tight control over the high-tech police-state apparatus, the idea that the oppressors of the people might eventually face inevitable comeuppance may seem far-fetched. Chinese history, however, is replete with examples of how putatively omniscient emperors – and their accomplices – have met with grievous fates for alienating themselves from the populace.

The contributions of the public sphere

For the foreseeable future, it seems unlikely that dissidents and NGO organizers can find sufficient chinks in the armor of the state-police apparatus to challenge socialist orthodoxy and CCP rule. Yet, as rebel leaders in Eastern Europe in the 1980s such as Václav Havel noted, when collective revulsion against dictatorial rule boils over, the opposition movement can coalesce and do battle with the façade of authority with unexpected ferocity. This is how Havel described the Charter 77 movement, one of the first pitched battles fought between severely out-gunned dissident groups in Soviet-ruled Czechoslovakia and the Czech Communist Party. In his landmark *The Power of the Powerless*, Havel wrote:

> Charter 77 would have been unimaginable without that powerful sense of solidarity among widely differing groups, and without the sudden realization that it was impossible to go on waiting any longer, and that the truth had to be spoken loudly and collectively, regardless of the virtual certainty of sanctions and the uncertainty of any tangible results in the immediate future.[132]

Despite the dissimilarity between 1977 Czechoslovakia and 2019 China, lessons can be learned as to whether outmaneuvered individuals and groups who stand on the right side of history could yet initiate changes in a political landscape dominated by a party championing falsehoods and tyranny.

Although new, bold calls for the expansion of the public sphere may have been suppressed in the media since the mid-2010s, the arguments of pro-civil-society academics – ranging from those published toward the end of the Hu Jintao era to those published during the ongoing Chinese–American Cold War – still sound as convincing as ever. The civil society is broadly seen as the logical conclusion of the emancipation of the individual. According to sociologist Zhou Xiaozheng, a professor at Beijing's Renmin University, "the entire dignity of the human race lies in humankind's ability to think." Zhou interpreted one of Deng Xiaoping's most acclaimed accomplishments – thought liberation – as liberation from the Maoist era of brainwashing. He sees as China's foremost task the nurturing of *gongmin* (which can be translated as "civil" or "citizens"), or people who can freely and responsibly make decisions regarding their behaviors. "China abounds in riffraff, rabbles, peasants or ignoramuses," he said. "Yet we are in dire need of citizens who have an innate aspiration for social justice."[133] At the same time, Zhou pointed out, the emergence of NGOs and other elements of a civil society is indispensable to this public education of gargantuan proportions.

For Professor Jia Xijin, the best solution not only for social management, but for the improvement of governance, is "to seek a partnership rather than an antagonistic relationship between society and the state." "The civil society is an innovative way of solving [sociopolitical] problems," said Jia, who teaches at Tsinghua University's School of Public Policy and Management. "It is a way of life … [and not just] a form of supplementary resources or manpower for the administrative power of the state." Yet, for the civil society to develop to the point where it could interact productively with the state machinery, there must be a recognition of the worth and innate self-sufficiency of the individual. "The civil society is a lifestyle based on the self-governance of citizens," Jia concluded. "It is a liberal institutional arrangement under the law, a society that is predicated upon individuals as basic units … and where the rights of the individual are the point of departure of social order." The sociologist sees the following as the "biggest challenge to Chinese civil society": whether China can make the transition "from collectivist concepts to individualistic concepts; from a uni-centric order of control to a multi-polar order of self-rule, and from worship of power to belief in the rule of law."[134]

Fellow academic Han Guozhi agrees. Unlike members of the Xi Jinping administration, Han sees no contradiction between state power and the civil society. The Inner Mongolia Nationalities University professor argued that, "the political state and the civil society could seek progress harmoniously." "We should affirm the autonomous and independent nature of the civil society, which enables it to maintain an adequate degree of tension with the political state," he wrote in 2014. Han added that mutual interaction between the state and the civil society should be premised upon "the coexistence of two self-sufficient entities, and not the absolute control and swallowing up of one [political] force by another."[135]

According to Chinese University of Hong Kong sociologist Chan Kin-man, while the Chinese civil society is at a low ebb, it must be remembered that organizations akin to NGOs have a tradition going back to the late 19th century. They first became active in the last decade or so of the Qing Dynasty. Chan citied members of the educated classes discussing politics in tea houses or in the grounds of temples. There were also charitable associations and even newspapers run by China's first generation of industrialists and merchants. At this stage of China's development, dissident intellectuals and forward-looking organizations can only patiently wait for a big change in the political set-up. According to Chan, one reason for optimism could be that Xi's efforts to reform the system are bound to fail, and that the weak links of the police state could be exploited by civil-society groupings. "Xi hopes that the CCP can reform itself internally, from the upper to the lower echelons," Chan wrote in 2015. "This is like a doctor performing heart surgery on himself." Despite the overwhelming oppression of the public sphere, the sociologist thinks that, "we should continue to safeguard our democratic awareness." "If not, we would be ill-equipped to [grab the chances of democratization] when opportunities arise," said Chan, one of the leaders of the 2014 pro-democracy Umbrella Movement in Hong Kong.[136]

Notes

1 Cited in "People power under attack: Findings from the CIVICUS Monitor," World Alliance for Citizen Participation, October 4, 2017, www.civicus.org/images/CM_Findings_7Oct_v1.pdf

2 For a discussion of growing labor unrest, see, for example, Harvey Thomlinson, "China's Communist Party Is Abandoning Workers," *New York Times*, April 2, 2018, www.nytimes.com/2018/04/02/opinion/china-communist-party-workers-strikes.html. The last estimate of the number of annual "mass incidents" was given by veteran sociology professor Sun Liping of Tsinghua University. He reckoned that there were 180,000 such incidents in the year 2010. Another reference was provided by labor NGO activist Lu Yuyu, who estimated that there were 30,000 mass incidents such as rallies, assemblies and protests in 2015. It must be noted, however, that the Tsinghua Sociology Department has a long record of studying social disturbances. Lu and his partner compiled the number of mass incidents mainly based on media accounts and information from their sources within the labor and other NGO spheres. See Yang Yang, "Mass incidents have exceeded 180,000; social disturbances have been exacerbated," *Deutsche Welle*, September 29, 2011, www.dw.com/zh/%E7%BE%A4%E4%BD%93%E4%BA%8B%E4%BB%B6%E5%B7%B2%E8%B6%8518%E4%B8%87%E4%B8%AD%E5%9B%BD%E7%A4%BE%E4%BC%9A%E5%8A%A8%E8%8D%A1%E5%8A%A0%E5%89%A7/a-15426349. See also "A volunteer called 'Non-news' and his girl friend proclaim that there were 30,000 mass incidents last year," Radio Free Asia, June 21, 2016, www.rfa.org/mandarin/yataibaodao/renquanfazhi/ql1-06212016103919.html

3 For a discussion of the increasing criticism that Xi faces within the party, see, for example, Willy Lam, "Who are Xi Jinping's enemies," *China Brief*, Jamestown Foundation, December 4, 2018, https://jamestown.org/program/who-are-xi-jinpings-enemies/. See also "Top Chinese officials forced to carry out self-criticisms," AFP,

December 27, 2018, www.channelnewsasia.com/news/asia/top-chinese-officials-for
ced-to-carry-out-self-criticisms-11067182

4   For a discussion of Xi Jinping's "concept of the battleground," see, for example, Cao
    Zhenghai, "We must boost our awareness of the battleground," *People's Daily*, November
    19, 2013, http://politics.people.com.cn/n/2013/1109/c1001-23483987.html

5   For a discussion of the rationales and manifestations of the "fourfold self-confidence,"
    see, for example, "The internal rationale and major significance of upholding 'fourfold
    self-confidence'," *Hebei Daily*, October 27, 2016, http://news.xinhuanet.com/poli
    tics/2016-10/27/c_1119795391.htm

6   Cited in "How many people of conscience has God left China," Bannedbook.org,
    December 8, 2015, www.bannedbook.org/bnews/zh-tw/sohnews/20151208/
    479245.html

7   Ibid.

8   For a discussion of Zhang Kangkang's ideas about the Chinese system, see, for exam-
    ple, "Zhang Kangkang: do not become a person who knows the most but who has
    the least [inclination for] thinking and reflection," *Xiaoshuo Yuebao (Novels Monthly)*,
    October 31, 2016, https://mp.weixin.qq.com/s?__biz=MjM5ODgwNjEyMg==&m
    id=2655339771&idx=1&sn=352974c06773669e4c2f2819a9ae10f0

9   "How many people of conscience has God left China," Bannedbook.org. For a dis-
    cussion of Zi's idea on the decline of Chinese culture, see also Zi Zhongyun, "I feel
    that we have the tendency of going toward savagery," Culture Sohu Net, January 11,
    2016, http://cul.sohu.com/20160111/n434152618.shtml

10 For a discussion of the "thought liberation" under Hu Yaobang and Zhao Ziyang, see,
    for example, Willy Wo-Lap Lam, *The Era of Zhao Ziyang*, Hong Kong: A.B. Books &
    Stationery, 1989, pp. 19–44.

11 For a discussion on the controversy surrounding Hu's statement on Marxism, see, for
    example, "China corrects a slip in ideology," Reuters, December 11, 1984, www.
    nytimes.com/1984/12/11/world/china-corrects-a-slip-in-ideology.html. See also Pico
    Iyer, "The Second Revolution," *Time*, June 24, 2001, http://content.time.com/tim
    e/magazine/article/0,9171,142530,00.html

12 For a definition of *wangyi zhongyan* ("make groundless criticism of the central party
    authorities"), see, for example, "The Central Commission for Disciplinary Inspection
    explains 'wangyi zhongyan'," *People's Daily Online*, November 2, 2015, http://politics.
    people.com.cn/n/2015/1102/c70731-27766237.html

13 For a discussion of Mao's views on *dangxing*, see "Mao Zedong talks about party con-
    struction: on individual characteristics and party characteristics," *Research on Party Con-
    struction* (Beijing), November 20, 2004, www.wutnews.net/news/news.aspx?id=4804/

14 See Mao Zedong, "Talks at the Yan'an Forum on Literature and Art" (1942) in
    Selected Works of Mao Tse-tung Online, www.marxists.org/reference/archive/mao/selec
    ted-works/volume-3/mswv3_08.htm

15 For a discussion of Lenin's concept of proletariats and party members being the "cogs
    and wheels of the revolution," see, for example, Paul Le Blanc, *Lenin and the Revolu-
    tionary Party*, Chicago: Haymarket Books, 1992, pp. xxv–xxvi.

16 Mao Zedong, "Talks at the Yan'an Forum on Literature and Art."

17 See "Mao Zedong on the qualifications and criteria of members of the Communist
    Party," *People's Daily Online*, June 12, 2016, http://dangshi.people.com.cn/n1/2016/
    0612/c85037-28425916.html

18 Cited in "Xi Jinping: ideological and propaganda work is an extremely important
    work of the party," Xinhua News Agency, August 20, 2013, http://news.xinhuanet.
    com/politics/2013–08/20/c_117021464.htm

19 See Yang Faxiang, "Party nature is the amelioration, sublimation and crystallization of
    human nature," *Study Times* (Beijing), August 19, 2013, http://opinion.hexun.com/
    2013-08-19/157199427.html

20 For a discussion of the "controversy over the surnames," see "Deng Xiaoping's talk in
    southern China has cut the dead knot about 'surnamed socialist' vs. 'surnamed

capitalist,'" Xinhua News Agency, November 18, 2011, http://news.xinhuanet.com/theory/2008-11/18/content_10373415.htm

21 Xi has on many occasions warned against the party making "subversive mistakes," that is, political or economic policies that could subvert the socialist system and threaten party rule. He even said, irrespective of how brilliant and effective a policy was, it should not be adopted if it could jeopardize the CCP's "perennial ruling party" status. In other words, only polices "surnamed socialist" should be considered. See Xi Jinping, "Subversive mistakes must not be made over fundamental issues," China News Service, October 8, 2013, www.chinanews.com/gn/2013/10-08/5347578.shtml

22 Cited in "Xi Jinping's speech at the seminar for literature and artistic work," Xinhua News Agency, October 15, 2015, http://news.xinhuanet.com/zgjx/2015-10/15/c_134715070.htm. It is significant that Xi, who fancies himself a "21st century Mao," likes to duplicate major meetings initiated by Chairman Mao. Another example took place in 2014, when Xi organized a meeting on political work in the military in Gutian, a village in Fujian Province that is famous for being the venue where Mao spoke in 1929 on army discipline and strategy. See "Xi Jinping makes major speech at seminar on military work for the army held in Gutian," Xinhua News Agency, November 1, 2014, http://news.xinhuanet.com/politics/2014-11/01/c_1113074055.htm

23 Like Mao, Xi has raised the crypto-liberal slogan of "let a hundred flowers bloom" on various occasions, but his suppression of artistic freedom recalls the harsh measures of the late chairman. See, for example, Xi's speech at a meeting of the China Federation of Literary and Artistic Circles. Cited in "Xi Jinping: raise high the spiritual torch of the people and blow loudly the horn of the advancement of the times," Xinhua News Agency, November 30, 2016, http://news.cctv.com/2016/11/30/ARTI3h9Xu62q2qaL6lVGSfZt161130.shtml

24 "Xi Jinping's speech at the seminar for literature and artistic work."

25 Cited in "Xi Jinping chairs over senior on literature and artistic work; he emphasizes that the arts should not be tainted by commercial interests," China News Service, October 15, 2014, www.chinanews.com/gn/2014/10-15/6683121.shtml

26 Cited in Zhang He and Xu Lei, "An interview with post-1980 Net author Zhou Xiaoping: we must uphold our own cultural values," *People's Daily*, October 24, 2014, http://politics.people.com.cn/n/2014/1024/c1001-25897492.html. See also Cary Huang, "Xi Jinping handshake has bloggers thrust into mainstream," *South China Morning Post*, November 2, 2014, www.scmp.com/comment/insight-opinion/article/1629999/xi-jinping-handshake-has-bloggers-thrust-mainstream

27 Cited in "Beijing's delineation of the 'new five black categories' has been criticized as [reminiscent of] Nazism," *Apple Daily* (Hong Kong), August 5, 2012, https://hk.news.appledaily.com/international/daily/article/20120805/16576327. See also Chang Ping, "How the 'new five black categories' are changing China," *Deutsche Welle Chinese*, August 2, 2012, www.dw.com/zh/%E6%96%B0%E9%BB%91%E4%BA%94%E7%B1%BB%E6%94%B9%E5%8F%98%E4%B8%AD%E5%9B%BD/a-16139544?&zhongwen=simp

28 Cited in Yuan Peng, "Where does the real challenge to China lie?" *People's Daily*, July 31, 2012, http://paper.people.com.cn/rmrbhwb/html/2012-07/31/content_1090137.htm

29 For a discussion of China's overarching plans to project its values and "soft power," see, for example, Eleanor Albert, "China's big bet on soft power," Council on Foreign Affairs, New York, February 9, 2018, www.cfr.org/backgrounder/chinas-big-bet-soft-power. See also "China soft power Part I: Beijing finds projecting soft power harder than it appears," Radio Free Asia commentary, May 15, 2017, www.rfa.org/english/commentaries/soft-power-05152017150724.html

30 See Liu Shaoqi, "On the cultivation of a Communist Party member," *People's Daily*, May 26, 2004, www.people.com.cn/GB/shizheng/8198/30513/30515/33955/2524494.html. See also Li Zengfu, "Liu Shaoqi and his 'On the cultivation of a Communist Party member,'" *People's Daily Online*, October 21, 2015, http://dangjian.people.com.cn/n/2015/1021/c117092-27722891.html

31   Cited in Chen Fang, "What kinds of demands has Xi Jinping made to thirty-six mass groups on fulfilling core values?" Phoenix Television, July 21, 2015, http://news. ifeng.com/a/20150721/44211209_0.shtml

32   For an elaboration of Xi's concept of socialist values, see "Xi Jinping's views on core socialist values," Xinhua News Agency, December 8, 2016, http://news.xinhuanet. com/politics/2016-12/08/c_129395314.htm

33   Ibid.

34   Cited in "Xi Jinping: render the core socialist values a matter of routine, [easy to] visualize, and a part of life," *People's Daily*, April 12, 2017, http://theory.people.com. cn/n1/2017/0412/c143843-29204288.html

35   For a discussion of the party's views on the manipulation of public opinion and information, see, for example, "The biggest politics lies in the people's heart; public opinion is a strong and powerful weapon," *Anhui News* Online, February 24, 2016, http://ll.anhuinews.com/system/2016/02/24/007231775.shtml

36   Cited in "Xi Jinping: we must do a better job in propaganda and ideological work," Gov.cn, August 20, 2013, www.gov.cn/ldhd/2013–08/20/content_2470599.htm

37   Cited in "At this stage, China cannot sustain the consequence of the loss of control over public opinion," *Seeking Truth*, August 16, 2013, http://media.china.com.cn/cm yw/2013-08-16/27056.html

38   Cited in "Number of NGOs in China grows to nearly 500,000," *China Daily*, March 20, 2012, www.chinadaily.com.cn/china/2012-03/20/content_14875389.htm

39   For a discussion of different categories of NGOs in China, as well as their potentials for changing sociopolitical norms, see, for example, Baogang He, *The Democratic Implications of Civil Society in China*, New York: Palgrave MacMillan, 1997; Qiusha Ma, *Non-Governmental Organizations in Contemporary China: Paving the way to Civil Society?* New York: Routledge, 2006; Li Fan, *Silent Revolution: Becoming Civil Society in China*, Toronto: Mirror Books, 1998; Fengshi Wu and Kin-Man Chan, "Graduated control and beyond: the evolving government–NGO relations," *Chinese Perspectives*, Issue 3, 2012, pp. 9–17; Deng Zhenglai, ed., *State and Civil Society: The Chinese Perspective*, Singapore: World Scientific, 2011; and Yu Keping, *Democracy is a Good Thing: Essays on Politics, Society and Culture in Contemporary China*, Washington, DC: Brookings Institution Press, 2009.

40   For a discussion of different categories of NGOs in China, see Yu Keping, "Chinese civil society: concepts, categorization and institutional environment," Aisixiang.com, June 9, 2006, www.aisixiang.com/data/9815-4.html. See also Jianyu He, "Mapping the Chinese NGO sector," Booksandideas.net, November 19, 2012, www.booksa ndideas.net/Mapping-the-Chinese-NGO-Sector.html

41   For a study of Hu Jintao's and Xi Jinping's policies toward social organizations, see, for example, Diana Fu and Greg Distelhorst, "Grassroots participation and repression under Hu Jintao and Xi Jinping," *The China Journal*, Vol 79, January 2018, www. journals.uchicago.edu/doi/abs/10.1086/694299?mobileUi=0&journalCode=tcj. See also Jessica C. Teets, "The future of civil society under Xi Jinping," China Policy Institute, Nottingham University, April 8, 2015, https://cpianalysis.org/2015/04/08/ the-future-of-civil-society-under-xi-jinping/; Chloe Froissart, "Changing patterns of Chinese civil society: comparing the Hu-Wen and the Xi Jinping era," in Willy Wo-Lap Lam, ed., *Routledge Handbook of the Chinese Communist Party*, Abingdon, UK: Routledge, 2018, pp. 352–371.

42   For a discussion of Deng Xiaoping's paranoia about Polish democratic ideas spreading into China in the mid-1980s, see, for example, Willy Lam, "The politics of Liu Xiaobo's trial," in Jean-Philippe Beja, Fu Hualing and Eva Pils, eds., *Liu Xiaobo, Charter 08, and the Challenges of Political Reform in China*, Hong Kong: Hong Kong University Press, 2012, p. 253.

43   Cited in editorial, "The lucky Jiang Zemin and the out-of-luck China," Radio Free Asia, September 3, 2002, www.rfa.org/cantonese/commentaries/88741-20020903.html

44 Cited in Wang Ming, "Analyzing civil society from different levels," *People's Forum*, No. 28, 2013, http://paper.people.com.cn/rmlt/html/2013-10/01/content_1308864.htm

45 Ibid.

46 Cited in "Li Fan: the current state of the Chinese civil society," Aisixiang.com, December 13, 2014, www.aisixiang.com/data/81270.html

47 Cited in Ji Dahe, *The Orientations of Xi Jinping*, Taipei, Leaders' Press, 2015, pp. 156–162.

48 "Li Fan: the current state of the Chinese civil society."

49 For a discussion of Beijing's fears about foreign NGOs interfering in domestic politics, see Liu Youping, "The situation and influence of the charitable activities of American NGOs in China," Aisixiang.com, August 15, 2015, www.aisixiang.com/data/91353.html

50 For a study of the impact on the enactment of Article 23 of the Basic Law in Hong Kong, see, for example, Elson Tong, "Reviving Article 23 (Part II): old wine in new bottles for Hong Kong's national security debate," February 18, 2018, www.hongkongfp.com/2018/02/18/reviving-article-23-part-ii-old-wine-new-bottles-hong-kongs-national-security-debate/

51 Cited in Yu Keping, "The emergence of Chinese civil society and its significance to governance," Cccpe.com, Winter 2002, www.ids.ac.uk/ids/civsoc/final/china/chn8.doc

52 For a discussion of Hu's reaction to the "color revolution" in Kyrgyzstan, see, for example, Willy Wo-Lap Lam, *Chinese Politics in the Hu Jintao Era*, Armonk, NY: M.E. Sharpe, 2006, pp. 173–174.

53 For a discussion of Hu Jintao's policy toward NGOs, see "Policy Brief No. 10: The 18th Party Congress and China's Civil Society," *China Development Brief* (Beijing), December 3, 2012, http://chinadevelopmentbrief.cn/articles/special-policy-brief-no-11-november-2012-the-18th-party-congress-and-chinas-civil-society/

54 Cited in "Hu Jintao makes important speech at start of seminar for major provincial leaders on social management and its innovation," Xinhua News Agency, March 20, 2011, www.most.gov.cn/jgdj/djyw/201103/t20110330_85718.htm

55 Cited in Willy Wo-Lap Lam, *Chinese Politics in the Hu Jintao Era*, pp. 243–44.

56 Cited in Chen Zhengxin, "Wang Yang: we will delegate to social organizations whatever they 'are capable to handle and manage well,'" *Guangzhou Daily*, November 24, 2011, http://news.cntv.cn/china/20111123/104830.shtml. See also "Guangdong social organizations need not have a sponsoring supervision unit when they are registered," Xinhua News Agency, November 24, 2011, http://news.cntv.cn/china/20111124/101449.shtml

57 Cited in Yaxue Cao, "Chinese authorities orchestrate surprise raid of labor NGOs in Guangdong, arresting leaders," China Change, December 10, 2015, https://chinachange.org/2015/12/10/chinese-authorities-orchestrate-surprise-raid-of-labor-ngos-in-guangdong-arresting-leaders/. See also "Guangdong labour activists to face trial by end of September," *China Labor Bulletin*, September 13, 2016, www.clb.org.hk/content/guangdong-labour-activists-face-trial-end-september

58 Cited in Zhou Tianyong and Wu Hui, "Develop the positive functions of people's organizations and religion," *People's Daily*, May 4, 2008, http://theory.people.com.cn/BIG5/68294/120979/120980/7191036.html

59 See Xu Yongguang, "2008: the first year of the Chinese civil society," People's Daily, June 3, 2008, http://politics.people.com.cn/GB/1026/7336201.html

60 See Yu Keping, "China must implement social renovation via nurturing a civil society," *People's Daily*, May 26, 2010, http://politics.people.com.cn/GB/14562/11707253.html

61 Cited in "The Beijing municipal government is spending 100 million yuan to purchase 300 counts of livelihood services," *China Securities News*, July 30, 2010, http://business.sohu.com/20100713/n273470264.shtml; "The government is buying welfare services from five social organizations," *Suzhou News Net*, July 19, 2014, http://news.subaonet.com/2014/0719/1364069.shtml

62 Cited in "Party central authorities confirm the setting up of party organizations in the leadership organs of social organizations," Xinhua News Agency, May 30, 2015, http://politics.people.com.cn/n/2015/0530/c70731-27078843.html

63 Cited in "Opinion on reforming the management system of social organizations and promoting the healthy and orderly development of social organizations," China News Service, August 21, 2016, www.chinanews.com/gn/2016/08-21/7979647.shtml

64 For a discussion of the plight of NGOs from 2012 onwards, see, for example, Carolyn Hsu, Fang-Yu Chen, Jamie P. Horsley and Rachel Stern, "The state of NGOs in China today," Brookings Institution, December 15, 2016, www.brookings.edu/blog/up-front/2016/12/15/the-state-of-ngos-in-china-today/. See also "People's organizations in the mainland have attracted the ire of the authorities," Cable News Hong Kong, March 27, 2015, http://cablenews.i-cable.com/ci/videopage/news/454866/%E5%8D%B3%E6%99%82%E6%96%B0%E8%81%9E/%E5%85%A7%E5%9C%B0%E6%B0%91%E9%96%93%E7%B5%84%E7%B9%94%E6%98%93%E6%83%B9%E5%AE%98%E6%96%B9%E5%8F%8D%E6%84%9F

65 For a discussion of the crackdown on the feminists, see, for example, Jinyan Zeng, "China's feminist five: 'this is the worst crackdown on lawyers, activists and scholars in decades,'" *The Guardian*, April 17, 2015, www.theguardian.com/lifeandstyle/2015/apr/17/chinas-feminist-five-this-is-the-worst-crackdown-on-lawyers-activists-and-scholars-in-decades

66 Cited in Zou Sheng, "China's premier protector of harbor seals Ding Jiguang's retrial," Thepaper.cn (Shanghai), May 17, 2017, www.thepaper.cn/newsDetail_forward_1686480

67 Cited in "A representative from people's organizations expects an even more tough going ahead," Cable News Hong Kong, November 13, 2015, http://cablenews.i-cable.com/ci/index.php/VideoPage/news/470304/

68 For a discussion of the animal rights movement, see, for example, Simon Denyer, "Activists gather 11 million signatures against China's infamous dog-meat festival," *Washington Post*, June 10, 2016, www.washingtonpost.com/news/worldviews/wp/2016/06/10/china-stop-eating-dogs-animal-rights-activists-campaign-against-annual-festival-of-slaughter/

69 Cited in Benjamin Haas, "China 'eliminating civil society' by targeting human rights activists – report," *The Guardian*, February 16, 2017, www.theguardian.com/world/2017/feb/16/china-eliminating-civil-society-by-targeting-human-rights-activists-report

70 For an explication and discussion of the Foreign NGO Law, see, for example, Kristin Shi-Kupfer and Bertram Lang, "Overseas NGOs in China: Left in Legal Limbo," *The Diplomat*, March 4, 2017, https://thediplomat.com/2017/03/overseas-ngos-in-china-left-in-legal-limbo/. See also Verna Yu, "Charity workers in China say NGOs being 'pulled out by the roots'," *South China Morning Post*, January 22, 2016, www.scmp.com/news/china/policies-politics/article/1903724/charity-workers-china-say-ngos-being-pulled-out-roots.

71 Cited in "An interpretation of the Management Law of Foreign NGOs within China," *Cishangongyi bao* ("Charity and Public Welfare Paper"), May 17, 2016, http://news.xinhuanet.com/gongyi/2016-05/17/c_128985970.htm

72 Ibid. See also Kenji Kawase, "China's new NGO law tightens the already short leash on civil society," *Nikkei Asia Review*, May 12, 2016, https://asia.nikkei.com/magazine/20160512-WEALTHIER-UNHEALTHIER/Politics-Economy/China-s-new-NGO-law-tightens-the-already-short-leash-on-civil-society?page=2

73 Cited in "Joint letter: Freedom House joins a call to repeal China's NGO Law," Freedom House, June 1, 2016, https://freedomhouse.org/article/joint-letter-freedom-house-joins-call-repeal-china-s-ngo-law

74 Cited in Nick Ching and William Ide, "US voices concerns about China's NGO Law," Voice of America, June 7, 2016, www.voanews.com/a/us-secretary-state-john-kerry-concerns-china-ngo-law/3365695.html

75 Cited in "Official media publishes article by Hu Angang: the people's society is superior to the civil society," *People's Daily Overseas Edition*, July 19, 2013, http://big5.xinhuanet.com/gate/big5/news.xinhuanet.com/politics/2013-07/19/c_125031886.htm

76 "Why is the people's society better than the civil society?" *People's Daily Overseas Edition*, July 19, 2013, www.people.com.cn/24hour/n/2013/0719/c25408-22246032.html

77 Cited in Wang Shaoguang, "The direction for constructing society: 'civil society' or people's society?" Aisixiang.com, November 28, 2014, www.aisixiang.com/data/80646-4.html

78 Cited in "Xi Jinping postulates perfecting the system of the people running their own affairs and developing socialist democratic politics," Xinhua News Agency, October 18, 2017, http://cpc.people.com.cn/19th/n1/2017/1018/c414305-29594502.html

79 For a discussion of the future of the Central Political-Legal Commission, see Sidney Leng, "China's domestic security commission gets renewed powers under restructuring plan," *South China Morning Post*, March 22, 2018, www.scmp.com/news/china/policies-politics/article/2138272/chinas-domestic-security-commission-gets-renewed-powers. See also Richard McGregor, *The Party: The Secret World of China's Communist Rulers*, New York: Harper Perennial, 2010, pp. 189–191.

80 For a discussion of the role and functions of the CNSC, see, for example, Joel Wuthnow, "Decoding China's new 'National Security Commission'," CNA China Studies, December 2013, www.cna.org/CNA_files/PDF/CPP-2013-U-006465-Final.pdf. See also "New Chinese agency to 'manage' social unrest," Radio Free Asia, November 12, 2013, www.rfa.org/english/news/china/agency-11122013140403.html

81 See "National security is a matter of prime importance: President Xi," Xinhua News Agency, April 15, 2014, http://english.cri.cn/6909/2014/04/15/2361s822190.htm

82 Ibid.

83 For a discussion of the composition of the CNSC, see, for example, Willy Lam, "Terrorism fears push muscular approach to 'overall national security'," *China Brief*, Jamestown Foundation, May 7, 2014, https://osintjournal.wordpress.com/2014/05/08/china-terrorism-fears-push-muscular-approach-to-overall-national-security/

84 For an explication of the role of the *zhengfa shuji*, see, for example, Cai Changchun, "The *zhengfa shuji* in many provinces are reshuffled; they no longer have joint appointments as head of the local police," *Legal Daily*, August 2, 2017, http://leaders.people.com.cn/n1/2017/0802/c58278-29443398.html. See also "Hebei Secretary for Political and Legal Affairs: take a firm grip on the new situation and symptoms of social risk," *Legal Daily*, November 25, 2015, www.chinapeace.gov.cn/2015-11/25/content_11284380.htm

85 Cited in "Expert: China needs a national security commission to lay out anti-terrorism strategies," *China Daily*, November 12, 2013, www.chinadaily.com.cn/dfpd/2013szqh18/2013-11/12/content_17100135.htm

86 Cited in Willy Lam, "Xi's power grab dwarfs market reforms," *Asia Times*, November 21, 2013, www.atimes.com/atimes/China/CHIN-01-211113.html

87 Cited in Chris Buckley, "China internal security spending jumps past army budget," Reuters, March 5, 2011, www.reuters.com/article/us-china-unrest/china-internal-security-spending-jumps-past-army-budget-idUSTRE7222RA20110305. See also Bruce Lui, "Let's estimate this year's *weiwen* budget," *Ming Pao*, March 9, 2016, https://news.mingpao.com/pns/dailynews/web_tc/article/20160309/s00012/1457459535343

88 See Guo Shengkun, "Deeply push forward the construction of a social law and order prevention-and-control system," Xinhua News Agency, May 24, 2016, www.gov.cn/guowuyuan/2016-05/24/content_5076376.htm

89 Cited in "Xi: national security 'a matter of prime importance,'" Xinhua News Agency, April 16, 2014, www.china.org.cn/china/2014-04/16/content_32104039.htm

90 For a discussion of the establishment of China's high-tech police state and the latest surveillance equipment used, see, for example, Zak Doffman, "Why we should fear China's emerging high-tech surveillance state," *Forbes*, October 28, 2018, www.forbes.com/sites/

zakdoffman/2018/10/28/why-we-should-fear-chinas-emerging-high-tech-surveilla nce-state/#dd473504c36b. See also Eva Xiao, "Armed drones, iris scanners: China's high-tech security gadgets," Phys.org, October 26, 2018, https://phys.org/news/ 2018-10-armed-drones-iris-scanners-china.html; Willy Wo-Lap Lam, "Beijing harnesses big data & AI to perfect the police state," *China Brief*, Jamestown Foundation, July 21, 2017, https://jamestown.org/program/beijing-harnesses-big-data-ai-to-perfect-the-poli ce-state/

91 For a discussion of how AI is aiding China's national security, see, for example, staff reporters, "Industries in the area of security and defense have become AI's 'first land-ing ground,'" *Auhui Daily*, July 11, 2017, http://difang.gmw.cn/roll2/2017-07/11/ content_119176930.htm

92 For a discussion of how AI-aided security instruments have facilitated surveillance over dissidents, see for example, Reuters, "Chinese activists fear increased surveillance under new security law," May 26, 2017, www.scmp.com/news/china/policies-poli tics/article/2095810/chinese-activists-fear-increased-surveillance-under-new. See also "China publishes new regulations on surveillance instruments," *Liberty Times* (Taipei), December 4, 2016, http://news.ltn.com.tw/news/world/breakingnews/1906960

93 Cited in staff reporters, "Fugitive in Wuhan has been arrested after he has been recognized by facial-recognition software," *Ming Pao*, July 10, 2017, https://news. mingpao.com/ins/instantnews/web_tc/article/20170710/s00004/1499674488848.
    For a discussion of the potency of the facial recognition facilities of the Chinese police, see Josh Chin and Liza Lin, "China's all-seeing surveillance state is reading its citizens' faces," *Wall Street Journal*, June 26, 2017, www.wsj.com/articles/the-all-seeing-sur veillance-state-feared-in-the-west-is-a-reality-in-china-1498493020

94 Cited in "Deep Glint CEO Zhao Yong on the real situation of face recognition and China's intelligent security and defense [network]," AI Technology Review, CPS.com [Beijing], March 9, 2017, http://news.cps.com.cn/article/201703/929929_2.html

95 For a discussion of the business potentials of Megvii Technology Inc., see, for exam-ple, Fan Feifei, "Megvii gives a digital meaning to face-reading," *China Daily*, January 12, 2017, www.chinadaily.com.cn/business/tech/2017-01/12/content_27931630.htm

96 For a discussion of the national security implications of the "social credit" network, see, for example, Alexandra Ma, "China is building a vast civilian surveillance network – here are 10 ways it could be feeding its creepy 'social credit system,'" Businessinsider. com, April 29, 2018, www.businessinsider.com/how-china-is-watching-its-citizens-in-a -modern-surveillance-state-2018-4. See also Charles Parton, "Social credit is just one part of China's new state control," November 17, 2018, www.spectator.co.uk/2018/ 11/social-credit-is-just-one-part-of-chinas-new-state-control/

97 Cited in Catherine Lai, "China announces details of social credit system plan, deemed 'Orwellian' by critics," Hong Kong Free Press, January 3, 2017, www. hongkongfp.com/2017/01/03/test-zone-proposed-for-chinas-orwellian-social-cred it-system/. See also "Push forward the establishment of a new-type surveillance and control mechanism based on social credit [systems]," Chinasafety.gov.cn, June 27, 2017, www.chinasafety.gov.cn/newpage/Contents/Channel_4140/2017/0627/ 290445/content_290445.htm

98 Cited in "Xinjiang establishes a DNA data bank to collect the DNA of Uighurs," Radio Free Asia, May 17, 2017, www.rfa.org/cantonese/news/DNA-05172017095946. html. See also "China: police DNA database threatens privacy," Human Rights Watch, May 15, 2017, www.hrw.org/news/2017/05/15/china-police-dna-database-threatens-p rivacy

99 See "Eradicating ideological viruses: China's campaign of repression against Xinjiang's Muslims," Human Rights Watch, September 9, 2018, www.hrw.org/report/2018/ 09/09/eradicating-ideological-viruses/chinas-campaign-repression-against-xinjiangs. See also Gerry Shih, "AP exclusive: digital police state shackles Chinese minority," The Associated Press, December 17, 2017, https://apnews.com/1ec5143fe4764a1d8ea 73ce4a3e2c570

100 Cited in "Xinjiang official defends 'education centers' for Uighur Muslims," BBC News, October 16, 2018, www.bbc.com/news/world-asia-china-45872356. See also Edward Wong, "U.S. weighs sanctions against Chinese officials over Muslim detention camps," *New York Times*, September 10, 2018, www.nytimes.com/2018/09/10/world/asia/us-china-sanctions-muslim-camps.html

101 For a discussion of Beijing's use of vigilantes, see, for example, "China forms huge army of vigilantes to fight terrorism," Press Trust of India, October 4, 2014, www.business-standard.com/article/pti-stories/china-forms-huge-army-of-vigilantes-to-fight-terrorism-114100400220_1.html

102 For a discussion of the use of "vigilante volunteers" to maintain stability during the Shanghai Expo 2010, see, for example, Willy Lam, "Beijing's blueprint for tackling mass incidents and social management," *China Brief*, Jamestown Foundation, Washington, DC, March 25, 2011, https://jamestown.org/program/beijings-blueprint-for-tackling-mass-incidents-and-social-management/

103 Cited in Zhang Hui, "Beijing to mobilize all residents to help manage the capital," *Global Times*, July 4, 2017, www.globaltimes.cn/content/1054815.shtml. See also "Beijing's security volunteers exceed 850,000," *New Beijing Post*, July 12, 2017, www.china.com.cn/shehui/2017-07/12/content_41198147.htm

104 For a discussion of the "anti-espionage" functions of residents of Chaoyang District in Beijing, see "Revealing the secrets of 'the Chaoyang masses': 130,000 people have registered, and activists can get a monthly subsidy of 500 yuan," *The Paper* (Shanghai), September 21, 2017, http://news.163.com/17/0921/15/CUS9AB8O000187VE.htm l. See also "Over 850,000 security volunteers have registered in Beijing, including 'Chaoyang masses' and the 'Aunties of Xicheng'," Xinhua News Agency, December 19, 2015, http://news.xinhuanet.com/politics/2015-12/19/c_1117516033.htm

105 See Guo Shengkun, "Develop the function of intelligence so that acts of terrorism can be prevented and controlled," *People's Police News*, November 27, 2015, www.xjpeace.cn/state/high_rise/201511/t20151127_910751.htm

106 Cited in Xue Lansuo, "Strategic thoughts on work on stability maintenance," *People's Daily*, March 15, 2012, http://theory.people.com.cn/GB/40537/17398861.html

107 See Tania Branigan, "Chinese police chief boasts of recruiting one in 33 residents as informants," *The Guardian*, February 10, 2010, www.theguardian.com/world/2010/feb/10/china-police-informants-surveillance

108 See, for example, the deployment of "village police" in Qinghai Province: "Police departments in Qinghai focus on training 4,530 newly employed 'village police,'" *People's Public Security News*, November 18, 2015, www.chinapeace.gov.cn/zixun/2015-11/17/content_11282331.htm

109 Cited in Didi Kirsten Tatlow, "China's 'dangerous love' campaign, warning of spies, is met with shrugs," *New York Times*, April 21, 2016, www.nytimes.com/2016/04/22/world/asia/china-foreign-spy-warning.html?_r=1. For an example of public education on national security, see, for example, "Xinjiang implements series of activities on 'First Day of the People's Education on State Security'," Huaxia.com (Beijing), April 18, 2016, www.huaxia.com/xjbt/xwsc/2016/04/4806038.html

110 Cited in Cheng Qian, "The significance of schools initiating education in state security should not be belittled," www.jyb.cn, April 17, 2017, www.jyb.cn/opinion/pgypl/201704/t20170417_699887.html

111 For a discussion of the influence of Facebook and the social media on the Arab Spring revolutions, see, for example, Rebecca J. Rosen, "So, was Facebook responsible for the Arab Spring after all?" *The Atlantic*, September 3, 2011, www.theatlantic.com/technology/archive/2011/09/so-was-facebook-responsible-for-the-arab-spring-after-a ll/244314/. See also Jose Antonio Vargas, "Spring awakening: how an Egyptian revolution began on Facebook," *New York Times*, February 17, 2012, www.nytimes.com/2012/02/19/books/review/how-an-egyptian-revolution-began-on-facebook.html. For a discussion of how the Internet could influence the development of China's

civil society, see, for example, Ziwue Tai, *The Internet in China: Cyberspace and Civil Society*, New York: Routledge, 2006.

112 For a discussion of the effectiveness of Beijing in imposing a collective amnesia on the June 4 massacre and other party-made disasters, see, for example, Julie Makinen, "Collective amnesia prevails in China 25 years after Tiananmen Square," *Los Angeles Times*, July 1, 2014, www.latimes.com/world/asia/la-fg-china-tiananmen-anniversary-20140601-story.html. See also Dan Long, "China marks 26th Tiananmen anniversary with collective amnesia," Ucanews.com, June 4, 2015, www.ucanews.com/news/china-marks-26th-tiananmen-anniversary-with-collective-amnesia/73729

113 See "Very few Chinese citizens know about Liu Xiaobo's aspirations for democratic reforms," Central News Agency, July 13, 2017, http://news.mingjingnews.com/2017/07/blog-post_267.html. See also Lin Li, "Hu Jia: after freeing Xiaobo, we start to free Liu Xia," *Citizen News* (Hong Kong), July 14, 2017, www.hkcnews.com/article/5384/%E5%8A%89%E6%9B%89%E6%B3%A2-%E5%8A%89%E9%9C%9E-%E9%80%9D%E4%B8%96-5389/%E9%80%9D%E4%B8%96

114 Cited in "Xi Jinping: the Internet could lead to the collapse of the Party and the state," *Apple Daily*, November 6, 2013, https://hk.news.appledaily.com/local/daily/article/20131106/18495692

115 Cited in David Barboza, "China's president will lead a new effort on cybersecurity," *New York Times*, February 27, 2014, www.nytimes.com/2014/02/28/world/asia/china-announces-new-cybersecurity-push.html?_r=0. See also "China's Xi to run Internet security body: state media," Reuters, February 27, 2014, www.reuters.com/article/us-china-hacking/chinas-xi-to-run-internet-security-body-state-media-idUSBREA1Q1EX20140227

116 Cited in "China has 3.5 million Web sites," Xinhua News Agency, March 24, 2014, www.chinadaily.com.cn/business/tech/2014-03/24/content_17373577.htm. See also Charles Custer, "The demise of Sina Weibo: censorship or evolution?" *Forbes*, February 4, 2014, www.forbes.com/sites/ccuster/2014/02/04/the-demise-of-sina-weibo-censorship-or-evolution/#4c83913b48f4

117 "China has 3.5 million Web sites."

118 For a discussion of the "gag order" on the Internet and Weibo, see, for example, Megha Rajagopalan and Adam Rose, "China crackdown on online rumors seen as ploy to nail critics," Reuters, September 18, 2013, www.reuters.com/article/net-us-china-internet/china-crackdown-on-online-rumors-seen-as-ploy-to-nail-critics-idUSBRE98H07X20130918. See also "China must crack down on critical online speech – Party journal," Reuters, August 16, 2013, www.reuters.com/article/net-us-china-internet/china-must-crack-down-on-critical-online-speech-party-journal-idUSBRE98A18Z20130916

119 Cited in Sarah Zeng, "Man jailed for 5½ years, fined US$76,000 for selling VPN in southern China," *South China Morning Post*, December 21, 2017, www.scmp.com/news/china/policies-politics/article/2125326/man-jailed-51/2-years-fined-us76000-selling-vpn

120 For a discussion of the case of Charles Xue, see, "Four months after prostitution arrest, influential investor Charles Xue remains uncharged," *South China Morning Post*, January 11, 2014, www.scmp.com/news/china-insider/article/1403009/four-months-after-prostitution-arrest-influential-investor/. See also "China releases blogger on bail, jails another amid rumor crackdown," Reuters, April 16, 2014, www.reuters.com/article/2014/04/17/us-china-blogger-idUSBREA3G04A20140417/

121 Cited in Qiu Yu and Liu Chang, "Expert: the importance of the Internet in Xinjiang's terrorist activities has significantly increased," *Global Times*, January 26, 2014, http://news.ifeng.com/mainland/detail_2014_01/26/33362950_0.shtml

122 Cited in "China's 'Internet sovereignty' marks the return of ideology: analysts," Radio Free Asia, December 4, 2017, www.rfa.org/english/news/china/internet-12042017113832.html. See also Phoebe Zhang, "China's cyber police take aim at 'negative information' in new internet crackdown," *South China Morning Post*, January 3, 2019, www.scmp.com/news/

china/article/2180608/chinas-cyber-police-take-aim-negative-information-new-internet-crackdown

123 See David Bandurski, "Can the Internet and social media change the Party," in Willy Wo-Lap Lam, ed., *Routledge Handbook of the Chinese Communist Party*, p. 384.

124 Cited in "Xi Jinping: Be wary of 'black swans' and take precautions against 'grey rhinos,'" *People's Daily*, January 22, 2019, http://paper.people.com.cn/rmrbhwb/html/2019-01/22/content_1905265.htm

125 Ibid.

126 For a discussion of the sentencing of two members of the now-defunct China Democracy Party, see, for example, Chris Buckley, "Two Chinese activists sentenced to over 10 years on subversion charges," *New York Times*, June 17, 2016, www.nytimes.com/2016/06/18/world/asia/china-lu-gengsong-chen-shuqing.html?_r=1

127 For a discussion of the authorities' treatment of the "Tiananmen mothers," including their leader, Ding Zilin, see, for example, Austin Tracy, "Tiananmen mother Ding Zilin is being 'forced into silence' on the 27th anniversary of the June 4 incident," *New York Times, Chinese Edition*, June 2, 2016, https://cn.nytimes.com/china/20160602/china-ding-zilin-tiananmen-mothers/. See also "Ding Zilin: I want to say a few words deep in my heart," Human Rights Watch, October 27, 2016, www.hrichina.org/chs/zhong-guo-ren-quan-shuang-zhou-kan/ding-zi-lin-wo-xiang-xiang-da-jia-shuo-ji-ju-xin-li-hua

128 For a discussion of the "Mingji Bajiuliusi" incident, see, for example, staff reporters, "A Sichuan man who sells wine labelled 'Mingji Bajiuliusi' has been accused of subverting the state," *Apple Daily*, May 30, 2016, https://hk.news.appledaily.com/local/daily/article/20160530/19633505

129 Staff reporters, "300 people are evicted and beaten up while visiting the grave of Lin Zhao, who was executed by the Communist Party 46 years ago," *Apple Daily*, April 30, 2014, https://hk.news.appledaily.com/international/daily/article/20140430/18704860

130 Cited in Simon Denyer, "In China, relatives of disaster victims are cast as troublemakers," *Washington Post*, November 9, 2015, www.washingtonpost.com/world/asia_pacific/in-china-disaster-victims-are-recast-as-troublemakers/2015/11/06/439693d6-7bef-11e5-bfb6-65300a5ff562_story.html

131 For a discussion of suicide cases among intellectuals in post-1949 China, see, for example, Yue Nan, "Pain and anxious thoughts: on the fate of intellectuals during the Cultural Revolution," *China Youth Daily Online*, March 26, 2013, http://cul.qq.com/a/20130326/000046.htm

132 Cited in Václav Havel, *The Power of the Powerless* (1978), available on the www.vaclavhavel.cz website, www.vaclavhavel.cz/showtrans.php?cat=eseje&val=2_aj_eseje.html&typ=HTML

133 Cited in "Zhou Xiaozheng: how will China advance toward a civil society," Phoenix TV (Hong Kong), December 8, 2012, http://news.ifeng.com/opinion/politics/detail_2012_12/08/19969549_3.shtml

134 See Jia Xijin, "Explaining the civil society: the relationship between the state, society and the individual," Xinhua Net, June 24, 2010, http://club.kdnet.net/dispbbs.asp?id=9157557&boardid=1

135 See Han Guozhi, "The benevolent interaction between the 'political state' and the 'civil society,'" *People's Forum*, Issue 10, 2014, http://paper.people.com.cn/rmlt/html/2014-04/11/content_1427927.htm

136 Cited in Chan Kin-man, "The development of China's civil society," Hong Kong Alliance in Support of Patriotic Democratic Movements in China, May 22, 2015, www.youtube.com/watch?v=kWvnyf7ndHI

2

CONTRIBUTIONS OF INTELLECTUALS

Emancipating the mind in the midst of ruthless suppression

Introduction:
irreconcilable contradictions between reform-oriented intellectuals and the hard-authoritarian party-state apparatus

Whereas poorly educated peasant leaders were often at the forefront of rebellions that toppled dynasties in pre-modern China, intellectuals have, since the Hundred Days Reform (1898) of the Qing Dynasty (1644–1911), been at the cutting edge of cataclysmic events such as the 1911 Revolution, the May Fourth Movement of 1919 and, of course, the victory of the Communist Revolution in 1949.[1] However, Mao Zedong, who was half-peasant and half-intellectual, made sure that men and women of learning would be in no position to challenge the authority of the Chinese Communist Party (CCP) and its Great Helmsman. This tradition has been followed by Xi Jinping, who has inherited the late chairman's statecraft, particularly ways and means to shackle the Chinese mind.

In a 2002 article entitled "The poverty of China's civil opposition," late Nobel Peace Prize winner Liu Xiaobo asked this question:

> Why is it that, to-date, China's civil opposition, having received both the attention and support of the international community, has not been able to form an organized civil pressure group … [and that] China's civil opposition forces have not achieved the results as in other countries that are going through transformation?

Liu ascribed the plight to the shortfall of intellectual-like figures. "The success or failure of civil opposition movements depends to a great extent on the actions of the civil society elite," he wrote. "A mature civil opposition movement must bring forth symbolic figures who can rally popular opinion, inspire courage, and enlighten the masses."[2] Liu's characterization of these "symbolic figures" matches most definitions of intellectuals (*zhishifenzi*) or public intellectuals (*gonggong zhishifenzi*) cited by scholars who have written about the traits and contributions of socially and politically influential educated elites.[3] For example, East China Normal University social scientist Xu Jilin, a recognized theorist of the Chinese intelligentsia, has laid down this definition of *zhishifenzi*:

> The modern meaning of intellectuals points to that group of cultured people who with an independent status and relying on the strength of knowledge and spirit express a fervent public concern towards society and embody a sort of public conscience and spirit of public participation.[4]

However, it is also due to the revolutionary tradition of intellectuals that Chairman Mao, who labelled the educated class "stinking category nine" during the Cultural Revolution, harbored the greatest distrust of well-educated and outspoken citizens who are capable of independent thinking. Leaders from Mao to Xi have demanded that intellectuals subsume their human nature, intelligence and aspirations under *dangxing* (the party's nature and prerogatives) – and to function as what Lenin called "cogs and wheels of the revolutionary machinery."[5] The punishment for members of the educated elite who dared rebel against Beijing's hard authoritarianism was exemplified by China's only Nobel Peace laureate Liu, who was denied basic medical care as he developed terminal liver cancer in an isolated jail in Liaoning Province.[6] Intellectuals live under such political pressure that, in the words of the acclaimed Nanjing University historian Gao Hua, "this is an era when intellectuals are prone to fall prey to cancer."[7] Gao (born 1954) himself died of liver cancer in 2011. It was discovered by his colleagues and students that Gao's life might have been extended for at least a few years if authorities at Nanjing University had allowed him to have access to U.S. or European medicine. Although Gao had written hardly anything directly challenging the CCP orthodoxy, he met with the same fate as disgraced State President Liu Shaoqi – and later, Liu Xiaobo: denial of proper medical treatment owing to their iconoclastic views.[8]

Yet in spite of Xi's control mechanisms, intellectuals ranging from exiled writers to professors expelled from universities have valiantly battled the CCP in their effort to build up a public space for citizens who refuse to live in Mao's proverbial one-voice chamber. For writer and blogger Ma Xiao, the CCP has never recognized that intellectuals are educated people who have their own way of thinking – and who can write and do their jobs without the supervision of the party. "CCP members view intellectuals through the prism of either 'if you don't support us, you are our enemies' or 'if you do not oppose us, you are our friends,'" said Ma, who called this frame of mind "extremely bigoted, narrow and selfish."[9] Veteran international relations professor Zi Zhongyun argues that it is difficult to find any nation where "intellectuals have come up against such devastating disasters while fulfilling their responsibilities as intellectuals." For her and other members of the intelligentsia, however, there is little choice but to persevere under horrid conditions. "While [the party-state] is [supposed to be] propagating rule of law, the law and the media are still 'high-risk professions,'" she added. "This shows that intellectuals face a tough path in trying to serve society with their independent moral integrity and individual conscience."[10]

This chapter chronicles the asymmetrical warfare between forward-looking intellectuals committed to upholding global norms on the one hand, and a CCP bent on stifling independence of thinking on the other. After tracing the tradition of the intelligentsia since the late Qing Dynasty, the author zeroes in on Mao Zedong's and Xi Jinping's policies concerning intellectuals. Emphasis will be put on how different sectors of the educated elite, ranging from dissidents to academics and "establishment intellectuals," try to beat back Beijing's repressive apparatus. The chapter appraises efforts by men and women of letters to emancipate the Chinese mind through means including exposing the defects of the "China model" and popularizing rule of law and other global norms. Focus will also be put on the role of intellectuals in enlarging the public sphere and in strengthening civil-society groupings that are geared toward challenging the CCP's monopoly on truth and on power.

The traditional role and contributions of intellectuals

The contributions – and limitations – of Chinese intellectuals must be gauged against the backdrop of Confucianism, which still forms an integral part of the Chinese mind-set despite the encroachment of alien worldviews ranging from Christianity to Marxism. Contrary to conventional wisdom, explicit concepts of democracy could be found in the multitudinous sayings of Confucius. Take, for example, this well-known dictum on the relationship between the ruler and the ruled: "Water can support a boat, but it can also capsize the vessel."[11]

A casual examination of Chinese history has revealed a sizeable number of intellectuals who have risked their lives to promote social justice and hasten the pace of political change. However, there is little doubt that, until the end of the Qing Dynasty in 1911, most learned Chinese cleaved to the quasi-Confucianist belief that they could best function as the "conscience of society" by unquestioningly serving their emperors and promoting evolutionary change within the system. The quintessential loyal official who committed suicide so as to sway the decision of the emperor was Qu Yuan (circa 340–278 bce). Qu is still honored today in the form of the Dragon Boat Festival.[12]

Mindful of the righteousness of Confucianist officials, feudal authorities were effective in co-opting men of letters partly through according them a prominent place in the sociopolitical hierarchy. The *shi* or *shidafu* – learned mandarins at the service of the monarch – were the cream of the nation. *Shidafu* were ranked ahead of farmers, industrialists and merchants in the long-standing pecking order of professions.[13] The imperial court was in charge of selecting the best – and most obedient – minds to become officials through the time-honored *keju* ("imperial government examination") system. For budding intellectuals down the centuries, the burning ambition of their life was to excel in the *keju* exams and bring honor to their clans by becoming a senior official. The idea that intellectuals could have an identity separate from the powers that be – and that they should take part in overthrowing evil emperors – simply did not develop within the tradition of learned mandarins.[14]

According to Chinese-American historian Ying-Shih Yu, intellectuals failed to develop a "group consciousness" – in the sense of a largely independent social sector that is separate from the regime – until China's defeat at the hands of the Japanese in the First Sino-Japanese War of 1895. The debacle led to a series of humiliations for the Qing government, including ceding Taiwan to the Japanese. Kang Youwei (1858–1927), a nationally known scholar-official, organized a signature campaign to urge the Qing court to adopt radical reforms. Intellectuals had a lot more room for maneuver after the fall of the Qing Dynasty in 1911. This was expressed fully in the May Fourth Movement of 1919, which Yu called "the first modern social movement organized by intellectuals."[15] The May Fourth Movement has been described as a Chinese renaissance that liberated the Chinese from not only the rule of corrupt monarchs, but also the yoke of feudalism. For the first time, Chinese intellectuals realized that each individual was a self-sufficient entity – not a mere adjunct of the authorities-that-be – and that a key role of intellectuals was to work together for the common good of society.[16] This renaissance, however, proved short-lived: the CCP, which was founded in 1921, would soon impose on the land a most stultifying form of Leninism with feudalist Chinese characteristics.

The role of intellectuals as serfs in the socialist system

Mao's policy on intellectuals

As discussed in Chapter 1, Mao's prescription for the role of intellectuals and educated classes in general was that they must shed their individuality – and even their *renxing* ("human nature" or humanity) – and serve the party with unquestioning fealty. Moreover, members of the educated class had to subsume their individuality under *dangxing*, meaning the "nature of the party," particularly the norms and requirements of the CCP. These ideas were laid out in the Great Helmsman's famous Yan'an Talks on Literature of 1942.[17]

In Mao's famous 1925 article on the classification of classes, he singled out five sectors: the "big bourgeoisie," the "middle bourgeoisie," the petty bourgeoisie, the semi-proletariat and the proletariats. The big bourgeoisie (otherwise known as the landlord class and the comprador class) incorporated compradors, major landowners, bureaucrats, warlords and *fandong zhishijieji*, or the "reactionary intellectual class." The reactionary and counterrevolutionary intellectuals were to be exterminated.[18] Mao was mostly interested in what he identified to be "a large number of high-class intellectuals" within the middle bourgeoisie. They consisted of personnel in banks and commercial enterprises, graduates from Japanese and Western universities, professors and lawyers. Intellectuals within the middle bourgeoisie can be divided into right and left wing. "The right wing was close to anti-revolutionaries," Mao said. "Members of the left wing may sometimes join revolutions; but they are prone to making compromises with the enemies." He added they could not "uphold their [revolutionary fervor] for long." The entire corps (of intellectuals) can be regarded as semi-counterrevolutionaries.[19]

It is therefore not surprising that, after 1949, Mao's basic policy on intellectuals was to "unify, educate and transform" them. The chairman urged intellectuals to learn from the workers and peasants. "If intellectuals do not synthesize themselves with the masses of workers and peasants, they will accomplish nothing," he said. He lectured that the ultimate criterion for determining whether an intellectual is a revolutionary, nonrevolutionary or counterrevolutionary was "whether they are willing and able to synthesize themselves with the masses of workers and peasants." The Great Helmsman's policy on intellectuals after Liberation amounted to rendering them "both red and expert." This meant that, apart from making contributions in their professions and areas of specialty, members of the educated class must be "red" – meaning they must become faithful followers of the CCP.[20] A party report issued in 1956 seemed to indicate that the CCP had finally taken intellectuals on board as useful citizens and significant contributors to the economy. The report said that, "we must recognize that the basic ranks of intellectuals have morphed into a part of the working classes. [...] In the task of constructing socialism, a union of workers, peasants and intellectuals has been formed."[21] As we shall see, however, intellectuals were again cast into limbo in the run up to the Anti-Rightist Movement (1957–1959) and the Cultural Revolution.

From a deeper perspective, however, the most iniquitous aspect of Mao's strategy concerning intellectuals was that theories about *dangxing* and the imperative of devotion to Marxism were but pretexts with which he marginalized and took out his critics and political foes. Intellectuals bore the brunt of Mao's ire and suspicions simply because members of the educated class had the requisite tools with which to expose Mao's deceitful and cynical game.[22] One of the first intellectuals to have been executed on the personal orders of Mao was Wang Shiwei (1906–1947), a brilliant writer who joined Yan'an out of a burning idealism to serve the revolution. Wang soon saw through the inequality – and basic inhumaneness – of Mao and other senior cadres. This was expressed in critical pieces such as *Wild Lilies* and *Politicians and Artists* (both 1942), which castigated grandstanding senior cadres for riding roughshod over junior party members, intellectuals and peasants. Wang was executed in 1947 without even a sham trial.[23]

The case of the "Hu Feng Anti-Revolutionary Clique" was an even more obvious illustration of how Mao smothered dissent under the grandiose pretext of eradicating unorthodoxy and saving the party from so-called conspirators. In 1955, gifted writer and literary theorist Hu Feng (1902–1985; real name Zhang Guangren) and about 2,000 of his associates and even casual acquaintances were arrested on trumped-up charges under the personal direction of Chairman Mao. Hu, a disciple of Lu Xun and the founder of the wartime literary magazine *July* – which inspired a generation of writers grouped under the name "July Circle" – was a zealous supporter of the cause of the CCP. The ostensible cause of what is sometimes referred to as the CCP's first large-scale miscarriage of justice was but a 300,000-character paper that Hu filed to the Politburo titled "Report on the state of the practice of literature and the arts since Liberation" (hereafter Report). The Report pointed out that party-mandated creative works, while supposedly serving the cause of the Marxist Revolution, had resulted in lifeless propaganda-like pieces that were bereft of authentic human feelings.[24] Although the Report could be interpreted as a direct critique of Mao's Yan'an lecture, Hu's major crime in Mao's eyes was challenging his authority as the unique dispenser of wisdom in the "one-voice chamber" the Great Helmsman was creating. On May 13, 1955, the *People's Daily* ran a long piece on the heinous crimes of the "anti-revolutionary clique." The "editor's note," which explained the need to crack down on the Hu Feng gang, was penned by none other than Mao himself.[25]

Both the Wang Shiwei and the Hu Feng cases explained why, just one year after proclaiming the successful "domestication" of the intelligentsia, the double-dealing Mao turned against disobedient writers, artists, professors and liberal-leaning cadres with the force of thunder and lightning. The Anti-Rightist Movement (1957–1959) and the Cultural Revolution (1966–1976) were masterminded by Mao for purposes including getting rid of his opponents in the party. Moreover, these two horrendous campaigns were also geared toward emasculating intellectuals, particularly those who dared raise objections to Mao's dictatorship. The Anti-Rightist Movement was preceded by a brief period of the so-called "Two Hundreds Campaign": "Let a hundred flowers bloom, a hundred schools of thought contend." It was a plot to, in Mao's words, "tempt the snakes out of their pits."[26] The Great Helmsman also used the metaphor of "luring the ants out of their holes." The snakes and ants, he contended, were professors and intellectuals "who no longer want the Communist Party." "They don't want CCP leadership and begin casting aspersions on socialism," he added. Mao concluded that intellectuals were so many poisonous weeds. "People who are not Marxists or who are anti-Marxists must be subjected to [harsh] rule," he concluded.[27]

Although Mao was a connoisseur of Chinese classics, a calligrapher and an accomplished poet, he had nothing but contempt for intellectuals. Many historians have speculated that his suspicions about and hatred of intellectuals stemmed from his humble days as a junior library assistant at Peking University, from 1918 to 1920, when he was snubbed by the university's famous professors.[28] He used the proverb "when the skin is no more, to what can hair attach itself?" to illustrate the subservient DNA of the *zhishifenzhi*. "Intellectuals must become intellectuals of the proletariat class," Mao said. "Otherwise there is no other option for them." The corollary of the chairman's verdict is that disobedient, trouble-making intellectuals must be subject to the "dictatorship of the proletariat."[29]

Mao's tyranny over intellectuals – and the fear with which the Great Helmsman was held by almost everybody – was illustrated by a conversation between Mao and the great translator Luo Jinan at the start of the Anti-Rightist Campaign in

July 1957. Mao was explaining the party's stringent policy toward the educated class to Luo and a group of 30 intellectuals in Shanghai. Luo asked Mao what would happen to Lu Xun (1881–1936) if he were still alive. Mao said, "As for Lu Xun, he might continue writing in prison, or he might keep his mouth shut." Everybody present was frightened to death. After all, Lu, perhaps the one writer and intellectual whom Mao held in the highest esteem, was eulogized as the "greatest and bravest standard-bearer of the new army of culture." Huang Zongying (born 1925), a well-known writer and actress who revealed the Mao–Luo exchange in 2002, said her hands sweated all over when she heard of Mao's shocking statement.[30]

Xi's revival of Mao's efforts to "transform" intellectuals

Xi Jinping also wants party authorities to ensure that all intellectuals and all branches of learning must subserve the cause of the revolution. First, knowledge, as discussed in schools and the media, must be politically aboveboard. Even more importantly, schools, newspapers, the Internet – as well as what is going on in the minds of all Chinese – are *zhendi* or "battlegrounds" that the ideological police must conquer and occupy. "If we do not occupy the *zhendi*, other people will do so," Xi said.[31]

The supreme leader divides knowledge and thinking into three categories: red, black and grey. Ideas and inclinations that are red, or politically correct, should be safeguarded by censors and commissars. "Black" areas refer to information and knowledge that have been corrupted by Western standards. "We must be bold enough to lay siege to black terrain and gradually implement a change of colors," Xi said. As for grey areas, Xi's recommendation is to turn them red – and prevent them from degenerating into black. In a genuflection to Mao's totalitarian views on "ideology and thought work," the general secretary told propaganda cadres in early 2014 that the party's mass-education campaigns must be so thorough and all-enveloping that "core socialist values" – shorthand for patriotism, loyalty to the party leadership and undying support for Chinese-style socialism – "should be as ubiquitous as the air."[32]

Although China in the 2010s was not yet a totally closed society in terms of culture and society, Xi insisted that party members, intellectuals and students devote themselves to building up the "calcium" of the spirit. "Ideals and beliefs make up the 'calcium' in the spirit of Communists," Xi said. "Without ideals and beliefs or if ideals and beliefs are irresolute, the spirit will 'lack calcium', and the result will be weak bones." But with what kinds of beliefs and values should party members – and by extension members of the educated elite – equip themselves? The answer is obvious. Xi's well-staffed PR team has repeatedly asked the public to follow the edicts of what influential foreign media call "China's New Emperor."[33] As deputy director of the party's Propaganda Department Wang Xiaohui pointed out in 2014, party members should "self-consciously arm their brains with and [use as] directions for their work the important series of talks by

Comrade Xi Jinping." "We must accurately get a firm grip on the scientific contents and spiritual substance of Xi Jinping's series of important talks," he added. The propaganda chief said that, if party members were to "arm their brains" with Xi's teachings and doctrines, the latter would "provide our spirit with additional calcium." President Xi's teachings, he added, would help every Chinese "establish their right view of the world, the right view of life, the right values and the right concept about [the use of] power."[34]

Revival of ideological campaigns and building a personality cult around the "Emperor for Life"

After Deng Xiaoping came to power in late 1979, the great reformer did two things to prevent a return to Maoist iniquities. The first was to say goodbye to the Great Helmsman's obsession with ideological purity – and commensurate ideological campaigns to "purify" cadres and intellectuals who had been poisoned by "bourgeois-liberal" ideas from the West. After all, one of the most important dictums issued by Deng was that, "the core task of the party is economic construction." The Great Architect of Reform also banned Mao-style ideological campaigns. Second, Deng also tried to put an end to the construction of personality cults around the top leaders of the party-state apparatus.[35]

Less than one year after coming to power, however, Xi began to water down Deng's dictums. In a talk to staff working in the party's ideology and media departments, Xi noted that, "while economic construction is the party's core work, ideological work is also the party's extremely important work." The orthodox leader added that, along with "the construction of material civilization," we must do a good job in "constructing spiritual civilization."[36]

In an apparent revival of Maoist norms, the Xi leadership instituted a nationwide "responsibility system for ideological work," whereby the party secretaries of provinces, cities and counties should be personally responsible for ideological and political rectitude within their areas of jurisdiction.[37] In an article in *People's Daily* in November 2015, Party Secretary of Hunan Xu Shousheng pointed out that,

> it is the prime task [of party leaders] to take a firm grip on ideological and thought work. [...] If we are not engaged [in ideology-related work], we have not done our job. If we do this job badly, this constitutes dereliction of duty.[38]

A college responsibility system was also established to ensure that heads of party cells in universities should take charge of political correctness in the lecture halls. Head of the Department of Propaganda in Guandong Province Shen Haixiong, who once worked with Xi in Zhejiang Province, noted in an early 2016 speech that party organizations in colleges must boost their "political consciousness, consciousness about the entire situation, consciousness about [being obedient to] the core of the party leadership, and consciousness about seeing eye to eye with the party leadership."[39]

Taking a leaf from Chairman Mao's theory about "perpetual warfare," Xi and his comrades have committed themselves to fighting a long-haul ideological battle. Under instructions from Xi, the Chinese Academy of Social Sciences set up a National Ideology Center (*guojia yishixingtai zhongxin*). Sixty experts from the universities, as well as party and government units handling culture, education, publication, propaganda and the Internet, have been given the job of "winning an ideological counter-attack warfare in the coming thirty years." Xi wanted scholars, intellectuals and other experts to help prove to both Chinese and the world that the "Chinese model," based on core socialist values with Chinese characteristics, was superior to universal values adopted by Western countries. In an apparent throwback to the Cold War, intellectuals have been forced to go against their own consciences as they bury themselves in the task of eulogizing CCP rule and casting aspersions on global values such as civil rights and the rule of law.[40]

In his seven years in power (at time of writing), Xi has meticulously built a personality cult around himself. It is therefore not surprising that ideological campaigns have been centered around the imperative of cleaving closely to the teachings of what some critics call the "Mao Zedong of the 21st century."[41] Take, for instance, the educational campaign that was code-named *liangxue yizuo* ("to study two [sets of materials] and to become [a qualified party member])." The movement was established in early 2016 in an apparent effort to improve the ideological purity of all 90 million party members. Officials and CCP members of all ranks are urged to study the Party Constitution, as well as the "series of important speeches" given by President Xi. Only through immersing themselves in the party charter and Xi's instructions could party members pass muster in terms of loyalty, competence and political rectitude.[42]

Particularly after Xi ascended to the status of "core" of the leadership at the 19th Party Congress, various grandiose titles such as *zuigaotongshuai* ("highest commander") and *renmindailuren* ("pathfinder for the people") have been conferred on the paramount leader. The hagiographic trend further intensified after the March 2018 Constitution amendment which abolished term limits to the post of state president. Xi's ideas and instructions were given grandiloquent formulations: "Xi Jinping Thought on Socialism with Chinese Characteristics for a New Era," "Xi Jinping's Economic Thought on Socialism with Chinese Characteristics for a New Era" and "Xi Jinping Thought on Diplomacy." Every word of wisdom spoken by Xi, beginning in his very early days as a rusticated youth in the village of Liangjiahe in Shaanxi, was given prominence in learned articles written by college professors.[43] His new slogans about building a "community of shared destiny" – a basic premise of his Belt and Road Initiative – were said to echo the Confucian ideal of China presiding over the *datong* or "grand commonality" of all mankind.[44] And, on the occasion of Beijing's celebration of the 200th birthday of Karl Marx in May 2018, propagandists deemed Xi Jinping Thought the worthy development of Marxism in the 21st century. And Xi was called the greatest Marxist of this century.[45]

Revival of Communist ideals and banishment of universal values

Since the end of the Cultural Revolution – and the demise of the Communist Party of the Soviet Union – the word "Communism" has seldom cropped up even in the most orthodox CCP journals. Deng famously pointed out, after the Cultural Revolution, that China was "at the preliminary stage of socialism" – and that this stage could last up to 200 years.[46] The Great Architect of Reform very seldom made reference to Communism. However, Xi and his like-minded ultra-conservatives have been reviving Communist ideals with gusto. This is despite the fact that not even Xi could pin down the exact shape or form in which Communism can be realized in the 21st century. After all, consumerism has taken over China, and the majority of Chinese are no longer employees of the state or state-owned enterprises (SOEs).

At a 2015 talk at the Central Party School for county-level cadres, Xi noted that, "we must never consider Communism as vague and ethereal." "The reason why we develop socialism with Chinese characteristics is to go forward in the direction of [realizing] Communism," instructed the paramount leader. As *China Youth Daily* commentator Wang Xiangming put it, "The gist of Xi's speech is to reiterate the Communist direction of socialism with Chinese characteristics, and to demand that all CCP members firm up their Communist faith."[47]

For ideologue Hou Huiqin, there can never be any doubt that "Communism is the soul of Marxist philosophy." In a late 2015 article in the journal *Red Flag Manuscripts*, Hou pointed out that, "if Marxist philosophy is rid of its Communist DNA, this philosophy will fundamentally be castrated and subverted." He called upon ideological workers to "push forward philosophical innovation through the synthesis of Marxist philosophy and Communism."[48] Similarly, Tian Xinming noted, in an article entitled "Beware of the theory that 'Communism is vague and ethereal,'" that CCP members must never lose sight of the ultimate goal of materializing Communism in China. "If we forget the bright future goal of Communism, the nature of 'socialism' as contained in the early stage of socialism will become vague," he argued. "We will lose our sense of direction and lose our energy and vigor." Tian, who is a senior cadre in the Ministry of Education, quoted Xi as saying that, "even as we uphold the belief of going down the road of socialism with Chinese characteristics, we must at the same time uphold the lofty ideals of Communism."[49]

The corollary of the Xi leadership's glorification of socialist – and even Communist – values is a wholesale attack on "universal values," which are a shorthand for Western liberal ideals, including parliamentary and multi-party democracy. Ideologue Su Changhe pointed out, in an article in the party's theoretical journal *Seeking Truth*, that party members and intellectuals must raise their self-confidence in the superiority of socialism with Chinese characteristics in the face of the onslaught of Western values. "For the past twenty years, Western [countries] have been pushing the values of 'democracy and peace' and 'universal values,'" Su wrote. "Yet the political materialization of this school of thought has brought about tragedies all over the world."[50] Similarly, the official *Beijing Daily* noted in a 2014 editorial that the party must "leave no space for international values." The conservative mouthpiece alleged that the Western alliance was trying to subvert CCP rule through infiltrating China with "universal values" such as constitutional governance and freedom of the media. "We must boost our sense of initiative, take a firm grip on our strong suit, and do well in the battle of striking first," the paper said. "We must be bold enough to take control [of ideological spheres] and to brandish the sword [against anti-party elements]."[51] In other words, intellectuals who are defending "universal values" must be prepared to pay a very heavy price.

The CCP's obsession with culture – and its ominous implications for intellectuals

The year 2016 being the 50th anniversary of the start of the Great Proletarian Cultural Revolution (GPCR; 1966–1976), not only intellectuals, but also relatively liberal officials have joined the discussion on whether it is possible for the Ten Years of Chaos to make a comeback in some form or shape. According to pop culture icon Cui Jiang, the Cultural Revolution is still not finished as long as Mao's portrait looms over Tiananmen Square. Even retired senior cadre Yu Youjun echoed this sentiment during a lecture he gave in late 2014 at Guangzhou's Sun Yat-Sen University. Yu, a former governor of Shanxi Province and party secretary of the Ministry of Culture, had this to say about the GPCR: "The soil for the Cultural Revolution is still fertile, especially when the people have no reasonable and profound knowledge of it. It may partially recur, under certain historical conditions."[52]

"Culture" has always been a loaded word in Communist China. Given the fact that the harsh, utopian tenets of Marxism-Leninism do not seem to fit in with Chinese values and beliefs, recent leaders ranging from ex-President Jiang Zemin to Xi Jinping have waxed eloquent on how the Communist regime has brought 5,000 years of Chinese culture to new heights. Both Jiang and Xi want to revive at least some strands of Confucianism, Buddhism and Taoism.[53] Yet it was Mao Zedong, whose living quarters in the Zhongnanhai party headquarters were chockablock with ancient Chinese classics, who was a past master in using "culture" to consolidate the Communist Party dictatorship. Not long after taking control of all of China, Mao noted that the "core tasks of the party and the people" consisted of waging a series of *douzheng* ("warlike struggles"). There would be a war against nature as well as herculean "efforts to develop our economy and our culture." There would simultaneously be an even crueler and more entrenched *douzheng* against "counterrevolutionaries," most of whom incurred Mao's ire and suspicions because they refused to be robot-like "cogs" of the revolution.[54]

The pretext of the Cultural Revolution was to "purify Chinese culture," which was a reference to the "corrupted" mentality of cadres, intellectuals, teachers and students. Just as in the case of the Anti-Rightist Movement of 1957–1959 – a precursor of the GPCR that victimized some 550,000 free-thinking academics and cadres – intellectuals bore the brunt of the madness and horror unleashed by the Red Guards. The Maoists placed members of the educated elites at the bottom of the barrel as far as the country's sociopolitical pecking order was concerned. Mao attributed the success of the CCP partly to its achievements in changing the worldview of the nation's intelligentsia. Key to what critics called "brain-washing" was getting rid of the "bourgeois-liberal mentality" – particularly pro-West inclinations – among relatively well-educated professors, journalists and writers.[55]

Authoritarian figures from Mao Zedong to Xi Jinping see "culture" as a means to impose on intellectuals norms such as uniformity of thinking and total fealty to the party. Despite Mao's love of the classics, untold quantities of rare books as well as objets d'art were burnt and destroyed, particularly during the first five years of the GPCR. Mao's infamous Little Red Book and the Gang of Four's instructions in the official media were all the reading materials that were approved by the leadership. Not only disgraced cadres, but also world-renowned men of letters such as the great novelist Lao She committed suicide, particularly during the first years of the GPCR.[56]

Even scholars deemed "national treasures" such as the great historian Chen Yanke, who was 76 at the start of the revolution, was not spared physical torture and mental torment at the hands of the Red Guards. Chen, who was denied any means to treat his eye and heart diseases, died in the most pitiful circumstances in 1969.[57] According to one report, 52 world-renowned scholars and men of letters committed suicide during the GPCR. These included the famous archaeologist Chen Mengjia, whose last words before ending his own life in September 1966 were: "I don't want to be duped and fooled like a monkey."[58] Although pretty much all of these illustrious artists and experts were given posthumous *pingfang* ("restoration of reputation"), few of their relatives received compensation. And the party has not released official archives detailing the cases of persecution during the Ten Years of Chaos.

One is reminded of the views of the recently deceased Du Runsheng, an acclaimed reformer whose disciples included PBSC member Wang Qishan. A handful of liberal scholars who have benefited from Du's teachings recently recalled the illustrious old man's judgment on the GPCR and similar ideological campaigns waged by Mao: "Without independent thinking, one billion brains are equivalent to just one brain. Mistakes made [by one person] are duplicated by everybody. We must take heed from these horrendous lessons of history."[59]

A graduate of Tsinghua University, Xi Jinping holds a degree in chemical engineering and a Doctor of Laws degree from this elite institute of higher learning, whose alumni include luminaries such as ex-President Hu Jintao and ex-Premier Zhu Rongji. Yet doubts have been cast about his academic credentials. For example, Xi studied in Tsinghua as a *gongnongbing xueyuan* (a "representative student" from among the peasants, workers and soldiers) before China's universities formally returned to normal in 1979.[60]

Questions have also been raised about the quality of his doctoral dissertation, which was an undistinguished treatise on agrarian reforms. Irrespective of whether Xi has ever received proper academic training, it is without doubt that Xi wants to project the image of a lover of learning and culture.[61]

Since he came to power in 2012, the president and party general secretary has begun a campaign to "resuscitate Chinese culture." Inherent in Xi's best-known mantra – the "Chinese dream" – is the concept of "the great renaissance of the Chinese nation." So-called cultural revival plays a big role in this super-nationalistic goal of a spectacular renaissance of Chinese values and worldviews. "The strength of a country and a people is underpinned by a vigorous culture," Xi said in late 2013 while visiting the home of Confucius in Qufu, Shandong Province. "The prerequisite of the great renaissance of the Chinese people requires the development and prosperity of Chinese culture."[62]

That Chinese culture dates from the glorious Confucian tradition is a key argument by Xi and his colleagues that citizens need not hanker after relatively recent "Western civilization," which, after all, might not suit Chinese conditions. "The Chinese are a great people," Xi said. "In more than 5,000 years of development of culture, the Chinese have made indelible contributions to the development of civilization. [...] CCP members are the faithful successors and developers of superior traditional Chinese culture." He argued that Chinese culture could be of great benefit in helping party members and citizens to "establish the correct worldview, philosophy of life and values."[63] "Traditional Chinese culture is deeply etched onto the DNA of the Chinese people," Xi said. "Our superior culture has provided nutrient for the renaissance of the Chinese people. It can be considered the 'calcium of the spirit.'" "We should adopt a position of historical dialecticism in studying Confucius and Confucianism," he added. "We must uphold [the philosophy of] using the ancient to serve the modern, to absorb the quintessence while jettisoning the dross ... so that Confucianism can develop positive influence in new historical conditions."[64]

It is clear, however, that for Xi and his colleagues working in CCP departments dealing with culture, propaganda and Internet censorship, "traditional culture" ultimately serves the utilitarian and politically expedient purpose of boosting the people's faith in "socialism with Chinese characteristics" – and supreme party rule. As Xi has repeatedly emphasized, "the most critical core of a country's comprehensive strength is cultural soft power." "We must firm up our self-confidence in the path, theory and system [of Chinese-style socialism]," he indicated. "Fundamentally, we also need to have cultural self-confidence."[65] Highlighting "cultural self-confidence" presupposes that supposedly unwholesome, Westernized and politically dubious culture – what Chairman Mao dismissed as "poisonous weeds" – can have no place in socialist China. On another occasion, Xi noted that culture is about "strengthening patriotism, collectivism, and socialist education." He urged writers and artists to "provide guidance to the people so that they can establish and uphold correct views" about history, the nation and culture. The paramount leader has reiterated his confidence about building up China into a *wenhua qiangguo*, or "cultural power" with Chinese characteristics.[66]

Xi not only talks about culture but frequently issues stern instructions to cadres working in cultural and propaganda departments to promote socialist values and to exterminate "bourgeois-liberal" ones. Like other Communist and socialist states that are committed to social engineering, the CCP administration has, since the 1950s, waged hundreds of ideological and educational campaigns to inculcate the right kind of culture and ideology in intellectuals and the people. In a national conference on literature and the arts held in Beijing in late 2014, Xi called upon "cultural workers" to "raise high the banner of the core values of socialism." "They should vividly and flamboyantly realize in their artistic creation the core values of socialism," said Xi, adding that writers and artists should "tell the people what should be affirmed and eulogized – and what should be opposed and negated."[67]

Like Mao Zedong, who stamped his ultra-radical ideals on a generation of students – and Red Guards – in the 1960s and 1970s, Xi is conscientious about molding young minds. While visiting Peking University in mid-2104, Xi noted that,

> the values of young people determine the values of the entire society of the future. [...] We must ensure that youths have the right kind of values from the very beginning. [...] It's like getting the buttons right when wearing a garment. If the first button is tied correctly, so will the subsequent buttons.[68]

Culture features prominently in China's 13th Five-Year Plan (FYP) for the years 2016–2020. A late-2015 article written by the Party Committee of the Ministry of Culture indicated that, "culture makes up an important component of a nation's core competitiveness." The goal of the 13th FYP was to ensure that China would cross the threshold of a "moderately prosperous society" by the year 2020. And the commissars in the Education Ministry noted that, "cultural construction is a critical component of the overall goal of building a moderately prosperous society." It says a lot about Xi's confidence in social engineering that he wanted a detailed blueprint on how "cultural construction" should be symbiotically linked with "economic construction, political construction, social construction, the construction of ecological civilization and party construction."[69]

The party's battle against liberal intellectuals

How intellectuals cope with "Democratic Proletarian Dictatorship"

Intellectuals such as Xu Jilin, Yu Jie and Zi Zhongyun are fully cognizant of the myriad strategies that the party is using to emasculate citizens who refuse to toe the line. They also know very well that their battle against the propaganda establishment, as well as the police-state apparatus, is an asymmetrical warfare with the authorities apparently holding most of the cards.

Beijing intensified its draconian tactics against dissidents – as well as NGO activists and rights defense lawyers – during the second half of the Hu Jintao era (2007–2012). Ostensible reasons cited by the CCP included heightened security concerns in the run-up to the Olympic Games in 2008, celebrations of the 60th birthday of the PRC in 2009 and the Shanghai Expo in 2010. Ethnic unrest in Tibet and Xinjiang flared up in March 2008 and July 2009, respectively. Then came the series of Arab Spring revolutions in countries such as Tunisia, Libya and Egypt. This revived the CCP's paranoia – first precipitated by the Polish Revolution in the early 1980s – that China could become the target of a "color revolution conspiracy."[70] Another factor that prompted the police to crack down harder on "destabilizing forces" was dissident writer Liu Xiaobo winning the Nobel Peace Prize in 2010. This was interpreted by the CCP leadership as an instance of "collusion" between dissidents and their "Western patrons." Yu Jie, a talented author who was at that time about to finish Liu's biography, was severely beaten up by police. He fled to the U.S. in 2012. In an op-ed article in the *Washington Post*, Yu quoted his secret-police tormentor as saying that the authorities had a list of "200 anti-Communist Party intellectuals" nationwide – and that, if need be, the state apparatus could easily round them up and bury them alive within a day or two.[71]

There are several areas where the Xi administration has gone way beyond the Jiang Zemin or Hu Jintao eras in exterminating "destabilizing elements" in society, particularly educated citizens who can think for themselves. Take, for example, the punishment of the close kin of noted dissidents. The wife of Liu Xiaobo, Liu Xia, was put under house arrest, and her brother, Liu Hui, was given a three-year jail term on what human rights organizations called trumped-up charges. Even after Liu Xia was allowed to seek medical treatment in Germany in 2018, her brother had to stay on in China as a "hostage" so as to ensure that she would not bad-mouth CCP authorities. The nephew of blind legal activist Chen Guangcheng – who was granted asylum in the U.S. in 2012 – was imprisoned for three years in late 2012 for apparently assaulting law-enforcement officers.[72]

Indeed, the persecution of the relatives of dissidents and activists has reached horrendous proportions under Xi. The best illustration is what happened to the spouses and relatives of the 300-odd legal professionals arrested on July 9, 2015 (see Chapter 4). The spouses of prominent rights attorneys, including Wang Quanzhang, Li Heping and Wang Yu, were either not informed of the whereabouts of the detainees or denied legal aid. Pressure was put on the relatives of the lawyers – and sometimes even those of their spouses – to persuade the victims of injustice not to launch public campaigns for their release. The son of well-recognized rights attorney Wang, Bao Zhuoxuan, was for a long period denied permission to pursue overseas studies. On the day of Wang's arrest, Bao, aged 16, was stopped at the airport and prevented from going to Australia to go to high school. Police claimed that the 16-year-old boy constituted a "national security threat." According to human rights lawyer Yu Wensheng, who was helping the Wang family, "the police have violated the human rights of Bao Zhuoxuan, who has not broken any law and who should have full rights of seeking an education abroad." Wang was released – but put under 24-hour surveillance – one year later after she made a "confession of guilt" under duress. Her son Bao was finally allowed to leave to study in Australia in early 2018.[73]

Xi also began the practice of targeting multimillionaire private businessmen who have gone beyond making liberal comments on political issues in providing financial support to dissident groupings. A case in point is billionaire real-estate and IT businessman Wang Gongquan, who was detained by police in September 2013 for allegedly "gathering a crowd to disturb public order." Wang's real "crime," however, could be that he was a keen supporter of civil-society and human rights activists such as well-known legal scholar Xu Zhiyong. Wang also initiated Internet signature campaigns to press the CCP leadership to pick up the threads of political liberalization.[74] President Xi and his colleagues are very nervous about private businessmen getting involved in activities that can be construed as politically destabilizing. Several entrepreneurs were behind the large-scale anti-nuclear demonstrations held in mid-2013 by more than 1,000 residents of the Guangdong city of Jiangmen. Guangdong authorities were forced to at least temporarily shelve the plan to build a nuclear power plant on the outskirts of the city.[75]

Moreover, the frequency with which state-security personnel bare their fangs at dissidents and intellectuals – even those whose only "crime" was to hold a dinner meeting to mark recent cases of gross injustice – has increased substantially under President Xi. In the run-up to and immediately after the 25th anniversary of the Tiananmen Square crackdown in mid-2014, a few hundred academics, lawyers, NGO activists, net-based opinion-makers and retired liberal cadres were hauled in for questioning by the police. In 2014, a dozen-odd critics of the regime – including prominent lawyer Pu Zhiqiang, who was dissident Ai Weiwei's counsel – were subjected to "criminal detention," meaning that they would likely be charged in court in the near future. The official pretext for harassing these intellectuals, whose "crime" was holding meetings in restaurants or hotels to mark the anniversary of the massacre, was that they were engaged in *xunxinzishi* ("picking quarrels and provoking troubles"), which could earn a convicted suspect up to five years in jail. A week or so after Pu and four friends were picked up for participating in a private Tiananmen-related saloon on May 6, his own lawyer, Qu Zhenheng, as well two journalist friends, Wu Wei and Xin Jian, were detained by Beijing police.[76] During the same period, the authorities arrested respected former journalist Gao Yu for allegedly revealing to a Hong Kong publication the contents of Central Document No. 9 of 2013, which forbids college teachers to touch on seven politically sensitive topics (see the following section). Also detained was freelance writer Xiang Nanfu, who was accused of supplying anti-government articles to the U.S.-based website Boxun.com.[77]

In 2016, the state-security apparatus started the scorched-earth policy of targeting the relatives of dissident intellectuals and journalists who have already left the country in search of breathing space. This followed the publication in March that year of an open letter on the Urumqi-based news website, *Wujie News* ("Without Boundaries"), calling on Xi to resign from his position of general secretary. The petition, which cited Xi's mistakes in both domestic and foreign policy, was allegedly signed by "a group of loyal party members." (Most analysts said the missive was likely penned by a China specialist in Hong Kong, Taiwan or the West.)

Police immediately swooped on the management and editorial team of *Wujie News*, which was subsequently closed down. Four editors and managers of the company were detained for lengthy interrogation.[78] What took even China critics by surprise was that the police briefly detained the relatives of two prominent bloggers and journalists, New York-based Wen Yunchao (whose penname is Bei Feng), and Germany-based Chang Ping, a well-known investigative journalist. The relatives were forced by police to put pressure on Wen and Chang to "come clean" on the circumstances behind the anti-Xi letter.[79] Both Wen and Chang denied any role in the protest. Chang disclosed that his siblings in Sichuan Province had been subjected to periodic harassment after he published articles critical of the Xi leadership in German and Hong Kong news outlets. "Every citizen has the freedom of speech to engage in comment or criticism of the political activities of state leaders," Chang said in a statement.[80]

The party's war against academics

The Xi administration's first salvo against academics consisted of Central Document No. 9 of 2013, which was disseminated by the CCP General Office. It forbade cadres and intellectuals – but mostly academics – from talking about seven taboo topics: universal values, media freedom, civil society, civil rights, aberrations in the party's history, the "crony capitalist class" and the independence of the judiciary.[81]

In late 2014, the Ministry of Education issued a document entitled "Opinion on long-lasting mechanisms for building and improving the construction of morality in colleges" (hereafter "Opinion"). The document said it was necessary to raise the moral levels of teachers because of their "direct influence on the development of young students' worldviews, philosophy of life and values systems." It forbade college staff from engaging in plagiarism and other acts of academic dishonesty. The document further warned professors and teachers not to make money through activities such as moonlighting or soliciting gifts from students and parents. Yet the essence of the Opinion was politics. The tough edict noted that college employees who "engage in activities detrimental to national interests" or who "run counter to the party's lines, goals and policies" would be penalized.[82] According to Central Nationalities University professor Zhao Shilin, the document was a slap in the face for liberal academics and administrators who were making efforts to promote the independence of the academic world. "In a country where politics and college teaching are merged and where there is thought control, it is difficult to promote the separation of politics and academic [pursuits]," he argued.[83]

This edict was followed in January 2015 by another official circular titled "Opinion on further strengthening and improving propaganda and ideological work in colleges under new situations." Three additional forbidden zones were added to the seven taboo areas laid down two years previously. As then-Minister of Education Yuan Guiren pointed out, the party and educational authorities would "definitely not allow views that attack and libel party leaders or that smear socialism to appear in the classroom." Second, teachers and students were not allowed to "express opinions that are counter to the Constitution and the law." Third, teachers were not allowed to "grumble, give vent to dissatisfaction, or transmit different types of unwholesome feelings to students." In an interview with the *China Disciplinary Inspection and Supervision Paper*, Yuan complained that party organizations and cadres in universities "lack political sensitivity and discriminatory ability regarding political [issues]." He urged party units in universities to do more to safeguard the political trustworthiness of professors, to step up the monitoring of classroom teaching and to keep an eye on student organizations as well as academic exchanges.[84]

Party mouthpieces have even periodically named what they consider to be academic troublemakers. Examples have included Peking University's He Weifang and Tsinghua University's Chen Danqing. "We need even more detailed regulations to eradicate 'negative energy' in colleges, and to ensure that engineers of the soul will not smear and dare not smear [Chinese-style socialism]," wrote propaganda official Xu Feng in a January 2015 piece in *Seeking Truth*. Xu suggested that more attention be paid to the blogs and other social-media vehicles maintained by Westernized professors.[85]

How effective are these fiats? Is it really possible to turn back the clock and reimpose Maoist-style "thought control" in the classroom? Some valiant professors are fighting back with gusto. "It is true that the authorities want to boost [ideological] dominance over colleges and to discipline liberal intellectuals," said Zhou Xiaozheng, a sociologist at Renmin University. "Yet things are getting out of the control [of the commissars.]" He added that liberal professors had the support of their colleagues and students because what the party was doing was "extremely inimical to freedom of expression and academic debate."[86] According to law professor He Weifang, it is difficult for the dictates of the commissars to be fully realized. "Liberal teachers including myself are still talking about Western theories and pro-liberal viewpoints in the classroom," he said. The popular professor added that knowledge and values propagated by intellectuals must be "independent of religion, politics, economics and other spheres of influence."[87]

Yet it is also clear that college party secretaries and commissars hold the ultimate weapons of dismissal, demotion or, in the case of Professor He, exile. Such pressure on college professors began with the Hu Jintao regime, but the situation has worsened significantly under Xi Jinping. In early 2009, a few months before the 20th anniversary of the Tiananmen Square massacre, Professor He was forced to leave his family behind in Beijing and to spend two years teaching in little-known Shihezi University in Xinjiang. Although Peking University said He's assignment was in line with the long-standing tradition of "coastal cities helping to build up Xinjiang," it was a clear case of punishment.[88]

Moreover, there is evidence to show that the Education Ministry and the MSS have recruited college students to spy on "suspicious professors." College professors routinely assume that full- or part-time "government informants" are recording every word they say in the classroom. Intellectual circles around the country were shocked when the official *Liaoning Daily* published a long front-page report in late

2014 entitled "Teachers: don't smear China." The *Daily* said its reporters had asked students in a number of universities about the "political attitude" of their professors. It quoted one unnamed student as saying, "Bad-mouthing China and cursing society has become a fashion. One teacher of mine sings the praises of foreign countries in every class and claims China must learn from them."[89]

President Xi has further strengthened control over the colleges by appointing ultra-conservative cadres as party secretaries – and in many cases also presidents – of universities. The top priority of these apparatchiks is to ensure that professors, including foreign professors, do not preach "pro-Western" values in the classroom. The academic community was shocked in late 2018 when Qiu Shuiping was appointed party secretary of Peking University (Beida). A lawyer by training, Qiu has skimpy academic credentials; he was, prior to his appointment, the party secretary or head of Beijing's municipal State Security Bureau, which is a local branch of the MSS charged with espionage and counterespionage. Upon his appointment, Qiu was quoted as saying he hoped Beida would "seize the opportunities in the new era and grow into a world-class university with Chinese characteristics."[90] A number of foreign academics were fired or even expelled from the country in 2018 for politically incorrect behavior. One of them was Christopher Balding, who lost his job as a finance professor in the Peking University HSBC Business School in the middle of the year. Shortly before leaving the country, soon after his dismissal, Balding wrote in his blog: "China has reached a point where I do not feel safe being a professor and discussing even the economy, business and financial markets."[91]

Intellectuals hit back as best they can

According to Central Nationalities University philosopher Zhao Shilin, the Chinese tradition has, for millennia, put the emphasis on the individual subsuming his interests and rights under a collective authority – first the imperial courts, and now the party. Zhao argues that China can only have democratic development if every individual can win back his or her right to self-development. The philosopher argued that Dr. Sun Yat-sen's teachings began to "shift the gravity [of politics] to the political, economic and cultural rights of the individual," a process of democratization that got a big boost from the democratic experiments in Taiwan in the 1980s. Zhao quoted revered thinker Liang Shuming (1893–1988) on the fact that, in the Chinese mentality, ordinary folks "are fundamentally not a 'person' – they are the properties of emperors, and they don't have their 'own selves.'"[92] As we have seen, the CCP has established a seamless police-state apparatus to keep Chinese intellectuals – and other potential "troublemakers" – in check. The first task of the intelligentsia, therefore, is to win back the dignity, rights and self-sufficiency of every citizen.

Zhizhuxing *versus* dangxing

Members of the educated class who have aspirations beyond being a "screw of the revolution" have fought back with gusto. Even politically alert intellectuals, however, have found it difficult to challenge CCP orthodoxy – and the virtual police-state regime that is backing it up. Apart from tight ideological control, most intellectuals – professors, artists, writers and performing artists – earn their living by working for state units, universities or companies that depend on official patronage. It was only in the 2010s that "freelance writers" and "freelance commentators," particularly those who are Internet-based, started to become more common in society. However, owing to Beijing's tight oversight, many net-based authors have found it hard to earn a living.[93]

Zhu Yongjia, a noted scholar and one-time adviser to the Gang of Four radicals, used a proverb previously employed by Mao to express the intimate connection between intellectuals and the powers that be: hair growing on skin. "There is this old saying that if the skin is no more, from where can hair draw its sustenance?" said Zhu. "In traditional Chinese society, intellectuals have little choice other than working for the administration. There were few other means of making a living."[94] According to writer and historian Wu Xiaobo, "Chinese in their heart of hearts are calling out for dictators. […] There is an old saying that goes 'it's better to be a dog in times of peace rather than a human being in times of upheaval.'"[95] Take the case of the quintessential sycophantic intellectual Guo Moruo (1892–1978), a friend of Mao's who was the president of the Chinese Academy of Sciences from 1949 until his death in 1978. The prolific writer, historian, philosopher and anthropologist was the doyen of Chinese intellectuals before the GPCR. However, he was widely condemned for licking the boots of Mao. When he faced persecution at the start of the Cultural Revolution, the Japan-educated Guo tried to save his own neck by penning hagiographic poems about Mao's wife Jiang Qing – and betraying his former literary and academic colleagues.[96]

Indeed, the majority of intellectuals do not have the wherewithal to take on the authorities. After the GPCR, there were no lack of acclaimed novels and other works of art dissecting the disastrous Ten Years of Chaos. Termed "Literature of the wounded," these novels, poems and plays gave vent to feelings of loss, betrayal and indignation. Perhaps the most famous of these works of art was *Six Episodes in the School for Cadres* by Yang Jiang (1916–2016), the wife of literary lion Qian Zhongshu who is a gifted translator in her own right.[97] Yet almost none of these big names in the circle of arts and academia – who have untold numbers of fans among China scholars and specialists in the West – came out to directly expose the horrendous crimes of Mao and his colleagues, or the inhumane and tyrannical nature of Chinese-style socialism.

Despite the high esteem in which Republican-period literary giants such as Ba Jin and Qian Zhongshu were held, quite a few liberal scholars have questioned whether they should not have been bolder in pointing a finger at the crimes of the powers that be. Public intellectual Zhu Xueqin, who teaches philosophy at Shanghai University, recalled how he had asked Ba Jin to more proactively lay bare the heinous crimes of Mao and his colleagues. Recalling how, in his last books, Ba had called upon young people to "tell the truth," Zhu had this to say to the literary giant: "Just say a few words please. A person cannot be contented with asking others to tell all while keeping mum himself. Why don't you leave behind a few words of truth to future generations?"[98] What Professor Zhu wanted Ba to say was how he – and members of his generation – had been systemically duped and suppressed by the party. As Wang Yi, a well-known pastor and writer who has done repeated battles with the authorities, put it: "the CCP has made it crystal clear to intellectuals that their knowledge and faith are insufficient for them to retain their *renge* [human dignity]." Wang recounted how Shanghai-based literary critic Wang Yuanhua cited two radical anti-party intellectuals – economist Gu Zhun and dissident Yu Luoke – as proof that "we intellectuals were not [totally] wiped out" during the Cultural Revolution. But did the nationally known Professor Wang put up a fight against the authorities so as to protect fellow intellectuals? Pastor Wang cited this comment from a critic of the literary celebrity: "Yes it is true that Gu Zhun stood his ground. But what has this to do with yourself?"[99]

Overwhelming odds notwithstanding, free-thinking Chinese have made a Herculean effort to wean themselves off political control – and to nurture independence and self-sufficiency within themselves. In an essay entitled "The quintessence of global values is to treat the individual as individual," Bao Tong, the former secretary of the late Party General Secretary Zhao Ziyang, pointed out that one of the greatest failings of the CCP was precisely its refusal to treat the people as individuals who can have aspirations and pursue agendas separate from those of the state. "The Four Cardinal Principles [of Marxism and party leadership] have led to the total degradation of the individual," he wrote.[100]

For much-translated writer Zhang Yihe, the first calling of intellectuals is to rediscover and relegitimize the primacy of *renxing*, literally "human nature" and, figuratively, humanity and the dignity of the individual. She argued that, since Mao's *Talk on Literature and the Arts in Yan'an* in 1945, *dangxing* has marginalized *renxing* to the point of extinction. In a 2016 essay on the lack of humanity as well as poverty of ideas among the present generation, Zhang wrote: "I feel that the major difference between ourselves and the older generation can be found in the issue of *renxing*." "Members of the older generation were so beautiful: they have a beautiful mind and their *renxin* is perfect," she wrote, adding that the *renxing* of the Republic-era intellectuals were "rich, complicated and wholesome." Echoing art critic Chen Danqing's point about the monotony and lifelessness of the pursuit of many intellectuals in the Communist era, Zhang wrote: "We don't have much of a story to tell … But members of the older generation have so many stories to tell, and all of them are so vivid."[101]

Similarly, Shanghai Huadong Normal University scholar Xu Jilin has waged a valiant battle against censors and commissars so as to defend the distinctive personality or *zizhuxing* ("initiative" and "innate self-sufficiency") of intellectuals. Xu contended that independent, self-respecting intellectuals must not only preserve their own *zizhuxing* but they must also ensure the *zhizhuxing* of knowledge itself. "The *zizhuxing* of knowledge and learning is fundamental to intellectuals' ability to reach [the goal of improving] public life and to implement the critique of the politics [of the day]," he added. The knowledge and values propagated by intellectuals must be independent of the requirements of the ruling regime, he indicated.[102]

Inchoate organizations of intellectuals

Xi Jinping has continued with efforts by Mao Zedong and other leaders to prevent members of the educated classes from forming any sort of organization, be it something as innocuous as a saloon for literary appreciation. Veteran author and party historian Hu Zhiwei, who is now based in Hong Kong, remembers how he was imprisoned for more than ten years for organizing a "club of poets" with his young friends and relatives in the 1950s. Also note that one of the apparent "crimes" cited against Gui Minhai, the Hong Kong publisher of books about elite Chinese politics who was kidnapped by state-security agents in Thailand in late 2015, was that he was a founding member of a Shenzhen-based organization of writers, journalists and intellectuals.[103]

In 2008, author and reform theorist Liu Xiaobo and several hundred of the nation's top academics, writers and public intellectuals signed Charter 08 so as to press for freedom of expression and rule of law. These citizen rights are enshrined in the PRC Constitution – but have never been carried out. The first batch of signatories included luminaries among men of letters, professors, lawyers, former cadres, businesspeople, as well as NGO activists. Until their Internet account was closed by the authorities, the Charter 08 website attracted more than 20,000 signatures; many of these enthusiasts were laborers, students, housewives and retirees. Equally significant was that the Charter 08 Movement gained international recognition. Although Liu eventually had to make the ultimate sacrifice of dying in jail, China's only Nobel Peace laureate has succeeded in drawing the world's attention to the plight of dissidents, intellectuals and NGO activists.[104]

For exiled intellectual Hua Yishi, the Charter 08 Movement had a similar significance to the Czech 77 Movement. "Since China fell prey to Soviet-style totalitarianism [in 1949], this was a collective resistance movement of the highest intellectual level," said Hua. "It was also a collective movement in non-obedience and civil protest." The Charter 08 statement represented "the spirit of modern human rights and democracy," Hua argued. "It has not only carried forward the mission of 'benevolent mandarins' of dynastic China but also laid out a new direction for the future of the country." Hua noted that, even though, in terms of the number of participants, the pro-democracy campaign of 1989 was much bigger, the demands of the students and professors were limited to asking the party to conduct reforms such as fighting corruption and relaxing press censorship. The 1989 protestors did not go so far as to question the legitimacy – and the dictatorial statecraft – of the party.[105]

The immediate effect of the prize, however, was that the state-security apparatus has become ever more wary of the formation of groups of intellectuals who might launch any shape or form of "political action." This was illustrated by the Chinese government's efficient clampdown on efforts on the part of dissidents to emulate the Arab Spring Revolution in early 2011. Inspired by the Jasmine Revolution in Tunisia, largely anonymous activists used the Internet to call for gatherings in big cities such as Beijing, Shanghai, Guangzhou, Shenzhen and Hong Kong in honor of the "Molihua Revolution." (The flower molihua is a Chinese variety of jasmine.) The slogans used by the Internet activists included "ending one party rule," "fighting for freedom of expression," and "promoting independence of the judiciary."[106] There was, however, no specific program of action. The first series of meetings took place on Sunday February 20, with the understanding that subsequent gatherings would be organized in the same venues every Sunday afterwards. The inaugural meeting in the capital, right outside a McDonald's restaurant in central Beijing, attracted several hundred spectators. However, police officers and plainclothes security personnel, in addition to diplomats and foreign journalists, far outnumbered the participants. The meetings were effectively stopped by the authorities that very day. Beijing detained for questioning no fewer than 100 suspects, including the artist Ai Weiwei, lawyers Teng Biao and Jiang Tianyong, blogger Ran Yunfei, and human rights activists such as Xiao Yong, Lu Yongxiang, Li Tiantian, Liu Guohui and Ding Mao.[107]

Yet another group of intellectuals who frequently rock the boat of police-induced stability consists of members of China's miniscule number of unofficial think tanks. According to the Think Tanks and Civil Societies Program of the University of Pennsylvania, the PRC had 512 think tanks in 2017, second only to the 1,872 in the United States.[108] Yet the great majority of these organizations are adjuncts of party and government departments, including civilian and military intelligence outfits. Only a small proportion of think tanks – for example, the Unirule Institute of Economics and The World and China Institute (TWCI) – are bona fide private organizations.

Take Unirule, for example, which is a pro-democracy institute that eschews street action. Mao Yushi (born 1929), a founder and principal researcher at Unirule, is a soft-spoken man who has never impinged upon the authority of either the CCP or its general secretary. A recipient of the Milton Friedman Prize for Advancing Liberty in 2012, Mao has for the past several years been under police surveillance.[109]

An engineer-turned-economist, Mao is one among a sizeable number of social scientists who have raised serious questions about not only the viability and sustainability of the "China model," but also whether it makes for a fair and just society. Mao's criticism of China's state-dominated "mixed economy" is particularly relevant given President Xi's refusal to give up party-and-state control of the economy. This has manifested itself in the top leadership's insistence on the primacy of 100-odd *yangqi*, or SOE conglomerates. Sometimes called China's *chaebol*, these conglomerates are given monopolies in strategic areas ranging from banking and insurance to telecommunications and oil and gas.[110] Mao thinks that the basic reason behind China's socioeconomic problems is the phenomenon of special privilege and the powerful – meaning clans and business groups with party backing – preying on sectors with no political connections. The only way to put an end to exploitation, he argued, was "through the advocacy of human rights, democracy, rule of law." "Only if we can hold high the banner of freedom and the rule of law … can China really become a major power in the world," he added.[111] Without any warning, the authorities closed down Unirule in July 2018. Burly agents shuttered the door of Unirule's office, even though five researchers were still at work in the premises. Mao has since been barred from leaving the country even for mundane reasons such as taking part in academic conferences.[112]

Could liberal "establishment intellectuals" sway the future of reform?

As of early 2019, there was no evidence that any civil-society organization established by intellectuals was potent enough to force the hand of the CCP on notable issues. It is possible, however, that so-called "establishment intellectuals" could sway the future of China, should there be a major crisis within the party-state apparatus. Establishment intellectuals consist of retired senior party cadres, members of prominent party clans, as well as influential academics who want to promote gradualist changes within the system – without necessarily bringing about the CCP's imminent collapse. They first made their mark in Chinese politics and society as the colleagues and underlings of two reformist icons of the 1980s: former General Secretaries Hu Yaobang (1915–1989) and Zhao Ziyang (1919–2005). Notable figures within this group include the two sons of Hu Yaobang, Hu Deping (born 1942) and Hu Dehua (born 1949); the former secretary of Mao Zedong, Li Rui (1917–2019); former director of the State Administration on News and Publications, Du Daozheng (born 1937); former Xinhua News Agency senior editor Yang Jisheng (born 1940); and the recently deceased former *People's Daily* chief editor Hu Jiwei (1916–2012).[113] It is also possible that avant-garde intellectuals with no connections to the system may work together with establishment intellectuals to ring in the new.

Intellectuals and retired cadres who used to be close to the party's liberal wing were marginalized after the Tiananmen Square incident of 1989. Almost none of them advocate the break-up of the CCP, but they have fulfilled the role of public intellectuals by not only lambasting the aberrations of the CCP system, but also offering novel solutions for governance. The advantage of this group of intellectuals is their seniority in party membership and their lofty moral station in society. Given the remnant Confucianism in Chinese society, fourth- and fifth-generation leaders, ranging from Hu Jintao to Xi Jinping (who typically joined the party between the 1960s and the early 1980s), have to show some degree of respect for these elders. This subset of *zhishifenzi* mostly makes itself heard through the printed word and in cyberspace, including interviews given to the Hong Kong and overseas Chinese media. Many of them were editors of and contributors to the vastly influential journal *Yanhuang Chunqiu*. Basically a journal of party history, *Yanhuang Chunqiu* carried scores of forward-looking articles on alternative, more liberal models of development that dovetailed with global norms.[114]

The *Yanhuang Chunqiu* group was responsible for pushing the "socialist democratic party (SDP) model" as an alternative for China. Their central idea is that the kind of humanitarian and democratic socialism found in Scandinavian countries has most aptly manifested the ideals of Marxism. In other words, SDPs in Europe, and not the CCP, have best lived up to the teachings of Marx and Engels. Thus, Xie

Tao (1922–2010), a former vice president of Renmin University in Beijing, argued in an article in the February 2007 issue of *Yanhuang Chunqiu* that, "the CCP's only way out is through [embracing] democratic socialism" of the Western European variety. "Only constitutional democracy can fundamentally solve the ruling party's problems of corruption and graft," he added. "Only democratic socialism can save China."[115] Some of Xie's ideas could have been partially incorporated into the Hu Jintao administration's "Scientific Theory on Development," one of whose central planks was to boost social welfare spending, particularly for peasants in the heartland provinces.[116]

Hu Dehua, the third son of Hu Yaobang, has boldly advocated the "Taiwan model" – the gradual liberalization measures laid down by the late president Chiang Ching-kuo in the mid-1980s – as a possible solution for China. Hu, who is a manager of a software company, said that, instead of continuing to rely on suppression and censorship, the CCP could also consider the path of "following the wishes of the people, telling people the truth, and getting the masses' forgiveness [for past wrongs done]." Hu cited Taiwan's Chiang as an example:

He was opposed to martial law and opposed to the reign of terror of spies. [...] He was able to attain reconciliation with the opposition parties and the Taiwan people. And even though [the Kuomintang] lost in elections [in 2000], they were re-elected [in 2008].[117]

At a time when President Xi Jinping – and his brand of orthodox "core socialist values" – is dominating the party-state apparatus, it would be difficult even for politically well-connected "establishment intellectuals" to influence the course of political development. There were reports in the *New York Times* as well as Hong Kong media that Hu Deping, whose friendship with Xi date back a few decades, had a long meeting with the princeling a few months before the latter assumed power at the 18th Party Congress. Hu was pulling out the stops to persuade Xi to rekindle the flames of political reform. After all, Xi Zhongxun, the father of Xi, was a close adviser to General Secretary Hu Yaobang. Hu, who used to be a vice-ministerial-level official at the CCP's Central United Front Work Department – one of whose jobs is to promote relations with non-party groupings – also lobbied Xi to expand the public sphere by giving more leeway to NGOs and politically inclined private businessmen.[118]

That the relatively few liberal "establishment intellectuals" have failed to make a dent on Xi's hardline policy was fully demonstrated by the closure of *Yanhuang Chunqiu* in July 2016. As usual, propaganda officials failed to give any reason. *Yanhuang Chunqiu* executive editor Hong Zhenkuai said that the demise of his journal would be a blow to intelligentsia interested in the fate of their country. "The magazine represented reformists within the party and liberals within the establishment," Hong said. "One of its key positions was to urge the party to advance political reform." Moreover, outspoken leaders of the *Yanhuang Chunqiu*, such as its former director Du Daozheng, have been told by officials not to give interviews to Hong Kong or overseas media.[119] In October of the same year, the *gongshiwang* (www.ccom.net), which since 2009 had provided a platform for both free-thinking and establishment intellectuals to air their views, was also closed down.[120]

Quite a few Sinologists think that, although the views of marginalized establishment intellectuals amount to little more than voices in the wilderness, they could pack a punch at times of a big split in the CCP due to either domestic or foreign crises. According to U.S.-based Sinologist Minxin Pei, who has forecast a seismic shift in Chinese politics by 2030, contradictions within the party might make possible a window for change. Pei noted that, should the Xi Jinping faction stumble, the other power blocs in the party might pick a new leader:

> There are two possibilities. One is that this post-Xi leader, who is pushed by the demand for fundamental political change, embarks on this path reluctantly. The other possibility is that this leader is merely a transition figure. His incompetence results in his quick removal from power and replacement by a genuine political reformer.[121]

The political scientist argued that, under both scenarios, the input of liberal cadres such as the sons of Hu Yaobang would be "critical" for the party to adopt a more reformist trajectory.[122]

Conclusion: achievements of intellectuals who fought back in 2018 and 2019

Meet Qiu Hao, an AI-enabled and fully digitalized news anchor who can belt out official propaganda in Chinese and English, 24 hours a day. At an international Internet convention held in November 2018, Xinhua News Agency and the Sogou search engine showed off a unique product of their joint research in AI: good-looking Qiu, who was wearing a red tie and an impeccably tailored suit. "Not only can I accompany you 24 hours a day, 365 days a year," intoned Qiu, who is capable of a wide range of tonal gradations and facial expressions. "I can be endlessly copied and present at different scenes to bring you the news." This robot newsman could be Xi Jinping's model of an intellectual "in the new era," one who is programmed to give voice to Marxist precepts – as well as the party's edicts of the day – as conceived by China's "pathfinder for the people."[123] The question for China's intellectuals is: how can they fight back against the party's multipronged attempts to subjugate them?

Continuation of the long-stalled emancipation of the Chinese mind

China's intellectuals have frequently been criticized for not daring to directly confront the CCP dictatorship. In light of the quasi-police-state apparatus, however, foreign observers might perhaps be unjustly taking them to task. At the very least, the intelligentsia has continued the task of enlightenment and thought liberation begun by the May Fourth generation of gifted thinkers from across the political spectrum, who ranged from the Westernized Hu Shih to Chen Duxiu, one of the founders of the CCP.

A number of noted intellectuals think that, although the first generation of liberal scholars raised the issue of "Mr. Science" and "Mr. Democracy" during the May Fourth Movement of 1919, the Chinese have not made enough headway in emancipating themselves from "feudalistic thinking." Instead of achieving a "scientific" or "democratic" way of thinking, even fairly well-educated Chinese lack basic criteria to think logically: to tell what is right or wrong. These pioneering thinkers are convinced that the Chinese need to be taught "what is logical" and not "just follow what the party says." One of internationally famous blogger Han Han's most famous sayings is that, "There are two kinds of logic in the world: one is logic, the other is Chinese logic."[124] For Yi Zhongtian, "Chinese logic" does not focus on what is right and wrong but on issues of "attitude, motivation and *guanxi* [connections]." For example, a censor or commissar could ban an article not because what the author said was wrong, but because he had the "wrong attitude and motivation of smearing the party or exposing embarrassing social situations."[125]

Similarly, writer Yu Ge has found that questions of what is right and wrong have been sidetracked – and badly politicized. In an article called "Chinese logic is not logic but the enemy of logic," Yu lamented the fact that the criteria of judgment had become totally warped. Yu noted that officials often used the pretext of *guoqing* ("national conditions") to justify imperfections in China. Similarly, what is logical or not is often based on "motivation." This means that, if an official or academic is imbued with a righteous desire to defend the party, it necessarily follows that what he says will never be wrong.[126] For noted jurist Jiang Ping, party cadres and propagandists often use two criteria on which to base their judgments: "stability is the overriding task" and "the theory that 'Chinese conditions' are special." In other words, arguments that fit officials' concern about stability above all else – and that seem to mesh with China's "special national characteristics" – always win the day.[127]

Listen, for example, to the heart-breaking testimony of Yan Lianke, an experimental novelist whose works have been translated into many languages. "I came to understand that darkness is not the mere absence of light, but rather it is life itself," Yan said in a speech while accepting the Franz Kafka Prize in October 2014.

> Darkness is the Chinese people's fate. [...] When I look at contemporary China, I see a nation that is thriving yet distorted, developing yet mutated. I see corruption, absurdity, disorder and chaos. Every day, something occurs that lies outside ordinary reason and logic. A system of morality and a respect for humanity that was developed over several millenniums is unraveling.[128]

Despite China's superficial wealth and glamor, Yan dares to ask this overwhelming question: "What is the price for abandoning the ideals of democracy, freedom, law and morality?"[129]

One of the lasting contributions of China's beleaguered intellectuals is to at least teach the nation how to distinguish between right and wrong – and to restore "logical thinking" based on standards of truth, justice and morality rather than the CCP's political exigencies. The educated elite has begun its arduous task of enlightenment by debunking the apparatchiks' claims about the glorious history of the party.[130] The CCP's insistence that it has always been correct has resulted in the hiding, molding and embellishing of the plethora of CCP-related blunders that ranged from China's entry into the Korean War to the Tiananmen Square massacre. After all, the Machiavellian use of information and propaganda – including self-serving interpretations of history – is a key weapon that has underpinned the CCP's success.

Following Mao, President Xi thinks that history has a "class nature and *dangxing* [party nature]." This means that, first, only historical knowledge that tallies with the party's goals should be taught in schools and talked about in the media. Second, the party is more than justified in deleting, whitewashing or repackaging past events.[131] In a 2010 lecture on compiling and doing research on the history of the party, then-Vice-President Xi Jinping contended that historians must "uphold the synthesis of *dangxing* and the scientific nature of historiography." This essentially meant that the research, teaching and overall dissemination of historical ideas and knowledge must be in sync with the party's interests. By "scientific" Xi meant "the scientific nature of the laws of China's social movements" – and not "scientific methodology" as is understood in the Western social sciences tradition.[132]

Since the start of the 21st century, muck-raking historians and writers have, thanks to relentless digging into central and local archives – plus interviews with witnesses of such horrendous events as the Three Years of Famine (1959–1961) – reconstructed a true picture of the party's mind-boggling aberrations. They started with China's participation in the Korean War, through the Great Leap Forward (1958–1962), the Anti-Rightist Movement (1957–1959) and, of course, the Cultural Revolution, which Xi has been so anxious to whitewash.[133] Zhu Xueqin, a liberal historian at Shanghai University, argued that "history books used in schools and universities have distorted history." "Students who grow up studying these books are equivalent to those who have consumed wolf's milk all their lives," he added.[134] Those intellectuals who have taken part in the battle to unveil the truth about the past have done their illustrious forebears, ranging from Qu Yuan to Lu Xin, proud.

Underscoring the importance of global norms

After the June 4, 1989 crackdown, only one Politburo-ranked official has openly said China should adopt *pushi jiazhi* ("universal values"), which, as discussed earlier in this chapter, are equated with potentially destabilizing ideas about "Western" democracy and civil rights. Wen Jiabao, who was premier from 2003 to 2013, said on several occasions in late 2002 that "science, democracy, rule of law, freedom and human rights are not unique to capitalism, but are values commonly pursued by mankind over a long period of history."[135] Other supporters of *pushi jiazhi* include the sons and colleagues of late party chief and liberal icon Hu Yaobang, with whom Wen worked closely in the 1980s. Liberal princeling Qin Xiao, the former head of the China Merchants Bank, also went on record praising *pushi jiazhi*. He said in 2010 that, "universal values tell us that government serves the people, that assets belong to the public and that urbanization is for the sake of people's happiness," he said. Supporters of the "China model," he added, believe the opposite: that people should obey the government, the state should control economic assets, and the interests of individuals are subordinate to those of local development.[136]

For CCP members who first joined the party in the 1930s and 1940s, however, the leadership's dismissal of "Western" or "universal values" such as freedom of expression and religion is as disturbing as it is ironic. After all, in public statements and interviews with the foreign press, Mao Zedong and Liu Shaoqi waxed eloquent about the fact that, after their victory, there would be universal-suffrage elections and opposition parties. Mao said in 1947, two years before taking power, that, "we support the abolition of one-party dictatorship." He added that the CCP would not "imitate the social and political order of the Soviet Union." Liu Shaoqi, who would become China's first president, said before Liberation that "one-party rule is against democracy; and the CCP will not institute one-party dictatorship."[137]

Testimonies by an older generation of intellectuals pointed to the fact that they joined the revolution precisely to fight for "Western values." Dai Huang (1928–2016), one of Xinhua News Agency's earliest journalists, had this to say on why he joined the New Fourth Army at the age of 16: "We wanted to sacrifice our lives to achieve 'liberty, democracy, equality and fraternity' for China," he said. "However, after the party had conquered heaven and earth [in 1949], these [ideals] vanished like ghosts."[138]

After President Xi came to power, however, the battle cry in favor of *pushi jiazhi* – which was first sounded by radical students and professors during the May Fourth Movement of 1919 – has been uttered by only a handful of liberal intellectuals. Peking University jurist He Weifang perhaps best exemplifies the intellectual who is prepared to risk all to introduce the most fundamental egalitarian ideas and institutions into China. There is no question in his mind that intellectuals should be closely involved in improving the country's sociopolitical standards. In an interview with the official *Southern Metropolitan News*, he cited figures such as Plato, Socrates, Locke, Montesquieu and Weber as men of letters who enlightened their countrymen. "They have been eulogized in history due to their concern for public issues," said Professor He. "They pay close attention to politics and society." Speaking as a legal academic, He said that "society is our laboratory." "If a legal scholar does not criticize and expose social problems or negative phenomena that go against the rule of law, his integrity as a legal specialist will be dented," he added.[139]

The acclaimed law professor has reiterated that the country was facing a dead end unless it picked up universal values of democracy and rule of law. "We may not be able to say this out loud," he wrote. "Yet it is certain that in the future we have to go down the path of for example, a multi-party system [and introduce] freedom of the press, real democracy and real liberty for the individual." He was even ready to tackle this taboo: Taiwan's largely successful democratization model. Saying that Beijing should take a hard look at political institutions in the "break-away province," He concluded, "This is perhaps the direction that China should take."[140]

For independent writer Liu Junning, the development of China's civilization hinges on its ability to absorb and abide by certain universal values, including those enshrined in the UN Charter. These include a democratic system, freedom of political participation by citizens and freedom of expression, particularly freedom to criticize the powers that be. "There are two prerequisites for democratic governance: one is participation by citizens; the second is their supervision of the powerful," wrote Liu, a former researcher in the Political Science Institute of CASS. "Freedom of expression is a tool for political participation [by the masses]; it is also a tool for supervision of the [current] leadership."[141]

Exposing the problems of the "China model"

Despite increasingly obvious chinks in the armor of the "Chinese economic miracle," not only official economists, but also many Western Sinologists have continued to sing the praises of the "China model."[142] For example, Daniel A. Bell has argued that the Chinese approach to governance, which he describes as "democracy at the bottom, experimentation in the middle, and meritocracy at the top," means at least that China is not a "'bad' authoritarian regime similar in nature to, say, dictatorships in North Korea and the Middle East."[143] A handful of notable Chinese social scientists, however, have for the past decade fulfilled their role as socially engaged intellectuals through spotlighting the failings of the Chinese governance model, which Beijing calls "socialism with Chinese characteristics."

For Du Runsheng (1913–2015), the grand old man of agrarian reform, the China model is but a synthesis of the two worst traditions in history: Soviet dictatorship and "Eastern despotism." "We must make a full assessment of the historical impact of long-standing Oriental despotism," he said shortly before his death in 2015. "Chinese history consists of a totalitarian society under imperial power." Millennia of dynastic rule has been exacerbated by Soviet intolerance, Du argued. "We lack a democratic tradition and independent thinking is lacking."[144]

Economist Hu Xingdou, who teaches at the Beijing University of Technology, is frequently sought after by both the domestic and foreign media for his views on domestic politics. Hu is devastatingly frank about his assessment of the China model. The professor thinks that "China is on the brink of becoming a failed state." "China is at a crossroads in terms of its development," he said in a 2013 talk to a cluster of Beijing-based Western diplomats. "China faces three paths: extreme leftism or Maoism; *quangui* ['aristocratic'] socialism or crony capitalism; and a system similar to constitutional democracy in the West." Hu favors the third path, yet he thinks that, unless the CCP is willing to gradually cede power to a civil society – and "to promote rule of law instead of rule by men and rule by the party" – this path is not possible.[145]

Hu has focused on several "core contradictions" in the Chinese system: over-concentration of political and economic power at the center; a mushrooming rich–poor gap; special privileges being accorded to top clans in the party; and lack of say – not to mention political power – on the part of the "lower classes," especially peasants. "The power of cadres has trumped civil rights," Hu said. "Central coffers have grown at the expense of the wealth of the people. And official propaganda has drowned out the voice of the populace." Although President Xi seems to have made some progress with his anti-graft campaign, social scientists agree that corruption, or "rent-seeking" is still serious. Hu quotes famed economist and government adviser Wu Jinglian's figure that rent-seeking accounts for 20–30 percent of GDP, which is a horrendous figure for a developing nation.[146] Hu is particularly worried about peasants, the disenfranchised 50 percent of the population who lack basic rights such as selling their plots for cash or moving around the country. Hu added a poignant note on intellectuals' responsibility to care for the downtrodden. "Intellectuals should be society's perpetual critics, and the custodian of social conscience," he pointed out. "It is not true that intellectuals want to become saviors of peasants," he added. "It's only that speaking from one's conscience is the innate mission of every intellectual."[147]

An equally dire prognosis has come from Sun Liping, one of China's most prominent sociologists. Like most of his colleagues, the Tsinghua University academic has shied away from direct criticism of the CCP or individual leaders. At a time when most experts point to the estimated 150,000 annual cases of social unrest to show what is behind the façade of glamor along the prosperous coast, Sun said the situation was worse. "The biggest threat to China is not social unrest but the *kuibai* [decay and collapse] of society," he said. "Unrest could mean a healthy body being hurt," Sun explained. "*Kuibai* means serious ailments have wreaked havoc on the body's cells; the cells are dying and the organs can't function."[148]

Catalysts of a vibrant civil society

For intellectuals who have been able to win back their *zhutixing* (self-sufficiency and independence), the next step to consolidate their hard-fought freedoms is to form groups of like-minded "campaigners" – and to expand the civil society. This is a tall order. As Tsinghua University professor Chen Danqing noted in 2010, "civil or public space" – as distinguished from sectors in the polity that are totally dominated by the party-state – "has not really come about in the country." "From whence can public intellectuals come?" he asked.[149]

For dissident writer Du Daobin, traditional Chinese society is dominated by the use of force, which is dependent on "the decision-making of just one brain, that of the dictator." The role of responsible citizens, including intellectuals, is to make possible the transition to a civil society, and eventually a nation of citizens who can fully take part in governmental and social decision-making. The first prerequisite for a viable civil society, wrote Du, is that "every citizen must be independent and is capable of taking his own initiative." "They must be willing to push forward the progress of society and country," he added. Given that the wherewithal of individuals is limited, Du advocated "cooperation among citizens to build up different types of citizens' groupings which are based on a consensus [of ideals] and mutually shared interest."[150]

Du's description of an "independent-minded" citizen fits the ideal of an intellectual who is determined to reject *dangxing* (party nature) and to embrace *renxing* (human nature) and *zhizhuxing*. For Shenzhen University professor Wang Xiaohua, the first calling of the intellectual is to maintain his independent status, meaning he should not be beholden to any political or economic vested interests. "The death of *zhizhuxing* is tantamount to the death of the public intellectual," he wrote in 2012. The public intellectual can only be born within a civil society or in the course of the establishment of a civil society. "The public intellectual can only thrive when the civil society thrives," he said. "The public intellectual acquires his legitimacy and meaning through building up and safeguarding the civil society." Like many other social scientists, Wang believes that the rise of the Internet has provided a relatively "democratic, egalitarian, extensive and non-utilitarian" platform for intellectuals to appeal to like-minded citizens in different corners of the nation. "When deficiencies in the system have exposed themselves or when citizens' interests are being hurt, the Internet provides space where the public intellectual can appear and have their say," he said.[151]

Xiao Gongqin, the renowned proponent of "neo-authoritarianism," believes in the indispensable role of the civil society in the modernization of Chinese politics and societies. The Shanghai Normal University professor noted that intellectuals could spearhead the formation of civil-society groups that could make possible the balance between a strong state and a strong society. "Only with the development of the civil society can there be effective societal supervision [of state power] and checks and balances," Xiao said. Chinese politics, said the professor, was characterized by "an extremely strong state coupled with an extremely weak society." He noted that individual citizens or intellectuals acting alone were not up to the task of supervising the state. "Only with the organization power of civil groups as well as independent social intermediary groups can social mechanisms that can effectively check and balance state power come into being."[152]

Although most intellectuals realize they might be going through a hard winter, they might be inspired by the encouraging words of Du Guang, a liberal theorist who used to work in the Theoretical Research Office of the Central Party School. Du pointed out in 2008 that intellectuals, being a key constituent of the civil society, represented the "brain and conscience" of the nation. He indicated that the growth and maturation of the civil society requires a benevolent environment, especially political democratization and freedom of the press. He argued,

> Yet we cannot sit and wait until political democratization and press freedom has been realized before we push forward the development of the civil society.

On the contrary, just because there is a lack of political democracy and press freedom, we should be all the more diligent and conscientious in reforming the social system and in forging ahead with nurturing a civil society.[153]

Intellectuals punch back in 2018 and 2019

Things began to stir some ten years after Du Guang's statement. In the last week of 2018, dissidents, intellectuals and NGO pioneers were pleasantly surprised by the appearance on the net of a public statement called "100 Chinese public intellectuals publish their thoughts on forty years of 'reform and the open door.'"[154] Although it was taken down by cyber cops in a matter of hours, the extraordinary outcry – which can be construed as a petition to the CCP – made its way quickly to dozens of websites run by Hong Kong, Taiwanese and overseas-Chinese media and NGOs. Within 24 hours, the impassioned plea for reform made its way back to China, or at least to the tens of millions of intellectuals who have ways of climbing over the Great Firewall of China. Although the "Petition of the Hundred" has so far not made an impact comparable to the Charter '08 Movement, it shows that pioneers of new thinking and freedom of expression could, sometimes with the help of "establishment intellectuals," be capable of delivering a shock to the system that might have a long-lasting effect. Moreover, although the bulk of the 100 were professors, writers and journalists, there were also representatives from legal, religious, business and NGO circles, as well as professionals affiliated with party institutions. This seems an indication that cross-sectoral NGO groupings, however loosely organized, are developing.

Although the aspirations, demands and suggestions made by these intellectuals might not be totally new, they amounted to a frontal challenge to President Xi. As will be fully discussed in Chapter 5, the stranglehold on power that is being exercised by the party and by Xi has been weakened owing to the Xi leadership's perceived inability to handle the multidimensional salvoes fired by the Trump administration. This is coupled with Beijing's apparent failure to solve socioeconomic problems owing to the "core leader's" refusal to push Deng Xiaoping's reforms forward. In Xi's December 2018 speech marking the 40th anniversary of the genesis of the reform era, he rejected Deng's advocacy of a market economy as well as his acquiescence on selected global norms. Instead, Xi merely emphasized boosting party leadership. He also reiterated that the party must guard against "subversive mistakes," a reference to reforms that would be detrimental to the party's – and particularly his own – monopoly on power.[155] The groundswell of discontent against Xi has created an opening for intellectuals and NGO groupings to make their voices heard.

The common theme of the signatories is that Xi has spurned all types of reforms that could undermine the party's control over education, the media, the business world and, indeed, what goes on in people's minds. Human rights and other civil liberties guaranteed by the Constitution have been trampled to the ground. According to Beijing-based political scientist Cheng Guangquan, "Reform means deepening reforms on all fronts." "There should be no taboos," he added. "Right now, the issue of human rights cannot be touched." For political commentator He Yanguang, "reform and the open door means reaching the standards of civilized countries." "Reform means changing our [identities], and opening up means learning from the U.S., Japan and other civilized societies," he argued. Similarly, Hubei entrepreneur Li Xueyuan contended that, "the open-door [policy] means keeping abreast with normal countries and civilized societies." Beijing-based economist Hu Xingdou was bold enough to insist that the CCP should "end 'reforms' that run counter to the marketplace and that are opposed to the rule of law." He added that China must "construct a real market economy as well as rule of law." For Peking University law professor Zhang Qianfan, the only way to improve the situation of human rights and rule of law is to develop universal-style political institutions such as "real elections." "Unless we breach the fortress of elections, there won't be real reforms," he argued.[156]

Although few among the petitioners pilloried Xi by name, there was indirect criticism of his obsession with imperial-style power – and his retaining the corrupt system of the elite monopolizing the biggest share of national income. Despite the position of Xi, who heads the army, the police and the secret police, seeming impregnable, the outburst of critical voices seems to indicate that his control over 1.4 billion people is much, much less than airtight. Should China's economic – and diplomatic – crises worsen, the possibility is real that a reinvigorated civil society, led by a team of dedicated intellectuals, could gradually steer the ship of state toward goals compatible with global norms.

Notes

1   Cited in Yu Ying-shih, "The re-creation of the spirit of the intellectual in a commercialized society," in Chen Ying-chen et al., *The Intellectual*, Taipei: Li Xu Cultural Enterprises Press, 2006, pp. 35–36.
2   Liu himself is a noted theorist on the traits and role of the Chinese intellectual; see Liu Xiaobo, *Contemporary Chinese Politics and the Chinese Intellectual*, Taipei: Tangshan Publishers, 1990.
3   Ibid.
4   Cited in Timothy Cheek, "Xu Jilin and the thought work of China's public intellectuals," *The China Quarterly*, No. 186, June 2006, p. 412; see also Xu Jilin, "What future for public intellectuals?" *China Perspectives* (Paris), No. 52, 2004, http://chinap erspectives.revues.org/799. For a representative sampling of the definitions of Chinese intellectuals given by scholars outside China, see Merle Goldman, *China's Intellectuals: Advise and Dissent*, Cambridge, MA: Harvard University Press, 1988; Merle Goldman and Edward Gu, eds., *Chinese Intellectuals between State and Market*, New York: Routledge, 2013; Timothy Cheek, *Propaganda and Culture in Mao's China: Deng Tuo and the Intelligentsia*, New York: Oxford University Press, 1998; Timothy Cheek, *Chinese Establishment Intellectuals*, New York: M.E. Sharpe, 1986; Yinghong Cheng, *Creating the New Man: From Enlightenment Ideals to Socialist Realities*, Honolulu: University of Hawaii Press, 2009; Edward X. Gu, "Cultural intellectuals and the politics of the cultural public space in Communist China (1979–1989): a case study of three intellectual groups," *The Journal of Asian Studies*, No. 2, May 1999, pp. 389–431; Wei Chengsi, *The Rise and Fall of Chinese Intellectuals*, Taipei: Ku Lao Cultural Enterprises, 2010; and Chen Ying-Zhen et al., eds. *The Intellectual*.

5   For a discussion of how Mao – and Xi – tried to subsume intellectuals under the *dangxing* of the party, see Willy Wo-Lap Lam, *Chinese Politics in the Era of Xi Jinping*, London: Routledge, 2015, pp. 282–290. See also Jean-Philippe Beja, "Reform, repression, co-optation: the CCP's policy toward intellectuals," in Willy Wo-Lap Lam, ed., *Routledge Handbook of the Chinese Communist Party*, London: Routledge, 2018, pp. 232–247.

6   For a discussion of the circumstances surrounding the death of Liu Xiaobo, see, for example, "Tyranny kills: Liu Xiaobo died from sickness," *Apple Daily* (Hong Kong), July 14, 2007, https://hk.news.appledaily.com/local/realtime/article/20170714/56953246. See also Chris Buckley, "Liu Xiaobo, Chinese dissident who won Nobel while jailed, dies at 61," *New York Times*, July 13, 2017, www.nytimes.com/2017/07/13/world/asia/liu-xiaobo-dead.html?_r=0

7   Cited in "The last 20 years of the life of Gao Hua," *Caixin Net* (Beijing), May 12, 2014, http://culture.caixin.com/2014-05-12/100675882.html

8   During the Cultural Revolution, numerous disgraced top cadres, not to mention intellectuals and academics, were denied medical treatment. Many committed suicide to protest their ill-treatment. See, for example, Xie Bing, "The question of suicide among Chinese intellectuals and members of other sectors during 1949 to 1976," Aisixiang.com, March 4, 2010, www.aisixiang.com/data/32030.html

9   Cited in Ma Xiao, "On intellectuals, dissidents and real Communist Party members," *Chinese Pen*, December 1, 2015, www.chinesepen.org/blog/archives/42267

10 See also "Zi Zhongyun: the words of an intellectual," Zi Zhongjun blog, July 8, 2016, http://zizjun.blogchina.com/3077079.html

11 This saying was attributed to Confucius in the *Chronicle of the Late Han Dynasty*, written by Fan Hua (398–445), http://chengyu.soouo.com/list/chengyu_9106.htm. For a discussion of the influence of Confucianism on the identity of the Chinese intellectual, see Edward Shils, "Reflections on civil society and civility in the Chinese intellectual tradition," in Tu Wei-ming, ed., *Confucian Traditions in East Asian Modernity: Moral Education and Economic Culture in Japan and the Four Mini-dragons*, Cambridge, MA: Harvard University Press, 1996, pp. 38–71.

12 For a discussion of Xi Jinping's views on Qu Yuan, see "On this occasion, Xi Jinping raises the issue of Qu Yuan," Xinhua News Agency, June 9, 2016, http://news.xinhua net.com/politics/2016-06/09/c_129048211.htm

13 For a discussion of the traditionally high sociopolitical status accorded intellectuals, see Tan Kai and Chen Xianchu, "Theories of 'the intelligentsia' in the media of Republican China," *Journal of Hunan University*, No. 5, 2001, www.cssn.cn/news/454395.htm

14 Cited in Yu Ying-shih, "The re-creation of the spirit of the intellectual in a commercialized society," in Chen Ying-chen et al., *The Intellectual*, pp. 35–36.

15 Ibid.

16 For a study of the genesis of the modern intelligentsia during the May Fourth Movement, see Vera Schwarcz, *The Chinese Enlightenment: Intellectuals and the Legacy of the May Fourth Movement of 1919*, Berkeley: University of California Press, 1986, pp. 55–93. See also Chow Tse-tsung, *The May Fourth Movement: Intellectuals in Modern China*, Cambridge, MA: Harvard University, 1960.

17 Cited in Mao Zedong, "Talks at the Yan'an Forum on Literature and Art, May 1942" from *Selected Works of Mao Tse-tung*, online, www.marxists.org/reference/archive/mao/selected-works/volume-3/mswv3_08.htm

18 Cited in Mao Zedong, "Analysis of the classes in Chinese society" (1925), *Minzufuxingwang (The People's Renaissance Net)*, October 7, 2017, www.mzfxw.com/e/action/ShowInfo.php?classid=21&id=92844. The English translation of the speech is available in "Analysis of the classes in Chinese society," March 1926, *Selected Works of Mao Tse-tung*, www.marxists.org/reference/archive/mao/selected-works/volume-1/mswv1_1.htm

19 Ibid

20   Cited in Tang Bingren, "On Mao Zedong's views on intellectuals," *People's Daily Online*, December 23, 2003, http://learning.sohu.com/2003/12/23/55/article217335569.shtml

21   Ibid.

22   For a discussion of Mao's innate suspicions about intellectuals, see, for example, Wang Laidi, "Mao Zedong's policy toward intellectuals," Aisixiang.com (Beijing), March 7, 2004, www.aisixiang.com/data/2770.html. See also Li Lienan, "A detailed look at the roots of the Cultural Revolution's big pogrom against intellectuals," *Huaxia Zhiqing Net*, April 10, 2013, www.hxzq.net/aspshow/showarticle.asp?id=7854

23   For a discussion of why Wang Shiwei ran foul of Mao, see, for example, Beja, "Reform, repression and co-optation," pp. 232–247. See also Timothy Cheek, "The fading of wild lilies: Wang Shiwei and Mao Zedong's Yan'an Talks in the First CPC Rectification Movement," *The Australian Journal of Chinese Affairs*, No. 11, January 1984, pp. 25–58.

24   For a recent study of Hu Feng and the Hu Feng Clique, see Louisa Wei, *Hu Feng: The Poet's Ideals and Political Storm*, Hong Kong: City University Press, 2017. See also Li Hui, *The Full Story of the Unjust Case of the Hu Feng Clique*, Wuhan: Hubei People's Press, 2003.

25   Ibid.

26   For a discussion of the origins of the Anti-Rightist Campaign, including the "Two Hundreds Campaign," see, for example, Li Rui, "There is evidence to show that the 'free airing of views' was an attempt by Mao to 'tempt the snakes out of their pits,'" *Yanhuang Chunqiu*, April 26, 2013, http://news.ifeng.com/history/shixueyuan/detail_2013_04/26/24688916_0.shtml. See also Li Shenzhi, "When did Chairman Mao decide to 'tempt the snakes out of their pits'?" Sohu.com (Beijing), April 14, 2015, www.sohu.com/a/10656075_114825; Xu Qingquan, "Uncovering a secret: Mao Zedong looks upon the 'Anti-Rightist Campaign' as a battle," *People's Daily*, January 19, 2012, http://history.people.com.cn/GB/205396/16920516.html

27   Cited in Wang Laidi, "Mao Zedong's policy toward intellectuals."

28   For a discussion of Mao's mentality, including his hatred of intellectuals as well as cadres with an "urban background," see Yingshih Yu, "The three stages of the life of Mao Zedong, the crook who won the world," *China in Perspective*, August 21, 2016, www.chinainperspective.com/ArtShow.aspx?AID=164092. Also see "Li Rui on the Anti-Rightist Movement: Mao has a deep bias against intellectuals because he was cold-shouldered by them," *People's Daily Online*, July 11, 2013, http://news.china.com/history/all/11025807/20130711/17939849_1.html. For a description of Mao's life in Beida, see, "The young Mao Zedong kept a low profile at Beida; his position was low and few people knew him," China News Service, July 5, 2011, www.chinanews.com/cul/2011/07-05/3159225.shtml

29   Cited in "Mao Zedong's talks on reforming the thoughts of intellectuals," 360doc.com (Beijing), January 24, 2010, www.360doc.com/content/10/0124/19/276775_14303503.shtml. See also Tang Bingren, "On Mao Zedong's views on intellectuals," *People's Daily Online*, December 23, 2003, http://learning.sohu.com/2003/12/23/55/article217335569.shtml

30   For a discussion of Mao's views on Lu Xun, see, for example, Shan Haifu, "Mao Zedong talked about 'if Lu Xun were alive today,'" China News Service, September 24, 2008, www.chinanews.com/cul/news/2008/09-24/1392893.shtml

31   Cited in "Xi Jinping's views on news and public opinion," *People's Daily*, February 25, 2016, http://theory.people.com.cn/n1/2016/0225/c40531-28148369.html. See also Li Qi, "Use mainstream thoughts and opinions to occupy ideological battlegrounds," *Liberation Daily* (Shanghai), September 27, 2013, http://theory.people.com.cn/n/2013/0927/c40531-23059778.html

32   Cited in "Xi Jinping: ideological and propaganda work is an extremely important work of the party," Xinhua News Agency, August 20, 2013, http://news.sina.com.cn/c/2013-08-20/191028001307.shtml?from=hao123_news_index_paihang_news/. See also "Xi Jinping: ensure that the effect of core socialist values will be as

ubiquitous as the air," Xinhua News Agency, February 26, 2014, http://news.ta
kungpao.com/mainland/focus/2014-02/2303281.html

33 Cited in "The party central authorities with Xi Jinping as general secretary put high
emphasis on construction of spiritual civilization," Xinhua News Agency, February 28,
2015, http://news.xinhuanet.com/politics/2015-02/28/c_127527324.htm

34 Cited in Wang Xiaohui, "Self-consciously arm one's brain and instruct one's
work with the spirit of the series of important talks given by Comrade Xi Jinping," *People's Daily*, July 7, 2014, http://theory.people.com.cn/n/2014/0707/
c40531-25245302.html

35 For a discussion of Deng Xiaoping's rationale behind putting an end to ideological
campaigns, see, for example, Tan Yuxi, "The historic change from organizing lots of
political campaigns to stopping the holding of political campaigns: learn from Deng
Xiaoping's idea of no more political movements," *Harbin Academy Journal* (June 2001),
www.cnki.com.cn/Article/CJFDTotal-HEBS200106011.htm; Kan Heqing and Chen
Changshen, "Rethinking on the history of political movements after 1949: Deng
Xiaoping's thoughts on 'stop organizing movements,'" *Journal of Yunnan Administration
Academy*, June 2004, www.doc88.com/p-1748774204372.html

36 For an assessment of Xi's attachment to ideological work, see, "Xi Jinping: ideological
work is extremely important work for the party."

37 For a discussion of the "responsibility system" for ideological and political work,
see, for example, "The No. 1 cadre should personally take care of ideological and
propaganda work," *People's Daily*, September 6, 2013, http://news.ifeng.com/mainla
nd/special/yishixingtai/content-3/detail_2013_09/06/29361832_0.shtml. See also Xu
Shousheng, "Earnestly take major responsibility for work related to ideology and
thought," *People's Daily*, November 11, 2015, http://politics.people.com.cn/n/2015/
1118/c1001-27826687.html

38 Xu Shousheng, "Earnestly take major responsibility for work related to ideology and
thought."

39 Cited in "Shen Haixiong puts emphasis on boosting ideological work in universities,"
Nanfang Daily, March 22, 2016, http://news.xinhuanet.com/local/2016-03/22/c_
128820811.htm

40 Cited in "The National Center on Ideology and Thought has established a New
Media Research Academy," *China Youth Daily*, November 12, 2015, http://news.
youth.cn/gn/201511/t20151112_7302366.htm

41 For a discussion about the personality cult built around Xi Jinping, see, for example
Willy Lam, "Xi Jinping presents himself as the new Mao," *Nikkei Asian Review*,
October 25, 2017, https://asia.nikkei.com/Viewpoints/Willy-Lam/Xi-Jinping-p
resents-himself-as-the-new-Mao. See also "Beware the cult of Xi," *The Economist*,
April 2, 2016, www.economist.com/news/leaders/21695881-xi-jinping-stronger-
his-predecessors-his-power-damaging-country-beware-cult

42 For a sampling of Xi Jinping's instructions regarding *liangxue yizuo*, see "Excerpts from
Xi Jinping's important talks on '*liangxue yizuo*,'" *People's Daily Online*, August 14,
2016, http://cpc.people.com.cn/xuexi/n1/2016/0814/c385474-28634283.html

43 For a discussion of the exacerbation of Xi's personality cult, see Chauncey Jung,
"How Beijing's propaganda dents China's image, rather than burnishes it," *South
China Morning Post*, September 2, 2018, www.scmp.com/comment/insight-opinion/
hong-kong/article/2162178/how-beijings-propaganda-dents-chinas-image-rather. See
also "Xi Thought on Diplomacy leads the way," *China Daily*, June 28, 2018, www.
chinadaily.com.cn/a/201806/28/WS5b34179da3103349141df593.html

44 For a discussion of Xi's views on *datong* or the "great commonality among nations,"
see, for example, Zhou Weiwei, Song Xiying and Ma Chang, "Xi Jinping's views on
relative prosperity and datong," *China Youth Daily*, March 30, 2017, http://news.
youth.cn/wztt/201703/t20170330_9385427_1.htm. See also Xi Jinping: "The great
commonality of the world: harmony, cooperation and co-prosperity," Xinhuanet.
com, April 12, 2018, www.xinhuanet.com/mrdx/2018-04/12/c_137104844.htm

45 For a discussion of the Xi personality cult after the 19th Party Congress, see, for example, "Xi Jinping has deified himself as the '21st century Marx'," Radio Free Asia, May 9, 2018, www.rfa.org/cantonese/features/hottopic/deify-05092018095100.html. See also Tetsushi Takahashi, "Xi carries Marx's torch, China says on 200th birthday of thinker," Asia.nikkie.com, May 8, 2018, https://asia.nikkei.com/Politics/Xi-ca rries-Marx-s-torch-China-says-on-200th-birthday-of-thinker

46 For a discussion of Deng's theory of the preliminary stage of socialism, see, for example, Li Zhongjie, "Deng Xiaoping and the basic line of the preliminary stage of socialism," *Chinese Communist Party History Journal*, February 10, 2010, http://cpc.people.com.cn/n/2014/0210/c69113-24310903.html

47 Cited in Wang Weiguang, "Insist on not forgetting our original intentions, and firm up our belief in ideals," *China Discipline Inspection Paper*, August 25, 2016, www.huanqiuzhiyin.com/hqgd/2016/08248403.html

48 Cited in Hou Huiqin: "Communism is the spirit of Marxist philosophy," *Hongqi wengao* (*Red Flag Articles*), October 13, 2015, http://sk.taizhou.gov.cn/art/2015/10/13/art_17284_487544.html

49 Cited in Tian Xinming, "Beware theories that 'Communism is ethereal and unreachable,'" *Hongqi wengao*, October 12, 2015, http://opinion.people.com.cn/n/2015/1012/c1003-27687276.html

50 See Su Changhe, "From where does Chinese self-confidence come?" *Seeking Truth*, September 30, 2015, www.qstheory.cn/dukan/qs/2015-09/30/c_1116695189.htm

51 For a discussion of the importance of banishing Western values and ideals, see, for example, "Editorial: leave no space for universal values," *Beijing Daily*, January 20, 2014, http://theory.rmlt.com.cn/2014/0120/220314.shtml. See also Cong Shouwu, "Assiduously render prosperous philosophy and social sciences with Chinese characteristics," *Huanqiu zhiyin* (Beijing), August 24, 2016, www.huanqiuzhiyin.com/tgzq/2016/08238388.html; Wang Simin and Zhang Sheng, "China, where the strongest voices of world Marxism are gathered," *Guangming Daily*, October 9, 2015, www.qstheory.cn/tjyd/2015-10/09/c_1116762620.htm

52 Cited in "Cui Jian: as long as the Mao portrait hangs over Tiananmen Square, the times have not changed," *Ming Pao* (Hong Kong), February 9, 2014, http://news.mingpao.com/20140209/cab1.htm. See also Jun Mai, "China's Cultural Revolution could happen again, warns ex-Shenzhen mayor and former rising political star," *South China Morning Post*, December 10, 2015, www.scmp.com/news/china/policies-politics/article/1889624/chinas-cultural-revolution-could-happen-again-warns

53 For a discussion of Jiang Zemin's views on "cultural construction," see "Comrade Jiang Zemin's important talks on the important status of cultural construction," China Culture Net, February 23, 2012, www.wenming.cn/ziliao/lingdaoren/zgldr/jiangzemin/201202/t20120223_518199.shtml

54 For a discussion of Mao Zedong's philosophy of *douzheng* ("struggle"), see, for example, Li Rui, "Philosophical ideas were the fundamental roots of Mao's mistakes made in his old age," *People's Daily Online*, September 30, 2013, http://news.china.com/history/all/11025807/20130930/18072583.html. See also Shi Zhongquan, "Summarizing Mao Zedong Thought as a philosophy of struggles does not dovetail with his ideas," CCP News Net, December 29, 2008, http://cpc.people.com.cn/GB/66888/77791/8594855.html

55 For a study of Mao Zedong's ideas about "thought reform" or brainwashing, see, for example, Jan Kiely, *The Compelling Ideal: Thought Reform and the Prison in China, 1901–1956*, New Haven: Yale University Press, 2014. See also Robert J. Lifton, *Thought Reform and the Psychology of Totalism: The Study of "Brainwashing" in China*, Chapel Hill: University of North Carolina Press, 1989.

56 For a discussion of the causes of Lao She's suicide, see, for example, "Literary stars during the Cultural Revolution: Lao She drowned himself after being beaten up by the mob," *Wenshi Yanjiu* (*Research on Literary History*), May 3, 2012, http://history.huanqiu.com/people/2012-05/2685315.html. For a discussion of the general trends of

intellectuals committing suicide, see Xie Bing, "The issue of intellectuals and members of other classes committing suicide from 1949 to 1976," Aisixiang.net, March 4, 2010, www.aisixiang.com/data/32030.html

57 For a discussion of the tragic death of Chen Yinke, see, for example, Tu Wenshu, "Chen Yinke and his wife passed away within one month during the Cultural Revolution," China Economy Net, October 7, 2013, http://history.sohu.com/20131007/n387513839.shtml

58 Cited in Sun Lizhao, "Fifty-two famous personages who committed suicide during the Cultural Revolution," Sohu.com, May 18, 2016, www.sohu.com/a/76033482_126685. See also Cary Huang, "China must let the dark deeds of the Cultural Revolution come to light," *South China Morning Post*, May 13, 2016, www.scmp.com/comment/insight-opinion/article/1943970/china-must-let-dark-deeds-cultural-revolution-come-light

59 Cited in Hua Sheng, "How should we thoroughly understand Du Runsheng?" *Financial Times Chinese Edition*, November 5, 2015. www.ftchinese.com/story/001064637?full=y

60 For a discussion of Xi's formal education, see, for example, Zhen Shuji, "Li Rui: although he only has primary school education, Xi Jinping is dictatorial and self-serving," Radio French International Chinese Edition, April 17, 2018, http://trad.cn.rfi.fr/%E4%B8%AD%E5%9C%8B/20180417-%E6%9D%8E%E9%8A%B3%E7%BF%92%E8%BF%91%E5%B9%B3%E5%8F%AA%E6%9C%89%E5%B0%8F%E5%AD%B8%E7%A8%8B%E5%BA%A6%E4%B8%94%E5%89%9B%E6%84%8E%E8%87%AA%E7%94%A8. See also Gao Xin, "Has Xi Jinping accused Baidu Encyclopedia of slighting gongnongbing students?" Radio Free Asia, August 23, 2017, www.rfa.org/mandarin/zhuanlan/yehuazhongnanhai/gx-08232017150256.html

61 Xi Jinping has in his speeches frequently used quotations from classical authors, including Confucius, Mencius and Han Fei. See his 304-page book, *Xi Jinping's Use of the Classics*, Beijing: People's Daily Press, 2015, http://theory.people.com.cn/GB/68294/394175/

62 Cited in "Xi Jinping talks about Chinese traditional culture in the House of Confucius," Cul.china.com.cn, November 28, 2013, http://cul.china.com.cn/2013-11/28/content_6494026.htm

63 For a discussion of Xi's ideas about traditional culture, see, for example, "Decoding Xi Jinping's traditional culture complex," Xinhua News Agency, June 10, 2016, http://news.xinhuanet.com/politics/2016-06/10/c_128921853.htm

64 Cited in Cui Xiaosu, "Why does Xi Jinping put so much emphasis on picking up traditional culture?" *People's Daily*, September 25, 2014, http://cpc.people.com.cn/n/2014/0925/c164113-25731729.html

65 For an explication of Xi's emphasis on cultural self-confidence, see, for example, "Xi Jinping on culture," www.wenming.cn, December 29, 2014, www.wenming.cn/djw/specials/djwwpt/wxgx/201412/t20141229_2374381.shtml

66 For a discussion about Xi's confidence in building China into a "cultural power," see, for example, "*Textbook on General Secretary Xi Jinping's Series of Important Talks*: on building a socialist cultural power," China.com.cn, December 12, 2014, http://cul.china.com.cn/2014-12/12/content_7438994.htm

67 Cited in "Xi Jinping's talk in a seminar on work on culture and the arts," Xinhua News Agency, May 15, 2014, http://news.xinhuanet.com/politics/2015-10/14/c_1116825558.htm

68 Cited in Zhan Yong, "Secure well from the very beginning the buttons of one's life," *People's Daily People's Forum*, May 5, 2014, http://opinion.people.com.cn/n/2014/0505/c1003-24973108.html

69 For a discussion of "cultural construction" during the 13th Five-Year Plan period, see, for example, the Party Organization of the Culture Ministry, "Use new developmental concepts to open up new vistas in cultural construction," *Seeking Truth*, December 15, 2015, www.qstheory.cn/dukan/qs/2015-12/15/c_1117452171.htm

70 For a discussion of the Hu Jintao administration's harsh reaction to color revolutions including the "Jasmine Revolution," see, for example, Wieland Wagner, "An unwelcome scent of jasmine: Chinese leadership fears its own people," *The Spiegel Online*, March 19, 2011, www.spiegel.de/international/world/an-unwelcome-scent-of-jasmine-chinese-leadership-fears-its-own-people-a-751467.html

71 Cited in Yu Jie, "The myth of China as a toothless tiger," *Washington Post,* February 10, 2012, www.washingtonpost.com/opinions/the-myth-of-china-as-a-harmless-tiger/2012/02/10/gIQAb7DxBR_story.html?utm_term=.6d09fd535ce1. See also Edward Wong, "From Virginia suburb, a dissident Chinese writer continues his mission," *New York Times*, February 25, 2012, www.nytimes.com/2012/02/26/world/asia/yu-jie-dissident-chinese-writer-continues-his-work-in-us.html?pagewanted=all/

72 For a discussion of the mistreatment of Liu Xiaobo's wife and relatives, see, for example, "Jailed Nobel dissident's wife seeks treatment in Beijing hospital," Radio Free Asia, February 20, 2014, www.rfa.org/english/news/china/liu-xia-02202014172456.html. See also "Liu Xiaobo's brother-in-law Liu Hui to serve 11 years after losing appeal," *The Guardian*, August 16, 2013, www.theguardian.com/world/2013/aug/16/liu-hui-loses-appeal-11-years-liu-xiaobo. For a discussion of the treatment of Chen's relatives, see, for example, Andrew Jacobs, "Chen Guangcheng's nephew given 3 years in prison for assault," *New York Times*, November 30, 2013, www.nytimes.com/2012/12/01/world/asia/nephew-of-chinese-dissident-chen-guangcheng-given-3-years-in-prison-for-assault.html

73 Cited in "The passport of the 18-year-old son of rights lawyer Wang Yu is voided," Thestandnews (Hong Kong), November 13, 2017, www.thestandnews.com/china/18%E6%AD%B2%E5%85%92%E5%AD%90%E8%AD%B7%E7%85%A7%E8%A2%AB%E5%89%AA-%E7%B6%AD%E6%AC%8A%E5%BE%8B%E5%B8%AB%E7%8E%8B%E5%AE%87-%E4%B8%80%E5%86%8D%E8%BF%AB%E5%AE%B3%E5%AD%A9%E5%AD%90-%E9%82%84%E6%9C%89%E4%BA%BA%E6%80%A7%E5%97%8E/. See also "Son of detained rights lawyers arrives in Australia after battle to leave China," Radio Free Asia, January 18, 2018, www.rfa.org/english/news/china/lawyer-son-01182018140246.html. For a discussion of the plight of Wang Yu, see, "The nightmare – an excerpt of lawyer Wang Yu's account of 709 detention and torture," Chinachange.org, November 13, 2017, https://chinachange.org/2017/11/13/the-nightmare-an-excerpt-of-lawyer-wang-yus-account-of-709-detention-and-torture/

74 For a discussion of the career of entrepreneur-activist Wang, see, for example, Simon Denyer, "In China, citizens rights activist Wang Gongquan is formally arrested," *Washington Post*, October 21, 2013, www.washingtonpost.com/world/chinese-citizens-rights-activist-wang-gongquan-is-formally-arrested/2013/10/21/888909ca-3a73-11e3-b0e7-716179a2c2c7_story.html?utm_term=.471588bf1d35

75 Cited in "1,000 people in Jiangmen, Guangdong protest against construction of nuclear raw materials factory," BBC News, July 12, 2013, www.bbc.com/zhongwen/simp/china/2013/07/130712_china_guangdong_nuclear_protest

76 Cited in staff reporters, "Five people including Pu Zhiqiang were arrested for taking part in a seminar on the June 4 incident," *Apple Daily*, May 7, 2014, https://hk.news.appledaily.com/local/daily/article/20140507/18712263. See also staff reporters, "Dissidents in Beijing planning dinner meetings to mark the anniversary of the June 4 crackdown were harassed by police," *Apple Daily*, May 23, 2016, http://hk.apple.nextmedia.com/international/art/20160523/19623862

77 For a discussion of the incarceration of Gao Yu and Xiang Nanfu, see, for example, Dexter Roberts, "Detained Chinese journalists forced to make televised confessions," *Businessweek*, May 14, 2014, www.bloomberg.com/news/articles/2014-05-14/detained-chinese-journalists-forced-to-make-televised-confessions. See also Tania Branigan, "US and EU criticise Chinese journalist's jailing for 'leaking state secrets,'" *The Guardian*, April 17, 2015, www.theguardian.com/world/2015/apr/17/gao-yu-and-document-no-9-china-jails-journalist-for-leaking-state-secrets

78   For a discussion of the case of the *Wujie News* incident, see, for example, John Sudworth, "China 'detained 20 over Xi resignation letter,'" BBC News, March 25, 2016, www.bbc.com/news/blogs-china-blog-35897905; Edward Wong and Chris Buckley, "China said to detain several over letter criticizing Xi," *New York Times*, March 25, 2016, www.nytimes.com/2016/03/26/world/asia/china-wujie-news-xi-jinping.html

79   For a discussion of the ill-treatment that police meted out to the parents of Wen Yunchao (Bei Feng), see, for example, "Suspected to be related to the 'open letter against Xi Jinping,' Bei Feng's parents and brother were kidnapped," Radio Free Asia, March 25, 2016, www.rfa.org/mandarin/yataibaodao/meiti/ql1-03252016104506.html

80   Cited in Philip Wen, "Overseas Chinese activists say families are being targeted over letter to Xi Jinping," Youngwitness.com.au, March 28, 2016, www.youngwitness.com.au/story/3816464/activists-say-families-targeted-over-open-letter/?cs=4195

81   For a discussion of the implications of Document No. 9, see, for example, Chris Buckley, "China takes aim at Western ideas," *New York Times,* August 19, 2013, www.nytimes.com/2013/08/20/world/asia/chinas-new-leadership-takes-hard-line-in-secret-memo.html. Also see "Editorial: China's pathetic crackdown on civil society," *Washington Post*, April 22, 2015, www.washingtonpost.com/opinions/chinas-pathetic-lockdown/2015/04/22/bddf8fdc-e548-11e4-905f-cc896d379a32_story.html?utm_term=.be931b91c232

82   Cited in staff reporters, "Seven red regulations strangle teachers' freedom of expression," *Ming Pao*, October 11, 2014, www.mingpaocanada.com/Van/htm/News/20141011/tcaa1.htm?m=0

83   Cited in "The CCP has pushed forward the 'seven red regulations'; educators say they have lost their freedom," DWnews.com, http://news.dwnews.com/china/big5/news/2014-10-10/59612622.html

84   Cited in staff reporter, "Minister of Education criticizes college teachers for challenging the political bottom line," *Ming Pao*, March 12, 2015, www.mingpaocanada.com/van/htm/News/20151203/tcba1.htm

85   See Xu Feng, "What are the difficulties involved in doing ideological work in institutes of higher learning?" *Seeking Truth Online*, January 24, 2015, www.qstheory.cn/wp/2015-01/24/c_1114113148.htm

86   Cited in "Peking University professor Zhou Xiaozheng: do not indiscriminately use enemy forces as an excuse," *Global Times*, December 12, 2015, http://news.ifeng.com/a/20151213/46648148_0.shtml

87   Cited in He Weifang, "The role of public intellectuals," Aisixiang.com, November 17, 2011, www.aisixiang.com/data/46717.html

88   For details about political pressure being applied on the academic activities of He Weifang, see, for example, Staff Writers, "He Weifang's speech at China University of Technology cancelled," *Ming Pao*, December 3, 2015, http://premium.mingpao.com/cfm/Content_News.cfm?Channel=ca&Path=168262545055/caa2.cfm. See also Peter Foster, "Leading dissident 'exiled' to Chinese northwest," *The Telegraph* (London), March 11, 2009, www.telegraph.co.uk/news/worldnews/asia/china/4974333/Leading-dissident-exiled-to-Chinese-northwest.html

89   Cited in "Liaoning Daily asked college teachers not to smear China during class; it has in the past two months sent reporters to investigate colleges," Thepaper.cn (Shanghai), November 14, 2014, www.thepaper.cn/newsDetail_forward_1278043

90   See "New Peking University leader former state security official," The Associated Press, October 30, 2018, www.nytimes.com/aponline/2018/10/30/world/asia/ap-as-china-peking-university-state-security.html

91   Cited in Elizabeth Redden, "Not feeling safe in China," Insidehighered.com, July 23, 2018, www.insidehighered.com/news/2018/07/23/american-academic-leaves-china-citing-concerns-about-physical-safety. See also Jason Lemon, "US professor fired from Chinese university after criticizing Communist government's censorship," Newsweek, July 18, 2018, www.newsweek.com/us-professor-fired-chinese-university-1030284

92   Cited in "Zhao Shilin: why an all-dimensional bottom-line crisis has appeared in Chinese society?" Cul.qq.com (Beijing), May 12, 2016, http://cul.qq.com/a/20160512/055583.htm

93   For a discussion of the difficulty of becoming a freelance writer, see for example, Liu Cixin, "Science fiction writers in China who can make ends meet do not number more than three," *Shanxi News Online*, September 11, 2015, http://cul.qq.com/a/20150911/025960.htm

94   Cited in Zhang Jianfeng, "Memorable things about the Shanghai writing team during the Cultural Revolution," *Southern Reviews* (Guangzhou), April 14, 2010, http://news.163.com/10/0414/17/648ECOQT00011SM9.html

95   See "Scholar Wu Xiaobo: Chinese in their heart of hearts are calling out for dictators," *National Humanity History* (Beijing), December 3, 2013, http://news.takungpao.com/mainland/focus/2013–12/2081847.html

96   For a discussion of the life and works of Guo, see, for example, Xu Jilin, "Why did Lu Xin label Guo Moruo as 'a man of talent and a blackguard'," Aisixiang.com, September 25, 2016, www.aisixiang.com/data/101524.html. See also Bao Ma, "Why are assessments of Guo Moruo so diametrically opposite," Guancha.cn, August 27, 2018, https://user.guancha.cn/main/content?id=36304&page=4

97   For a study of the significance of Yang Jiang's work, see, for example, Margo Gewurtz, "The afterlife of memory in China: Yang Jiang's Cultural Revolution memoir," Ariel, Vol. 39, No. 1–2, 2008, https://journalhosting.ucalgary.ca/index.php/ariel/article/viewFile/31444/25524

98   For a discussion of Zhu Xueqin's views on Ba Jin, see, for example, "Remembering Ba Jin: an interview with Shanghai University history professor Zhu Xueqin," *Southern Weekend* (Guangzhou), October 21, 2005, http://news.sohu.com/20051021/n227270285.shtml

99   Cited in "Wang Yi: Christian rightists in 1957," Quora.com, June 17, 2014, www.quora.com/profile/Simon-Lee-22/Hermons-World/%E7%8E%8B%E6%80%A1%EF%BC%9A1957%E5%B9%B4%E7%9A%84%E5%9F%BA%E7%9D%A3%E5%BE%92%E5%8F%B3%E6%B4%BE%E5%88%86%E5%AD%90%E4%BB%AC

100 Cited in Bao Tong, *A Collection of Essays by Bao Tong*, Hong Kong: New Century Media, 2012, p. 479.

101 See Zhang Yihe, "The biggest difference between ourselves and our forebears is about *renxing*," www.mingjingnews.com (New York), May 24, 2016, www.mingjingnews.com/MIB/news/news.aspx?ID=N000147600

102 Cited in Xu Jilin, "From the specialized to the common: the possibility of the emergence of public intellectuals in the age of specialization," in *Theoretical Studies of Intellectuals*, Vol. 1, Nanjing: Jiangsu People's Press, 2002, www.aisixiang.com/data/37021.html?page=1/

103 Author's interviews with Hu Zhiwei in Hong Kong, June 2017. For a discussion of the career of Gui Minhai and why he ran foul of the CCP, see, for example, Fred Hiatt, "Why is China afraid of this man?" *Washington Post*, July 29, 2017, www.washingtonpost.com/opinions/global-opinions/china-is-trying-to-muzzle-gui-minhai-these-poems-tell-his-story/2018/07/29/c75b18dc-91bc-11e8-b769-e3fff17f0689_story.html?utm_term=.50de45cb19c8

104 For a discussion of the significance of Liu Xiaobo's ideas and contributions, see, for example, Li Hongyu, "'Charter 08' is a declaration and a program of action for building a democratic China," 08charterbbs.blogspot.hk, December 10, 2012, http://08charterbbs.blogspot.hk/2012/12/blog-post_1640.html

105 Cited in Hua Yishi, "'Charter 08' and its democratic seeds," Minzhuzhongguo.org (U.S.), December 20, 2014, http://minzhuzhongguo.org/ArtShow.aspx?AID=48080

106 For a discussion of the party leadership's reaction to the "Molihua Revolution," see for example, Andrew Jacobs and Jonathan Ansfield, "Catching scent of revolution, China moves to snip jasmine," *New York Times*, May 10, 2011 www.nytimes.com/2011/05/11/world/asia/11jasmine.html?_r=0

107 For a discussion on liberal intellectuals harassed or arrested during the Molihua Movement, see, for example, Gloria Davies, "Discontent in digital China," in *The China Story 2012*, Australian Centre on China in the World, Australian National University, www.thechinastory.org/yearbooks/yearbook-2012/chapter-5-disconten t-in-digital-china/

108 Cited in James G. McGann, *Global Go-To Think Tank Index Report*, University of Pennsylvania, January 31, 2018, https://repository.upenn.edu/cgi/viewcontent.cgi? article=1012&context=think_tanks

109 For a discussion of the contributions of Mao Yushi, see, for example, "Mao Yushi: winner of the 2012 Milton Friedman Prize for Advancing Liberty," Cato Institute, April 2012, www.cato.org/friedman-prize/mao-yushi

110 See "Mao Yushi: the basis of the reform of state-owned enterprise is that the government beats a retreat from enterprises," *Netease Finance*, December 1, 2015, http://m oney.163.com/15/1201/18/B9P657MK002556KR.html

111 Cited in "Mao Yushi: only through democracy and rule of law can China become a rich and strong country," China50plus.com, September 14, 2015, www.china50plus. com/%E8%8C%85%E4%BA%8E%E8%BD%BC%EF%BC%9A%E5%8F%AA%E6%9C %89%E6%B0%91%E4%B8%BB%E6%B3%95%E6%B2%BB%E6%89%8D%E8%83% BD%E4%BD%BF%E4%B8%AD%E5%9B%BD%E8%B5%B0%E5%90%91%E5%AF% 8C%E5%9B%BD%E5%BC%BA%E5%9B%BD/. See also Simon Montlake, "China's 'privilege powers': an interview with Mao Yushi," *Forbes International*, April 25, 2012, www.forbes.com/sites/simonmontlake/2012/04/25/chinas-privilege-powers-an-inter view-with-mao-yushi/#3ae532786f0f

112 See "Shuttering of liberal Chinese think-tank part of 'long-term plan,'" Radio Free Asia, July 17, 2018, www.rfa.org/english/news/china/thinktank-closure-07172018144752.html

113 For a discussion of the "older generation" of liberal Chinese intellectuals within the party, see Feng Chongyi, "Democrats within the Chinese Communist Party since 1989," *Journal of Contemporary China*, 17, no. 57, 2008, pp. 673–688.

114 For a discussion of the significance of the *Yanhuang Chunqiu* magazine, see Du Daozheng, "The systemic exploration of *Yanhuang Chunqiu* is successful," *Yanhuang Chunqiu* (Beijing), March, 2012, www.cqvip.com/qk/80474x/201203/41070166.html

115 Cited in Xie Tao, "The democratic socialist model and China's future," *Yanhuang Chunqiu*, Issue 2, 2007, http://blog.renren.com/share/234535725/768916220/

116 For a discussion of the socialist roots of the Hu Jintao administration, see, for example, Willy Wo-Lap Lam, *Chinese Politics in the Hu Jintao Era: New Leaders, New Challenges*, Armonk, NY: M.E. Sharpe, 2006, pp. 38–44.

117 Cited in "Hu Dehua's speech at the gathering of *Yanhuang chunqiu*," China.com, June 17, 2013, http://club.china.com/data/thread/1011/2761/38/84/0_1.html

118 For a discussion of the reformist views of Hu Deping and his relations with Xi Jinping, see, for example, Edward Wong and Jonathan Ansfield, "Many urge next leader of China to liberalize," *New York Times*, October 21, 2012, www.nytimes.com/2012/ 10/22/world/asia/many-urge-chinas-next-leader-to-enact-reform.html?_r=0

119 For a discussion of the background of the closure of *Yanhuang Chunqiu*, see, for example, Oiman Lam, "Chinese reformist magazine shuts down to resist authorities' hostile takeover," *Global Voices*, July 26, 2016, www.hongkongfp.com/2016/07/26/ chinese-reformist-magazine-shuts-down-to-resist-authorities-hostile-takeover/

120 Cited in "21ccom.net, well-known Chinese website for ideology and culture, was closed down several days ago," Radio Free Asia, October 2, 2016, www.rfa.org/ma ndarin/yataibaodao/meiti/yf2-10022016111634.html

121 Author's interview with Minxin Pei, Hong Kong, February 2016.

122 Ibid.

123 Cited in Lily Kuo, "World's first AI news anchor unveiled in China," *The Guardian*, November 9, 2018, www.theguardian.com/world/2018/nov/09/worlds-first-a i-news-anchor-unveiled-in-china. See also Li Tao, "Xinhua News Agency debuts AI

anchors in partnership with search engine Sogou," *South China Morning Post*, November 8, 2018 www.scmp.com/tech/innovation/article/2172235/xinhua-news-a gency-debuts-ai-anchors-partnership-search-engine-sogou

124 Cited in "The sayings of Han Han," *Apple Daily* (Hong Kong), May 26, 2010, http s://hk.lifestyle.appledaily.com/lifestyle/columnist/6781865/daily/article/20100526/ 14067110

125 See Yi Zhongtian, "On logic and 'Chinese logic,'" www.aisixiang.com, September 2, 2011, www.aisixiang.com/data/43801.html

126 Cited in Yu Ge, "Chinese logic is not logic, but the natural enemy of logic," www.360doc.com (Beijing), February 12, 2015, www.360doc.com/content/15/ 0212/02/362669_448038421.shtml

127 Cited in "Old men on reform," Caixin Net (Beijing), April 6, 2012, http://opinion.ca ixin.com/2012-04-06/100376567.html

128 Cited in Yan Lianke, "Finding light in China's darkness," *New York Times*, October 22, 2014, www.nytimes.com/2014/10/23/opinion/Yan-Lianke-finding-light-in-chinas-darkness.html?emc=eta1

129 Ibid.

130 Cited in "Mao Yushi – from the Anti-Rightist Movement to the Cultural Revolution," RTHK (Hong Kong), May 27, 2016, www.youtube.com/watch?v=8cda lHZ9-7w. Among historical research that has shocked the world were two books about the Three Years of Famine penned by ex-Xinhua journalist Yang Jisheng and University of Hong Kong historian Frank Dikotter. For a discussion of these and other works on the famine years, see, for example, Ian Johnson, "Finding the facts about Mao's victims," *New York Review of Books*, December 20, 2010, www.nybooks.com/ blogs/. See also Susanne Weigelin-Schwiedrzik, "Trauma and memory: the case of the great famine in the People's Republic of China (1959–1961)," *Historiography East and West*, No. 1, 2003. For a discussion of Yang Jisheng's research of famine-related issues, see, for example, Verna Yu, "Chinese author of book on famine braves risks to inform new generations," *New York Times*, November 18, 2008, www.nytimes.com/2008/ 12/18/world/asia/18iht-famine.1.18785257.html?pagewanted=all&_r=0/

131 Cited in "Xi Jinping: the study of party history is a science; we must uphold the unity of *dangxing* and science," *People's Daily*, July 22, 2010, http://dangshi.people.cn/ GB/151935/196989/196997/12218213.html

132 Cited in Shi Zhongquan: "Research of party history is the synthesis of the nature of the party and the nature of science," CCP News Net, July 30, 2010, http://theory. people.com.cn/GB/12303209.html

133 For a discussion on the controversy over the origin of the Korean War, see, for example, Shen Zhihua, "The China–Soviet alliance and the origin of the Korean War," Culture.21ccom. net, February 21, 2014, http://news.takungpao.com/his tory/dongjian/2014-02/2292026.html. An analysis of the Anti-Rightist Movement can be found in Judith Shapiro, *Mao's War against Nature: Politics and the Environment in Revolutionary China*, New York: Cambridge University Press, 2001, pp. 21–66. See also "Fifty years on, deaths, persecution of Anti-Rightist era still taboo in China," Radio Free Asia, June 19, 2007, www.rfa.org/english/china/china_antir ightist-20070619.html. For a discussion of how the CCP has imposed a collective amnesia on the Tiananmen incident, see, for example, Louisa Lim, *The People's Republic of Amnesia: The Legacy of Tiananmen Square*, New York: Oxford University Press, 2014.

134 Cited in "Scholar Zhu Xueqin thinks new history textbooks have shown some improvement," Xinhua News Agency, October 16, 2006, http://news.163.com/06/ 1016/07/2THO73KC000120GU.html

135 Cited in "Wen Jiabao: On several questions about the historical tasks of the pre-liminary stage of socialism and China's policy toward other countries," Xinhua News Agency, February 26, 2007. http://news.xinhuanet.com/politics/2007-02/26/con tent_5775212.htm

136 Cited in Qin Xiao, "The Chinese road needs to develop universal values," Phoenix Television (Beijing), October 29, 2010, http://finance.ifeng.com/news/20101029/2796138.shtml

137 Cited in Xiao Zhu, ed., *The Harbingers of History: Earlier Pledges by the Chinese Communist Party*, Hong Kong: University of Hong Kong Media Centre, 2013, pp. 340–360.

138 Cited in "Dai Huang: be a person who speaks the truth," Chinesepen.org, February 20, 2016, www.chinesepen.org/blog/archives/46936

139 He Weifang, "The role of public intellectuals."

140 For a discussion of He's views on Taiwan, see, for example, Lu Sumei, "Peking University professor praises Taiwan for having successfully undertaken a democratic change of government," Chinatimes.com (Taipei), October 7, 2013, www.chinatimes.com/newspapers/20131007000777-260302

141 Cited in Liu Junning, "A civilized society and freedom of expression," Aisixiang.com, February 10, 2015, www.aisixiang.com/data/83857.html

142 For a study of the China model, see, for example, Suisheng Zhao, "The China Model: can it replace the Western model of modernization?" *Journal of Contemporary China*, 2010, Vol 19, Issue 65, pp. 419–436; Weiwei Zhang, "The allure of the Chinese model," *International Herald Tribune*, November 2, 2006, www.sinoptic.ch/textes/articles/2006/20061102_zhang.weiwei.model-en.pdf; Wenfang Tang, *Populist Authoritarianism; Chinese Political Culture and Regime Sustainability*, New York: Oxford University Press, 2016, pp. 20–41; Daniel A Bell, *The China Model, Political Meritocracy and the Limits of Democracy*, Princeton, NJ: Princeton University Press, 2016, pp. 151–198; and Ding Xueliang, *The China Model: Agree or Disagree*, Hong Kong: Oxford University Press, 2014, pp. 171–222.

143 Daniel A. Bell, *The China Model*, p. 140.

144 Cited in Hua Sheng, "How should we thoroughly understand Du Runsheng?"

145 Cited in "Hu Xingdou: a China that has lost direction," Nandu.com (Beijing), May 14, 2013, http://news.nandu.com/html/201305/14/59740.html

146 Cited in Wu Jinglian: "The main reason for the gaping rich–poor divide is corruption and monopoly," *Southern Daily Net*, October 31, 2010, http://news.sina.com.cn/pl/2010-10-31/080721386516.shtml

147 "Hu Xingdou."

148 Cited in Sun Liping, "The decay of Chinese society has accelerated," Aisixiang.com, March 28, 2010, www.aisixiang.com/data/32648.html

149 Cited in Chen Danqing, "We are slaves, slaves who can't see the end," Chinavalue.net (Beijing), April 25, 2010, www.chinavalue.net/Group/Topic/36002/

150 Cited in Du Daobin, "How can we construct a civil society," Radio France International, August 7, 2011, http://cn.rfi.fr/%E4%B8%AD%E5%9B%BD/20110807-%E6%88%91%E4%BB%AC%E6%80%8E%E4%B9%88%E5%BB%BA%E6%9E%84%E5%85%AC%E6%B0%91%E7%A4%BE%E4%BC%9A%EF%BC%9F

151 See Wang Xiaohua, "The rise of the public intellectual and the definition of his role," www.doc88.com (Beijing), July 25, 2014, www.doc88.com/p-2981006578670.html

152 For a discussion of Xiao Gongqin's views on the civil society, see, for example, Xiao Gongqin, "The Chinese path to developing civil society," Aisixiang.com, July 26, 2012, www.aisixiang.com/data/55833.html. See also Xiao Gongqin, "Certain thoughts on the reconstruction of China's civil society," Guancha.cn (Beijing), November 7, 2011, www.guancha.cn/politics/2011_11_07_61433.shtml

153 See Du Guang, "Push forward the growth and maturation of the civil society," Minzhuzhongguo.org, June 28, 2008, www.tiananmenmother.org/Forum/forum080823004.htm

154 Cited in An Delie, "More than 100 Chinese public intellectuals cry out for reform," Radio French International, December 30, 2018, http://cn.rfi.fr/%E4%B8%AD%E5%9B%BD/20181230-%E5%8E%86%E5%8F%B2%E5%85%B3%E5%A4%B4-%E4%B8%AD%E5%9B%BD%E7%99%BE%E4%BD%99%E5%85%AC%E5%85%B1%E7%9F%A5%E8%

AF%86%E5%88%86%E5%AD%90%E4%B8%BA%E6%94%B9%E9%9D%A9%E5%A5%8B%E8%BA%AB%E5%91%90%E5%96%8A

155 Cited in "Xi Jinping's speech on the conference celebrating the 40th anniversary of Reform and the Open Door," Xinhua News Agency, December 18, 2018, www.xinhuanet.com/2018-12/18/c_1123872025.htm

156 An Delie, "More than 100 Chinese public intellectuals cry out for reform."

3

HUMAN RIGHTS LAWYERS' STRUGGLE AGAINST XI JINPING'S "SOCIALIST RULE BY LAW"

Introduction: which is more powerful – the party or the law?

It has been two decades since Tsinghua University political scientist Pan Wei made a call to the Chinese leadership to introduce "consultative rule of law." The U.S.-educated scholar's point is that, although it might be difficult in light of China's sociocultural background to develop democracy and rule of law at the same time, the country's *guoqing* ("national conditions") would dictate that legal modernization should come before parliamentary or multiparty democracy.

Professor Pan, deemed a relatively conservative scholar, laid down strict stipulations regarding what constitutes rule of law. First of all, "law is the manifestation of the synthesis of *pubian gongyi* [common justice] and abstract moral principles." Rule of law means a dedicated corps of professional civil servants administering the country according to law in a "strict, [politically] neutral, fair, clean and highly efficient manner." There is no room for "a system of power politics exercised by a 'leader,'" he added. Moreover, *fazhi* (rule of law) should be distinguished from *yifazhiguo*, meaning "rule by law" or, more exactly, running the country according to laws that have been enacted under the guidance of the Chinese Communist Party (CCP). This is despite the fact that the English services of Xinhua News Agency or *People's Daily* usually translate *yifazhiguo* as rule of law or, sometimes, rule of law with Chinese characteristics. In a 2001 article entitled "The rule of law and China's political system," Pan envisaged a 25-year program for realizing his recommendations for good governance. The first five years would be devoted to public consultation and mass education about the importance of rule of law. Strict separation of party and government – as well as the establishment of a politically neutral civil service – would take up the next decade. The final decade would be earmarked for the transition from rule by law to rule of law. By that time, China would have attained the level of political maturity seen in Hong Kong and Singapore, where rule of law coexists with less-than-perfect democratic mechanisms.[1]

What has been happening in the past 20 years – and particularly since President Xi Jinping came to power in 2012 – has been a stunning retrogression in the CCP's commitment to abiding by the Constitution and the law. According to Peking University law professor He Weifang, "law in China must be subject to the will of the party." He noted in a speech at the Brookings Institution in the U.S. in 2012 that, although concepts of universal norms such as freedom of speech and inviolability of private capital are generally accepted among Chinese intellectuals and a large sector of the population, the CCP elite still believes that it has the monopoly on truth – and the sole right to shape the Constitution and laws. "China has had its own Constitution, but to our dismay, it always fails to play the role assigned to it," Professor He said. "Various rights granted in the Constitution are not strictly guaranteed, and the mutual checks and balances of power provided for in the Constitution have never been implemented."[2]

Beijing's shabby track record in upholding the law clashes with the Xi administration's painstaking efforts to offer the China model or the "China approach" as a possible alternative to the global norms embraced by most Western – and increasingly Asian – countries.[3] Wuhan University law professor Qin Qianhong noted that, apart from depriving ordinary Chinese of legal protection, Beijing's disregard for the rule of law has severely undermined China's global status. Citing Margaret Thatcher's well-known remark that China is not a country worthy of respect owing to its lawlessness, Qin noted in 2012 that "human rights and constitutional governance constitute a country's birth certificate." "They are also what protects a country," he said. "If a country rejects the slogans of 'human rights, constitutional governance and democracy,' this country will be barred from the currents of the world."[4]

The most notable sign of retrogression is Beijing's scorched-earth policy toward the 400-odd human rights lawyers in China. Torturing attorneys who "make trouble" for the regime by defending Christians, Falun Gong affiliates, labor union organizations and victims of "land grab" began in the Hu Jintao era (2002–2012). Gao Zhisheng, an internationally known rights lawyer who, from the mid-2000s, was repeatedly jailed, "disappeared" and held incommunicado in remote places, was so cruelly tortured in custody that, when he was last seen in mid-2017, the 54-year-old could hardly be recognized by his relatives and friends.[5] Things got much worse after Xi came to power in 2012. The licences of rights lawyers are routinely revoked, and entire law firms are closed down. The wives and children of rights attorneys are often subjected to detentions and harassment. Imprisoned lawyers are forced to make "scripted TV confessions" before they are released – after which they are often held under virtual house arrest and subjected to 24-hour police surveillance.[6]

This chapter looks at apparent efforts by the Xi administration to promote "rule by law with socialist characteristics."[7] Although Xi has committed the party to acting within the parameters of the Constitution and the law, it is clear that the

CCP reserves to itself full rights to amend the Constitution and to enact laws so as enhance the party's near-absolutist control over the polity. A convert to legalist Han Fei's (280–233 BCE) belief in "ruling the country with stern laws and harsh punishments," the supreme leader has enacted a plethora of statutes for purposes ranging from buttressing state security to reining in NGOs. Valiant attempts by rights lawyers and related NGO pioneers to defend the people's freedoms of expression, publication and religious beliefs will be discussed. Also analyzed will be Beijing's ferocious efforts to muzzle and stifle these lawyers, including the swoop on 300-odd rights attorneys and legal personnel on July 9, 2015. The chapter ends by looking at how suppressed and outgunned rights lawyers, as well as legal scholars and professionals, are determined to expand awareness of legal precepts in China's civil society and to uphold the rule of law as defined by global norms.

Xi Jinping's "rule by law" mechanism

Xi's dubious commitment to yifazhiguo

Given his father Xi Zhongxun's ill-treatment under Chairman Mao Zedong – and his own experience during the lawless Cultural Revolution – it is not surprising that Xi should be personally concerned with the establishment of party-controlled rule by law. After the princeling took power in late 2012, Xi has on numerous occasions expressed views that could be construed as supportive of some form of socialist rule by law.[8] At a Politburo study session in early 2013, the general secretary underscored what Western analysts call rule by law with Chinese characteristics. "We must push forward scientific law-making in a comprehensive manner," he said. "We must seriously implement the law." "There must be a fair judicial system, and all citizens must abide by the law," Xi added. "We must insist on the simultaneous implementation of running the country according to law, [conducting] politics according to law, and [ensuring] public administration according to law." The paramount leader argued that, "all organizations and individuals must conduct themselves within the parameters of the law." It was made clear, however, that what Xi was referring to was "socialist rule by law." As he indicated, "we must uphold the unity, dignity and authority of the socialist legal system." In the CCP tradition, a socialist legal system is different from a capitalist one to the extent that, in the former case, the party controls the law-making processes as well as court proceedings.[9] Similarly, Xi said on another occasion that the CCP leadership "must acquit ourselves well in providing leadership to the people in instituting the Constitution and the laws, so that the party can uphold its leading position in the course of administering the country according to law.[10]

On the 30th anniversary of the promulgation of the 1982 Chinese Constitution, Xi again made a solemn pledge regarding the imperative of upholding the Constitution. "We must closely follow the principles of the Constitution, propagate the spirit of the Constitution and implement the mission of the Constitution," he said. "No organizations or individuals have the special privilege of overriding the

Constitution and the law," he added. "All actions that run counter to the Constitution and the law must be held to account." Although this seemed to be a declaration of unreserved deference to the rule of law, it seems clear that the fifth-generation leader viewed the Constitution as having crystallized the "will of the party and the people." "Safeguarding the authority of the Constitution means safeguarding the authority of the joint will of the party and the people," he said. Xi added that the Constitution had "endorsed the theoretical system of socialism with Chinese characteristics."[11] In other words, following the newly revised Constitution – which has repeatedly emphasized the supreme leadership role of the party in all political arenas – means not straying from party directives and the tenets of socialism with Chinese characteristics.[12]

Liberal intellectuals have urged the Xi administration to live up to its pledge of *xianzheng*, or constitutional governance, by ensuring that all the liberties granted to the people by the supreme charter – including freedoms of expression, publication and assembly – should be fully honored. Writing in response to Xi's statements in 2012, retired liberal cadre Hu Deping, who is the son of the late General Secretary Hu Yaobang, argued that China should gradually adopt some form of tripartite division of power. "The authority of legislation, administration and the judiciary should be substantiated and legitimized under the Constitution," he wrote. He added that *xianzheng* manifested itself in "administration according to the Constitution, [undertaking] judicial procedures according to the Constitution, and making laws according to the Constitution."[13] It would soon become apparent, however, that, despite the close comradeship between Xi's father, Xi Zhongxun, and Hu Yaobang, President Xi did not share the two liberal icons' respect for rule of law as understood universally.[14]

Xi himself weighed in on the issue that "the people's democracy in our country and the so-called 'constitutional governance' in the West are fundamentally different." "When we talk about running the country according to the Constitution, this does not mean negating or giving up party leadership," said Xi in a 2014 speech to senior provincial leaders. "We are in fact stressing the fact that the party leads the people in establishing the Constitution and the laws, and in executing the Constitution and the laws."[15] Conservative commissars and ideologues also responded with a rash of articles saying that the very idea of "constitutional governance" was a bourgeois-liberal concoction that applied only to capitalist countries. Writing in the official *Party Construction*, theoretician Zheng Zhixue pointed out that the ideal of *xianzheng*, or constitutional governance, was a plot to "sabotage the socialist regime in China." Zheng claimed that "constitutional governance" or "constitutionalism" was a distinctly capitalist concept that did not apply in China. "The goal of *xianzheng* is very clear," Zheng wrote. "It is to abolish the leadership of the Communist Party and to subvert the socialist regime."[16] Ma Zhongcheng, a scholar at the Chinese Academy of Social Sciences, asserted that *xianzheng* was a propaganda tool whereby the U.S. sought to "globalize American liberal economics and [the American] legal system." "If socialist countries adopt

American-style constitutional governance, this will open up the way for the capitalist class to take over political power," Ma argued.[17]

The 2014 Fourth Plenum on rule by law and its aftermath

Xi Jinping's apparent commitment to legal governance was highlighted in October 2014, when the CCP, for the first time, devoted an entire Central Committee plenum to constitutional, legal and judicial issues. The Fourth Plenum of the 18th Central Committee, held in October 2014, passed a Decision on Certain Major Issues Concerning Comprehensively Advancing Rule of Law (hereafter "Decision"). The party and state apparatus pledged to establish a system serving "the socialist rule of law with Chinese characteristics" and to build a country under "socialist rule of law" principles.[18] In fact, the phrase *fazhi* (rule of law) was cited 19 times in the Decision. Xi vowed that "law-based governance" would protect people's rights and interests, and that it would allow them to supervise civil servants' exercise of power. Also mentioned were citizen's rights to share in the fruits of reform. A key thrust of this legal initiative was to give judges more independence and to prevent local cadres from unduly influencing court rulings. According to the Decision, officials would be given demerits or held accountable if they were found to be interfering in judicial cases. "Officials will be criticized in public notices if they influence judicial activities or meddle in a particular case," the document added. "Judicial injustice can inflict a lethal damage to social justice."[19]

To further boost judicial independence, the Supreme People's Court (SPC) would set up circuit courts to facilitate the handling of judicial cases, especially complaints filed by local communities. The leadership would explore the possibility of establishing courts and procuratorates with jurisdictions spanning different administrative regions, according to the Decision. The document also indicated that trial judges and prosecutors would assume lifelong accountability for their cases, and public participation would be ensured in judicial procedures. No illegal mitigation of a sentence would be allowed, and the handling of judicial cases should not be influenced by personal connections, favors or bribery.[20]

Professor Ma Huaide, vice-president of the China University of Political Science and Law, noted that this was the first time that the CCP leadership had, in a high-level party document, explicitly banned officials from meddling in judicial cases and vowed to hold violators accountable. "Only by ensuring judicial organs' independent practice of justice [and] independence from influences such as administrative orders, personal relations or money, could the public feel the fairness and justice in the judicial process," he said.[21] Jiang Ping, one of China's best-known liberal jurists, noted that all obstacles to judicial reform should be removed:

> Judicial power belongs to courts, and courts should adhere to the Constitution and laws while passing verdicts. There is an intricate link among China's efforts to promote political institutional reform, rule of law, and judicial reform, because rule of law is an important aspect of political

institutional reform while judicial reform plays a crucial role in promoting the rule of law.[22]

China's jurists, however, are pessimistic about the realization of any semblance of "independence of the judiciary" as interpreted in the West. The Decision made it very clear that the country should fully support the CCP's leading role in its quest for rule of law, citing stern party leadership as "the most fundamental guarantee" of the process. "The CCP's leadership is consistent with the socialist rule of law," the Decision noted. It further explained that the realization of rule of law required CCP leadership, and the CCP's administration should be underpinned by rule of law. Given that the Constitution has enshrined the principle of the party's leadership over all aspects of the polity, the party should take the lead in promoting rule of law, the Decision said. "Only if the CCP rules the country in line with the law will people's rights as the master of the nation be realized and the state and social affairs be handled in line with the law," the document added.[23] It is thus obvious that, despite its billing, the Fourth Plenum did not move beyond the hackneyed concept that the party would be in full control of the legal and judicial apparatus.

Feeble efforts in judicial reforms

Actually, the Third Plenum of the 18th Central Committee, which was held in late 2013, already contained what some regarded as a new dispensation for the country's judges. The document passed by the Third Plenum, entitled the Decision on Certain Major Issues Concerning Comprehensively Deepening Reforms (hereafter "Deepening Reforms"), pledged that the authorities would "guarantee that judicial powers and prosecutorial powers are exercised according to the law, independently and fairly." The party also committed itself:

> to reform judicial management systems, to promote the unified management of human resources in courts and procuratorates at the provincial and lower levels, to explore the establishment of jurisdiction systems that are suitably separated from administrative areas, and to guarantee the uniform and correct implementation of state laws.

Deepening Reforms made it clear, however, that the party's goal is to put together a "high-efficiency and authoritative socialist judicial system" – that is, one that tallies with the values of socialism with Chinese characteristics.[24]

A number of specific reformist measures were introduced, and some of them were speedily implemented. For example, the much-maligned *laojiao* – or reform-through-labor system, which allows the police to lock up suspects for up to four years – was officially abolished on January 1, 2014. However, in provinces such as populous Henan, other penal institutions administered by the police, such as "discipline and education centers" for petitioners, are still flourishing.[25] Torture as a means of extracting confessions was supposedly abolished. The number of crimes carrying the death penalty was also reduced. Grassroots judges and prosecutors below the provincial level would, by 2017, be appointed by provincial courts and procuratorates – and not by the party secretaries of local administrations. Local-level courts and procuratorates would also be funded by their superior units at the provincial level. Owing to the fact that the salaries of county and municipal judges and prosecutors used to be paid by party and administrative units of the same level, the latter were often in a position to exert political influence on the judicial system.[26]

Yet neither the Third Plenum nor the Fourth Plenum documents came close to tackling the crux of the problem, that is, the fact that the courts and procuratorates are under the direct supervision of the party's *zhongyang zhengfa wei*, or Central Political-Legal Commission (CPLC), headed by Politburo member Meng Jianzhu (2012–2017) and Kuo Shengkun (2017–2022). The CPLC, in turn, is controlled by the superagency Central National Security Commission (CNSC), which is headed by Xi himself.[27]

Since taking office as CPLC chief in 2012, Meng claimed on different occasions that the commission would not tamper with judicial procedures. For example, Meng indicated, at a nationwide meeting of law-enforcement officials in early 2013, that the CPLC would not interfere with individual cases, and that procuratorial and judicial units would be given full independence in enforcing the law. "China is a big country with 1.3 billion people," Meng pointed out. "The most fundamental guarantee of clean governance, social equality and stability is the rule of law."[28] Reuters News Agency cited two senior law professors in Beijing on the fact that an internal regulation had been drafted by the CPLC to reduce "coordination" – meaning judges consulting with the CPLC and other party organs – in the process of adjudication. Peking University law professor Jiang Ming'an quoted Meng as saying in an internal meeting that, "officials are not allowed to intervene in specific [court] cases."[29]

However, it is difficult to envisage the party not meddling in the judicial apparatus, which is an integral part of the *zhengfa* ("political-legal") system. Particularly after Xi assumed the position of "leader for life" at the 19th Party Congress, Politburo member and CPLC head Guo Shengkun urged different senior officials of the *zhengfa* system, including police officers, prosecutors and judges, to pledge their allegiance to the party – and to "leadership core" Xi in particular. For example, at a March 2018 meeting of *zhengfa* departments directly under the leadership of the CPLC, it was spelled out that cadres of all *zhengfa* units must "earnestly ensure that their thoughts and actions be unified under the party leadership's arrangements ... and resolutely safeguard the authority and united leadership of party central authorities with comrade Xi Jinping at its core."[30]

And what about the attitude of the SPC, which in theory is the highest judicial authority in the land? Zhou Qiang, who became president of the SPC in early 2013, is deemed a relatively liberal cadre who has a genuine commitment to improving the quality of the judiciary. A former first secretary of the Communist Youth League and party secretary of Hunan Province, Zhou (born 1960) had previously been thought to be a potential successor to former General Secretary Hu Jintao.[31] After becoming the equivalent of China's chief justice, Zhou lost no time in trying to raise the low esteem in which the judiciary was held. "Transparency is our general principle – and non-transparency an exception," Zhou said at a conference of senior judges in July 2013. He added that the courts would uphold the law with the utmost vigor, and that judicial fairness would be safeguarded. Moreover, Zhou even made an oblique reference to the "independence of the courts." "The people's courts will go about its adjudication independently and fairly in accordance with the law," he said.[32]

Yet it was also clear that Zhou would not challenge the party's direct and absolute leadership over the *zhengfa* apparatus, which includes all the courts. In an oral work report submitted to the PBSC in January 2015, Zhou indicated that he and his colleagues would "insist on upholding the concentrated and unified leadership of the party central authorities, and that they would resolutely go down the path of socialist rule by law with Chinese characteristics." He also pledged to observe Xi's instruction that, "the party would be in charge of the direction, policy, principles and personnel [involved] in political-legal work."[33] Speaking at a 2014 conference on "political and ideological construction" within the judicial system, Zhou called upon judges and other personnel to "arm their brains with the theoretical system of socialism with Chinese characteristics." "We must prevent and overcome [the tendency] of separating the party's policy from the legal codes or adopt the mistaken view of pitting party leadership against fair adjudication," he added. By 2017, Zhou's views had become more conservative as President Xi asserted the party's control over the police and judicial departments. In a meeting of the party cell of the SPC, the chief justice pointed out that judicial cadres must "firmly uphold the party's leadership over the courts and insist on unswervingly going down the road of socialist rule by law with Chinese characteristics." He also called upon judges to "remain in the highest level of unison with the party central authorities with comrade Xi Jinping as its core."[34]

Xi forces through a major constitutional change without any consultation

According to Guanzi, a sage in the Age of the Spring of Autumn (circa 771–476 BCE) who predated Han Fei, there are two types of laws: *wangfa* (the emperor's law) and *yuefa* (laws made through consultation). "*Wangfa* is laid down by the emperor and no discussion or give-and-take is possible," Guanzi said. Guanzi also divided a country's citizens into three categories: emperors and aristocrats who make laws, officials who implement the laws and citizens who obey them. "Officials and citizens have no right to establish laws," said famous classical scholar Yi Zhongtian. For emperor's laws, he added, "There is no seeking of public opinion or casting of votes."[35]

President Xi's "imperial approach" to the law was fully illustrated by his suspiciously hasty revision of the State Constitution with the main purpose of abrogating term limits for the posts of state president and vice-state president. Despite the CCP's long-standing record for neglecting the law, the revision of the Constitution used to be regarded as a major affair involving relatively broad consultation of members of the NPC or the legislature, and those of the top government advisory council, the Chinese People's Political Consultative Conference. Respected jurists were often also consulted. After Deng Xiaoping came to power in late 1978, he decided to revise the Maoist Constitution – a reference to the first-ever Constitution promulgated in 1954, which had been subjected to two revisions, in 1975 and 1978. Deng's consultative exercise began almost two years before the 1984 Constitution was promulgated. There was thorough discussion among senior party cadres, members of the eight "democratic parties" were consulted, and constitutional experts and legal professors were allowed to publicly air their views.[36] When ex-President Hu embarked upon the revision of the 1984 Constitution, he allowed a full year of public discussion before the 2004 Constitution was promulgated; this was despite the fact that the radical views of liberal scholars such as the late Cao Siyuan were spurned by the party media.[37]

The news that the 2004 Constitution would be revised was only revealed on December 27, 2017 after a meeting of the Politburo. The 25-member ruling body announced that the Second Plenum of the 19th Central Committee, to be convened in January 2018, would be devoted to discussing possible changes to the Charter.[38] The revision of the Constitution was passed by the NPC on March 11, 2018. What was striking was the lack of consultation among even senior party cadres. Legal scholars were not allowed to express their view in public. And, in the run-up to the NPC, which opened in Beijing on March 5, constitution experts and law professors were given explicit instructions by the party secretaries of their relevant CCP cells not to talk to the Hong Kong or foreign media on the sensitive issue. Xi was so anxious that the revision would be passed by the greatest possible majority of NPC deputies that the delegates – including 200-odd from Hong Kong – were strongly advised to stay in Beijing and cast their votes. Eventually, the revision was endorsed by the legislature with only two negative votes and four abstentions.[39]

Apart from removing the clause that limited the tenure of the president and the vice-president to two terms of five years each, the 2018 Constitution revived the spirit of the 1954 Charter by reinserting several clauses about CCP leadership into the main body of the supreme document. This was a slap in the face for Deng Xiaoping. The 1982 Constitution had removed clauses such as "the CCP is the leading core of all Chinese people" – which affirmed the supreme position of the party – from the main body of the Charter; CCP leadership was only mentioned in the preamble to the document.[40] The official justification for changes embodied in the 2018 Constitution was that, as the CCP Constitution contained no limits on the tenure of the general secretary, there should be a unification of the standards of the state and party charters. A March 2018 Xinhua commentary called this *sanwei yiti*, or "the same system for the three positions" of the head of the party, the military and the state, meaning that the holders of these positions now have the same tenure system.[41] Moreover, the restitution of clauses on CCP leadership in the body of the 2018 Constitution, such as "CCP leadership is the most fundamental characteristic of socialism with Chinese characteristics" – was in line with Xi's reemphasis on the party's leadership role over other political entities, including the State Council (or central government), the legislature, the judiciary, and both public and private companies.[42]

Towards a legalistic control apparatus

Xi's ascendency as arguably the most powerful leader since Mao Zedong has coincided with a barrage of new statutes dealing with state security and ways and means to bolster "proletariat dictatorship." More dissidents, underground Christians and rights attorneys have been jailed under vague and blanket crimes such as "gathering a crowd to disturb public order," "picking quarrels and provoking trouble" and "subverting state power." Televised confession, whereby statements made by suspects – usually under duress, including threats to their relatives – to public security officials in police stations are broadcast on TV stations and other media well before court dates have been set, has become common. A spokesperson for the Human Rights Watch expressed worries that the series of national security-related laws passed by the Xi administration, as well as the use of unorthodox methods to criminalize lawful protest activities, could "reduce the capacity of civil society to criticize the government and hold the government accountable."[43]

Xi Jinping and ancient legalist philosopher Han Fei

Law professor He Weifang noted that one important reason why universal-style rule of law had not come about in China was that, "in its 2,000 years of history, China has never had the tradition of the rule of law." "Countries which have the tradition of the rule of law will not accept socialism or Communism," he added.[44] Top leaders, including Mao Zedong, Jiang Zemin, Hu Jintao and Xi Jinping, are well versed in ancient Chinese philosophy, and they have elevated the status of sage-like scholars in the past who put their emphasis on the heaven-given right of monarchs to rule by decree. Jiang and Hu honored Confucius, who had been lionized by untold numbers of emperors in dynastic China for his arguments favoring the perpetuation of the status quo by "saint-like wise men" running the country.[45]

Xi's favorite ancient philosopher is the Machiavellian realist Han Fei. The progenitor of the "legalist tradition" in Chinese philosophy, Han preached that "stringent and clear-cut laws" were the emperor's best weapons for ensuring stable and unchallenged rule. Xi has repeatedly cited one of Han Fei's best-known dicta – "Strong implementation of the law will bring forth [national] strength, while lax implementation of the law will result in weakness" – in his arguments about pushing forward rule by law with Chinese characteristics.[46]

As a general rule, the legalist philosopher noted, countries cannot be strong and victorious forever; nor will they be forever weak and impoverished. What matters is the degree to which monarchs and officials can rule by clear-cut laws, rewards and punishments. As the *People's Daily* said in a 2015 commentary, Xi has used Han Fei's narrative to emphasize that "rule by law is the fundamental mechanism for governance," and that leading cadres in charge of making laws, as well as members of the judiciary, should implement the law fairly.[47] Xi neatly summed up Han Fei's philosophy in this short quote: "A system that preaches private gain will bring forth chaos; one that preaches the law will produce orderly governance."[48]

Han Fei is also a master psychologist in devising ways and means whereby monarchs can pick the best officials – and ensure their loyalty. The legalist did not go for the kind of benevolence and compassion advocated by Confucius or his disciple Mencius. For Han, it is all a question of the cynical but effective dispensation of rewards and punishment. Han noted that the relationship between an emperor and his officials was dictated merely by materialistic calculations. "There is nothing resembling the kindred feelings between father and son," he wrote. "Ministers pull out all the stops to impress emperors, while emperors reward this with senior positions [and material rewards]." Han also urged emperors to establish their patriarchal dominance over ministers and citizens. "Mothers love their kids twice more than fathers do," Han liked to say. "Yet orders coming from fathers are ten times more effective than those of mothers. Officials harbor no loving feelings for the people, yet their orders are ten thousand times more efficacious than those of fathers."[49]

Another criterion for good personnel management recommended by Han Fei is that awards and punishments must be clear-cut. According to the great legalist, "saintly monarchs run their countries through judicious laws and prohibitions." "If the laws and prohibitions are clear-cut, the officials will be clean and efficient," he wrote. "The awards and punishments must be thoroughgoing. If the awards and punishments are fair, the people will be willing to do the best [for the regime]." Han noted that awards and punishments were the most effective tools for governance. "The emperor uses these tools to control the ministers," he added. "But if the ministers get hold of these tools, the emperor will be obfuscated." Xi has certainly awarded officials faithful to him – particularly members of the so-called Xi Jinping Faction – with big promotions. The fifth-generation potentate has also used hefty punishment to drive fear into the hearts of corrupt officials.[50]

Xi has repeated Han's teaching that, "prime ministers must begin their careers in the regions and grassroots while generals must work all the way up from the rank and file." Xi himself started his career from the grassroots, as deputy party chief of Yongding County in Hebei Province. Han's instruction has also helped justify the supreme leader's penchant for elevating dozens of his former underlings – who worked under Xi when the latter served as a senior regional cadre in Fujian (1985–2002) and Zhejiang Provinces (2002–2007) – most of whom have solid grassroots experience.[51] For Xi, a cadre's unquestioned personal loyalty to himself certainly takes pride of place over the official's grasp of modern management ethos such as universal-style rule of law.

A made-to-order legal maze to snuff out dissent

According to a Zhejiang-based lawyer, Xi's "rule by law" is a far cry from the rule of law as understood in democracies in Asia or the West. "Xi and his colleagues want to have a complete set of laws to counter all possible challenges to the CCP," he said. "Their purpose is to have a legal pretext or justification for suppressing citizens' civil rights through stringent applications of catch-all legal codes."[52] Here, we examine laws and regulations that have a direct bearing on national security, including statutes on espionage and fighting terrorism. Other laws and State Council regulations, such as those concerning religious activities and NGOs, are examined in other chapters.

A sweeping national security legislation

The NPC passed on July 1, 2015 an overarching National Security Law that is sweeping in providing justifications for state actions against any challenge to the regime. The statute, which was passed on the 94th anniversary of the founding of the party, empowers law-enforcement and other relevant units to safeguard "the country's state power, sovereignty, unity, and territorial integrity; its people's well-being; its sustainable economic and social development; and other major interests." The law also ensures that these core interests are "free of any threat from both within and without."[53]

The legislation authorizes party and state authorities to call upon the army to prevent and resist invasions by hostile foreign forces, and to stop "armed subversion and separatism" originating from within China. Military action can also be taken "to safeguard the nation's overseas interests." Other clauses deal with the establishment of mechanisms for the protection of cyber and information security, as well as "the prevention of social conflicts." The statute also tackles threats from terrorism, religious cults, interference in religious issues by "overseas forces," as well as efforts to jeopardize China's delicate ethnic harmony. One clause underscores the imperative of buttressing "the [party's] guiding authority in the ideological sphere" and the prevention of the infiltration of "harmful moral standards" from abroad. The party is empowered to take initiatives geared toward establishing "a centralized, efficient and authoritative national security leadership system."[54]

As with most Chinese laws, the courts, which are directly controlled by party organs, are given full leeway to interpret what actions or public statements constitute threats to state security or national interests. For example, do "harmful moral standards" refer to Western political values that are denigrated on a daily basis by official media? Do demands made by Uighurs or Tibetans for a higher degree of autonomy amount to threats to "ethnic harmony," and are they therefore tantamount to acts of treason? Zheng Shu'na, with the NPC's Legislative Affairs Commission, said the law was crucial in the face of "ever-growing security challenges." "We face dual pressure," she said. "Externally, the country must defend its national sovereignty as well as security and development interests. Internally, it must also maintain political security and social stability." She argued that a comprehensive legislation that safeguards the country from "all kinds of security threats and risks" is needed, as the latter are "more complicated than any other times in history."[55]

It is significant that the law empowers the police and courts to clamp down on ideological offenses such as spreading so-called "Western" standards and norms. The code also criminalizes efforts by intellectuals or civil-society groups to criticize party policies through means ranging from posting articles on the Internet to holding street demonstrations. Nicholas Bequelin, East Asia director of Amnesty International, said the definitions of the law were "dangerously over-broad." He said the categorization of many activities as "national threats" would stifle debate and suppress objective analysis of social problems.[56] Eva Pils, an expert on Chinese law at King's College London, argued that the statute reflected the Xi administration's rejection of the rule of law as well as universal values. She noted that the law had been drafted on the basis of neo-Maoist, neo-totalitarian political ideas. "It re-emphasizes the leading position of the party in protecting China from its perceived enemies, by references to the 'people's democratic dictatorship' and by apparently giving formal backing to the role of the new national security commission," she said.[57]

The Cybersecurity Law

Implemented in November 2017, the Cybersecurity Law (CSL) is the legal manifestation of President Xi's oft-repeated mantra that "a country without cybersecurity is a country that has no national security."[58] The CSL has crystallized numerous government regulations restricting Internet freedom, particularly the freedom of China's 800 million netizens to express their views through blogs, chat-rooms or the social media. Since 2013, for example, netizens have been charged with "defamation" or other crimes if "online rumors" they create are visited by 5,000 Internet users or reposted more than 500 times. Although frequent government critics using the Internet or social media are all under 24-hour surveillance, the party-state apparatus wants to legitimize its draconian control through the CSL.[59]

The harsh statute forbids individuals, groups and service providers to "endanger cyber-security" or to make use of the net to "endanger state security" through "instigating subversion of state power, overthrowing the socialist system, inciting separatism, harming national unity [or] propagating terrorism, extremism, hatred among the nationalities." Also proscribed are acts construed as spreading fake information so as to "disturb the economic and social order." The CSL also provides the legal basis for police to lock up dissidents or NGO activists found guilty of using the net to contact organizations outside China or to pass on so-called "state secrets" to individuals and units in Hong Kong or the West. A regulation requiring both domestic and foreign Internet products and services that may affect national security to undergo a security review came into effect on the same day as the CSL.[60]

Attempts by enforcers of the CSL to keep close tabs on foreign Internet companies and service providers that are based in China led to widespread opposition among multinationals. For example, the statute says that operators of key information infrastructure in the areas of public communications and information services, as well as energy and finance, are required to store locally personal information and other vital data collected and produced by their services in China. China-based IT companies, which are already subject to stringent control, believed that the new law would oblige them to share privileged information, possibly including IPRs, with the Chinese. James Zimmerman, chairman of the American Chamber of Commerce in China, said the law was "a step backwards for innovation in China that won't do much to improve security."[61] A petition by scores of multinationals to Premier Li Keqiang was rebuffed. According to the Cyberspace Administration of China, the law "does not restrict foreign companies or their technology and products from entering the Chinese market, nor does it limit the orderly, free flow of data."[62]

The Counterespionage Law

The NPC passed a counterespionage law on July 1, 2014 that was geared toward tightening state security and helping build a "comprehensive" national security system. The law allows authorities to seize any equipment and properties linked to activities deemed harmful to the country. Persons found to have "illegal possession of documents, materials or other objects that belong [in the realm of] state secrets" may have committed a criminal offense. Police and other security-related units can also demand that organizations or individuals modify or refrain from activities deemed detrimental to China's national interests. Refusal to comply with the statute will result in enforcement agencies detaining suspects or confiscating relevant materials and properties. Possession of espionage equipment, as defined by state-security authorities, is also illegal.[63]

Similar to other security-related laws, the definitions of what constitute espionage, "national interests," or "state secrets" are vague – and open to interpretation by the police and the courts. The law urges citizens to beware of "actions that endanger the country's security, honor and interests." It particularly warns against "collusion between departments, organizations and individuals within Chinese boundary" and counterparts outside China.[64] Analysts have pointed out that the law gives more authority for state-security agents to monitor individuals, human rights lawyers and NGOs that have relationships with foreign entities. Murray Scot Tanner, a veteran Sinologist at the U.S.-based CNA Corporation, said the law could enable the authorities to "more closely monitor the relationships between [Chinese] citizens and the international community."[65]

An important facet of the law is its advocacy of a Mao-style "mass line," or mass mobilization, to help police and anti-spy agencies foil alleged espionage attempts. The ordinance stipulates that, "citizens and organizations should facilitate or provide help to anti-espionage work." It calls upon national security agencies to "rely on the support of the people," adding that state units should "mobilize and organize the people to prevent and stop spy activities that will jeopardize state security." The Counterespionage Law also provides the legal and theoretical justification for periodic propaganda exercises held in major cities, in which residents, including students, are encouraged to report on "spies" in return for huge rewards.[66]

The Counterterrorism Law

The Counterterrorism Law, which came into effect in January 2016, has given unprecedented powers to the police, state-security departments, courts, procuratorates, in addition to the PLA and the PAP, to fight terrorism. It indicated that the state will spare no financial or other resources to attain key objectives contained in the country's counterterrorist master plan. Moreover, professional anti-terrorist forces will be established by police and state-security departments, as well as the People's Liberation Army. The term "terrorism," which is often mentioned in conjunction with "extremism," is given a broad definition. It refers to statements and actions that are aimed at attaining political and ideological goals through generating social panic, undermining public security, endangering citizens and infringing upon property rights, as well as menacing government organs and international organizations.[67] Terrorism suspects are said to employ means of violence, sabotage or intimidation to achieve their nefarious goals. "[China] opposes all [brands of] extremism that seeks to instigate hatred, incite discrimination and advocate violence by distorting religious doctrines," the statute said, adding that the authorities will do all they can to eradicate the ideological basis for extremism. The law also obliges local and foreign IT companies to provide services, such as de-encryption, that would help Chinese police crack terrorist cases.[68]

Li Shouwei of the NPC Standing Committee Legislative Affairs Commission, said the legislation accorded with the actual work needed to fight terrorism and was "basically the same as those of other major countries […] The law reflects lessons China has learned from other countries and is a result of wide solicitation of public opinion," he said. "[The law] will not affect companies' normal business nor [allow police to] install backdoors to infringe intellectual property rights," Li said, adding that "citizens' freedom of speech on the internet and their religious freedom will not be affected."[69]

Many Western observers, however, have expressed concerns that Beijing could use the pretext of "fighting terrorism" to suppress expressions of dissent, including efforts by Uighurs and Tibetans to fight for more autonomous rights. "The definition of terrorism and extremism in this law is very vague, and 'extremist' behavior could include any criticism of policies, laws and regulations," said Patrick Poon, a Hong Kong-based researcher at Amnesty International. "While the Chinese authorities do have a legitimate duty in safeguarding their citizens from violent attacks, passing this law will have negative repercussions for human rights," he added.[70] Given the wide-ranging definitions of acts that would "generate social panic or undermine public security," attorneys defending "terrorism suspects" such as Uighur intellectuals or Tibetan monks would also be implicated.

Regulations on Measures for the Administration of Law Firms

Apart from laws, the party-state apparatus has passed regulations impinging upon the rights – and restricting the parameters – of law firms as well as lawyers. An Amendment to the Regulations on Measures for the Administration of Law Firms (hereafter "Regulations") was introduced by the Ministry of Justice in September 2016. The amendment emphasized that it was the duty of all law firms to follow CCP leadership, uphold party rules and "uphold socialist rule by law." Lawyers must not express views "that negate the fundamental political order and fundamental principles established by the Constitution … and that will endanger state security."[71]

The Regulations point out that lawyers are forbidden to use so-called "extra-legal" methods such as holding rallies, publishing open letters and organizing petitions to "create public-opinion pressure in order to attack and slander judicial organizations or the judicial system." Nor must they "make use of the Internet and the media to instigate discontent against the party and government … or to support, participate in or implement activities that endanger state security." Law firms whose members have violated such rules will have their licenses revoked, according to the Regulations. This is a reaction against the practice of lawyers broadcasting their cases – or the plight of victims of miscarriages of justice – in the public media, or in some cases organizing street rallies to highlight injustices that fail to be addressed by the courts.[72] Under the Law of the PRC on Lawyers, which came into effect in 2008, the licenses of lawyers are renewed once a year by the Ministry of Justice. Fear of losing their license is a big disincentive for many lawyers when they consider whether to take up political or religious cases.[73]

The Regulations also empower regional Bureaus of Justice in provinces and cities to freely investigate law firms' "compliance with laws, rules, and regulations," as well as their "internal management." According to Human Rights Watch, Bureaus of Justice officials from Beijing, Guangdong, Guangxi, Henan, Hunan and Yunnan, along with local branches of the government-controlled All-China Lawyers Associations, had, as of late 2017, instituted "comprehensive evaluations" of, or conducted "research" into, the management of at least seven law firms. Lawyers told Human Rights Watch that in some cases the officials came for "chats" during which they collected data about the management of the firms, the number of criminal cases they had undertaken in the past year, and how much they charged. In one case, a lawyer said investigators wanted to see all his contracts and receipts for the year. Personnel from the Beijing Bureau of Justice told the director of a local firm that they planned to scrutinize their lawyers' "online speeches." Another firm in the capital was told by investigators that they wanted to speak individually to all 20 lawyers under employment.[74] Attorneys' offices could have their license revoked if just one of their lawyers is found to have infringed regulations such as that forbidding attorneys to seek public support through the Internet.[75]

Even though the Regulations were promulgated not long after the July 9, 2015 swoop on about 300 lawyers (see below), opposition to the draconian rule was vehement. According to Guangzhou-based lawyer Yu Pinjian, the Regulations' prohibition of lawyers' bid to appeal to public opinion in support of their cases was in contravention of the Constitution and the law. "The Constitution and the law recognize civil rights and liberties … including sit-ins, wielding of banners, shouting of slogans and rallying for support in public" for victims of a miscarriage of justice, wrote Yu in his blog.[76] More than 40 lawyers called for the dismissal of the Minister of Justice in a petition sent to the State Council and the NPC. The petition letter, signed by 44 lawyers and 375 members of the public, said:

> In recent years, the Ministry of Justice, headed by Wu Aiying, has introduced several regulations that seriously violate the Constitution and the law, beefed up the ministry's power and severely infringed upon the lawful rights of lawyers and law firms, while burdening them with extra obligations.[77]

The rise of rights attorneys

The emergence of rights-defending lawyers

Given the apparent importance that President Xi has attached to Chinese-style rule by law, it is ironic that *renquan lv'shi* (human rights lawyers) should be considered "trouble-makers" and even criminals who "incite subversion to state power." As mentioned in Chapter 1, "human rights lawyers," together with the underground church, dissidents, Internet opinion leaders and *ruoshishequn* ("disadvantaged sectors" of society), are among the new "five black categories" of people who are deemed by the CCP regime to be the most destabilizing agents.[78]

The emergence of rights attorneys as "the collective conscience of society," or fighters for civil rights, has followed a haphazard pattern. The estimated 400 *renquan lv'shi* make up a miniscule percentage of the 300,000 legal professionals in practice in the country. Being loose-knit, net-based associations, these socially committed lawyers did not have any formal organizations or registered offices. It was not until September 2013 that a relatively formal organization was set up: around 270 rights lawyers established a China Human Rights Lawyers Group (CHRLG). The group, which was led by Wang Cheng, Tang Jitian and Jiang Tianyong, has remained a virtual network with neither an office nor a secretariat.[79] Immediately after the authorities' swoop on rights lawyers and other legal activists on July 9, 2015 (see the following section), the group issued a statement expressing solidarity with those behind bars.[80] Said CHRLG representative Yu Wensheng, "After the July 9 incident, we have received supportive messages from hundreds upon hundreds of lawyers. Dozens of young lawyers have vowed to join our cause." Yu, who had worked with the incarcerated lawyers, was instrumental in calling international attention to the largest crackdown on rights attorneys in Chinese history. However, Yu himself was arrested for alleged "subversion against the state" in April 2018.[81]

The rise of rights attorneys has coincided with the popularity of social media throughout both urban and rural China. As one Beijing-based lawyer put it:

"When one colleague hears of a particularly outrageous case of the strong preying on the weak, such as poorly educated villagers or underground Christians being ill-treated by the authorities, we just spread the word on the Internet." "Those attorneys with the needed expertise – and who can afford the time and expenses – would agree to meet at a certain hotel near the scenes of the actions," he added.[82] Such activities have continued despite the authorities' apparent success in censoring the Internet, including social media.

A Hangzhou-based attorney said that there were more disadvantages than advantages to having a formal office. "The party is very nervous about 'trouble-makers' establishing organizations," he said. "Moreover, such a formal office would be subject to constant surveillance and harassment." Other attorneys also agreed that a formal organization would hand the CCP the excuse of "getting rid of an anti-party secret organization." At the same time, relevant departments such as the MPS and the MSS maintain 24-hour surveillance over the activities of these rights lawyers. They are regularly summoned to police units in their cities for "sessions of political education," which could last for 24 hours.[83] And the Ministry of Justice – which is the unit overseeing the professional and "political" standards of lawyers – and the official All-China Lawyers Association keep close tabs on the activities of *renquan lv'shi*. The practicing licenses of disobedient lawyers are routinely revoked.[84]

Groups of human rights lawyers have bonded with each other while performing largely pro bono work for the underprivileged who are being squeezed by powerful cadres and business interests. According to lawyer Wei Rujiu, rights attorneys have focused on the following areas: religion (involving Christian house churches and the quasi-Buddhist Falun Gong practitioners); "land grab" cases; petitioners (elements of disadvantaged sectors who have grievances against officials); ethnic issues (defending Uighur and Tibetan dissidents); labor issues; and litigation on behalf of victims of miscarriages of justice in Chinese courts.[85]

The year 2003 could be regarded as the turning point for many attorneys who began to shift their focus from lucrative commercial cases to righting the wrongs of society through legal action. After becoming party general secretary at the 16th CCP Congress in November 2002, Hu Jintao was keen to demonstrate a *xinzheng* ("new order") marked by relative tolerance toward outspoken voices in society. Hu and Premier Wen Jiabao also wanted to distinguish themselves from the Jiang Zemin era, which was marked by the stringent measures taken to suppress dissent. Although the so-called "Hu–Wen *xinzheng*" only lasted one year, legal scholars and attorneys found an opening to pool their resources so as to better promote rule of law and social justice.[86] The following incidents were landmarks in the emergence of one of the most powerful sectors of China's civil society.[87]

The Sun Zhigang case: inviolability of the rights of migrant workers

Sun Zhigang was a 27-year-old college-educated industrial designer from Hebei Province who was employed by a Guangzhou factory. According to China's stringent *hukou* or residence permit system, migrant worker Sun had to carry his work permit at all times. On March 20, 2003, however, he was picked up by police because he could not produce the relevant papers. According to the Regulations on the Detention and Deportation of Vagrants and Beggars in the Cities (hereafter "Regulations"), Sun was locked up in a Guangzhou detention center. Perhaps because he failed to offer money to staff at the center, he was beaten up and certified dead the next day.[88]

Owing to a timely and reliable report in the media – and lobbying by legal scholars in both Guangzhou and Beijing – the Sun case became a litmus test of whether the new Hu administration was willing to abide by its *yiren weiben* ("putting people first") governing credo. Eight established scholars with doctoral degrees in law, including Yu Jiang of the Law School at Huadong University of Science and Technology, Teng Biao of the China University of Political Science and Law, and Xu Zhiyong of the Law School of Beijing University of Posts and Telecommunications, wrote petitions to the NPC. Teng and Xu would subsequently become full-time rights lawyers. A key point of their argument was that the Regulations were against the principles of civil rights, including freedom of movement, enshrined in the Chinese Constitution. These scholars also urged the authorities to do away with the *hukou* system altogether.[89]

In June, a Guangzhou court slapped hefty jail terms on the 18 people accused of causing Sun's death. More significantly, the Regulations were replaced by a new instrument called Administrative Means to Help Vagrants and Beggars in Cities Who Have No Means of Livelihood. The police were deprived of the authority to lock up "vagrants" – or to solicit bribes from their relatives. The speedy resolution of this glaring social injustice was a big boost to the morale of rights-concerned scholars and legal activists. Lawyer Xu later recalled that he was moved to tears by the quick response of the CCP leadership. However, the Hu–Wen administration began turning progressively more hardline after 2004. And a host of laws and practices that violate rights guaranteed in the Constitution, including the *hukou* system, are still in force today.[90]

Lawyers versus land grab: protecting citizens' property rights

The phenomenon of land grab, whereby the apartments and farming plots of workers and peasants are illegally appropriated by powerful developers, who are often acting in collusion with corrupt officials, was the underlying cause of more than half of the estimated 150,000 cases of riots and disturbances that took place in China every year. In 2003, 152 lawyers in Shanghai set up an informal organization to help residents who failed to get rightful compensation after having been forcibly evicted from their homes. These committed lawyers came from 78 law firms scattered among the city's 19 districts. They charged a nominal fee – and often no fee at all – for providing advice to the victims of land grab or for representing them in court.[91]

What could be termed the "radicalization" of Shanghai lawyers was the well-known case of local attorney Zheng Enchong, a courageous rights attorney who was, in 2003, charged by the police with "illegally obtaining state secrets." Although his lawyer's license was revoked in 2001, he was at the forefront of those fighting greedy developers, many of whom had ties to the Chinese Mafia. The trumped-up charge was an apparent reference to his passing on information to journalists in Shanghai and around the country. Several prominent lawyers, including Guo Guoding and Pu Zhiqiang, took part in Zheng's defense. When the Ministry of Justice revoked the license of Pu, the defense was taken over by young lawyers Zhu Jiuhu and Li Heping.[92] Zheng was sentenced to three years in jail in 2003. After his release in 2006, he was put under 24-hour surveillance. Police routinely summon him for questioning, and his apartment has been searched dozens of times. Although Zheng might never be able to gain full freedom, the crusade against "land grab" has galvanized lawyers from different cities – and confirmed their commitment to justice.[93]

Lawyers in defense of religious freedom

The next cause célèbre that prompted concerted action by groups of lawyers was the CCP authorities' increasingly hash suppression of underground Christian and Catholic churches, Falun Gong practitioners, as well as members of Islamic groups. In 2005, Cai Zuohua, a charismatic pastor who ran an unauthorized place of worship in the capital, was arrested under the pretext of "illegal operation of a business" – specifically printing bibles without a license – and sentenced to three years in prison. His wife was also slapped with a two-year jail term. Several lawyers, including Gao Zhisheng, Xu Zhiyong, Teng Biao, Zhang Xingshui, Fan Yafeng and Wang Yi, jointly took part in what would later be described as "the first major court case involving the Chinese house church."[94] As we will see Chapter 4, rights lawyers have, since 2014, played a pivotal role in the battles between churches in Zhejiang and other provinces, on the one hand, and authorities who are intent on imposing the party's edicts on members of the faithful, on the other.[95]

The struggle to protect small investors in Shaanxi Oilfields

Beijing's commitment not only to fair play in general but also to the sanctity of private property was put to the test in the so-called Shaanxi Oilfields scandal. At the turn of the century, the government of the resource-rich western province gave permission to private companies to drill for oil.[96] Some 1,000 companies – in addition to 60,000 individual investors – pooled their resources to begin prospecting work in more than 5,000 small oilfields. Without any forewarning, however, the cities of Yulin and Yan'an, together with 15 counties in the neighborhood, declared that the oilfields had been taken over by the government. Apart from taking care of the interests of the regional administrations, local officials were also acting on behalf of Petrol China, one of the three giant state monopolies in the oil and gas sector. Owing to the fact that the compensation was a mere fraction of their investments, thousands of investors took to the street to protest.[97]

In June 2004, Beijing-based lawyer Zhu Jiuhu took over the case. Zhu spent almost a year gathering evidence in Shaanxi. He tried to persuade the investors to stop the protests and to put their trust in the legal system. However, Zhu was arrested by Yulin police in mid-2005 on the grounds of "illegal assembly" and "gathering a crowd to create disturbances." Five experienced lawyers, including Gao Zhisheng, Li Heping and Zhang Qinghua, volunteered their services to secure Zhu's release. But law-enforcement officials in Shaanxi did not even allow them to see Zhu. Although Zhu was eventually freed four months later, he was forced to quit the oilfield cases and prevented from talking to the media. To this day, the hapless investors in the Shaanxi Oilfields have not received their rightful compensation.[98]

Rights lawyers have also been active protecting the commercial rights of small-scale private businesspeople, who are often squeezed by corrupt local officials, including the police. An early case in point was Sun Dawu, a rags-to-riches peasant who ran an animal husbandry business in Hebei. In 2003, he was arrested for alleged economic crimes, including illegally acquiring funds from 4,000-odd individual investors. Sun (born 1954), who maintained that he had broken no laws and that his investors were properly paid, was defended by respected rights attorneys including Zhu Jiuhe and Zhang Xingshui. The millionaire's supporters asserted that Sun was harassed by authorities because he was also an active critic of the CCP, frequently posting political commentary on the net. Together with five law professors, the rights lawyers wrote a petition to the NPC asking for the protection of private property as well as the right of private businesspeople to raise capital. Sun was eventually given a suspended sentence of three years. In summing up his defense of Sun, lawyer Zhu said: "I think lawyers must necessarily be fighters, who look upon the law with fervent faith." "Judicial improvement requires the cooperative input of [different sectors] of society, and non-state entrepreneurs should not play a passive role," he added.[99]

The case that brought most of China's rights-conscious attorneys together

The one incident that arguably brought the largest number of lawyers together was what jaded China observers would call a "run-of-the-mill case" of police brutality. On May 2, 2015, a thinly built, middle-aged farmer named Xu Chun'he was travelling through the crowded railway station in Qing An County, Heilongjiang Province, with family members including his elderly mother and three children. He got into an altercation with a police officer, Li Lebin. TV footage showed that the elderly farmer was beaten up by the burly cop; then, for reasons that have been never disclosed, Li shot Xu dead. Within a few days, several lawyers from different cities paid their own travel expenses and descended upon An Qing to help the family of deceased Xu. These attorneys included You Feizhu, Ge Yongxi, Ma Wei, Ma Lianshun, Tang Tianhang, Xu Zhong, Zhai Yanmin and a couple of staff from the Feng Rui Lawyers Office in Beijing. Security officials forbade Xu's mother from contacting the lawyers.[100]

The lawyers not only failed to get information from the authorities, but were subject to detention and harassment on account of "picking quarrels and stirring up troubles" and other allegations. A few of the rights attorneys were held incommunicado, and all were denied legal assistance. News of their plight was instantly made available on the WeChat social media site, blogs and other Internet channels frequently used by socially conscious lawyers. More than a dozen lawyers, including You Zhonghong, Xie Yanyi, Xie Yang, Liu Shuqing, Li Zhongwei, Liu Weiguo, Zhao Yonglin, Feng Yanqiang, Zhang Junjie and Wang Wanqiong, travelled to Qing An to "rescue" the initial batch of attorneys and to show their solidarity.[101]

A petition signed by more than 600 attorneys and legal professionals was presented to the authorities. The lawyers wanted a clear account of the incident – together with explanations of why the dozen-odd lawyers who had helped the Xu family were briefly detained and harassed by police, both in Qing An and in nearby counties. Tens of thousands of netizens also expressed their support for the rights lawyers on the Internet. By June 9, most of the lawyers had been released. Yet none of the officials involved in the harassment of the concerned rights attorneys were penalized. Moreover, the authorities failed to deliver an investigation into the death of farmer Xu.[102]

The views of well-known rights lawyers

By the middle of the 2000s, human rights lawyers were seen as torchbearers of social justice – in addition to being pioneers in using China's legal system to challenge the often unconstitutional, if not also illegal, activities of the party and state.[103] University of Hong Kong Law School Professor Hualing Fu had this to say about the particularly bold missions of China's rights lawyers: "The parameters of some lawyers have transcended issues of the law," he wrote. "They have raised political viewpoints and taken part in politics." "Lawyers have directly or indirectly challenged the police as well as the abuse of judicial procedure," he added. "They are also challenging a judicial system that lacks [the power of] independent decision-making."[104] Actually, many rights attorneys are determined, even in the early days of their legal apprenticeship, to bring about changes in the political system, which inevitably involves challenging the near-omnipotence of the CCP.

As in the case of attorneys working in countries without universal-style democratic institutions, China's rights lawyers believe that, instead of just arguing cases in court on behalf of members of disadvantaged sectors, they should go one step further by trying to promote the modernization of the legal system – and the reform of the entire political system. After all, injustices in the legal system are a function of the party's iron grip over law-making procedures and the courts. It is emblematic of their moral commitment that a good proportion of rights attorneys are ready to suffer reprisals from a regime that still views its critics as "destabilizing agents" or even state enemies who collude with "hostile anti-China elements" in the West.[105]

The development of the thinking of Pu Zhiqiang, one of China's best-known legal activists, bears close examination. A student protestor during the 1989 Tiananmen Square crisis, Pu has always been interested in the correlation between politics and the law. He has represented controversial figures ranging from dissident artist Ai Weiwei to Chen Jiadi, the author of *Investigations of the Chinese Peasants*, a respected book on peasant rights. Pu has also defended Falun Gong practitioners, as well as members of the underground Christian church.[106] Yet his political views were best illustrated in his attack on the *wei-wen* ("stability maintenance") system instituted by former PBSC member Zhou Yongkang. Zhou was a minister of public security from 2003 to 2007 and a Politburo member in charge of security from 2007 to 2012. In an open deposition attacking Zhou and his colleagues, Pu pointed out that draconian efforts by Beijing to lock up dissidents and other "destabilizing agents" of society had resulted in "the drastic fall in people's trust in the government's authority and in the judicial system." The only way for stability to be maintained would be to abandon the quasi-police-state apparatus and "build up rule of law and constitutional governance," Pu argued way back in 2007. "China must establish the authority of the judicial process, not the authority of the party," he concluded. Pu has also cited the democratization of Taiwan as a possible way out for China.[107]

Similarly, the career of Gao Zhisheng, China's internationally recognized rights attorney who has been nominated for the Nobel Peace Prize, best illustrates why human rights lawyers also inevitably take on the role of a social and political crusader. Coming from a destitute background, Gao passed the bar examination in 1995 largely through studying on his own. In 2001, he was among a list of ten attorneys who received commendation from the Ministry of Justice for services rendered to the disadvantaged sectors of society.[108]

However, Gao soon came under 24-hour police surveillance after participating in several controversial cases. He was a key attorney in the defense of underground Christian pastor Cai Zuomu, as well as members of the Falun Gong spiritual sect. In 2005, Gao and a host of well-recognized lawyers, including Teng Biao, Xu Zhiyong, Guo Feixiong, Tang Jingling, Guo Yan, Zhang Xingshui and Li Heping, provided legal advice to villagers in Tai Shi County, Guangdong Province, who wanted to throw out their corrupt village leaders. The peasants' demand for a re-election was crushed by local authorities, who called in thousands of police and the PAP.[109] Gao's lawyer's license was revoked in November that year. In early 2006, Gao, together with well-known dissident Hu Jia and a host of rights lawyers and activists, held China's first-ever "cross-provincial hunger strike" against Beijing's treatment of petitioners and underground religious personnel. Dozens of activists from 13 provinces and the major cities of Beijing, Tianjin and Shanghai took part in the huge protest.[110]

Gao was convicted in 2006 of "inciting subversion to the state" and given a three-year jail term, suspended for five years. Throughout his five-year probation, Gao was under police control and was held incommunicado for months on end. In 2010, the illustrious lawyer was put inside a jail in remote Xinjiang for having "seriously violated probation rules." Although Gao was, in theory, released in 2014, his whereabouts remained unclear. The public only got to know his thinking through petitions and writings he managed to smuggle out of different detention locations. In 2007, he sent a petition to the United States Congress asking the U.S.

to boycott the 2008 Olympics. Gao cited eight counts of severe violation of human rights by the Chinese government, including "bloody suppression of religious freedom," "wanton attack on people's freedoms," and "cruel oppression of human rights movements."[111]

As Gao Zhisheng put it in an open letter to the CCP leadership in 2005: "If we were to confine ourselves to legal issues, it is difficult for us to fulfil our civil responsibility of protecting the rights [of the downtrodden]." The calling of rights defenders could not be limited to the legal sphere, Gao said. "The responsibility of contemporary lawyers should be much broader." At the very least, Gao thinks that rights lawyers and other social activists should find out and publicize the truth behind the authorities' persecution of Falun Gong practitioners and other disadvantaged members of society. In an open petition to then-President Hu Jintao and then-Premier Wen Jiabao, Gao wrote: "The state uses continuous and public measures of terror to warn people that it is very dangerous to get to know the truth and to tell the truth." "Yet it is both proper and necessary for ordinary people to investigate the truth," he added. "The future of our people is closely related to the value that we put on truth."[112]

Scholar-turned-rights attorney Xu Zhiyong has followed a similar trajectory. He was also among the first group of rights attorneys to go beyond defending the underprivileged in court by initiating social movements. Xu committed himself to a life-long career of legal activism soon after gaining his law doctorate from Peking University in 2003. He has carried out pioneering research into the lives of petitioners who were holed up in virtual ghettos in Beijing as they awaited replies to their petitions – usually about gross injustices suffered at the hands of the police and corrupt cadres – from various party and government units in the capital. In 2003 and 2006, Xu also ran successfully for the position of deputy to the district-level People's Congress of Beijing.[113] In his electoral campaign statement of 2004, Xu noted that, "we should treat the law, our compatriots and our government with full sincerity." "And we must take action," he added. "Only with action will there be progress in legal and judicial institutions." Xu also expressed hope in legal reforms. "The legal profession [in many countries] is a conservative one," he said. "Yet in China, it is an 'innovative' profession that is spearheading the realization of citizen rights."[114]

In 2005, Xu and several other legal scholars and attorneys set up an Open Constitution Initiative (hereafter Gongmeng). It was committed to investigating breaches of human rights across China and providing legal services for citizens ranging from dispossessed peasants to migrant workers. Gongmeng published a "China Human Rights Development Report" in 2006. It was the first rights-oriented study by an NGO in Chinese history. In 2009, Gongmeng was closed down by the authorities, which also fined the NGO 1.46 million yuan for "dodging taxes."[115] In 2010, Gongmen changed its name to New Citizens' Movement (NCM). Its influence was augmented owing to the participation of influential lawyers and public intellectuals, including Teng Biao, Li Fangping, Wang Gongquan and Li Xiongbing. The movement's most important contribution was to initiate a series of peaceful protests – either on the streets of big cities or on the Internet – to demonstrate citizens' rights to air their views. Given that the theme of the protests – asking officials to make public their assets and those of their close kin – dovetailed with President Xi's anti-graft drive, the movement was guaranteed a moral high ground. Beijing's suppression of the crusade, although in line with expectations, received unusually harsh condemnation from Chinese intellectuals at home and abroad.[116]

Xu was detained by police in 2013 and, a year later, sentenced to four years in jail for "gathering a crowd to disturb public order." "In today's China, social injustice is being exacerbated," Xu said in his court statement. "Unfair distribution of political power is the source of social injustice as well as other kinds of injustices." "One privileged interest group has monopolized state power as well as economic resources," said Xu, who added that the only solution was "democratic, constitutional governance." He called upon the judges and prosecutors to be "loyal to the law and to their conscience" and not to "trample upon the dignity of rule of law."[117] Despite his harsh treatment at the hands of the authorities, Xu's pioneering work has inspired a new generation of rights attorneys. Moreover, Xu has remained perhaps the most eloquent legal professional in explaining why rights lawyers have to go one step further in reforming the Chinese political system. When commenting on the Shaanxi Oilfields scandal, Xu noted that this case of "bureaucratic monopolistic capital and regional bureaucratic interest groups trampling upon [the interests of the people] is similar to the Chinese situation a century ago." "Controversies surrounding the oilfields in north Shaanxi are fundamentally an economic problem," he added. "Unfortunately in China, all problems can develop into political problems."[118]

The July 9 swoop on 309 lawyers, legal personnel and activists

The administration of Xi Jinping has adopted progressively more draconian tactics against rights lawyers and other sectors of the civil society. In the year ending March 2014, at least 100 lawyers and legal activists were harassed or arrested for reasons ranging from publicly supporting "constitutionalism" to defending dissidents. In July 2013 alone, some 44 lawyers were beaten up or otherwise barred by police and other security officials from routine operations such as meeting their clients.[119] Yet few observers were prepared for the large-scale swoop on the legal community on July 9, 2015.

An unprecedented attack on rights attorneys

On July 9, 2015, the police and related law-enforcement agencies dealt a frontal blow to the rights-concerned legal community by detaining 309 lawyers, legal assistants, as well as activists who had provided help to the lawyers. Several were affiliated with the Beijing-based Fengrui Law Firm whose attorneys had gained fame for taking up civil rights cases involving ethnic minorities, forced demolitions of people's homes, unauthorized Christian churches or the banned spiritual sect Falun Gong. In terms of geographical distribution, 60 of the incarcerated were from Beijing. An additional 45 were from the southern city of Guangzhou, 25 from Jiangsu Province, 17 from the Guangxi Zhuang Autonomous Region and 16 from the Shanghai metropolis.[120]

Attorneys who lost their freedom in what has become known as the 709 Incident included nationally and internationally recognized rights lawyers such as Zhou Shifeng, Wang Yu, Wang Quanzhang, Li Heping, Xie Yang, Li Chunfu and Liu Sixin. Zhou and the two Wangs were attorneys of the Fengrui Law Firm. Zhou Shifeng (born 1964) first gained recognition for representing the parents of the victims of melamine-tainted milk produced by the San Lu Group in 2008. Zhou announced in 2015 that he would set up an 8 million yuan "China Lawyers Weiquan Fund" to provide monetary assistance to the families of persecuted lawyers. Wang Yu (born 1971), who won the Ludovic Trarieux International Human Rights Prize in 2016, achieved national acclaim for defending human rights activist Cao Shunlin, who died under suspicious circumstances while in police custody in 2014. She was also a co-defender of Uighur scholar Ilham Tohti, who was sentenced to life imprisonment in 2014 for allegedly promoting separatism and "spreading racial hatred." Wang Quanzhang (born 1976), who is not related to Wang Yu, is a veteran attorney for persecuted Falun Gong practitioners. Wang was detained for ten days by police when he was defending a group of practitioners in Jing Jiang, Jiangsu Province, in April 2013. This precipitated a petition by 100 lawyers demanding Wang's release. Li Heping (born 1970) is a Christian lawyer who has represented house church members, Falun Gong practitioners, as well as political dissidents. In 2008, he received the Democracy Award for Religious Freedom given by the Washington-based National Endowment for Democracy. Li was among a group of lawyers and intellectuals who met President George W. Bush at the White House that year. He also won the Human Rights Award offered by the Council of Bars and Law Societies of Europe (CCBE) in 2008.[121]

It is a testimony to Beijing's failure to abide by its self-defined "rule by law" principles that, as of early 2019, the fate of a good number of attorneys detained in the 709 swoop remained unsettled. Six attorneys, including Zhou Shifeng and Jiang Tianyong, were in jail. Li Hipeng, Gou Hongguo and Zhai Yanmin were given suspended sentences. Five were released on bail, and four were set free upon completion of their sentences. However, the great majority of the 709 lawyers have been put under illegal 24-hour surveillance. At least 41 were barred from leaving China. Among those released or given bail to await medical treatment, Li Chunfu, Li Heping, Li Zhuyun, Gou Hongguo and Ren Quanniu, told their relatives that they had been severely beaten. In a departure from similar cases, these lawyers were also force-fed medicines that were suspected to be psychiatric drugs.[122]

The most egregious case involving Beijing's blatant disregard of its own laws involved the prolonged "disappearance" of Wang Quanzhang. For almost three and a half years after July 2015, his wife Li Wenzu was not told of Wang's whereabouts. Nor was she allowed to seek legal help. In April 2018, when Li undertook a 100-kilometre walk to the Tianjin Detention Centre to protest the 1,000-day disappearance of Wang, she was stopped halfway and forcibly taken back to her humble Beijing apartment. Several foreign and Hong Kong reporters who tried to interview Li were roughed up by security personnel who were posted at the entrance of the apartment building on a 24-hour basis. Eventually, the authorities scheduled a trial for Wang on December 26, 2018, during which the well-recognized lawyer was accused of "subversion of state power." Neither Li, nor Wang's fellow attorneys, nor Western diplomats were allowed to attend the half-day trial. In late January 2019, Wang was given a four and a half year jail term for subversion of state power and "collusion" with foreign NGOs in endangering national security.[123]

Colleagues and relatives of the detained have difficulty obtaining legal assistance. The relatives of Zhou Shifeng, one of the major targets of the authorities, originally engaged the services of Beijing attorney Yang Jinzhu. However, the authorities deprived Yang of the right to defend Zhou. Saying that he and his staff had faced intimidation from the police, Yang launched an Internet petition in mid-2016 to safeguard his rights as a lawyer. The petition was signed by 240 lawyers within one month. In many instances, the spouses of the detained were prevented from liaising with lawyers, and lawyers who had initially promised to help the detainees were forced to withdraw after rounds of intimidation by the police. Take the case of lawyer Xie Yanyi (born 1975), who gained fame in 2003 for challenging the constitutional propriety of Jiang Zemin's remaining chairman of the Central Military Commission after having retired from the Politburo in late 2002. His wife Yuan Shanshan failed to get any information from the police or judicial authorities when he was "disappeared" on July 9. It was only in January 2016 that she was told that Xie would be charged with "incitement to subvert state power." The family-appointed lawyer had been dismissed and replaced by a government-appointed counsel, but neither lawyer was allowed to visit Xie. When Yuan demanded to know why, she was told she "did not need to know." After Xie's arrest, she was also forcibly evicted from their Beijing apartment.[124]

Some 20 international legal and human rights NGOs signed a petition to Beijing asking President Xi to "uphold the rule of law in China" in the treatment of the 709 case. Signatories included the Hong Kong-based China Human Rights Lawyers Concern Group, the Amsterdam Bar Association, the Australian branch of the International Association of People's Lawyers and the International Commission of Jurists. Said Sophie Richardson of the New York-based Human Rights Watch: "Every day these people languish in detention, Beijing harms ordinary people's access to justice, dissuades other lawyers from taking sensitive cases, and deepens the stain on China's reputation." King's College London's Eva Pils said the government under Xi appeared more confident in resorting to "rule by law with Chinese characteristics" in tackling dissident lawyers. Before Xi came to power, Pils argued, "you had oppression but it was kept more hidden, the government wanted to avoid criticism." "There is a new assertiveness in the Xi era with the claims that we're running the legal system our way," she added.[125]

In a July 2016 commentary, the party-run paper *Global Times* said the Western media had exaggerated the importance of the 709 Incident because the number of lawyers in detention was a miniscule percentage of the few hundred thousand lawyers in the country. "How come the arrest of this extreme minority of lawyers could be used to buttress the claim that 'there is no rule by law' in China?" the paper asked. *Global Times* did admit, however, that the fact the lawyers had still not been put on trial one year after their detention was "slower than people's usual expectations." Equally significant is the fact that, if the CCP authorities were genuinely convinced of the lack of significance of the 709 Incident, they would not have deployed the party's formidable propaganda machinery to try to discredit the rights lawyers and their relatives.[126]

Extra-legal steps to silence lawyers and their relatives

Within a week of his arrest on July 9, the principal partner of Fengrui Law Firm, Zhou Shifeng, was seen on national TV making the following confession of his "guilt." The video was recorded while Zhou was being interrogated by Beijing police in an undisclosed detention center in the capital. "Our firm only became a partnership firm in 2012, and could not compete with established law firms," said Zhou in the televised confession. "We wanted to fabricate several big cases and become famous, after which we can earn more money easily." Zhou noted that he was able to politicize cases by means including saturating the social media with sympathetic reports about the suspects, as well as organizing "petitioners" to hold noisy protests outside court rooms. "I allow and encourage my staff to engage in illegal activities while handling court cases," said Zhou. "I bear irrevocable responsibility for harming social stability."[127]

At about the same time, CCTV aired a 10-minute confession made by a lawyer and two employees from the same law firm. Labeled "criminal suspects" on the screen, the three described how they organized paid protests, hyped public sentiment and disseminated online rumors to put pressure on court decisions in sensitive cases. Staring into the camera, lawyer Huang Liqun said that the major shareholder of Fengrui, Zhou Shifeng, was behind the cases. Huang said Zhou was "motivated by unspeakable political purposes ... He has the final say over the finances [of the firm]. And he is very lecherous."[128]

The authorities also used tough tactics to intimidate the spouses, relatives and children of the incarcerated attorneys. Perhaps the most criticized – and inhumane – weapon used by law enforcement officials was not to disclose the whereabouts of the detainees. In July 2016, the wives of five of the lawyers, Li Heping, Xie Yanyi, Zhai Yanmin, Wang Quanzhang and Xie Yang, managed to shake off police surveillance and went to Tianjin, where the lawyers were thought to have been incarcerated. They told stories of the miscarriage of justice to a dozen-odd reporters from the foreign and Hong Kong press.[129] Earlier, Li Wenzu told the foreign media that police had visited her parents' home in Shandong Province to intimidate her father and sister. Law-enforcement officials even threatened her sister by saying that her children might not be able to find schools if Li did not stop her advocacy activities. "I feel guilty because my family has been dragged in," Li said. "I am scared of what they might do to my parents and my sister's family."[130]

Also consider the serious maltreatment accorded lawyer Wang Yu, one of the most illustrious female rights attorneys in the country. Her 16-year-old son Bao Zhuoxuan was held as a hostage and prevented from leaving China for overseas studies for a few years.[131] Wang suffered ill-treatment akin to torture in jail: at one point, she was stripped naked by female guards in a cell with security cameras. In August 2016, Wang was forced to make a "confession of guilt," which was broadcast on several pro-Beijing Hong Kong media. Subsequently, she and her husband were released – but they were forced to live under tight police surveillance and given strict warnings not to talk to foreign media.[132]

Conclusion: the calling and strategy of rights lawyers

The real and potential influence of China's relatively limited number of rights attorneys could be gauged through exploring the reasons behind Beijing's particularly harsh treatment of Wang Quanzhang, the "709 lawyer" who suffered the longest incarceration before being subjected to a show trial in late 2018. It is notable that, at least on the surface, Wang did not seem to have as strong a track record in defending the weak and the suppressed as, for example, Xu Zhiyong or Gao Zhisheng. Wang's strength was organization – setting up a network of law-related "help centers" across China and also liaising with lawyers' groups and charitable organizations abroad. According to court documents as well as revelations by his Swedish collaborator, NGO activist Peter Dahlin, Wang set up a company in Hong Kong in August 2009 with the goal of establishing a network of "legal aid stations" in different Chinese cities. The Hong Kong office was instrumental in securing foreign donations and providing training to mainland lawyers and legal assistants in running the legal-aid grid in China. In other words, Wang aspired to feed into and bolster China's inchoate civil society – and to promote a symbiotic working relationship between lawyers on the one hand, and journalists, jurists, intellectuals and foreign NGO personnel on the other.[133] Beijing's scorched-earth policy toward Wang's set-up has paradoxically revealed the potential of lawyers' participation in a gradually expanding civil society.

How rights lawyers conserve their strength under the party's "proletarian dictatorship" – and speak out whenever circumstances allow

A 43-year-old Guangzhou-based lawyer interviewed by this author is aware of the severe limitations under which rights attorneys labor. "We are a very small minority among China's legal professionals," he said in late 2016. "We are aware that the great majority of lawyers do not share our sense of commitment to justice; they may even despise us for creating unnecessary confrontation between our profession and the authorities." He added that, by and large, the overwhelming propaganda machinery of the CCP was effective. Even among members of the educated and professional classes, only a minority was aware of the work of human rights lawyers – and even fewer people would think of risking their well-being to support them.[134]

Other lawyers are also not optimistic about progress in what party authorities call "legal construction," or about more tolerance from the regime regarding "troublemaking attorneys." The series of draconian legal and administrative measures introduced particularly in the Xi Jinping era has highlighted the David versus Goliath nature of the asymmetrical struggle. Take the TV confessions for example. "Televised confession may seem like a gross concoction to people in the West," said a 48-year-old lawyer in Shanghai. "However, there are many Chinese who believe in what they see on television. The psychological damage wreaked on the suspects making the confession – as well as their relatives – cannot be over-stated." Another sign of deterioration is the increased participation of the police – and sometimes triad elements employed by the police – in intimidating and sometimes beating up attorneys and their relatives. "In the early days, punishment to lawyers who had run afoul of the authorities were meted out mostly by the Ministry of Justice, which wields the powerful weapon of revoking the licenses of legal professionals," the Shanghai lawyer added. "But increasingly, the police and occasionally agents of the MSS are deployed when authorities want to clamp down on rights lawyers."[135]

A minority of rights attorneys have even cast doubt on the strategy of using "extra-legal" means – such as organizing street protests or launching appeals on the Internet – to press cases. "Some rights lawyers think we should just stick to the law," said a veteran Hangzhou-based lawyer. This is despite the fact that, in most cases involving the use of political means – for example, mobilizing victims of land grab to hold public demonstrations – justice is on the side of the attorneys and their clients.[136] The majority of nationally known legal activists, however, seem to gravitate to the view of icons such as Gao Zhisheng, Teng Biao, Pu Zhiqiang, Xu Zhiyong and Zhou Shifeng that lawyers should fight for justice on two fronts: in the law courts and through tactical political maneuvers. This pathway first became obvious during the Charter 08 Movement – a net-based petition that called on the party to fully honor human rights as enshrined in the Chinese Constitution – initiated by intellectuals including Nobel Prize winner Liu Xiaobo. Thirty or so among the first batch of signatories of 500-odd pro-democracy activists were law professors, lawyers or legal assistants. They included attorneys, legal scholars and commentators He Weifang, Yu Haocheng, Zhang Sizhi, Zhang Zuhua, Teng Biao and Xu Youyu, and lawyers Tang Jingling, Pu Zhiqiang, Mo Shaoping, Zheng Enchong, Zhu Jiuhu, Jin Guanghong, Fan Yafeng and Wu Baojian. It must be noted that political campaigns such as Charter 08 or the New Citizens Movement never challenged the CCP's power to rule. Activists were merely asking the leadership to honor its oft-repeated reassurance about "running the country according to law" and "honoring the Constitution and the laws."[137]

A 36-year-old Shenzhen-based lawyer is convinced that, apart from litigation work, legal professionals should embark on the dual task of expanding the public sphere as well as educating the public about international values such as justice and independence of the judiciary. Rights lawyers are comforted by the fact that the 709 Incident notwithstanding, more attorneys are committed to the task of defending disadvantaged sectors of society. "I have known many newly qualified lawyers who are taking up human rights cases," said the Shenzhen lawyer interviewed by this author. "The only difference is that given the extra-tough stance of the police apparatus, rights lawyers nowadays are for the time being more circumspect in using extra-legal means such as organizing protests and on-line petitions."[138]

Citing Chairman Mao's famous adage − "the more suppression there is, the more resistance" − a Xiamen-based lawyer with more than 12 years of experience was adamant that the spirit of rights lawyers could not be crushed by strong-arm tactics. "We are spending more time trying to promote our cause among attorneys who are mostly focused on ordinary commercial cases," said the lawyer. "We are also cementing relations with other sectors of the civil society such as intellectuals, scholars, and religious activists." The Xiamen lawyer believes that, despite the promulgation of the new law on foreign NGOs − which may make it difficult for Hong Kong and Western legal organizations to render support to lawyer groups in the PRC − rights attorneys should also promote ties with counterparts overseas. "Awards given to outstanding rights lawyers such as Gao Zhisheng and Wang Yu by American or European human rights organizations lift up our morale," she added. "Despite the Xi administration's aggressive public persona, it is very much concerned about how the CCP regime is perceived in the West."[139]

Lawyers as long-term catalysts in civic and legal education for the public

On May 29, 2012, Xu Zhiyong published an article regarding the need to organize a mass movement to promote civil rights. "China needs a new citizens' movement," he wrote:

> This movement is a political movement in which this ancient nation bids farewell to authoritarianism and completes the civilized transformation to constitutional governance; it is a social movement to completely destroy the privileges of corruption, the abuse of power … and to construct a new order of fairness and justice; it is a cultural movement to bid farewell to the culture of autocrats and servants and instead create a new nationalist spirit.[140]

Despite heavy-handed state control of the Internet and the media, Xu and his comrades are convinced that their valiant struggles against injustice on the political, social and cultural fronts could serve to persuade ordinarily nonpolitically minded citizens to join the attorneys' battle for justice and equality.[141]

Li Boguang (1968–2018), a prominent lawyer based in Beijing, believed that lawyers could change the worldview of the oppressed by motivating the latter to use the law as a weapon for protecting rights guaranteed by the Chinese Constitution and UN covenants. Li, who had a law doctorate from Peking University, kept a relatively low profile compared with other rights attorneys who talk regularly with the Chinese and foreign media. After becoming a Christian in 2007, he devoted his attention to promoting "rights awareness" among members of house churches who had been regularly harassed by police. "Some less-educated Chinese have confused the concepts of 'rule of law' with 'law and order,'" said Li. "They are not aware that a key role of the law is to protect citizens' rights – and not just to maintain political stability." "Compared with victims of 'land grab', members of houses churches tend to be more timid and submissive," Li added. "Yet when the police see that their suspects are citing relevant statutes during their interrogation, the former are taken aback. In some cases, the police meted out a more lenient punishment." For Li, the law is both a sword and a shield:

> The law can protect victims of injustice. Yet it can also serve as an efficacious weapon. For example, we can sue officials, judges as well as members of the procuratorate. We can raise petitions to deprive officials of their status as local-level members of the People's Congress.[142]

According to a rights lawyer with more than 15 years of experience in Guangdong Province, he and his colleagues have used a plethora of laws to sue officials for issues ranging from abuse of power to dereliction of duty.

Efforts have also been made by lawyers and their clients to strip errant officials of their titles as deputies to grassroots level People Congresses or Chinese People's Political Consultative Conferences. The relevant legislations include the Law of the PRC on Administrative Supervision (1997), the Law of the PRC on Public Servants (2005), the PRC Administrative Litigation Law (revised, 2015) and the Organic Law of the Local People's Congresses and Local People's Governments of the PRC (2007). "The success rate of our litigation against individual cadres or civil servants is not high," said the Guangdong lawyer. "However, members of law-enforcement units in most provinces now know that their otherwise clean CVs could be sullied – and that this could have a detrimental impact on their promotion prospects."[143]

The irreplaceable role of rights attorneys

For Peking University's Professor He Weifang, one of the most respected legal scholars in China, rule of law is the fairest means to strike a balance between the aspirations and demands of China's disparate interest groups. He noted that the rule of law and democracy make for a society of compromise and civilized intercourse. Instead of a dog-eat-dog world, he said, "democracy can promote [the spirit of] compromise, and legitimize the maintenance of the power [structure]." "Rule of law can render society more orderly, and independence of the judiciary can improve the orderly functions of society," he argued. Moreover, rule of law and independent courts can resolve disputes among citizens and between citizens and the government in a just and rational manner. And rule of law is only made possible by courageous lawyers who risk their freedom defending citizens deprived of basic rights that are guaranteed by the Constitution and the law.[144]

Apart from improving the legal system and helping victims of miscarriages of justice, can China's relatively small number of rights attorneys spearhead a civil-society movement so as to put pressure on the CCP administration to make changes? Beijing-based lawyer Wei Rujiu gave high marks to rights lawyers defending disadvantaged groups including dissidents, the Falun Gong, house churches, members of ethnic communities, private businesspeople, non-official candidates for grassroots-level elections, victims of land grab, petitioners and disadvantaged citizens involved in "mass incidents" (a reference to riots and disturbances). Pointing to the hundreds of lawyers who were founders of Taiwan's ruling party, the Democratic Progressive Party (DPP), Wei argued that, "it was not yet possible for rights attorneys [in China] to coalesce into a social movement, let alone form a political party." Owing to factors including "the inherent weakness of rights attorneys such as lack of resources for grassroots mobilization," Wei noted that these committed lawyers could amount to only "a social phenomenon, not yet a social movement."[145]

Other observers are convinced that China's 400-odd rights lawyers have emerged as a pillar of the civil society, a public sphere that is valiantly battling the inexorable oppression of the Xi Jinping regime. As lawyer Zhu Jiuhu said in the early days of the development of the *weiquan lv'shi* phenomenon, lawyers need to work together with other elements of the inchoate civil society. "I think lawyers should be fighters," he said in 2003. "Legal and judicial progress requires the coordinated efforts of [different sectors of] society." Zhu, who had acted on behalf of non-state-owned enterprises, argued that private businesspeople could do more to advance the rule of law.[146] Despite the ruthless clampdown by the authorities, scholar Cao Zhi pointed out in 2015 that rights attorneys had used an array of ways and means to expand society's public sphere. "Apart from running law firms, lawyers have set up groupings on the Internet and the social media," Cao wrote. "They have also established NGOs, and worked together with scholars to start campaigns to intervene in large-scale cases of confrontation between officials and the people. Lawyers have also taken part in local-level elections."[147]

For former Peking University professor Xia Yeliang, one reason why the CCP was paranoid about rights attorneys was that they could spearhead a popular crusade to clamor for citizen rights and democratic values. "The civil society has developed slowly in China," he said. "Yet lawyers have played an active role in pushing the inchoate civil society forward." Xia argued that the CCP should realize that lawyers actually serve to resolve social contradictions. He noted that, if the people were to totally lose their confidence in the law, they might become radicalized and start using violent means to overthrow the party-state apparatus.[148]

According to Chinese law expert Eva Pils, one reason why the authorities are so paranoid about rights attorneys is the increasingly substantial influence they wield in Chinese society and politics. "Since so many lawyers started openly identifying with human rights causes and coordinating their advocacy campaigns, they are one of the closest things China has to a political opposition," she said immediately after the July 2015 mass arrests. "What rattles [Beijing] is that civic-minded lawyers have the capacity to get together in such large numbers to protest [against] what they see as illegal behavior on the part of the state," Pils added.[149] For the time being, Xi's quasi-police-state apparatus seems to have the upper hand; yet seeds for social transformation via mass movements seem to have been planted among not only legal professionals and political crusaders, but also increasingly large swathes of Chinese society.

Notes

1 Cited in Pan Wei, "The rule of law and the future of the Chinese political system," Aisixiang.com, September 17, 2001, www.aisixiang.com/data/67.html. See also Wei Pan, "Toward a consultative rule of law regime in China," *Journal of Contemporary China*, Vol. 12, No. 34, 2003, pp. 3–43; Pan Wei, "What is the rule of law?" Aisixiang.com, January 11, 2004, www.aisixiang.com/data/2674.html

2 Cited in He Weifang, *In the Name of Justice: Striving for the Rule of Law in China*, Brookings Institutions, November 5, 2012, www.brookings.edu/book/in-the-name-of-justice/

3 Cited in "Xi Jinping's Political Report to the 19th CCP Congress," Xinhua News Agency, October 18, 2017, http://news.youth.cn/sz/201710/t20171018_10888424. htm. Propagating "Chinese wisdom" (which includes Chinese rule by law) is part of the CCP's ambitious soft-power projection. See "Xi Jinping's views on 'cultural soft power,'" Chinareform.org, February 9, 2015, www.chinareform.org.cn/Explore/sa ying/201502/t20150209_218421.htm

4 See Tong Zhiwei and Qin Qianhong: "The reform of the judicial system must go down the road of judicial independence," Calaw.cn, September 13, 2012, www.cala w.cn/article/default.asp?id=7535

5 For an overall assessment of the Gao case, including Gao's ideas on legal reform and his torture in prison, see, for example, Isolda Morillo, "AP interview: Chinese lawyer not giving up despite torture," Associated Press, June 14, 2016, http://bigstory.ap. org/article/6979d11445eb4596beb8a0367b167262/ap-interview-chinese-lawyer-not-giving-despite-torture

6 For a discussion of trials made under duress and "televised confessions," see, for example, Amnesty International, "China: assault on human rights lawyers and activists escalates with convictions after sham trials," August 4, 2016, www.amnesty.org/en/la test/news/2016/08/china-assault-on-human-rights-lawyers-and-activists-escalates-with-convictions-after-sham-trials/

7 For a discussion of Chinese rule by law and its relationship with regime stability and political reform, see, for example, Benjamin L. Lieban, "China's law and stability paradox," in Jacques deLisle and Avery Goldstein, eds., *China's Challenges*, Philadelphia: University of Pennsylvania Press, 2015, pp. 157–177; Susan Trevaskes and Elisa Nesossi, "Control by law," in Jane Golley, Linda Jaivan and Luigi Tomba, eds., *Control*, Canberra: ANU Press, 2017, pp. 41–60; Young Nam Cho, "Governing the country according to the law: China's rule of law policy as political reform," *Journal of International & Area Studies*, Vol. 21, No. 1, June 2014, pp. 21–36; Eva Pils, "The party and the law," in Willy Wo-Lap Lam, ed., *Routledge Handbook of the Chinese Communist*

Party, London: Routledge, 2018, pp. 248–265; Eva Pils, *China's Human Rights Lawyers: Advocacy and Resistance*, London: Routledge, 2014.

8   For a sampling of Xi's remarks on rule of law with Chinese characteristics, see *Chinese Law and Government*, Vol. 48, No. 6, 2016, pp. 468–474.

9   Cited in "Xi Jinping stresses running the country according to law and administrating according to law," Xinhua News Agency, February 24, 2013, http://news.xinhuanet. com/politics/2013–02/24/c_114782088.htm

10   Cited in Chen Xixi, "The theoretical contribution of General Secretary Xi Jinping's ideas on governance and administration to the development of 21st century Marxism," *People's Daily*, August 17, 2017, http://theory.people.com.cn/n1/2017/0817/ c83859-29476801.html

11   Cited in "Xi Jinping's talk at the conference hosted by different circles in Beijing to commemorate the 30th anniversary of the promulgation of the 1982 constitution," Xinhua News Agency, December 4, 2012, http://news.xinhuanet.com/politics/ 2012-12/04/c_113907206.htm

12   For a discussion of the enshrinement of party leadership in the newly revised Constitution, see, for example, Jun Mai, "Xi Jinping is changing the constitution, but what's his endgame?" *South China Morning Post*, March 12, 2018, www.scmp.com/ news/china/policies-politics/article/2136676/xi-jinping-changing-constitution-wha ts-his-endgame

13   Cited in "Hu Deping: the constitution presupposes constitutional governance; without constitutional governance, the constitution itself will be sullied," *Economic Observer Post* (Beijing), August 10, 2013, http://nb.ifeng.com/gngj/detail_2013_08/10/1091519_0. shtml. See also Hu Deping, "How to solve the questions raised in l'Ancien Régime et la Révolution," EEO.com.cn, Beijing, August 11, 2013, http://business.sohu.com/ 20130811/n383892863.shtml

14   For a discussion of Hu Yaobang's ideas on legal issues, see, for example, Zhu Houze, "Hu Yaobang's complete views on reform," *Yanhuang Chunqiu*, No. 7, 2010, http:// xueshu.baidu.com/usercenter/paper/show?paperid=a991eb887a2cc88e946af06da2fa 871d&site=xueshu_se

15   Cited in "Xi Jinping on rule by law: 'whether the party or the law is more powerful' is a fake question and a political trap," *People's Daily*, May 11, 2015, http://cpc.people. com.cn/xuexi/n/2015/0511/c385475-26978527.html

16   Cited in Zheng Zhixue, "The goal of constitutional governance is to abolish the leadership of the party," *Party Construction* (Beijing), May 30, 2013, http://news.takungpa o.com/mainland/focus/2013-05/1651218.html

17   Cited in Ma Zhongcheng, "The essence of 'constitutionalism' is a kind of weapon in propaganda warfare," *People's Daily*, August 5, 2013, http://money.163.com/13/ 0805/09/95GLMPT700254TI5.html

18   See "CCP Central Committee decision on certain major issues concerning comprehensively advancing rule of law," Xinhua, October 28, 2014, http://politics.people. com.cn/n/2014/1028/c1001-25926121.html

19   Ibid. See also Qiao Xinsheng, "Party congress promotes rule of law," *China Daily*, October 23, 2017, www.chinadaily.com.cn/newsrepublic/2017-10/23/content_33628001.htm

20   Cited in "CCP Central Committee decision on certain major issues."

21   Cited in Ma Huaide, "The Fourth Plenum has blown loudly the horn of comprehensively pushing forward [the principle of] running the country according to law," *Guangming Ribao* (Beijing), October 30, 2014, www.wenming.cn/xj_pd/ssrd/201410/ t20141030_2261631.shtml

22   Cited in Martin Sieff, "Rule of law must follow China's path," *China Daily*, October 23, 2014, www.chinadaily.com.cn/china/2014cpctps/2014-10/23/content_18793552.htm

23   See "CCP Central Committee Decision on Certain Major Issues."

24   See "Decision on certain major issues concerning comprehensively deepening reforms," English.court.gov.cn, October 8, 2015, http://english.court.gov.cn/2015-10/08/con tent_22130532.htm

25 For a discussion on the *laojiao* system, see, for example, "China abolishes reeducation through labor," Xinhua News Agency, December 28, 2013, www.chinadaily.com.cn/china/2013–12/28/content_17202294.htm; see also Fang Yang, "Reeducation returns in new form in Henan," *Global Times*, February 13, 2014, www.globaltimes.cn/content/842351.shtml

26 For a discussion of legal-judicial reforms from late 2013 onward, see, for example, Stanley Lubman, "An encouraging sign for (limited) legal reform in China," *Wall Street Journal*, February 25, 2014, http://blogs.wsj.com/chinarealtime/2014/02/25/an-encouraging-sign-for-limited-legal-reform-in-china/. See also Sui-Lee Wee and Li Hui, "With legal reforms, China wants less interfering in cases, fewer death penalty crimes," Reuters, March 9, 2014, www.reuters.com/article/us-china-parliament-legal/with-legal-reforms-china-wants-less-interfering-in-cases-fewer-death-penalty-crimes-idUSBREA2804S20140309; "In China, brutality yields confessions of graft," Associated Press, March 7, 2014, www.usatoday.com/story/news/world/2014/03/07/china-brutality-yields-confession/6179431/

27 For a study of the evolution and functions of the CPLC, see, for example, Zhong Jinyan, "The history and evolution of the Central Political-Legal Commission," *Yanhuang chunqiu*, September 2012, www.yhcqw.com/71/8977.html. See also Liu Zhong, "The constitution of the Central Political-Legal Commission and its work style," Guancha.cn, September 3, 2017. Since the creation of the Central National Security Commission in 2014, much of the CPLC's work has been subsumed under the CNSC. On the rationale for setting up the CNSC, see Wang Yong "The historical mission of the National Security Commission and ways of improvement," Aisixiang, com, June 11, 2014, www.aisixiang.com/data/75395.html

28 Cited in "The Central Political-Legal Commission will reform itself to ensure that it does not interfere with individual cases," *Southern Metropolitan News*, July 14, 2013, http://news.takungpao.com/mainland/focus/2013–07/1758629.html

29 Cited in Sui-Lee Wee and Li Hui, "With legal reforms, China wants less interfering in cases, fewer death penalty crimes," Reuters, March 9, 2014, www.reuters.com/article/us-china-parliament-legal/with-legal-reforms-china-wants-less-interfering-in-cases-fewer-death-penalty-crimes-idUSBREA2804S20140309

30 Cited in "Guo Shengkun presides over the Central Political-Legal Commission's plenary session and transmits the spirit of the party's Third Plenum of the 19th Central Committee," *Legal Daily*, March 2, 2018, www.chinadaily.com.cn/micro-reading/2018-03/02/content_35775772.htm

31 For a discussion of Zhou Qiang's political career, see Zhou Xin, "Why Zhou Qiang has lost to Hu Chunhua in leadership sweepstakes," Radio Free Asia, January 25, 2017, www.rfa.org/mandarin/zhuanlan/yehuazhongnanhai/gx-01252017153445.html

32 Cited in "Zhou Qiang: transparency is our principle and nontransparency is the exception," China News Service, July 5, 2013, www.chinanews.com/fz/2013/07-05/5005275.shtml. See also "Zhou Qiang: what people are most dissatisfied about the work of courts are unjust adjudication and corrupt judges," *People's Daily*, August 16, 2013, http://cpc.people.com.cn/n/2013/0816/c64094-22590447.html

33 Cited in Zhou Qiang, "Insist upon the concentrated, unified leadership of the party central authorities," *People's Daily*, April 3, 2015, http://theory.people.com.cn/n/2015/0403/c83846-26794639.html

34 For a discussion of Zhou's views on party leadership of the courts, see "Guard against the wrong idea of putting the party's leadership against judicial fairness," *Legal Daily*, September 24, 2014, www.chinanews.com/fz/2014/09-24/6623787.shtml; "Zhou Jiang lays emphasis on seriously studying General Secretary Xi Jinping's important talks on the construction of rule by law," Court.gov.cn, April 17, 2013, www.court.gov.cn/xwzx/fyxw/zgrmfyxw/201304/t20130417_183384.htm. See also "Zhou Qiang: firmly uphold the party's leadership over the courts," China News Service, January 12, 2017, www.chinanews.com/gn/2017/01-12/8121430.shtml

35 Cited in Zhang Shaoliang and He Fangi, "The legal ideas of Guanzi and its modern significance," Qilu Net (Beijing), April 10, 2014, http://news.iqilu.com/other/20140410/1946232.shtml. See also Yi Zhongtian, "Rule by law in China and Chinese culture: why Chinese are not adept at using the law to protect themselves," 360doc.com September 24, 2016, www.360doc.com/content/16/0924/11/7300976_593242396.shtml

36 See "The constitutional revision is passed; what are the changes involved in past revisions?" News.163.com, March 12, 2018, http://news.163.com/18/0312/09/DCMGI8T90001875N.html

37 For a study of the process of the revision of the Constitution undertaken by ex-President Hu Jintao, see Willy Wo-Lap Lam, *Chinese Politics in the Hu Jintao Era*, New York: M.E. Sharpe, 2006, pp. 121–122, 151–152.

38 See "China will revise its Constitution: the Politburo has unveiled this important information," Xinhua News Agency, December 29, 2017, http://shizheng.xilu.com/20171229/1000010001021860.html

39 See staff reporters, "NPC passes constitutional revision with two negative votes and three abstentions," *Ming Pao* (Hong Kong), March 11, 2018, https://news.mingpao.com/ins/instantnews/web_tc/article/20180311/s00004/1520751176572; Li Chun, "Some Hong Kong NPC delegates take leave of absence at the final moment before vote-casting to revise the constitution," *United Daily News* (Taipei), March 11, 2018, https://udn.com/news/story/11311/3024237

40 See staff reporters, "Proposals in the revised constitution abrogate term limits for state president; mainland Chinese commentator: undermining Deng Xiaoping's reforms," *Ming Pao*, February 26, 2018, https://news.mingpao.com/pns/dailynews/web_tc/article/20180226/s00001/1519583438872. See also Salvatore Babones, "China's constitutional amendments are all about the Party, not the president," *Forbes*, March 11, 2018, www.forbes.com/sites/salvatorebabones/2018/03/11/chinas-constitutional-amendments-are-all-about-the-party-not-the-president/#1f1ac6e11615

41 Cited in "It's a successful experience to have 'the three most powerful positions having the same [tenure] system,'" Xinhua News Agency, March 1, 2018, www.xinhuanet.com/comments/2018-03/01/c_1122469831.htm

42 For a discussion of the controversy over whether to enshrine "CCP rule" into the body of the PRC Constitution, see, for example, Chun Chiubei, "Deng Xiaoping abrogates party leadership but Xi Jinping has once again enshrined it into the Constitution," DwNews.com (Beijing), March 2, 2018, http://culture.dwnews.com/history/news/2018-03-02/60043390.html

43 For the latest assessments of legal issues in China, see "China, Events in 2017," in *World Report 2018*, Human Rights Watch, New York, 2018, www.hrw.org/world-report/2018/country-chapters/china-and-tibet

44 Cited in "He Weifang: The cultural impediments to the construction of the Chinese legal system," Hong Kong Trade Development Council, July 24, 2010, www.hktdc.com/info/mi/a/tdcnews/sc/1X070LMN/1/DATASOURCE-DESCRIPTION/ARTICLE-TITLE.htm

45 For a discussion of Jiang Zemin and Hu Jintao's partial revival of Confucianist ideals, see, for example, Richard Spencer, "China rediscovers Confucius in drive for social harmony," *The Telegraph*, March 16, 2005, www.telegraph.co.uk/news/worldnews/asia/china/1485772/China-rediscovers-Confucius-in-drive-for-social-harmony.html

46 Cited in "Xi Jinping on 'rule of law': rulers who forcefully implement the law will render their country strong," *People's Daily*, March 16, 2015, http://cpc.people.com.cn/xuexi/n/2015/0316/c385476-26697660.html

47 For a discussion of "legalism" and its implications for Chinese governance, see, for example, Paul R. Goldin, "Persistent misconceptions about Chinese 'legalism,'" *Journal of Chinese Philosophy*, Vol. 38, No. 1, March 2011, pp. 88–10.

48 Cited in "The rule by law section of *Xi Jinping Uses the Classics*," *People's Daily*, March 16, 2015, http://theory.people.com.cn/n/2015/0316/c394175-26697262.html

49 Cited in "Viewing Xi Jinping's ideas on governance and administration from the way he uses the classics," *People's Daily Online*, March 1, 2015, http://news.sohu.com/20150301/n409241785.shtml. For a discussion of Han Fei's use of the father–son analogy to explain how emperors should control ministers, see, for example, Gao Dang, "On Han Fei's reinterpretation of the Confucianist view of filial piety," *Nanchang Education Institute Journal*, 2011, Vol 26, No. 4, https://wenku.baidu.com/view/63fe8509804d2b160a4ec029.html

50 Cited in "Xi Jinping: speech on the party's summing-up conference on the practice of education on the mass line," Xinhua News Agency, October 8, 2014, www.xinhuanet.com/politics/2014-10/08/c_1112740663.htm

51 "Xi Jinping's views on human resources: the top priority of governance is to use talents properly," *People's Daily*, August 4, 2015, http://cpc.people.com.cn/xuexi/n/2015/0804/c385474-27405703.html

52 Author's interview with a Hangzhou-based human rights attorney, March 2018. For an official view of the national security-related laws passed in the 2013–2018 period, see "National security legislation safeguards China's core interests: report," Xinhua News Agency, March 11, 2018, www.chinadaily.com.cn/a/201803/11/WS5aa4ee88a3106e7dcc140e48.html

53 See "China adopts national security law," Xinhua News Agency, July 1, 2015, www.chinadaily.com.cn/china/2015-07/01/content_21150783.htm. See also Edward Wong, "China approves sweeping security law, bolstering Communist rule," *New York Times*, July 1, 2015, www.nytimes.com/2015/07/02/world/asia/china-approves-sweeping-security-law-bolstering-communist-rule.html

54 Ibid.

55 See "National People's Congress Legal Work Committee explains in detail the new National Security Law," China News Service, July 1, 2015, http://politics.people.com.cn/n/2015/0701/c70731-27239185.html

56 Cited in staff reporter, "Beijing passes sweeping national security law, but legislation 'will not be directly implemented in Hong Kong,'" *South China Morning Post*, July 1, 2015, www.scmp.com/news/china/policies-politics/article/1830383/chinas-contentious-national-security-law-due-be-passed

57 Ibid.

58 Cited in "Xi Jinping gives important speech at the first conference of the Central Leading Group on Cybersecurity and Informatization," Xinhua News Agency, February 27, 2014, www.cac.gov.cn/2014-02/27/c_133148354.htm

59 See "The People's Republic of China Cybersecurity Law," NPC.gov.cn, November 7, 2016, www.npc.gov.cn/npc/xinwen/2016-11/07/content_2001605.htm. See also Jonathan Kaiman, "China cracks down on social media with threat of jail for 'online rumors,'" *The Guardian*, September 10, 2013, www.theguardian.com/world/2013/sep/10/china-social-media-jail-rumours

60 Cited in "The People's Republic of China Cybersecurity Law." See also "China Internet regulator says cybersecurity law not a trade barrier," Xinhua News Agency, May 31, 2017, www.chinadaily.com.cn/business/2017-05/31/content_29563471.htm

61 See Sherisse Pham, "China's 'draconian' new cybersecurity law slammed by rights groups and businesses," CNN.com, November 7, 2016, http://money.cnn.com/2016/11/07/technology/china-cybersecurity-law/?iid=EL

62 Cited in "China Internet regulator says cybersecurity law not a trade barrier."

63 Cited in "China passes Counterespionage Law," *China Daily*, November 1, 2014, www.chinadaily.com.cn/china/2014-11/01/content_18839915.htm

64 See "The Counterespionage Law of the People's Republic of China," Xinhua News Agency, December 7, 2017, www.mod.gov.cn/regulatory/2017-12/07/content_4799261_5.htm

65 Cited in Didi Kirsten Tatlow, "China approves security law emphasizing counter-espionage," *New York Times*, November 2, 2014, www.nytimes.com/2014/11/03/world/asia/china-approves-security-law-emphasizing-counterespionage.html

66 For a discussion of how authorities are mobilizing the masses to enhance the effectiveness of the Counterespionage Law, see, for example, D.D. Wu, "Anti-espionage: a new mass line campaign in China?" *The Diplomat*, April 17, 2017, https://thediplomat. com/2017/04/anti-espionage-a-new-mass-line-campaign-in-china/. See also Simon Denyer, "To catch a spy: Beijing offers $70,000 reward — and a cartoon video to help in the hunt," *Washington Post*, April 10, 2017, www.washingtonpost.com/news/ worldviews/wp/2017/04/10/to-catch-a-spy-beijing-offers-70000-reward-and-a-ca rtoon-video-to-help-in-the-hunt/?noredirect=on&utm_term=.7e46b4251d00

67 See "People's Republic of China Counter-Terrorism Law," Xinhua News Agency, December 27, 2015, www.xinhuanet.com/politics/2015-12/27/c_128571798.htm

68 Ibid. See also "Counter-Terrorism Law of the People's Republic of China," Human Rights in China, December 2016, www.hrichina.org/en/counter-terrorism-law-peop les-republic-china

69 Cited in "China adopts first counter-terrorism law," Xinhua News Agency, December 27, 2015, www.xinhuanet.com/english/2015-12/27/c_134955905.htm

70 "China set to pass controversial anti-terrorism law," Deutsche Welle, December 22, 2015, www.dw.com/en/china-set-to-pass-controversial-anti-terrorism-law/a-18935003

71 Cited in "Regulations on Measures for the Administration of Law Firms," Gov.cn, September 6, 2016, www.gov.cn/gongbao/content/2016/content_5109321.htm

72 Ibid.

73 One recent case of a lawyer's license being revoked involved Yu Wensheng, who wrote an online missive criticizing Xi Jinping's "totalitarian" legal system. See Christian Shephard, "China rights lawyer says legal license revoked after criticizing President Xi Jinping," Reuters, January 16, 2018, www.reuters.com/article/ us-china-rights/china-rights-lawyer-says-legal-license-revoked-after-criticizing-presi dent-xi-jinping-idUSKBN1F5067

74 See "China: Justice Ministry pressures law firms; defense lawyers face new round of official scrutiny, intimidation," Human Rights Watch, New York, September 19, 2017, www.hrw.org/news/2017/09/19/china-justice-ministry-pressures-law-firms

75 See June Mai, "Chinese law firms face punishment under amended rules if lawyers exert pressure on judicial authorities," *South China Morning Post*, September 25, 2016, www.scmp.com/news/china/policies-politics/article/2022318/chinese-law-firms-fa ce-punishment-under-amended-rules

76 Cited in Yu Pinjian, "Angrily denounce the ten defects of the Regulations for the Administration of Law Firms," Yu Pinjian blog, October 16, 2016, http://blog.sina. com.cn/s/blog_4cf0b9a70102wu06.html

77 See Nectar Gan, "Chinese lawyers call for justice minister's dismissal over 'unlawful rules that violate rights,'" *South China Morning Post*, October 12, 2016, www.scmp. com/news/china/policies-politics/article/2027340/chinese-lawyers-call-justice-minis ters-dismissal-over

78 Cited in "The CCP's establishment of the 'five black categories' is slammed as an act of Nazism," *Apple Daily*, August 5, 2012, http://hk.apple.nextmedia.com/internationa l/art/20120805/16576327

79 Cited in "Make sacrifices to illuminate the future, commemorating the fifth anniversary of the founding of the China Human Rights Lawyers Group," www.chrlawyers. hk, September 13, 2018, www.chrlawyers.hk/en/content/forward-make-sacrifice s-illuminate-future-commemorating-fifth-anniversary-founding-china

80 See Didi Kirsten Tatlow, "Despite crackdown, Chinese lawyers vow to press for human rights," *New York Times*, September 16, 2015, https://sinosphere.blogs.nytim es.com/2015/09/16/china-lawyers-human-rights-crackdown/

81 See Gao Feng, "Chinese human rights attorney formally arrested for 'subversion,'" Radio Free Asia, April 20, 2018, www.rfa.org/english/news/china/lawyer-yuwen sheng-04202018135248.html

82 Author's interview with Beijing-based attorney, May 2017.

83 Author's interview with rights lawyer based in Hangzhou, January 2018.

84 Human Rights Watch has launched a campaign to put pressure on Beijing to reinstate lawyers' licenses that have been revoked. See "China: free rights lawyers, reinstate law licenses; ahead of '709' anniversary, justice minister tells lawyers to support Communist Party," Human Rights Watch, July 5, 2016, www.hrw.org/news/2018/07/05/ china-free-rights-lawyers-reinstate-law-licenses

85 Cited in "Wei Rujiu: worries about China's human rights lawyers," Gongfa.com, January 18, 2015, www.gongfa.com/html/gongfazhuanti/minquanyuweiquan/ 20150118/2759.html

86 See David Kelly, "Citizen movements and China's public intellectuals in the Hu–Wen era," *Pacific Affairs*, Vol. 79, No. 2, Summer 2006, pp. 183–204.

87 For a list of the typical cases handled by rights attorney, see, for example, Cao Yaxue, "Typical cases in which rights lawyers are involved (2003–2015)," Voice of America, August 7, 2015, www.voachinese.com/a/caoyaxue-china-lawyers-20150806/ 2904574.html

88 For a discussion of the significance of the Sun Zhigang incident, see, for example, Lam, *Chinese Politics in the Hu Jintao Era*, pp. 119–120. Also see Teng Biao, "The Sun Zhigang incident and the future of constitutionalism: does the Chinese Constitution have a future?" Occasional Paper, Centre for Rights and Justice, Faculty of Law, the Chinese University of Hong Kong, December 30, 2013, www.law.cuhk.edu.hk/en/ research/crj/download/papers/2013-tb-szg-constitutionalism.pdf

89 Ibid.

90 Cited in "A new approach to vagrancy," China.org.cn, July 4, 2003, www.china.org. cn/english/2003/Jul/68913.htm

91 For a detailed description of the first corps of lawyers who defended victims of "land grab," see "Demolished: forced evictions and the Tenants' Rights Movement in China," Human Rights Watch, March 24, 2004, www.hrw.org/report/2004/03/24/ demolished/forced-evictions-and-tenants-rights-movement-china

92 For a discussion of the unique contributions of Zheng Enchong, see, for example, "Case summary of Zheng Enchong," Committee to Support Chinese Lawyers, June 4, 2013, http://csclawyers.org/cases/ZhengEnchong/

93 For a discussion of the plight of Zheng in more recent times, see "China's rights attorneys: upholding principles in the course of wind and rain," Radio French International, Chinese Service, January 30, 2016, http://cn.rfi.fr/%E4%B8%AD%E5%9B% BD/20160130-%E4%B8%AD%E5%9B%BD%E7%BB%B4%E6%9D%83%E5%BE%8B %E5%B8%88%EF%BC%9A%E9%A3%8E%E9%9B%A8%E4%B8%AD%E7%9A%84% E5%9D%9A%E6%8C%81. See also Joseph Kahn, "Lawyer who exposed Shanghai scandal is jailed for 3 years," *New York Times*, October 28, 2003, www.nytimes.com/ 2003/10/28/international/asia/lawyer-who-exposed-shanghai-scandal-is-jailed-for-3- years.html

94 For a discussion of the early interactions between underground church leaders and rights lawyers, see, for example, Min Xia, "Rights 'crusaders' and the legal profession: the emerging civil society," *New York Times*, n.d. https://archive.nytimes.com/www. nytimes.com/ref/college/coll-china-politics-004.html

95 Ibid.

96 Chinese businesspeople are still wary of making private investments owing to improper legal protection. See, for example, Maggie Zhang, "Private investment proving to be Chinese economy's Achilles' heel," *South China Morning Post*, August 17, 2016, www.scmp.com/news/china/policies-politics/article/2001728/private-investment-p roving-be-chinese-economys-achilles

97 For a discussion of the scandal over the illegal confiscation of the private oilfields in northern Shaanxi Province, see "The case of private oilfields in Northern Shaanxi: the rights-protection movement rises again," Radio Free Asia, November 18, 2008, www. rfa.org/mandarin/yataibaodao/weiquan-11182008082136.html. See also Liu Xiaobo, "Protests on behalf of rights attorney Zhu Jiuhu," Boxun News, June 30, 2005, www. peacehall.com/news/gb/china/2005/06/200506300253.shtml

98   For a discussion of how lawyers from different provinces came to the aid of private oilfield owners, see, for example, Li Heping, "The contest and development of the case of Northern Shaanxi Oilfields and its possible directions," Aisixiang.com, September 26, 2005, www.aisixiang.com/data/8878.html

99   For a discussion of the Sun Dawu case, see, "Billionaire Sun Dawu was arrested: is it economic crime or punishment for his [political] views?" *Southern Metropolitan News*, July 11, 2003, www.people.com.cn/GB/jingji/1045/1964100.html. See also "Sun Dawu in support of rights lawyers: what can you do in the fact of terror," China Citizens Movement, July 19, 2015, https://cmcn.org/archives/20059

100 For a discussion of the Qing An case, see, for example, "Lawyers cast doubt on the results of official investigation into the Qing An shooting incident," VOA, May 15, 2015, www.voachinese.com/a/qingan-shooting-incident-questioned-20150514/2767717.html. See also "Several lawyers from Beijing's Feng Rui Law Firm have been criminally detained," *New Beijing Post*, July 12, 2015, www.xinhuanet.com/legal/2015-07/12/c_128010444.htm

101 Cited in Tan Mintao, "Lawyers intend to prosecute Qing An police, and to 'punish' those who have misused their powers," Blog of lawyer Chen Guangwu, June 6, 2015, http://blog.sina.com.cn/s/blog_63aeaff70102vsle.html. See also Hai Yan, "Qing An authorities boosted measures to uphold stability and arrested several lawyers and citizens," VOA, June 1, 2015, www.voachinese.com/a/qing-an-security-lawyers-arrest/2802865.html

102 For a discussion of the longer-term significance of the Qing An incident, see, for example, Shi Ying, "The Qing An shooting incident: the gunshot that shattered the Chinese dream," Minzhuzhongguo.org, May 15, 2015, http://minzhuzhongguo.org/MainArtShow.aspx?AID=52729

103 The high level of respect in which rights attorneys are held was demonstrated when 14 lawyers appeared on the front page of *Yazhou Zhoukang*, a weekly Hong Kong news magazine, as men of the year for the year 2005. See *Yazhou Zhoukang*, Hong Kong, December 25, 2005.

104 Cited in Fu Hualing and Richard Cullen, "Climbing the Weiquan ladder: a radicalizing process for rights-protection lawyers," *China Quarterly*, Vol. 205, March 2011, pp. 40–59.

105 For a recent description of how rights attorneys fight against the party's hard authoritarianism, see, for example, Eva Pills, *Human Rights in China: A Social Practice in the Shadows of Authoritarianism*, New York: Polity Press, 2018.

106 For a discussion of lawyer Pu's views, see, Chu Bailiang, "What were the views of rights lawyer Pu Zhiqiang that got him arrested?" *New York Times, Chinese Edition*, February 2, 2015, https://cn.nytimes.com/china/20150202/c02pu/

107 Cited in Wen Yuqing, "Pu has accused Zhou Yongkang of implementing ten years of dictatorial rule to uphold stability," Radio Free Asia, February 7, 2007, www.rfa.org/cantonese/news/complaint_a-02072013083522.html?encoding=simp

108 For a discussion of the legal and political views of Gao Zhisheng, see, Isolda Morillo, "AP interview: Chinese lawyer not giving up despite torture," Associated Press, June 14, 2016, https://apnews.com/6979d11445eb4596beb8a0367b167262/ap-interview-chinese-lawyer-not-giving-despite-torture

109 For a discussion of the involvement of Gao Zhisheng and other lawyers in the democratic movement of villagers in Tai Shi Village, Guangdong, see, for example, "China's rights attorneys elected 'men of the year,'" Radio Free Asia, December 19, 2005, www.rfa.org/mandarin/yataibaodao/weiquan-20051219.html

110 Cited in "Interview with lawyer Gao Zhisheng (10): China rulers' suppression and the response of hunger strikers from different cities," Radio Free Asia, February 18, 2006, www.rfa.org/mandarin/zhuanlan/xinlingzhilyu/zhongguominjianweiquanjishi/gaozhisheng/mind10-05152014132456.html

111 Cited in "Yellow ribbon campaign for human rights at the Olympics are concerned about the persecution of Gao Zhisheng," Radio Free Asia, November 1, 2007, www.rfa.org/mandarin/2008-Auyun/gao-20071101.html

112 Cited in "Famous rights attorney Gao Zhisheng's open letter to China's leaders," Radio Free Asia, December 12, 2005, www.rfa.org/mandarin/yataibaodao/gaozhisheng-20051212.html

113 For a description of Xu's rise to prominence as a rights attorney, see "Xi Zhiyong: I want to use action to prove that the times will definitely move forward," *Southern People Weekly*, April 18, 2006, http://finance.sina.com.cn/leadership/crz/20060418/21512510549.shtml. See also Tom Mitchell, "Xu Zhiyong, the quiet lawyer holding Beijing to account," *Financial Times*, January 25, 2014, www.ft.com/content/d9a136da-838d-11e3-86c9-00144feab7de

114 Cited in "Xu Zhiyong: for the sake of ideals and responsibility," China Citizens Movement, March 5, 2017, https://cmcn.org/archives/29101

115 See Tania Branigan, "China officials shut legal aid centre," *The Guardian*, July 18, 2009, www.theguardian.com/world/2009/jul/18/china-shuts-legal-aid-centre

116 For a discussion of the pioneering work of the New Citizens' Movement, see, for example, Michael Caster, "The contentious politics of China's New Citizens' Movement," Opendemocracy.net, June 6, 2014, www.opendemocracy.net/civilresistance/michael-caster/contentious-politics-of-china%e2%80%99s-new-citizens-movement.

117 See "Xu Zhiyong's statement in court: For the sake of freedom, justice and love," Radio Free Asia, January 22, 2014, http://cn.rfi.fr/%e9%a6%96%e9%a1%b5/20140122-%e8%ae%b8%e5%bf%97%e6%b0%b8%e6%b3%95%e5%ba%ad%e9%99%88%e8%af%8d%ef%bc%9a%e6%9c%80%e5%90%8e%e4%b8%ba%e4%ba%86%e8%87%aa%e7%94%b1%c2%b7%e5%85%ac%e4%b9%89%c2%b7%e7%88%b1.

118 Cited in He Sanwei, "Xu Zhiyong: I want to use my actions to prove that the times must be improving," *Nanfang People Weekly*, April 18, 2006, http://finance.sina.com.cn/leadership/crz/20060418/21512510549.shtml

119 Cited in Malcolm Moore, "Chinese lawyers targeted as Xi Jinping tightens control," *The Telegraph*, August 20, 2013, www.telegraph.co.uk/news/worldnews/asia/china/10254632/Chinese-lawyers-targeted-as-Xi-Jinping-tightens-control.html

120 For an overview of the massive crackdown on attorneys in July 2015, see, for example, Verna Yu, "What China's crackdown on lawyers says about authorities' fear of burgeoning rights defense movement," *South China Morning Post*, July 16, 2015, www.scmp.com/news/china/policies-politics/article/1840611/what-chinas-crackdown-lawyers-says-about-authorities. See also Andrew Jacobs and Chris Buckley, "China targeting rights lawyers in a crackdown," *New York Times*, July 22, 2015, www.nytimes.com/2015/07/23/world/asia/china-crackdown-human-rights-lawyers.html?_r=0

121 For a discussion of the careers of some of the incarcerated lawyers, see, for example, "Wang Quanzhang: human rights lawyers' database," www.chrlawyers.hk, December 31, 2017, www.chrlawyers.hk/en/content/wang-quanzhang. See also "Jailed Chinese lawyer Li Heping force-fed medication, wife says," AFP, May 24, 2017, www.straitstimes.com/asia/east-asia/jailed-chinese-lawyer-li-heping-force-fed-medication-wife-says; "Zhou Shifeng: Chinese law firm founder jailed for subversion," BBC News, August 4, 2016, www.bbc.com/news/world-asia-china-36972206; Mimi Lau and Viola Chau, "A crackdown hasn't cowed China's most prominent woman human rights lawyer," *South China Morning Post*, July 10, 2018, www.inkstonenews.com/china/chinese-human-rights-lawyer-wang-yu-remains-defiant-709-crackdown-anniversary/article/2154627

122 Cited in *2017Annual Report on China Human Rights Lawyers*, Hong Kong: China Human Rights Lawyers Concern Group, 2018, pp. 6, 20. Also see "Chinese lawyers are force-fed medications; the media cannot remain in silence," *Apple Daily*, May 20, 2017, https://hk.news.appledaily.com/local/daily/article/20170520/20027279

123 Cited in Mimi Lau, "Chinese '709' rights lawyer Wang Quanzhang stands trial as his wife is forced to stay away," *South China Morning Post*, December 27, 2018, www.scmp.com/news/china/politics/article/2179524/chinese-rights-lawyer-wang-quanzhang-court-final-case-2015. See also Lily Kuo, "Wang Quanzhang: China sentences

human rights lawyer to four years in prison," *The Guardian*, January 28, 2019, www. theguardian.com/world/2019/jan/28/wang-quanzhang-china-sentences-human-right s-lawyer-to-four-years-in-prison

124 For a discussion of the ill-treatment accorded Zhou Shifeng and his lawyer Yang Jinzhu, see, Zheng Zhou, "The 709 swoop: lawyers Zhou Shifeng and Yang Jinzhu may become new targets for suppression," New Citizens' Movement, July 23, 2016, https://cmcn.org/archives/26295. See also John Sudworth, "'I didn't see the sunlight for six months': how rights lawyer Xie Yanyi was tortured in prison," BBC Chinese Service, October 28, 2017, www.bbc.com/zhongwen/simp/chinese-news-41758287

125 Cited in "China: free rights lawyers held secretly for a year," Human Rights Watch, July 7, 2016, www.hrw.org/news/2016/07/07/china-free-rights-lawyers-held-secretly-year. Author's interview with Dr. Pils in Hong Kong, May 2018.

126 Cited in "Human rights lawyers not above the law," *Global Times*, August 8, 2014, www.globaltimes.cn/content/874997.shtml; Also see "West willfully provokes over rights lawyers," *Global Times*, July 11, 2016, www.globaltimes.cn/content/993417. shtml

127 For a discussion of the forced confessions of rights attorneys in China, see, for example, Rishi Iyengar, "Alleged confessions from detained Chinese lawyers prompt fears of an unfair trial," *Time*, July 20, 2015, http://time.com/3963913/china-lawyers-deta ined-confession-beijing-fengrui-zhou-shifeng/

128 Cited in "China is using televised confessions to shame detained lawyers, journalists and activists," Chinese Human Rights Defenders, Chrdnet.com, July 17, 2015, http://chrdnet.com/2015/07/china-is-using-televised-confessions-to-sham e-detained-lawyers-journalists-and-activists/. See also Human Rights Watch, "China: confessions, closed trials mock justice," HRW.org, August 3, 2016, www. hrw.org/news/2016/08/03/china-confessions-closed-trials-mock-justice

129 See "Wives of China's human rights lawyers protest in Beijing," BBC, July 4, 2016, www.bbc.com/news/blogs-china-blog-36704380; "Wives of detained human rights lawyers in China fight on a year after husbands held by authorities," Agence-France Press, July 7, 2016, www.scmp.com/news/china/policies-politics/article/1986569/ wives-detained-human-rights-lawyers-china-fight-year

130 For a discussion of the plight of Li Wenzu, see, for example, Wang Zhicheng, "Wife of human rights lawyer on 100 km march to break the silence on husband's arrest," Asianews.it, April 5, 2018, www.asianews.it/news-en/Wife-of-human-rights-lawyer-on-100-km-march-to-break-the-silence-on-husband's-arrest-43535.html. See also "Li Wenzu, wife of disappeared lawyer Wang Quanzhang, was sent back to Beijing," Radio French International, April 9, 2018, http://cn.rfi.fr/%E4%B8%AD%E5%9B% BD/20180409-%E7%BB%B4%E6%9D%83%E5%BE%8B%E5%B8%88%E7%8E%8B% E5%85%A8%E7%92%8B709%E5%A4c%B1%E8%81%941000%E5%A4%A9%E5% 85%B6%E5%A6%BB%E6%9D%8E%E6%96%87%E8%A6%B3%E5%A4%A9%E6% B4%A5%E5%AF%BB%E5%A4%AB%E9%81%AD%E9%81%A3%E4%BA%AC

131 For a description of the maltreatment of Wang Yu while in jail, see, for example, Michael Caster, *The People's Republic of the Disappeared*, New York: Safeguard Defenders, 2017, pp. 65–84. For a discussion of threats being made against Wang's son, see "Teenage son of Chinese lawyer arrested as crackdown sweeps China," News.com.au, July 22, 2015, www.news.com.au/finance/work/leaders/teenage-son-of-chinese-la wyer-arrested-as-crackdown-sweeps-china/news-story/ 304cb5849fb006e9fbdc9f84c4437a98

132 See *2017 Annual Report on China Human Rights Lawyers*, p. 19–21. See also "Son of detained rights lawyers arrives in Australia after battle to leave China," Radio Free Asia, January 18, 2018, www.rfa.org/english/news/china/lawyer-son-01182018140246.html

133 For a discussion of Wang's indictment and its implications for the Chinese civil society, see, for example, "Chinese human rights lawyer tried in secret on subversion charges," Radio Free Asia, December 26, 2018, www.rfa.org/english/news/china/chinese-huma n-rights-lawyer-tried-in-secret-12262018104855.html. See also Peter Dahlin, "Statement

on Wang Quanzhang's indictment," rsdlmonitor.com, December 26, 2018, http://rsdlm onitor.com/statement-wang-quanzhangs-indictment-peter-dahlin/

134 Author's interview with lawyer in Guangzhou, May 2017.

135 Author's interview with lawyer in Shanghai, March 2018.

136 Author's interview with Hangzhou-based lawyer, October 2017.

137 See "Full signatures of the 08 Charter Movement," *China Digital Times*, n.d., https://china digitaltimes.net/space/%E3%80%8A%E9%9B%B6%E5%85%AB%E5%AE%AA%E7%AB %A0%E3%80%8B%E7%AD%BE%E5%90%8D%E4%BA%BA%E5%91%98%E5%90% 8D%E5%8D%95%E6%B1%87%E6%80%BB%EF%BC%88%E5%85%B1%E4%BA% 94%E6%89%B9%EF%BC%89

138 Author's interview with Shenzhen lawyer, January 2018.

139 Author's interview with lawyer in Xiamen, November 2017.

140 For a discussion of Xu Zhiyong's political ideals, see Xu Xing "Xu Zhiyong and the New Citizens' Movement," *Open Magazine* (Hong Kong), September 7, 2013, www. open.com.hk/content.php?id=1485#.W_kNj_ZuLbJ

141 Ibid.

142 For a sampling of the views of Li Boguang, see, for example, "Chinese rights attorney passed away under suspicious circumstances: he is seen as a 'Hunan mule' by his friends," BBC news, February 27, 2018, www.bbc.com/zhongwen/simp/chinese-news-43207806

143 Author's interview with Guangdong lawyer, in February 2018.

144 Cited in "He Waifang: the role of a public intellectual," Aisixiang.com, November 17, 2011, www.aisixiang.com/data/46717.html

145 Cited in "Wei Rujiu."

146 Cited in "Case 20 of suppressed attorneys: Beijing lawyer Zhu Jiuhu," Aisixiang.com, May 20, 2014, www.aisixiang.com/data/7599.html

147 Cited in Cao Zhi, "The logic of the movement of Chinese lawyers," Aisixiang, May 14, 2015, www.bdppfw.com/data/87928.html

148 Author's interview with Professor Xia, September 2017.

149 Cited in Verna Yu, "China's crackdown." See also Bochen Han, "China's human rights lawyers: political resistance and the law; Eva Pils on the shrinking space China's rights lawyers have to operate within," *The Diplomat*, February 11, 2016, http://thedip lomat.com/2016/02/chinas-human-rights-lawyers-political-resistance-and-the-law/

4

A NEW AWAKENING FOR CHINA'S OPPRESSED CHRISTIANS

Introduction: Christians' fight against the party's unremitting suppression

According to public intellectual Xiao Jiansheng, "one of the biggest flaws of the Chinese mentality is that Chinese do not have religious beliefs." In his remarkable work *Chinese History Revisited*, Xiao wrote that "Christianity has played a critical role in the establishment of democratic and constitutional institutions in the [Western] political order."[1] CCP founder Chen Duxiu indicated that Christianity was the "foundation and propellant of Western Civilization." Chen noted in a 1921 article that, "I hope to instill in our blood the lofty and great personality of Jesus, in addition to his profound passion."[2]

The growing popularity of Christianity after the Cultural Revolution (1966–1976) – particularly the proliferation of underground or "house" churches – is one of the most significant social-cultural phenomena in contemporary Chinese history. There is no concrete evidence that the majority of the estimated 80 million Protestants and Catholics have joined the church so as to seek sociopolitical changes. It is, however, obvious that the Christian faith has filled a spiritual vacuum caused by Chinese people's wholesale loss of faith in the ideals of socialism and communism.[3]

Unlike dissidents, human rights lawyers and NGO activists – who make up a small percentage of the population – the number of Christians and Catholics is overwhelming. President and CCP General Secretary Xi Jinping, who seems paranoid about "destabilizing forces" in society, has adopted increasingly draconian tactics to control both "legal" and underground Christians. Xi has repeatedly warned of "hostile anti-China forces in the West" colluding with religious groups in China to wreak havoc on the CCP and its legitimacy. As Xi pointed out, whether "religious questions" are correctly handled "has a direct impact on the development of socialism with Chinese characteristics … on social harmony, unity of the nationalities, state security and national unification."[4] Using Maoist language, Wang Zuo'an, the director of the State Administration of Religious Affairs (SARA) – a ministerial-level unit under the party's Central United Front Work Department (CUFWD) that deals with all Chinese religions – said the relationship between the authorities and Christianity was characterized by both "contradictions between ourselves and the enemy" and "contradictions among the people." In the Maoist tradition, contradictions between the party and its enemies could only be resolved through the thorough elimination of the "enemies."[5]

Xi's policy toward Christianity and other creeds is significantly different from that of his predecessors Jiang Zemin and Hu Jintao. There is no doubt that the two former presidents were keen to prevent foreign religions from subverting CCP power. Yet both Jiang and Hu also indicated that Christians should be encouraged to make contributions to the economic modernization of China. It is Xi who started the policy of the sinicization of Christianity – to change the nature of Western religions and render them "Chinese" – so that Christianity could, somewhat like Buddhism, be transformed into a creed that would prop up the orthodoxy of the powers that be.

The forced removal of more than 1,500 crosses from churches – including state-sanctioned places of worship – in coastal Zhejiang Province has testified to the Xi leadership's brutal tactics. Moreover, large numbers of church personnel – as well as lawyers supportive of churches – have been incarcerated on trumped-up charges of embezzlement and other "economic crimes." Although the majority of church leaders and believers seem to have been cowed into silence, a significant number of Christians have undergone a kind of baptism of fire. Convinced that there can be no religious freedom until the authoritarian Chinese system is drastically reformed, politicized members of the congregations are determined to fight back.

Meanwhile, there is evidence that the outwardly fierce Xi administration is afraid that even party members have succumbed to the siren songs of foreign religions. In February 2016, the party's Central Committee and State Council issued a circular ordering retired officials never to succumb to the appeal of religion. The document stated that, "retired cadres cannot believe in religion, cannot participate in religious activities and must resolutely fight against cults." Retired officials must distinguish between "ethnic customs" and "believing in religions," it said.[6] Previously, only personnel serving in the machinery of the dictatorship of the proletariat – soldiers, PAP officers and the police – were forbidden to have beliefs other than Marxism-Leninism. One year later, it was announced that no party members must be allowed to become a convert to any religion. In a July 2017 article in the party theoretical journal Seeking Truth, SARA's Wang warned that, "party members are not allowed to have religious beliefs." "This is a red line which each party member must not touch," he added. This top religious commissar added that party members must observe Marxist atheism. "They must never seek in religion their own values and beliefs."[7] The authorities have a good reason to be nervous about the spread of religion among cadres and party members. According to surveys conducted in 2007 by Purdue University's Center on Religion and Chinese

Society, 84 percent of party members admitted to some kind of religious belief, including Christianity.[8]

This chapter looks at the religious policy of ex-Presidents Jiang Zemin and Hu Jintao – and particularly that of President Xi Jinping. How Christians react to Beijing's efforts to "sinicize" and "harmonize" Western religions will be analyzed. To sharpen the focus of the discussion, this report will lay emphasis mainly on Protestants, who outnumber Catholics by a ratio of five to one.[9] Questions will be asked as to the extent to which the Xi administration's tough tactics have politicized and, in some cases, even radicalized the believers – and what impact the reawakened churches will have on the development of the civil society and the latter's determination to promote human rights and political liberalization.

Christianity's perceived threat to the regime

The CCP has never been reticent about what it perceives to be imperialistic powers – now referred to as "hostile anti-China forces" – using religion to infiltrate China and subvert the rule of the party. Almost immediately after the establishment of the PRC, then-Premier Zhou Enlai told religious figures, including Christian leaders, to "cut off links with the imperialists." "We want churches in China to be run by Chinese," he said. "Materialists and non-materialists can cooperate and co-exist politically," he said. Although Zhou warned that "black sheep in religious circles and the extreme minority of running dogs and Judases should be flushed out," the relatively moderate leader noted that, "there would be no [political] movements against Christians."[10] This promise, of course, was broken during the waves of anti-Christian movements in the 1950s and throughout the Cultural Revolution. Even after a more "rational" policy toward Christianity was introduced by ex-Presidents Jiang Zemin and Hu Jintao, several aged Catholic bishops and priests continued to languish in jail.[11]

Since the end of the Cultural Revolution, CCP authorities have used official and quasi-official entities to ensure that Christians do not step out of line. At the apex of the party-state apparatus are two organs handling religious issues: SARA and the State Ethnic Affairs Commission (SEAC), which are both subsumed under the higher-level CUFWD, which is headed by Politburo member You Quan. SARA and, to a lesser extent, SEAC map out major policies under policy guidance from the CUFWD. (Both SARA and SEAC used to be ministerial-level units under the State Council; they became party organs in March 2018 – as adjuncts of the CUFWD – in accordance with Xi's teachings about the party being supreme.)[12] At the regional levels, provincial, municipal and county-level *minzuzongjiao shiwuju* (ethnic and religious affairs offices; ERAOs) are charged with implementation of the policies of SARA while at the same time receiving policy guidance from the party-state apparatus of the same level of government.[13] The two state-sanctioned religious bodies under SARA – the Three-Self Patriotic Movement (TSPM) of the Protestant Churches in China and the China Christian Council (CCC; collectively known as the *lianghui* or "two associations") – serve as a conduit between administrations of various levels and the churches.[14] Except for harassing or detaining the leaders and members of underground or house churches, the country's *zhengfa* ("political and legal") apparatus – which includes the MPS, the MSS and the para-military PAP – was usually not heavily involved in religious affairs during the Jiang Zemin and Hu Jintao eras.

In theory, Xi has not closed the door to seeking a dialogue and even reconciliation with the Vatican and Protestant organizations. A breakthrough in Vatican–CCP relations was reached in the autumn of 2018, involving an unpublicized arrangement for the joint appointment of bishops. Earlier in the year, a senior Vatican official told the Reuters News Agency that, "It is not a great agreement but we don't know what the situation will be like in 10 or 20 years. It could even be worse." The source added that, after mutual recognition between the Vatican and China, "we will still be like a bird in a cage but the cage will be bigger."[15] Hong Kong's outspoken Cardinal Joseph Zen, however, has blasted advisers to the Pope for failing to ensure that both "legal" and underground Catholics would get more protection after the proposed diplomatic deal. "Better no deal than a bad deal," the cardinal told the Catholic media. He added that, in recent years, the Vatican policy had left the church in China "much weakened than before." This has harmed our negotiating power, Zen said, as "from a weak position you cannot get anything in a negotiation."[16]

Sheer numbers – and a close-knit organization – amount to a threat

Numbers matter. Every year, the CCP's Organization Department publishes the latest tally of party members. And even though some Xi advisers once mentioned plans to whittle down unqualified and undesirable members, the party still spends tremendous resources recruiting college students, young professionals and businesspeople. It is clear, however, that the number of Christians will soon overtake CCP affiliates. According to official statistics, there were, in the year 2011, 23 million Protestants attending "official" as well as house churches.[17] Yet senior religious bureaucrats have admitted privately that there could be more than 70 million Christian converts, 80 percent of whom are rural citizens.[18]

Western estimates are much higher than official Chinese ones. The Pew Research Center's Forum on Religion and Public Life pointed out that there were, in 2010, more than 58 million Protestants in China compared with 40 million in Brazil and 36 million in South Africa.[19] Professor Fenggang Yang, a sociologist at Purdue University, believes that the total Chinese congregation will swell to around 160 million by 2025. That would likely put China ahead even of the United States, which had around 159 million Protestants in 2010. "By my calculations China is destined to become the largest Christian country in the world very soon," Professor Yang said. "It is going to be less than a generation. Not many people are prepared for this dramatic change."[20]

The party-state apparatus in China, however, is well prepared. Among Chinese officials who are nervously watching the proliferation of Christians – and actively preparing to quell the influence of Western religion – are senior cadres in charge of state security and propaganda. Apart from sheer numbers, the party leadership is paranoid about organization per se. Since Deng Xiaoping initiated the Reform and Open-Door policy in 1978, there have been relatively liberal periods when dissident intellectuals were allowed to publish articles in print or electronic media that were critical of the regime. However, once these members of the opposition crossed the "red line" by organizing a political party or some form of regular organization, the quasi-police-state apparatus immediately swung into action.[21] As Li Xiaobai, a pastor in Beijing's Shouwang Church, pointed out: "China's rulers have always considered congregations of masses as a big threat." It was reported that one reason why the Qing Dynasty forbade the opening of large mines was the fear of large congregations of people.[22]

The CCP's reaction to religious organizations with a national network was fully illustrated by ex-President Jiang Zemin's pogrom against the quasi-Buddhist Falun Gong organization, which first came to prominence in the early 1980s. The party took a largely tolerant attitude toward the sect, partly because a relatively large number of prominent retired cadres and even scientists were adherents. However, the Falun Gong made a mistake by showing off their political strength on April 25, 1999, when they staged a daring sit-in demonstration: more than 10,000 members surrounded the Zhongnanhai Party Headquarters. After this show of political muscle, however, the CCP reacted with brutal force.[23]

One of the ways in which Beijing and the official church authorities have controlled Christians is by restricting the activities of clergy and congregation to their specific *muqu*, or parishes. Three-Self churches in different counties and cities are not supposed to liaise – let alone set up formal organizations – with colleagues in other *muqu*. Cross-provincial religious activities are discouraged, if not banned outright. This is in accordance with the well-practiced principle of "fixed venues, fixed personnel, and fixed localities." This stipulates that worship activities must be held in designated venues, missionaries and clerics must be licensed or registered with local authorities, and church personnel must work in their designated locality. The last stricture also means that church personnel must not attempt to set up organizations that span villages, districts, cities or provinces.[24]

Many churches – particularly house churches – however, have defied governmental restrictions by establishing province-wide or even cross-provincial organizations. The China Gospel Fellowship (CGF; *zhonghua fuyin tuanqi*), a denomination with Pentecostal leanings that practices faith-healing, is a good example. Although it originated in a rural county in central Henan province, the CGF has spread throughout the province and won converts throughout China. Estimates of its affiliates range up to 7 million.[25] "Teams lived and worked in accordance with the frugal and egalitarian 'Spirit of Yan'an,'" wrote Christian scholar Karrie J. Koesel. "They sought to broaden their base through face-to-face interaction with peasants, and armed themselves only with ideology." Koesel noted that one reason CCP authorities might harbor misgivings about cross-provincial church movements is that there are similarities between the organization and networking of Christian *tuanqi* and the underground CCP cells before the party came to power in 1949. The CGF also followed the Maoist strategy of "surrounding the cities from the countryside" when it spread from the villages to the cities. Different units are often insulated from each other both horizontally and vertically, so that, when one unit is put down by the authorities, the damage to the activities of other units is kept to a minimum. "The Church's organizational structure became its greatest asset when navigating the inhospitable landscape" of a country dominated by authoritarian one-party rule, Koesel wrote.[26]

"Collusion with foreign forces"

As indicated in Chapter 1, President Xi Jinping cited 11 major threats to national security, which included Western ideology and religious beliefs. He particularly highlighted the danger emanating from the collusion between anti-party forces within China and "anti-China foreign forces."[27] This is despite the fact that, in the early phase of the Reform and Open-Door Policy, Deng Xiaoping's views about Western religions were relatively mild. Perhaps in view of the damage to churches, monasteries and mosques during the Cultural Revolution, Deng advocated relatively tolerant measures toward Christians and members of other religions. The Deng leadership's religious policies were spelt out in a 1982 party document, "On our country's fundamental viewpoints and fundamental policies regarding religious questions in the socialism period" (known as Party Document 19). "The party's fundamental policy toward religious issues is to respect and protect freedom of religious belief," Document 19 said. "And this is a long-term policy." The paper warned, however, against "infiltration by all types of enemy forces within foreign religions."[28] Deng's views toward religion noticeably hardened after seeing the role of the Catholic and Christian churches in undermining Communist parties in Eastern Europe in the 1980s.

Chinese suspicions were also aroused by statements made by prominent U.S. personalities who visited churches during their China tours. While visiting the Chinese capital for the 2008 Summer Olympics, then-President George W. Bush toured the Kuanjie Protestant Church. "I feel very strongly about religion," Bush said, adding that the church visit had instilled in him a "spirit-filled feeling." Bush added that, "it just goes to show that God is universal, God is love and no state, man or woman should fear the influence of loving religion."[29] And, during a visit to China in 2015, then-U.S. First Lady Michelle Obama hinted at concerns over religious freedom in China. She told a student gathering: "When it comes to expressing yourself freely, and worshipping as you choose, and having open access to information – we believe those are universal rights that are the birthright of every person on this planet."[30]

Although the CCP has long regarded Protestantism and Catholicism as ideological agents geared toward infiltrating China and undermining socialism, the Xi administration has raised counter-infiltration to the highest level of national security. As Professor Ying Fuk-tsang of the Divinity School of the Chinese University of Hong Kong put it, the recent suppression of both official and house churches represented "a return of the Cold War mentality." He cited the Chinese leadership's concern about "religious infiltration, state security, and ideological struggle" as clear-cut indications of the Maoist mentality of the Xi leadership. Illustrative of the CCP's siege mentality was the controversial documentary *The Silent Contest* put out by the National Defense University in 2013. Ying said the video warned that the party and state apparatus must take measures against "surreptitious missionary activities" and "the infiltration of Western religious systems into the lower stratums of Chinese society."[31]

Yet another influential article revealing the Western "conspiracy" behind missionary work was theorist Wang Xiaoshi's 2014 piece in the hawkish *Global Times*, where he asserted that Christianity was a key American weapon to "bring down and win over China." Wang argued that the U.S. was "using Christianity as a cloak to spread American political views and values." "Using religious freedom as a shield," Wang wrote, "parties in the U.S. are doing political brainwash in an effort to subvert the masses' identification with the legitimacy of the Chinese Communist administration."[32]

Church leaders – and lawyers who defend the churches – have been harassed or detained for "colluding with foreign forces." A case in point was Christian lawyer Zhang Kai, who was arrested in Zhejiang in August 2015 shortly before he was due to meet with an official from the U.S. State Department. He was accused of "stealing, spying into, purchasing, or illegally providing state secrets or intelligence" to foreign actors and "disturbing public order." In a televised confession in February 2016, Zhang, who represented dozens of churches in their fight against persecution, confessed to making a fortune through receiving "consultancy fees" of at least a few thousand yuan from each church.[33] Yet Zhang's biggest "crime" was perhaps his relationship with foreign Christian organizations, including China Aid, a U.S.-based NGO active in promoting religious freedom in China. Zhang admitted in his confession – which was likely made under duress – that he had received donations from China Aid, an organization that was determined to "change China's political system."[34]

One sign of Beijing's nervousness about "collusion" between Chinese and foreign Christians is much closer scrutiny of the activities of Hong Kong Special Administrative Region's (SAR) 1,500 churches, about 60 percent of which had outreach programs on the mainland. Mainland pastors and believers are often barred from attending international Christian conferences in the SAR. Staff in both official and house churches have found it more difficult to obtain permission to attend seminaries in Hong Kong to gain degrees in divinity. Cases of active Hong Kong pastors being summoned to Shenzhen for lectures by cadres of SARA have also been reported.[35] The Liaison Office of the Central People's Government in the Hong Kong SAR (usually referred to as the Central Liaison Office), which is Beijing's de facto mission in Hong Kong, periodically performs "united front work" by inviting Christian leaders and scholars for talks in its well-guarded head office near Hong Kong's Central District.[36]

The spread of Christianity in the countryside – and rural cadres' failure to stem the tide

The Xiu Yuan or Longway Foundation, a think tank made up of mainstream scholars and business leaders that was registered with the Beijing Civil Affairs Bureau in 2009, undertook fairly extensive surveys of the Christian Church in different parts of China in 2013 and 2014. It published a lengthy report in September 2014 entitled *The State of Western Religions Spreading in Chinese Villages* (hereafter "Report"). Xiu Yuan researchers found that Christian churches had made speedy progress in rural areas in provinces north of the Yangtze, where 10–15 percent of the population had fallen for the siren songs of Christianity. In individual villages, as many as 95 percent of residents believed in one form or other of Christianity. Most disturbing, said the report, was that, in these villages, "the underground church [house church or 'cult'] held sway over 70 percent of Christians." "Traditional forms of beliefs in northern villages are crumbling," it said. "They are unable to meet the large-scale spiritual needs of the people." The situation was somewhat better in the villages in southern China. Yet the study found that, "[traditional] systems of beliefs in the south are also in the process of unravelling." "Antigens against Western religions are being cast into doubt and jettisoned by the people," the paper added.[37]

Xiu Yuan analysts have also detected increasing sophistication with which missionaries and church personnel try to boost recruitment. "Teachers of the faith firstly target disadvantaged sectors in society, including retirees, women, and poor families," the Report said. "Afterwards, they pay more attention to young people, intellectuals and people with high [social] positions." The church also provided education, medical treatment and other services that are beyond the reach of peasants.[38] Despite oft-repeated boasts by the party that it will, by 2020, lift all destitute Chinese out of poverty, living conditions in many parts of China, including the three northeast rust-belt provinces, are poor.

Xiu Yuan's survey of Henan Province, long a bastion of different Christian denominations, was particularly significant. It pointed out that, as of 2003, more than 4 million residents belonged to Three-Self churches. There were 2,411 churches, in addition to 3,402 "meeting areas." However, adherents to house churches were "more than double" those who patronized official places of worship. Most of the believers were in the age group of 35–50. Although worshipping ancestors at temples was still practiced, the Report noted that the religious components of such activities had diminished – and that remembering forebears had become a mere act of filial piety instead of a religion. These trends were reflected in the other provinces. One interesting phenomenon was the increase in young worshippers, as well as female believers. The Report noted that, in a Shaanxi rural township, "women who became Christians in the 1980s did not have the courage to admit their faith in front of strangers." "After just ten years, they feel that [being Christians] is a badge of honor," the paper added.[39]

At the same time, grassroots party and government administrations seem disinclined and ill-equipped to handle the onslaught of the Christian soldiers. Since the start of the reform era, the state has beaten a retreat from the villages; grassroots administrations have withdrawn from both the public and the private arenas of rural life. "The great majority of functions regarding social management and construction have been given to rural society," the Report said. "The rights of the people have advanced even as state power is in recess. The state has also retreated from the private sphere, including the psychological and spiritual aspects of families and individuals."[40] Equally irksome to the authorities is the fact that it is not uncommon for village cadres to become Christians. "The ease with which we do missionary work in rural areas varies from area to area," according to a Guangdong-based house church poster. "In one village, the authorities might threaten to lock us up. Yet in the next village, we find that the Head of the Village Administration Committee is a fervent Christian and we have no problem with the police there."[41]

A survey of female Christians in rural Zhejiang conducted in the early 2010s by sociologist Wang Hongfang showed that they derived immense spiritual satisfaction from worshipping in house churches. Wang, who teaches at Jinhua Polytechnic in Zhejiang, estimated that 60–70 percent of Christians in villages in the province were women – and that those below 50 were gaining in numbers. For example, in Huaqiao Village near Wenzhou, 52 percent of female Christians were under 39 years of age. They were also better educated than previously thought. Twenty-three percent of the faithful surveyed had high school education or above. "A good proportion of interviewees chose to believe because they are moved by the moral attributes of Christians," Wang wrote. Among villagers who faced economic pressures or who felt lonely, Christianity offered a relief because "they could let Jesus Christ handle their sufferings." That Christianity is expected to remain a viable force can be attested to by the fact that, according to Wang, 58 percent of female Christians "occasionally or often engaged in missionary work."[42]

Rationale behind the suppression

Policies under ex-Presidents Jiang Zemin and Hu Jintao

Following long-standing CCP precepts, former-President Jiang, who was in power from 1989 to 2002, repeatedly warned against "hostile anti-China forces" using religion to infiltrate China and to undermine the CCP rule. One of his major instructions regarding the treatment of Christianity and other religions was "to enthusiastically provide instruction to religions [so as to render them] compatible with a socialist society."[43] He cited two ways of achieving this. One was to ensure that "the activities of religious [organizations] must be within the parameters of the law." Second, he indicated, "religious activities must be subsumed under – and they must provide service to – the highest interests of the state and the comprehensive interests of the people." "People in the religious sector should be patriotic, progressive, and they should make more contributions to national reunification, the unity of the nationalities and social development," he said.[44]

From more perspectives than one, however, the Jiang administration could be interpreted as having softened the party-state's policy toward religions, including Christianity. Jiang was a fervent Buddhist who visited monasteries during the Chinese New Year and other occasions. Christian churches, in addition to Buddhist ones, were the targets of "united front work," meaning that they would be co-opted by the party-state authorities in order to promote stability and national unity and to make contribution to the economy. "The principle under which we handle relations with our religious friends is unity and cooperation in politics and mutual respect in the areas of thoughts and beliefs," Jiang said in 1991. "We respect each other in terms of ideas and beliefs. And this will never change."[45] More significant was the fact that Jiang warned against using "leftist" – meaning "ultra-conservative" or Maoist-style – tactics against religion. "We should not use a 'leftist' attitude toward religious beliefs just because Communists are atheists," he said in 1990. "We cannot indiscriminately interfere with the beliefs of non-party members. Otherwise, the relationship between the party and masses with religious beliefs will be hurt, and stability and unity [of the nation] will be affected."[46]

Optimistic interpreters of Jiang's dictum could even come to the conclusion that the CCP did not discriminate between officially registered churches and underground places of worship. In a 1999 book titled *Tell the American People the Real Situation of Religion in China*, then SARA chief Ye Xiaowen said that, although the government wanted all unofficial churches to register themselves, "this registration is voluntary, not obligatory." Whether churches are officially registered or not is not a criterion for determining whether laws have been broken. He added that, "whether [the churches] are registered or not, they [believers] can pursue prayers and reading from the bible."[47]

Jiang's stance toward religion was largely unchanged under the Hu Jintao administration (2002–2012). This was despite the fact that Beijing's policy toward creeds it considers toxic and dangerous – particularly Tibetan Buddhism in the Tibet Autonomous Region (TAR) and Islam in the Xinjiang Uighur Autonomous Region (XUAR) – undertook a harsh turn. After all, one reason why Hu was chosen in 1992 by Deng Xiaoping as a future general secretary was his ruthless suppression of "splittists" and "rioters" in Lhasa just a few months before the Tiananmen Square massacre in 1989.[48]

The Hu leadership's policy toward Christians could be discerned from a SARA circular issued in 2011, one year before Hu's departure from the scene. "We must strengthen the regularization and management of the activities of Christians," the circular said. It noted that members of house churches and other underground congregations must be incorporated in "registered worship places" so that religious activities could be held in a "normal and organized" manner. "We must support religious sectors to discover and develop the concept of harmony in their religious doctrines, culture and morality," the paper added. Although SARA warned against "hostile forces outside China using religion to undertake infiltration activities [against the party]," there were during the Hu era relatively few cases of the authorities deploying police to detain believers or to damage church properties.

Nor was there any attempt to sinicize Christianity or to inject "socialism with Chinese characteristics" into Christian doctrines.[49]

Ex-President Hu's policy of relative restraint was demonstrated in a speech on united front work in 2006. Following past leaders, Hu underscored the imperative of "ensuring that the broad masses of believers will support the leadership of the CCP and the socialist order." The fourth-generation leader also repeated the need for "compatibility between religion and the socialist society." However, he urged cadres responsible for united front work and religious affairs to "help and support different religious bodies to *jiaqiang zishen jiangshe* ['strengthen their self-construction']," thus at least giving a hint that religious organizations should have some leeway in pursuing faith-related work. Hu also urged relevant party cadres to "comprehensively and correctly implement the party's policy regarding the freedom of religion, insist upon unity and cooperation in political [issues] and mutual respect in terms of beliefs."[50] Hu Jintao's *Political Report to the 17th Party Congress* of 2007 painted religious groups in a largely positive light. Hu noted that, "we must bring into play the positive function of personnel in religious sectors and the masses of believers in promoting economic and social development."[51]

At a Politburo study session on religious policy held after the Party Congress, Hu noted that, "we must as much as possible unite all [sociopolitical] forces that can be united, and give play to all positive factors that could be deployed." The fourth-generation leader stressed that, "we must develop the positive effect of religious personages and the masses of believers ... in comprehensively building up a relatively prosperous society." Hu, one of whose major political slogans was "constructing a harmonious society" also dwelled on the party's intention to "assiduously develop the positive role of religion in promoting social harmony [so as] to materialize the wholesome situation of religion and society getting along harmoniously ... and the general public who are believers getting along harmoniously with non-believers." Overall, Hu has continued Jiang's key dictum on religions, including Christianity – that is, "seeking unity and cooperation in politics, and [maintaining] mutual respect regarding beliefs."[52]

The relatively liberal trend was evidenced in a quasi-official document called *Storming Fortifications: A Research Report on the Reform of China's Political Structure after the 17th Party Congress* (hereafter *Research Report*), which was written by professors from the Central Party School and other leading universities. *Research Report* said that, "in the area of social construction, the negative impact of religions is decreasing while the positive impacts are increasing." "We must not render political beliefs into something religious," the document added. "At the same time, we should not politicize religious beliefs." This essentially meant that there should not be excessive political interference in the activities of believers.[53]

Xi Jinping's new harsh deal

Xi Jinping has applied the broadest definition to the term "cultural security," which includes preventing religious, political and other ideas from the West from infiltrating

China. As Vancouver-based minister Hong Yujian pointed out, so-called "cultural security" is being used by the Communist Party "to manufacture a closed cultural environment through eliminating dissident culture and through negating the principle of cultural pluralism." "The authorities are afraid of freedom," he added. "They can only feel security through thought control and the closing [of the Chinese mind]."[54]

Xi's policy toward religions ranging from Tibetan Buddhism to Christianity has taken a significantly leftist and ultra-conservative turn since he gained power in late 2012. The supreme leader's views on religion were made known in April 2016, when Xi held what was regarded as the highest-level-ever national conference on religion. All PBSC members, together with representatives from different department and regions were on hand. Xi underscored the imperative of the party's ironclad control over all religions, including Christianity.[55] "In handling relations with religions, we must tightly uphold the leadership of the party and consolidate the party's leading position," he said. While Xi noted that religions must never interfere with the country's administration, judiciary or education departments, he said, "[we must] insist on the government's management of religious affairs [in areas involving] state interests and society's public interests." For the first time in the party's history, Xi insisted that all religions observe – and incorporate into their teachings – "core socialist values." The party chief instructed that adherents of religions and creeds should "support CCP leadership, embrace the socialist order, insist upon going down the road of socialism with Chinese characteristics, and enthusiastically implement socialist core values." Although, in this and other speeches, Xi went through the motions of repeating the dictums of his predecessors – "seeking unity and cooperation in politics, and [maintaining] mutual respect regarding beliefs" – there seemed little doubt that he demanded absolute obedience to party edicts.[56]

In a speech at the headquarters of UNESCO in Paris, Xi noted that, for the past millennia, three belief and cultural systems – Confucianism, Taoism and Buddhism – had had the most profound impact on Chinese civilization. He singled out Buddhism as having made the best contribution to the flowering of China's culture. Xi said of the three creeds, "Buddhism has had a relatively benevolent development."

> Buddhism has become the most important *zaiti* ['receptacle and embodiment'] of the renaissance of Chinese culture. ... Chinese Buddhism since the new millennium has developed a cultural consciousness and it has on its own initiative plunged itself into the historical currents regarding the creative transformation and the innovative development of Chinese civilization.[57]

This betrays the views of Xi and other top leaders that Christianity should emulate Buddhism by seeking the patronage of the powers that be and by incorporating quintessential Chinese values into its development.

Former SARA chief Ye Xiaowen, who is noted for his hawkish views, has compared sinicized foreign religions to the children of mixed marriages. Yet the emphasis is on control by the reigning authorities, meaning the CCP. "God's ways must follow *rendao* ['the people's way'], and God's power must be dependent on political power," he said in a 2015 speech. Similar to Xi, Ye saluted Buddhism as the creed that has best served the *rendao*. "As a foreign culture, Buddhism has after multiple failures found its rebirth," he said. "This is due to Buddhism's capacity to adapt itself to the development of Chinese society through making ceaseless internal and external adjustments." There is little doubt that these "adjustments" referred to individual monks' and nuns' willingness to follow the political leadership of the party.[58]

The sinicization of Christianity

Xi has radically changed the policy of relative acquiescence toward the churches, or at least religious organizations not seen as posing frontal threats to national stability. In theory, he has cleaved to the dictum used by both his predecessors: "provide positive guidance to [ensure] the compatibility between religions and socialist society." Yet the "core leader" of the party was the first CCP general secretary to have coined the slogan: "We must uphold the direction of the *zhongguohua* ['sinicization'] of religion."[59] At a Central United Front Work Conference of May 2015, Xi made his much harsher policy toward religions – particularly those that originated in the West – crystal clear. He laid down this "four must-dos" policy:

> We must uphold the direction of *zhongguohua* ['sinicization']; we must uphold the legal level of religious work; we must dialectically view the social function of religion; we must put emphasis on developing the [sociopolitical] functions of members of religious circles.[60]

Of the four instructions, "sinicization" is the most important – and has the farthest-reaching consequences for state–church relations. The supreme leader wants to subsume the churches – Christian doctrines and Christian activities – under not only the authority of the party-state, but also the kind of culture with Chinese characteristics that is promoted by the Xi leadership. Zhi Jiangping, an official commentator for *Zhejiang Daily*, noted in an article in mid-2015 that the "direction of sinicization of religion means the political affirmation [of the socialist order], compatibility with Chinese society, and assimilation with Chinese culture."[61] Or, as one house church activist from Shandong Province told this author: "Xi is a keen promoter of Chinese culture with socialist characteristics." "He wants to change the nature of the Christian church by injecting into it elements of Chinese civilization and the Chinese way of doing things," he added.[62]

The modus operandi for realizing the sinicization of Christianity was made clear in a speech given by Wang Zuo'an to religious figures in Beijing at the end of 2014. The SARA chief urged Christians to "continue to push forward the construction of theological thought, and to discover contents where Christian doctrines are *xiangtong* [compatible] with the core values of socialism." "We must counter efforts by [forces] outside China to use Christianity to infiltrate China ... and we must provide leadership to believers to make contributions to the realization of the Chinese Dream," he added.[63] It must be noted that there is a big difference between "rendering Christianity compatible with Chinese society" (which was the norm under Jiang and Hu), on the one hand, and "rendering Christianity compatible with the core values of socialism," on the other. The former merely meant that Christian doctrines and activities must not disrupt Chinese society; the latter called for making changes in Christian dogma and practice so that they would dovetail with the CCP's socialist values and policies. Moreover, Wang for the first time made a linkage between the evolution of Christianity in China and the realization of the Chinese dream, which is President Xi's super-nationalistic slogan about the "great renaissance of the Chinese people."[64]

"The Path of the Sinicization of Christianity" was the title of a conference held in Beijing in November 2015. Although the organizers were the China Religion Academy, the World Religion Research Institute, and the Christianity Research Center of the Chinese Academy of Social Sciences (CASS), as well as the Beijing municipal *lianghui*, there was no doubt that the viewpoints expressed by Chinese experts reflected the thinking of the top echelons of the party. According to the chairman of the Beijing Christian Three-Self Patriotic Movement Committee, Cai Kuai, the core of the concept of the sinicization of Christianity was "how Christianity can develop healthily and harmoniously in the context of Chinese culture."[65] Chairman of the China Religion Academy Zhuo Xinping noted that the sinicization of Christianity was not "a narrow path of self-isolation." He claimed that the interaction between Christianity and Chinese culture since the Tang Dynasty (618–907) represented "the process of the ocean absorbing a hundred streams," which is an often-used idiom to show how Chinese culture has absorbed and transformed alien systems of belief. "The Sinicization of Christianity demonstrates how superior elements of world culture have been reborn and rejuvenated within the Chinese people," he argued. "It is also the materialization of Chinese culture in the lives of Christians."[66] What Zhuo chose not to point out was that, except for individual periods such as the Boxer Rebellion (1899–1901), Christian missionaries and scholars were never subjected to the level of tight control that is being exercised by the Xi administration. From the Tang to the Qing Dynasties (1644–1911), quite a number of European missionaries became highly respected advisers to members of the Imperial Court.[67] According to Christian scholar Guo Baosheng, "the purpose of the 'Sinicization of Christianity' is to render Christianity into a Communist and socialist [vehicle] so that it will become an obedient tool of the Communist Party."[68]

That Christianity must subserve the political requirements of the CCP was demonstrated in a paper that Zhuo delivered at a European conference. He contended that Christianity should play the cultural and political role of persuading Western society to accept Chinese-style modernization. "Christianity may play the role of active reconciliation and guidance in its mother body – the Western society – so as to enable the latter ... to react constructively to China's modernization process," he wrote. He called upon Christian workers in China to shed their "condescending and arrogant attitude" and instead help to promote harmony – with the proviso that "such 'harmony' should be Chinese," meaning as interpreted by party authorities.[69]

The rest of President Xi's "four must-dos" policy was quite straightforward. Regarding the objective of using "rule by law" methods in handling religious affairs, it must be noted that this is different from global norms of rule of law (see later). "We must dialectically view the social function of religion" simply means that religions – be they Christian, Buddhist or Muslim – must not be used by anti-socialist and anti-China elements at home or abroad to undermine CCP authority and social stability. As Xi put it, "religious organizations should work hard to serve [the goals of] promoting economic development, social harmony, cultural prosperity, the unity of the nationalities, and the unity of the motherland."[70]

The last of Xi's "four must-dos" regarding religious work – "we must put emphasis on developing the [sociopolitical] functions of members of religious circles" – also demonstrates the much more aggressive and interventionist stance of the paramount leader. As Xi noted at the United Front Work Conference,

[W]e must pay attention to nurturing teams of patriotic religious teachers and staff, adopt effective measures to raise the quality of personnel working in religious sectors, and ensure that the leaderships of religious organizations are firmly held by officials who love the country as well as their religions.

SARA's Wang added that party and government leaders of all levels should provide "political help" to religious leaders so that they will become "politically reliable, distinguished in their learning [and] able to submit [to party instructions]."[71]

The wujin *and* wuhua

Cadres responsible for religion in 2013 laid down the draconian policy of the so-called *wujin* (literally, the "five penetrations" or "five introductions") and *wuhua* (literally, the "five transformations"), which were first tried out in Zhejiang Province. *Wujin* consists of the following: "Policies, laws and regulations must be introduced to churches"; "Health and medical treatment must be introduced to churches"; "The culture of popular science must go inside churches"; "[The concept of] supporting people in need must be introduced to churches"; and "[The idea of] the construction of harmony must go inside churches." The *wuhua* include the following concepts: "religion must be localized," "the regularization of the management of churches," "the *bendihua* [indigenization] of theology," "rendering transparent the finances of churches" and "rendering church doctrines *shiying* ['compatible' with socialism]."[72]

The wording of the new regulations is clearly loaded. For example, the promotion of "popular science" presupposes that churches are spreading "unscientific" creeds or even cults.[73] The concept of "harmony" has, since the days of ex-President Hu

Jintao, been interpreted as values that fit CCP doctrines and the party's norms about social stability. *Wuhua* is more disturbing. "Localizing and indigenizing" churches and church doctrines clearly mean that they should be sinicized. This was illustrated by a talk to Protestants and Catholics given by SARA's Wang at the end of 2014. He urged Christian leaders to "further push forward the construction of theological ideas, and to discover contents within Christian theology that are commensurate with the core values of socialism."[74] A BBC report on Xi's policy toward Christians quoted a senior party official as saying Beijing wanted to develop the country's unique version of Christianity, which boasted "a Chinese Christian theology." Such a theology needs to be compatible with China's political development and subservient to the party's edicts.[75]

There has been another marked change in religious policy after Xi's rise to power. First, the country's *zhengfa* system (or quasi-police-state apparatus that incorporates the police, state-security personnel and the courts) has been playing a significantly bigger role in clamping down on religious organizations and activities deemed threatening to the regime. In different parts of the country, such as Zhejiang, the police were given powers to rough up church personnel and believers in addition to tearing down crosses or even entire churches. The frontal role played by the police was the direct result of the party committees running provinces and cities – particularly the party secretary and the member of the regional party committee responsible for the *zhengfa* apparatus – taking direct control of the policy and practice of muzzling religious freedom.[76] In many instances, local authorities did not find it necessarily to consult with central-level departments such as the UFWD or SARA. The main reason probably had to do with the fact that *weiwen* ("upholding stability") – as well as crushing "foreign infiltration" – had become one of the most important tasks for party organizations at all levels. At the same time, the status and influence of SARA – and particularly the *lianghui* – have declined. As we shall see, the persecution has become so severe in different parts of China that supposedly subservient leaders of the *lianghui* rose in protest against the dismantling of churches and crosses.[77]

The "rule by law" solution to religious issues

In an apparent attempt to reassure both Chinese and foreigners that the CCP had morphed from rule of personality to rule of law, the Xi Jinping leadership convened the party's first-ever Central Committee plenum that was devoted to legal and judicial issues. The Fourth Plenary Session of the 18th Central Committee in October 2014 passed a resolution on "comprehensively advancing *yifazhiguo*," or running the country according to law. According to the Xinhua News Agency, the communiqué issued by the Central Committee highlighted:

> the need to speed up the building of a law-abiding government, to ensure judicial justice, to improve the credibility of judicial system, to promote public awareness of law, to enhance the building of a law-based society, to

improve team building and to sharpen the CCP's leadership in pushing forward rule of law.

"Only if the CCP rules the country in line with the law, will people's rights as the master of the nation be realized and the state and social affairs be handled in line with law," the statement said.[78] (See Chapter 3.)

What are the implications for the party's religious policies? In theory, the party-state apparatus is committed to "administering religious policies in accordance with the law." As Wang Zuo'an pointed out at a meeting to plan work for the year 2015, SARA would "push forward the *fazhijianshe* [rule by law construction] relating to religious work." He added that "we must uphold rule-by-law methods in implementing religious work."[79] However, *yifazhiguo*, or Chinese-style rule by law, also means all sectors and organizations must follow laws and regulations laid down by party authorities. The party leadership – not the law courts – has ample latitude to interpret vaguely worded statutes relating to sensitive areas such as national security, infiltration and state secrets. It is therefore not surprising that Wang went on to emphasize that,

> the religious work *xitong* ('hierarchy') of the entire country must closely rally around the party central authorities with comrade Xi Jinping as General Secretary, and resolutely uphold the major decisions and plans of the party central authorities regarding religious work.[80]

The philosophy behind the "legalization of the suppression of religion" was elucidated by former SARA chief Ye Xiaowan. In an article explicating Xi's address at the United Front Work Conference of mid-2015, Ye noted that the quintessence of the party's religious policy revolved around this question: "Which is bigger, the deity or the law?" "Abiding by the Constitution and the law is the basic responsibility of every citizen," he indicated. "No places of worship, no religious personnel, and no church can exist outside the law," Ye said. "People in the religious sector should stand at the forefront of countering religious extremism."[81] The veteran party cadre, however, failed to mention that "freedom of religion" was enshrined in the Chinese Constitution. What is becoming more obvious, however, is that the first of the "five introductions" stipulated by religious cadres in Zhejiang Province – *zhengcefagui jinjiaotang* ("introducing policies, laws and regulations into churches") – actually means different party and government departments, particularly *zhengfa* units, using a plethora of laws and regulations to clip the wings of dissent in religious circles.[82]

That the law has become a "weapon" whereby the party-state apparatus can further constrict religious freedom was demonstrated by the enactment in early 2018 of a new State Council Regulation for Religious Affairs. In about 10,000 characters, the regulation includes sections on general legal provisions, regulations on religious bodies, sites for religious activities, religious personnel, religious property, legal liability and religious activities. Section 4 pointed out that activities relating to worship and spreading of the faith should take place "in registered sites for religious activities." Religious units must secure "registration certificates for sites for religious activities" from relevant authorities. This amounted to a further blow to the legal status of house churches whose personnel were exposed as never before to harassment and even imprisonment by the police. Churches and all religious organizations must follow lawful practices in finance, accounting and law-enforcement. Churches have to accept regular "supervision and inspection" by relevant government religious units. Financial and other contributions from religious or political units overseas are forbidden. Moreover, schools run by religious organizations must be approved by the authorities and will be subject to strict supervision by educational and law-enforcement departments. Most significant is the stipulation that religious activities "must not endanger state security, damage social order ... or hurt national interests." Nor will religious organizations and individual believers be allowed to "damage national unity, split up the nation or perpetrate terrorist activities."[83]

Beijing passed in early 2017 a Law on the Management of Foreign NGOs, which is seen as an effort to restrict the activities of foreign NGOs in fields ranging from religion to labor rights. The legislation obliges China-based NGOs and charities to submit to relevant departments regular reports about their finances and their relations with Chinese organizations. The ordinance also empowers the police to enter the premises of foreign NGOs and seize documents and other kinds of information. Above all, the statute points out that foreign organizations "must not endanger China's national unity, national security, or ethnic unity."[84] Although there are only a limited number of foreign religious organizations based in China, the law would make it difficult for China-based human rights organizations in general to come to the aid of the downtrodden churches. In theory, the law does not apply to the dozens of Protestant and Catholic NGOs based in the SAR of Hong Kong. However, given the ease with which state security agents in China could operate in the SAR, the law will have a chilling effect on Hong Kong's religious and human rights NGOs.[85]

Since 2015, a number of prominent church leaders have been arrested – and in some cases given severe jail terms – for breaking Chinese laws. In 2015, Zhejiang-based Pastor Bao Guohua and his wife Xing Wenxiang were sentenced, respectively, to 12 years and 10 years in jail for allegedly accepting bribes, embezzlement and "gathering people to disturb public order." The couple were also accused of holding frequent fund-raising activities – and pocketing the donations of Christians. The Zhejiang court confiscated 600,000 yuan from Bao and 92,000 yuan from his wife. Both church staff worked for a state-approved church in the city of Jinhua.[86] In January 2017, Pastor Yang Hua (whose real name is Li Guozhi) was sentenced to two years for "leakage of state secrets." Pastor Yang, who served in the Huo Shi Church in Guiyang, Guizhou, was one of the most respected religious leaders in southwest China. Yang's wife Wang Hongwu was not allowed to attend the trial, and one of Yang's lawyers was forced to leave the city. His alleged crime was putting materials on the Internet about the party-state's religious policy.[87]

Despite rhetorical commitment to honoring the Constitution and the law, the Xi administration's supposedly law-based measures toward religion represent a pronounced retrogression from the days of Jiang Zemin. In a talk to the CUFWD in 1992, Jiang pointed that, "when we boost the management of religion according to law, this does not mean changing the policy of freedom of religion and beliefs." "We want to safeguard the healthy and normal execution of religious activities," the former president indicated. He added that, while countering efforts by hostile foreign forces to use religion to infiltrate China, "we must forcefully guard against the superficial interpretation of [this principle] or the simplification of actions [to achieve this goal]."[88] Although Jiang could definitely not be called a liberal, his knowledge of the Western world is vastly superior to that of Xi. After all, Jiang grew up in the cosmopolitan city of Shanghai. He speaks English fairly well. And he had more than a decade of experience dealing with Western businesspeople when he was mayor and party secretary of Shanghai and when he worked on the establishment of the special economic zones.[89]

The Zhejiang experience: worst religious persecution since the Cultural Revolution

It was a Manichean struggle the pathos of which recalled that of the primordial battles fought between the embryonic Christian church and the much more powerful infidels in the first centuries after Christ. In March 2014, word spread in Wenzhou, one of the most prosperous – and religious – cities in coastal China, that the authorities were about to demolish the Sanjiang Church. Protestant believers from all over the city and neighboring regions flocked to defend the recently built monument to Christianity.[90] By early April, as many as 5,000 Christians, including the old and the infirm, began to form a human shield around the 8,000-square-meter place of worship. Hundreds of believers took turns keeping watch against the police and demolishers. All to no avail. In the early hours of April 28, the authorities mobilized 1,000-odd PAP to disperse the crowd. With the help of powerful bulldozers, the police razed the 6-million-yuan building to the ground in less than 12 hours.[91]

Hopes that the Zhejiang government would heed the voices of harmony, a watchword of the Communist Party, disappeared. After all, although it was by no means rare for the police – often aided by thugs – to harass and beat up members of house churches, Sanjiang is a church regulated by the Zhejiang and Wenzhou *lianghui*. Moreover, the official reason given by the Wenzhou authorities – that the church was built on illegally obtained ground – went against the effusive praise that many cadres had heaped on it as a demonstration of Wenzhou's openness not only to commerce, but also to interactions with the Western world. Some of the biggest donors to both official and underground churches in this city were millionaire Christians, and the latter used to enjoy close ties with officials.[92] In its April 2014 edition, the official *Zhejiang Daily* defended the authorities' tough action, asserting that church leaders had been given the chance to demolish "illegal" parts of the building themselves but had "failed to live up to their commitment." It also blamed believers for "spreading online rumors" about religious persecution and "inciting illegal gatherings inside" the now broken church.[93]

The demolition of crosses, and sometimes entire churches, in Zhejiang would prove a watershed in the demise of trust between the CCP and members of even moderate, sanctioned Christian organizations. "It is outrageous and utterly unjust," said Chen Yilu, the head of the official Nanjing Union Theological Seminary and a respected authority on Christianity. Chen railed against the government's "crude and hardline" handling of the churches, which, he said, could damage the CCP's image and harm "social stability."[94] Chinese University of Hong Kong scholar Ying Fuk-tsang noted that the offensive against Zhejiang churches was the most ferocious attack on Christianity since the end of the Cultural Revolution. "The total resources of an entire province have been mobilized to demolish the churches," Ying said. "The Zhejiang pogrom signifies a much-enhanced level of contradiction and confrontation [between the party and Christianity]."[95]

Why Zhejiang and why Wenzhou?

As of late 2017, more than 1,500 crosses from as many Christian churches in Wenzhou and other cities in Zhejiang had been forcibly removed, despite opposition from members of both the official and underground churches. The party-state apparatus has continued to defy condemnation from Christian organizations in Hong Kong, Taiwan, the United States and other countries and regions.[96]

Why did the Xi Jinping administration pick Zhejiang, and particularly the quasi-capitalistic city of Wenzhou? At least two factors were at play. The first was that, as party secretary of Zhejiang from 2002 to 2007, Xi is familiar with the relentless growth of the Western creed in the province.[97] Zhejiang Province now has an estimated 2 million Christians, just behind the traditionally strong Christian centers of Henan and Anhui Provinces.[98] An estimated 1.2 million out of the 8 million population of Wenzhou – known as "China's Jerusalem" – are Christians. Moreover, given Wenzhou's status as a coastal port for the past several centuries, the city has had a long history of religious contact with foreign countries. Wenzhou churches have links with counterparts in not only Hong Kong, Taiwan and Southeast Asia, but also the United States and Europe.[99]

Wenzhou was also one of the first Chinese cities where *tuanqi* (Christian fellowships) of businesspeople were set up. Such *tuanqi* consisted of Christian entrepreneurs who were active in making donations to churches in addition to other charities. Owing to their close relationship with local officials (some of whom were actually "silent partners" in private firms), Christian businesspeople were often able to act as an effective conduit between TSPM and house churches on the one hand and municipal officials on the other. By the time of the crackdown on Zhejiang, Wenzhou *tuanqi* had brought their message to several coastal provinces and cities, where similar "rich men's fellowships" were set up.[100] The suppression of the

Zhejiang faithful, however, demonstrated that well-heeled believers were unable to use their *guanxi* (political connections) to help their churches.

The persecution of Christians in Wenzhou is the handiwork of former-Party Secretary Xia Baolong, a protégé of President Xi who served as the province's No. 1 official from 2014 to 2017. According to Zhejiang Christians, Xia's declaration of the war on churches was first revealed when he visited Baiquan Township in early 2014. "How come the crosses are so tall?" Xia reportedly said. "Is this the world of the crosses? Or is it the world of the Communist Party?"[101] The first salvo for the unprecedented dismantling of crosses and other church properties took the guise of an administrative order issued by the Zhejiang government in February 2013, three months after Xi Jinping's ascent to the top of the leadership. Zhejiang Government Circular (2013) No. 12 said all levels of administration in the coastal province should implement the *sangai yichai*, or "three transformations and one demolition" program, from 2013 to 2015. *Sangai yichai* refers to the modernization and gentri-fication of old residential areas in cities and towns, old factory districts and "villages within cities," as well as the "dismantling of illegal architectural structures." The executive order made no reference to religion or even to politics in general. It merely said that the goal of the *sangai yichai* was to "expedite development, expand [urban] space, improve the environment, promote stability and boost standards of living."[102]

Yet tidbits from the province-wide *sangai yichai* meetings conducted by Hang-zhou authorities made it clear that the movement was targeting the "three exces-ses" of Christianity in the coastal province: "excessively fast development [of Christianity]; excessive numbers [of worshipping places] and excessive degree of enthusiasm [among believers]."[103] Although there was, in the early days, specula-tion that the Zhejiang anti-Christian crusade was a local initiative, there were signs aplenty that it enjoyed the blessings of the top-level party-state apparatus. The Hong Kong weekly *Yazhou Zhoukan* quoted a Hangzhou-based believer as saying that "they [the authorities] spent 6 million [yuan] dismantling the San Jiang Church." "The bill for taking down the crosses of small churches comes to a few hundred thousand yuan each. Such huge sums could only have been approved by superior departments in Beijing," he added.[104]

Zhejiang and Wenzhou authorities were at pains to reassure local Christians as well as foreigners that what had happened was not an anti-Christian crusade. A spokesman for the *sangai yichai* office in Zhejiang claimed that the urban renewal project was not targeted at religions. He asserted that properties owned by different religions accounted for only 0.26 percent of the total illegal areas closed down by his office. Moreover, Christian churches took up a mere 2.3 percent of the total construction areas taken down by the authorities.[105] The official Wenzhou media pointed out in mid-2015 that, since the demolitions began, local party chief Chen Yixin and other leaders had conducted 42,000 meetings with the personnel of Christian and other religions. Moreover, "practical questions" regarding 1,301 places of worship had been solved. Wenzhou officials even claimed that this model of reconciliation through dialogue would be applied to the rest of the province.[106]

That this was window dressing was illustrated by signs of revolt by senior *lianghui* personnel in Zhejiang and Wenzhou. One lasting impact of the Zhejiang persecution is the growing contradiction between the *lianghui* and official churches on the one hand and the authorities on the other. This is despite the role of the *lianghui* as a bridge between the party-state apparatus and Christians. In July 2014, the Zhejiang branch of the CCC issued an open letter to the Zhejiang Province ERAO, asking provincial and municipal authorities to stop dismantling the crosses. The letter said acts of destroying church properties "were against the spirit of running the country according to law," and such actions must be halted immediately.[107] The ERAO responded by taking away the official seal of the Zhejiang CCC Committee. The head of the CCC, Pastor Joseph Gu Yuese, was practically expelled from the council. On January 27, 2016, Pastor Gu and his wife were taken away by local police. The Hangzhou *lianghui* issued a statement claiming that Gu was under investigation for "economic crimes such as suspected embezzlement of funds."[108]

The Zhejiang suppression also illustrated how the police successfully exploited its control over the media and the Internet to crush both active – and relatively passive – opposition from church clerics and believers. The net police closely monitored the Internet and social media communications of clerics and believers. Consider, for example, what happened to an elder in a church in Yongjia County, Wenzhou, in mid-2015. After the elder sent out *weibo* messages to two believers that contained the words "demonstration" and "rally," all three of them were briefly detained by local police. Newspapers and TV stations also started broadcasting the alleged corrupt practices of clerics and even confessions of guilt when they were interrogated by police.[109]

How are Zhejiang Christians coping?

By late 2016, the demolition of the crosses seemed to have petered out in a number of provinces and regions. However, a "new normal" of sustained and rigorous suppression of both official and underground churches had begun to set in. There is not the slightest relaxation of the ironclad surveillance of the church by police and state-security personnel. TSPM churches in different provinces were, in 2016 and 2017, forced to install cameras and video facilities – many of which are equipped with facial recognition technology. Known activists from the house churches are not allowed to leave the country; most of them are under 24-hour surveillance.[110]

In an interview conducted with this author in early 2017, a *dixiong* (brother) from Wenzhou summarized the harsh new regime of fear in his city. "The authorities are trying to impose unprecedented ideological control over the churches," he said. "Most pastors of TSPM Churches as well as house churches are not allowed to leave the country." Church officials have to regularly report their activities to ERAO cadres or neighborhood committees. For example, church personnel have to provide the authorities with data about their sources of finances, expenditures and the number of attendees in functions such as group prayers or pilgrimages. Visits by and donations from religious organizations and NGOs from abroad must be reported. Both TSPM and house churches are forbidden to run summer camps for youths and children. Christian schools are under grave threats of closure. "The authorities' goal is to threaten our autonomy and sever our links with the civil society in both China and abroad," he concluded. Churches are much more careful about spreading the gospel. Recruitment of new believers is usually done among friends and relatives of existing members of the congregation.[111]

The most intense religious persecution since the end of the Cultural Revolution has shocked Christians in Zhejiang – but they are not bowed. Among other things, more Christians realize the importance of seeking independence not only from the political order, but also from the *lianghui* structure. There is a broad realization that registration with the authorities can protect neither their crosses nor their freedom of worship. The bulk of the forcibly removed crosses were from TSPM churches. Another realization is that pastors and other personnel in registered churches are on the receiving end of particularly tough and unfair treatment once they are found not to bow to official demands. SARA and other units consider disobedience on the part of members of TSPM churches as an act of betrayal – and that these traitors and black sheep must be severely penalized.[112]

It is in this context that Pastor Wang Yi of Chengdu's Early Rain Reformed Church, one of the best-known religious leaders in the country, called upon the faithful to guard their spiritual independence above all else. "Give up tangible church properties but safeguard intangible church properties," he said. "Give up church properties that can be seen, but safeguard church properties that cannot be seen." Wang asked congregations not to risk making personal sacrifices by defending the churches because "believers can gather in any place if they invoke the name of God." "We should totally cut ourselves off from the TSPM, the CCC, SARA and the CUFWD," he said.[113]

A Hong Kong theology lecturer who had carried out extensive interviews in Zhejiang said that, although a relative minority of church leaders and followers wanted to confront the authorities head-on, the majority were lying low. "Many affiliates of official churches have tried to seek refuge in house churches," said the academic. Underground Christian leaders are mainly working to improve their organization and networking. Some house church members have forged links with nationwide *tuanqi* such as the CGF. Others have beefed up contacts with and sought guidance from churches that have nationwide appeal, such as the Shouwang Church in Beijing and the Early Rain Reformed Church in Chengdu. Despite the large number of "Christian attorneys" who have been detained or jailed, most house church affiliates realize that they have to form closer links with like-minded sectors of the civil society, such as Christian writers and human rights lawyers.[114]

On the surface, many Christians who have fallen victim to the horrendous persecution seem to be enduring their fate with patience. A popular activity of churchgoers who belong to churches whose crosses have been demolished is to make small wooden crosses which they hang up in inconspicuous places in their homes.[115] Yet, the unprecedented suppression of religious freedom has brought about a qualitative change in Christians' assessment of the party-state apparatus. Also evident is a paradigm shift regarding how members of the faithful will conduct their protracted struggle with the powers that be.

Religious persecution in other regions

Experts on Chinese Christianity are divided over the reasons behind the Xi leadership's decision not to apply the experience of the mass demolition of crosses in Zhejiang to other provinces. At the much-talked-about National Conference on Religion of 2016, four provinces and regions – the provinces of Hebei, Jiangsu, Guangdong and the Ningxia Autonomous Regions – were singled out for praise. Zhejiang failed to make the grade. As Chinese University of Hong Kong's Ying pointed out, Jiangsu's religion-related cadres were praised for "curtailing extremist incidents involving individuals or mass incidents due to simplified and *cubao* ['crude and brutal'] work methods." "It seems the Jiangsu experience is the opposite and antithesis" of the horrendous events in Zhejiang, Ying noted. Moreover, Zhejiang Party Secretary Xia Baolong, long deemed a confidant of Xi's, retired from his powerful post in April 2017, when he was transferred to a pre-retirement sinecure job at the NPC.[116]

Yet, even assuming that the Xi leadership realized the negative impact of the Zhejiang experience on the prestige of the party and China's global soft power, tough tactics toward both official and underground places of worship have continued throughout China. As discussed, the 2018 Regulation for Religious Affairs authorized much tighter supervision of church activities by religious-affairs cadres as well as police. Churches have been forbidden to organize educational activities. Children in general are not allowed to take part in either official or underground churches. And the demolition of symbolic churches in other provinces has continued, even though the number of crosses and church properties destroyed was lower than in Zhejiang.[117]

Take, for example, Henan, which has one of the largest concentrations of Christians in China. In May 2017, Shuangmiao Christian Church in the city of Shangqiu, Henan, which was still under construction, was destroyed by 300 police officers and inspectors. Forty parishioners who tried to stop the demolition were beaten up and detained by the police. Just as the in case of Zhejiang, Henan was subject to intense religious persecution starting in 2014. In April that year, Ding Cuimei, a parishioner in Zhumadian, Henan, died when she and her husband stood in front of a bulldozer that was about to wreck a small house church. The workmen simply ran over the couple, burying them in mud and concrete. Ding was killed in the process, although her husband, Li Jiangong, managed to escape. "Bulldozing and burying alive Ding Cuimei, a peaceful and devout Christian woman, was a cruel, murderous act," said China Aid President Bob Fu in a statement. "This case is a serious violation of the rights to life, religious freedom and rule of law."[118]

Several churches in Guangzhou, Dongguan and Foshan in Guangdong Province were raided by the police in mid-2016. A few dozen house church personnel and believers were briefly detained. According to Pastor Ma Ke of the Guang Fu house church in Guangzhou, the police were using dubious pretexts as well as brutal tactics to terrorize the places of worship. "They closed down our church for two weeks under the pretext that we had not paid taxes," he said. The police and state-security personnel also put pressure on property owners not to let apartments to churchgoers. The electricity and water supplies of some churches were cut off.[119] The clampdown even reached the predominantly Muslim Xinjiang Uyghur Autonomous Region, which is home to a relatively small community of Christians. During the Chinese New Year in 2017, some 80 members of house churches in the Xinjiang districts of Urumqi, Kuytun and Shawan were detained. It was one of the largest anti-Christian swoops in of the XUAR since the Cultural Revolution.[120]

Cadres involved with religious work, together with members of the *weiwen* ("stability maintenance") apparatus, have particularly targeted congregations with the following attributes: churches – especially those led by charismatic leaders – that have immense influence within the cities or regions in which they are located; unofficial churches with cross-provincial networks; and churches that have contacts with religious NGOs in Hong Kong and abroad. Thus, the Shouwang and Zion Church in Beijing, Wanbang Church in Shanghai, Golden Lampstand Church in Shanxi, Early Rain Reformed Church in Chengdu, and the Huo Shi Church in Guizhou have been subject to frequent harassment and 24-hour surveillance by local police.[121]

Persecution of Beijing's well-known Shouwang Church began to intensify in 2015. After the establishment of Shouwang in 1993, it was able to conduct house church activities in apartments or office spaces that the congregation had rented in the capital. From 2009, however, property owners in Beijing were warned by the police not to let space to Shouwang – which has since been holding prayers meetings in public parks. In October 2015, Shouwang activists Zeng Miao, Huang Danyi, Guan Shanyue and Sun Huibo were arrested by police for "disturbing public order" and detained for 10 days. The tense standoff between Shouwang and Beijing police is ongoing. In a note to worshippers in July 2017, the church leadership said Shouwang had entered into a "stage of fierce warfare" with its persecutors.[122] The latest swoop against an influential unofficial church was the arrest in early December 2018 of a few hundred regular worshippers at the Chengdu Early Rain Reformed Church. Its charismatic pastor Wang Yi and his wife were detained for "incitement to subvert state power." Police tracked down a few hundred worshippers and forced them to sign confessions which said they would never again attend church services.[123]

The authorities have also wreaked havoc on a host of churches in other provinces under the campaign against "evil cults." In mid-2014, the official media published a list a 20 *xiejiao*, or "evil cults." This came with insinuations in the public media that a number of Christian churches, particularly in rural areas, were in fact "fronts" for cults that had reportedly been responsible for the deaths or financial losses of adherents. As liberal author Murong Xuecun noted, "The anti-cult campaign has been extended to more mainstream religious practices." Murong cited the official media as saying that, "underground churches and evil cults are spreading like mushrooms ... the problem is very urgent."[124] Given the spiritual vacuum – and the crisis of confidence – hitting the nation in the wake of the horrendous personality cult being built around President Xi, however, many converts to the faith might be convinced that what the CCP was pursuing sounded a lot more "cultist" that even non-mainstream, unorthodox Christian orders.

Christians' baptism of fire – and their pursuit of civil rights

Christians must re-examine their dependence on the party-state – and assert their spiritual independence

Although interactions between the church and the much more powerful party-state apparatus have always been asymmetrical, a rough quid pro quo had existed during long periods of PRC rule. "We observe the restraint of not promoting Marxist-Leninist propaganda in churches and our friends from religious circles must observe the restraint of not doing missionary work on the streets," Zhou Enlai said during a meeting with religious figures from Beijing, Shanghai and Tianjin in the mid-1950s.[125] For Christians in the early 1950s, Zhou's relatively conciliatory approach could look like a compromise, a tacit understanding between the government and religions. What has happened since Xi came to power, however, has amounted to an effort by the all-powerful state to subjugate the church and to adulterate its doctrines. The law of survival seems to dictate that it is impossible for even the humblest individual – let alone one who thinks God is on his side – not to try fighting back by calling on the CCP to honor religious and other freedoms guaranteed by the Chinese Constitution.

Many Christians have drawn inspiration from the stormy interactions between the church and the state in the past century or so by reexamining how even the most devoted missionaries and pastors were forced to compromise by either joining the official TSPM or putting an end to publicly and independently propagating the faith. Immediately after Liberation, the party-state apparatus used strong-armed tactics to cow Christians into subservience. Upon the instruction of then-Premier Zhou, patriotic Christian leader Wu Yaozong initiated a Christian proclamation entitled "The path of China's Christianity in assiduously constructing the new China."[126] China's estimated 8,000 missionaries and 840,000 Christians were forced to sign the de facto declaration of loyalty to the party. By April 1951, 180,000 Christians had signed the document, which emphasized the party leadership of the church. By the time the TSPM was established in 1954, 416,000 had done so.[127]

In light of the recent persecution of Zhejiang Christians, the vicissitudes of the lives of several well-known early Christian leaders have been reexamined. These included prominent theologian Jia Yumin (1880–1964), who was the head of a number of seminaries and divinity schools at the time of Liberation. Jia, who had earlier proclaimed that "joining the TSPM is against the will of God," became the vice-chairman of the national committee of the TSPM.[128] Ni Tuosheng, a vocal advocate of Christian independence and an early opponent to the TSPM, was forced to change his mind in 1952. Calling the church a cup and the government a tray, he said that, "it is natural that the cup must anchor itself on the tray." Despite his apparent betrayal of Christian independence, Ni was arrested by the authorities in 1952 and he died in jail in 1972.[129] Ni's statement echoed that of Ding Guangxun, a veteran CCP member who became perhaps China's most prominent "official Christian." He had this to say about the delicate church–state balance: "My belief does not consist of a circle with only one center. My belief is an ellipse that has two centers – Christ and the country."[130]

More Christians have begun to celebrate the example laid down by Pastor Wang Mingdao, the iconic Christian leader whose lifelong struggle against the CCP has inspired generations of believers. Wang was first imprisoned in 1955 as the head of the so-called "Wang Mingdao Anti-Revolutionary Sect." By the time he was released in 1980 – four years after the end of the Cultural Revolution – Wang had spent 23 years in jail. In 1984, seven years before his death in 1991, he resumed house church activities in his tiny flat in Shanghai.[131] One of Wang's most famous sayings goes like this: "In the history of mankind, there is this war between Christ and Satan … [As Christians] we can only advance; there is no way we will retreat." "If we retreat one inch, it will soon be two inches, one foot, three feet, one mile, five miles, ten miles … until total defeat," he added.[132]

The reason why, since the TSPM was set up in 1954, at least half of the country's Protestants decided to join the official church was that this would afford some form of protection from persecution from the atheistic party-state authorities. This bears some similarity to the trajectory of Chinese Buddhism, which first flourished in the Tang Dynasty. A key reason for its fast development was that senior monks obtained the patronage of monarchs and the nobility.[133] Xi Jinping's resumption of what some critics call a scorched-earth policy against Christians, however, has thrown into sharp relief the futility of seeking refuge in a regime that does not observe either rule of law or civil and religious rights guaranteed by the Chinese Constitution.

A spiritual and political awakening: religious freedom cannot be attained unless there are basic changes in the political system

The spirit of both legal and underground congregations has remained uncowed in the face of the most severe religious persecution since the Cultural Revolution. Members of the faithful have put up passive resistance by installing crosses of different sizes and shapes in their homes. More significantly, they have begun to debate the path ahead, particularly in light of the fact that President Xi will likely stay in power at least until 2032.[134]

It is true that a significant number of Christians are convinced that, instead of confronting the authorities, they should patiently wait until the next major change of Beijing's policy toward religion. The horrendous treatment of churches and mosques during the Cultural Revolution was halted by Deng Xiaoping, and his successors, Jiang Zemin and Hu Jintao, switched to a more human tactic of seeking "cooperation" with the churches. As a 47-year-old house church leader in central Henan Province put it, "We have to bear the cross in our hearts." This church leader said more resistance by parishioners could invite harsher suppression. "I'm not in favor of putting up resistance, which could become the excuse for the police to continue using force against the churches," he said. "Moreover, trying to rally the support of the churches in Hong Kong, Taiwan and the Western world could convince the Beijing leadership that there is some kind of 'collusion' between anti-China foreign forces and the Christian community in China." He added that it is better for members of the underground church to conserve their strength and wait for the current wave of ultra-leftist policies associated with President Xi to wane.[135]

Yet, for the majority of worshippers in both official and house churches, the ongoing crackdown has served as a wake-up call. Even those members of the faithful who eschew confrontation with the authorities believe that they have to establish a raison d'être that is outside the party's purview: Christians have to buttress and expand their room for maneuver in the public space. More importantly, they have realized that religious freedom cannot be achieved in a vacuum: Christians have to fight for a China that embraces civil liberties and social justice as understood not only in the West, but also in Asian countries that have undergone democratization. As another house church member in Wenzhou put it: "Ordinary believers have become mistrustful of authorities, if not anti-government." "They have become more aware of their rights as citizens," he added. "Growing numbers of my church are clamoring for freedom of expression, freedom of assembly and the right to be protected by the laws."[136] As Pastor Huang Yizi said in a message to Christians in China and Hong Kong soon after his release from jail, "the attacks against the church have awakened believers who were in deep slumber." "We are citizens of China and if we see injustice in this country, we must uphold justice."[137]

Actually, the first major Chinese Protestant figure who spearheaded a movement for religious freedom and civil liberties was Pastor Wang Mingdao, who, in 1955, penned a moving manifesto to unite Christians who refused to join the TSPM entitled "We – for the sake of faith." Wang called upon Christians to differentiate between the rule of men and the rule of God. "When the institutions of men and the orders of men are in conflict with the will of God, we can only serve God and we cannot serve men," he noted. Wang added that, normally, sons and daughters should follow the instructions of their parents. "But if the parents tell their children to tell lies, they should no longer abide by their parents' instructions," he wrote.[138] On May 13, 2011, pastors and personnel from 17 house churches nationwide issued a public petition – also entitled "We – for the sake of faith," – to the then-chairman of the NPC and PBSC member Wu Bangguo. The pastors and elders were from churches in Beijing, Shanghai, Xian, Wenzhou and Wuhan. They asserted their rights as Chinese citizens to freedom of worship and a full range of civil liberties enshrined in both the Chinese Constitution and United Nations human rights covenants. "Freedom of religion includes freedom of assembly and forming organizations, freedom of speech, education and doing missionary work," the petition said. "Christians in the great majority of countries in the world enjoy these freedoms." They also demanded that Wu investigate whether the Beijing municipal government had violated the Constitution and the law by denying the more than 1,000 Shouwang Church affiliates a regular place of worship.[139]

The idea that persecuted Christians should somehow "fight back by asserting their civil rights" was shared by vocal Hong Kong-based pastor Hu Zhiwei:

> The Wenzhou incidents have shown up the contradiction between the pledge that the state has made to its citizens about religious freedom and the actual practice of this policy ... If we do not do deep reflection on this issue, do not differentiate [between right and wrong] and do not fight back, we are acquiescing in the existence of evil.[140]

The vice-president of the Nanjing Union Seminary, Chen Yilu, has highlighted the need for persecuted Christians to relentlessly pursue not only human rights, but also a more open, transparent and rational form of government. The ruthless tearing down of the Sanjiang Church and others, he wrote, was a "wanton trampling of human rights." The issue is no longer just a religious affair. Chen saw in the Zhejiang authorities' treatment of both official and unsanctioned churches a glaring example of misrule by the CCP administration. "The ironclad means [adopted by Beijing] have run afoul of the principles and wisdom of modern [government] management," said the respected theologian. "A blow has been dealt the image of the party-state [apparatus], the relations between the party and the masses as well as social stability."[141]

Similar sentiments were echoed in the so-called Beijing Manifesto, which represents the more radical wing of unsanctioned churches in Beijing and the surrounding areas. The manifesto, which was penned by members of underground churches in different cities, appeared on a number of Chinese and overseas-Chinese websites in late 2015. "The history of the Christian church far predates the setting up of the new regime [in China] in 1949," it said. "Church doctrines were revealed by God; and the church cannot and will absolutely not bear the shame of submitting to a temporary new administration." Reflecting the ideas of other "reawakened" – and in a way radicalized – church members, the manifesto took a more broad-brush approach to church–state contradictions. "Politics should be separated from religion," the document said. "The state and the ruling party cannot use public power to guide or force Christians to amend their standards of belief." The manifesto ended with the relatively radical view that only in a democratized China could its citizens enjoy real religious freedom. "We advocate that China must become a country with constitutional democracy, market economy, political democracy, and freedom of expression," the document said. "The church should and must be a catalyst for the future Chinese order of governance."[142]

Compared with dissident intellectuals or human rights lawyers, church leaders have not yet spun out concrete visions for a government that will safeguard universally accepted citizen rights and rule of law. Yet it seems clear that Christian scholars and believers are aware of the necessity of participation in the civil society and the public sphere. In an article entitled "A Church that has been thrust into the public sphere," respected Chinese Christian commentator Yang Jun summed up the much-enhanced cooperation between house churches, on the one hand, and other civil-society organizations, on the other, in fulfilling their common aspiration of seeking China's democratization. "Even though in terms of converts the Chinese church has grown exponentially in the past few decades, it has remained conservative and introverted at least in theological realms," Yang said. The horrendous impact of the destruction of the crosses, however, meant that religious persecution in China had become an international phenomenon that has been covered by the Hong Kong, Taiwan and global media. "Whether it is willing or not, the Church has been thrust into the public sphere," Yang argued. He added that, for the first time since 1949, members of both official and unofficial churches had no choice but to "make themselves heard in the public sphere." According to Yang, sanctioned and underground pastors, Christian intellectuals and other friends of the church have become more mature and they are ready to "spread its doctrines and beliefs in an expanded space."[143]

The apparent radicalization of Christians had aroused intense concern in the party leadership even before Xi came to power. This was reflected in a 2010 article in the party mouthpiece *Global Times*. In a commentary on the Shouwang Church affair, *Global Times* warned Shouwang and its supporters "not to engage in politics" such as establishing a sizeable organization. "Setting up a large organization is something that is always treated with seriousness," the paper said. "This cautious attitude has been formed over the past few decades and the government's ... management [of mass organizations] has always been relatively severe." It added that whether a relaxation of this policy is required is a "major political issue for the entire society." "The church should not become a radical force of change in this sensitive matter," it warned.[144]

Interactions between Christians and other sectors of the civil society

According to Chinese University of Hong Kong theology professor Ying Fuk-tsang, the police are cracking down particularly hard on pastors and missionaries who want to form a solid alliance with the civil society. Ying cites as example the leader of Chengdu's Early Rain Reformed Church, Wang Yi, who has been subject to police harassment for more than a decade. "Wang, who is a former lawyer, believes the church should make contribution to building up China's civil society through joining hands with expanding civil society groupings ranging from dissident intellectuals to human-rights attorneys," said Ying. "The authorities are

paranoid about the Christian church spearheading a national civil-society movement." Apart from his church work, Wang is an active campaigner for the rights of
dissidents and for causes such as overturning the official verdict on the 1989 student
movement.[145]

Involvement of human rights lawyers

Church leaders have to some extent formed a united front with human rights
lawyers, the 300 or so attorneys who are at the forefront of fighting for the constitutional and legal rights of civil-society units, including house churches. (See
Chapter 3.) The first China Christian Human Rights Lawyers Group was established in January 2006. It included five prominent legal scholars and lawyers: Gao
Zhisheng, Wang Yi, Li Boguang, Teng Biao and Fan Yafeng. Apart from working
for Protestants and Catholics, rights lawyers were at the forefront of providing legal
aid to the Falun Gong group, Tibetan Buddhists and Muslims in Xinjiang.
According to lawyer Teng Biao, who was forced go to into exile in the U.S.,
about a quarter of China's human rights lawyers are Christians. The visiting professor at Harvard Law School pointed out that human rights lawyers were routinely
harassed by the authorities. "Without God or a belief, a rights lawyers would feel
hopeless," Teng said.[146]

After the crosses were torn down in Zhejiang in 2014, several dozen lawyers
from all around the country converged upon Wenzhou and other cities to offer
pro bono services to clerics. One of them was well-known lawyer Zhang Kai, who
was based in Beijing. Either upon Zhang's referral or independently, more than
30 lawyers from all over the country descended upon Zhejiang to help churches in
the cities of Wenzhou, Chaozhou, Jinhua and Lishui.[147] Zhang proved particularly
irksome to the authorities because he was stirring up the congregations' resolve to
defend their civil rights. Together with colleagues and assistants from his firm, who
included Yang Xingquan, Liu Peng and Fang Xiangui, the 37-year-old Zhang first
came to Zhejiang in mid-2014 to defend the well-respected Pastor of the Jiu'En
Church, Huang Yizi. After Huang was sentenced to one year in jail, Zhang organized an Internet petition of 1,000 Christians followed by a small-scale demonstration. What the authorities could not tolerate was that Zhang also initiated a
series of lectures and seminars for Christians on how to use Chinese law to defend
their religious and civil rights. In August 2015, Wenzhou police arrested Zhang
and his assistant Liu Peng, who were both charged with the offences of "gathering
crowds to disturb social order and obtaining and illegally providing state secrets and
intelligence to [units] outside China." Shortly before his incarceration, Zhang told
foreign reporters that, "the relationship between political [authorities] and the
church has become very difficult." "Yet we must tell Christians to fight for their
rights as citizens."[148]

The Zhang Kai case became a cause célèbre among lawyers and Christians,
particularly in Zhejiang and Beijing, owing to the obviously illegal ways in which
Zhang and his associates were treated by local police. Lawyers Zhang Lei and Li

Boguang, who had taken up the cases of Zhang Kai and Liu Pang, issued an open letter to the Zhejiang Province Procuratorate outlining how local police had failed to follow legal procedures. For example, the lawyers were not allowed to get in touch with either Zhang or Liu. The relatives of the accused were not informed where the two were held. Even more outrageous was the fact that Zhang and Liu were apparently forced to sign papers saying they no longer required the services of Zhang and Li.[149]

With the support of lawyers and legal experts, more church members are demanding that Beijing enact a proper law on religion so as to delineate the mode of interaction between churches and the party-state. Despite the fact that, after Xi's ascendency to power, the NPC rushed through a plethora of statutes on areas ranging from national security and counter-terrorism to the activities of foreign NGOs, the CCP apparatus has postponed indefinitely the promulgation of a law on religion.

"The authorities are still relying on 'rule of personality' and not rule of law," said Liu Peng, director of the Pu Shi Institute for Social Science in Beijing. Liu proposed a law on religion that would stipulate clearly that, "the country implements the separation of politics and religion." Liu subscribed to the paradigm of "rendering to Caesar the things that are Caesar's, and to God the things that are God's." "The separation of politics and religion is the fundamental principle for handling the relations between political [institutions] and religion in modern societies with rule of law," he noted. The professor added that, "many problems have arisen due to a lack of legal basis to delineate the relations between political power and religion."[150]

Yu Canrong, a leading sociologist at the CASS, has asked the authorities to depoliticize their treatment of Christians – and to instead approach the issue of religions from the legal point of view. "The fact is that if China's masses of Christians correctly follow Christian doctrines, the sky won't fall down," said the respected public intellectual. "We must trust the wisdom of these several tens of thousands of Christians … it will not be easy for people [outside China] to make use of them." Yu noted that, instead of cracking down on the house churches, it was more advisable to allow them to become legally recognized organizations and to conduct their activities openly. "We should allow house churches to register under a form of self-ruled Christian mass organizations that are to their liking," the sociologist argued. Yu said house churches should be allowed to be registered under organizations other than the TSPM. "It's better that they become legal organizations and that [all operations] become transparent," he added.[151]

The role of Christian intellectuals

As Professor Ying Fuk-tsang of the Chinese University of Hong Kong put it, it is not too easy for members of the Christian Church to build up and consolidate their relations with intellectuals. "The Church does not have many attributes that can attract well-educated young men and women," he wrote. For some sectors in society, Christianity still carried with it the "original sin of having colluded with the imperialists." "The [government-induced] mainstream narrative about the relationship between Christianity and imperialism has rendered intellectuals reluctant to maintain open and intimate ties with the Christian church," he noted. Ying pointed out that, compared with the late Qing Dynasty and early Republican Period, it would be difficult to propagate outstanding groups of Christian intellectuals.[152] Christianity flourished during the early Republican Period partly because prominent political figures in the early decades of the 20th century were converts. The latter included Father of the Revolution Dr. Sun Yat-sen, Kuomintang leader Chiang Kai-shek and "Young Marshal" Zhang Xueliang. However, the fact that many respected Christian leaders chose to abandon their autonomous status and bow to the leadership of the CCP also detracted from the reputation of Christian intellectuals active from the 1930s to the 1950s.[153]

Yet, at the same time, it is precisely because so many Chinese intellectuals have suffered under the whiplash of a dictatorial order that Christianity has provided them with inspiration for the pursuit of a better spiritual and moral life. The best example is Lin Zhao (1932–1968), a gifted writer who was one of the few intellectuals who dared to denounce the excesses of Maoism. Labelled a "counter-revolutionary," she was jailed in 1960 for anti-party offences. Before her execution in 1968, she wrote hundreds of letters in her own blood denouncing Chairman Mao's dictatorship. A devout Christian, Lin had this to say about her insistence on keeping the faith: "As a Christian, my life belongs to God and my beliefs," she noted. Lin added she was willing to sacrifice her life "so as to uphold my path and my direction, which is the direction of God's servant and the direction of Christ's governance."[154] Lin's tragic story has been told and retold by Christians to remind themselves of the purity and holiness of Christian martyrs.

The big challenge facing Christians is whether they can galvanize a new generation of well-educated intellectuals sympathetic to the Christian cause. Several of the big-name Christian intellectuals who played prominent roles in defending not only freedom of religion, but also civil rights for Christians and other Chinese have gone into exile. They included essayist and Xi Jinping biographer Yu Jie (born 1973), as well as Tiananmen Square activists Yuan Zhiming (born 1955) and Zhang Boli (born 1957). (Both Yuan and Zhang converted to the Christian faith and became pastors after they left China to flee persecution by the authorities for their role in the 1989 "counter-revolutionary turmoil.")[155] After being forced into exile in the U.S., Yu has been a vigorous campaigner for religious freedom in China. Yu compared Xi to a Nietzchean "spiritual tyrant" who claims to hold the monopoly of truth. "It is easy to understand why Xi has used all means to suppress religion," wrote Yu. "Xi not only wants to become emperor; he also wants to become God."[156]

By the 1990s, a group of Christian intellectuals had appeared on the scene: they believe that their primary task is not so much getting involved in direct struggles with the CCP authorities as fostering and propagating "Christian culture" in society. Representative figures include spiritual novelist Bei Cun, commentator and philosopher Wang Yi (leader of the outspoken Early Rain Reformed Church in Chengdu) and writer Yu Jie (before his exile to the U.S.). Their idea is that spreading Christian ideas and culture among intellectuals is a good way to plant the seeds of faith in a society where the powers that be are unlikely to wind down their oppression, particularly toward Christianity. Their message was evident in the foreword to their short-lived publication *Fang Zhou*, which was first published in 2005. "Christian faith and Christian values have still not become important elements among the multiple faiths and values of Chinese society," it said.

> One important reason is that for a long time Chinese Christians, evangelists and Church [leaders] have seriously neglected the merits of writing … and the creation of Christian literature, music and art as well as academic research have long been stagnant.[157]

In his 2016 article on culture-focused Christian intellectuals, University of Gothenburg scholar Fredrik Fällman also cited the artworks of Xia Kejun and Zha Changping. According to Fällman, these artists believe that, "art can bridge areas and spheres within societies and assist in expressing ideas and emotions otherwise difficult to formulate." Specifically, art enables the "cross-fertilization" between aesthetic appreciation and the nurturing of Christian faith. Many of the novels, commentaries and works of art of these Christian intellectuals do not directly ask fellow Chinese to convert to Christianity or any other religion. However, their stunning portrayals of the importance of faith in an anti-religious, hard-authoritarian state have served to broaden the appeal of Christianity at least to members of the educated and professional classes.[158]

Conclusion: the battle of the century shapes up

As discussed in Chapter 2, the brutal clampdown on religion is part of President Xi Jinping's Cultural Revolution-era control over the ideology and thought of every citizen. The "leadership core" and *zuigao tongshuai* (Supreme Military Commander) will not tolerate any ideas or activities that will challenge the supremacy of the party – or of himself. Apart from Christians, sectors such as liberal college professors, NGO activists, even feminist groups have been targeted.

For a good number of Christians, however, Xi's scorched-earth policy toward the church marks a point of no return. The battle of the century has begun. Renmin University Professor Wei Dedong noted that the enhanced suppression of Christianity as symbolized by the Zhejiang experience has demonstrated the "public fissure and the split-up between religious circles and the state." There would be no going back to the old system of uneasy coexistence whereby the legal churches – and, to some extent, a good number of house churches – sought patronage from the government so as to avoid harassment by the police.[159]

According to noted Christian commentator Li Xiangping, the best way that believers can combat the "ecology of power" that has ridden roughshod over the church since 1949 is to "socialize religion": turn Christianity from an individual's faith to a community-based religion. "What Chinese lack most is a community of faith [based on] countless individual believers, that is, a 'society of the faithful,'" he wrote. This communal faith platform, he said, "lies outside the state and the market – and could provide service to society." Li saw the future of Christianity as "the nurturing of a Chinese civil society, the democratization of Chinese politics, and the diversification of Chinese culture."[160]

One path ahead could be that churches expand their influence in China's civil society, however circumscribed it may be. According to a pastor who has worked in Shanghai for ten years, the position of official – and particularly house – churches will never be secure unless churches become anchored in a civil society that is recognized by the all-encompassing party-state apparatus. "Religions for and by the people must be in sync with the idea of a modern country and modern civil awareness," he said. "Believers must be liberated from a religious model that is tied to the state."[161] For blogger and public intellectual Ren Yunfei, who converted to Christianity in the 1990s, the church needs "public space" to survive. Moreover, it is possible that, like NGOs, Christian churches may spearhead the movement to create a larger public sphere in China. This is what Ren said:

> If this country wants to develop well it needs faith. It also needs NGOs. [Most] Chinese intellectuals don't get [the significance of] NGOs. NGOs are necessary in the same way that churches are. The unregistered churches are public spaces. They're maybe the only real public space in China right now.[162]

Although many government-sanctioned and underground churches do not seem to consider themselves NGOs, they do have clear-cut attributes of organizations outside the purview of the party-state. A 2017 Council on Foreign Relations background report on Christianity drew attention to the fact that Chinese Christians were attracted to the faith's "sense of fellowship, comprehensive moral system, organized structure, and solidarity as part of an international movement."[163] At the very least, churches in poor areas have fulfilled the function of a charitable non-profit organization. As Hong Xiaomei, a professor in Northeastern University, said, religious organizations used the funds they had collected to build homes for the elderly and orphanages. "They provide assistance to the handicapped, migrant workers and people with leprosy and other ailments," she added. "Churches amount to a major social force in building a civil society."[164]

It can thus be argued that Christian churches already constitute the largest NGO grouping in China. This is despite the fact that churches have never tried to register themselves as NGOs with the Ministry of Civil Affairs or relevant government departments. According to Carsten Vala, a U.S.-based expert on the Chinese church, the tens of millions of Protestants who worship in unregistered churches may "contribute to a civil society that offers alternative values, defends church interests, and seeks to limit state authority." Vala argued that Protestant groups in China sought to do more than forge "autonomous social spaces" based on

Buddhist-like, partially sinicized ethics and charitable giving. "They strive to carve out such spaces through public activism that combines religious worship with protest and defends the priority of religion over state domination of society." He added that many Christian churches and bodies did not want state registration because they wanted to remain independent.[165]

Li Fan, a respected scholar on grassroots political movements, noted in the late 2000s that the estimated 800,000 to 1 million Chinese church organizations qualified as religious-oriented NGOs. "From the point of view of social organizations, the Christian church has provided Chinese society with the foundation of a kind of social structure," said Li. "This [the church] is a strong civil society with adherents numbering 100 million." Li argued that, whether it is willing or unwilling, passive or active, conscious or unconscious, Christianity has in reality played an important role in rendering society stronger – and in enabling society to be well organized. Li added that the church's role in organizing a civil society could "result in major changes in the relationship between society and state in China."[166] Terry Halliday, an expert on Chinese Christianity at the American Bar Foundation, said:

> From the point of view of the top leaders, Christians might present a particular danger because they are the largest civil society grouping in China, they are increasingly connected to each other and therefore they might have an increased capacity to mobilize if their freedoms are harmed further.[167]

At this stage, it is difficult to predict whether – and how – this civil-society subset called the Christian Church could bring about changes in the political system. In theory, radicalized congregations could be a catalyst for a significant degree of social mobilization and transformation. Wang Ce, a Hong Kong-based Christian commentator, even argued that Beijing's harsh policy to suppress Christianity could precipitate a wholesale revolution comparable with the series of "color revolutions" that shook countries and cities, ranging from "velvet revolutions" in Eastern Europe to the Sarong Revolution in Myanmar. "If the campaign against the churches were to continue, China's Christians could wage a Revolution of the Crosses," wrote Wang. "The faithful will rush out to the streets to protect the dignity and glory of the cross – as well as their religious freedom and civil liberties."[168]

Although it may be difficult to conceive of Christianity in China playing a political role similar to that of the Catholic Church in Poland in the 1980s, U.S.-based pastor Guo Baosheng has proposed that Christian leaders and congregations seek to transform Chinese society by using Christian ideals including peace, tolerance and equality under God. "Instead of the Sinicization of Christianity, we should [bring about] the Christianization of Chinese culture," he said. The idea of the "Christianization of Chinese culture" was first raised by the late Christian minister Zhao Tian'en. Zhao wrote that, "the Christianization of Chinese culture means using Christian thoughts to affect Chinese culture, perfect Chinese culture ... so that [Christian ideas] will occupy a leading position and become the dominant ideology in Chinese culture." Zhao also raised the possibility of using Christian ideals to transform not only the cultural sector, but also "sectors including thought and ideology, education, politics, and society." Guo expressed confidence that "this is an era for the deepening of faith ... This is the era for [expanding] our belief in exerting the mighty influence of the 'City on the Hill.'"[169]

The battle line is drawn between the Xi Jinping leadership's efforts to sinicize Christianity in accordance with the values of socialism with Chinese characteristics, on the one hand, and religious crusaders' attempts to "Christianize Chinese society," on the other. The latter pursuit would go hand in hand with Christian scholars' argument that both the official and underground churches should leverage their organizational strength in nurturing and strengthening a civil society. On the surface, Xi's hard-authoritarian approach seems to be winning. However, Chinese and world history shows that social and spiritual transformation is a long-term game. Given the ironclad methods that leaders from Mao to Xi have used to clamp down on alien religions and "cults," the speedy spread of Christianity after the Cultural Revolution is nothing less than phenomenal. The possibility that faith can eventually prevail over a political party that seems to have lost all moral and spiritual bearings cannot be discounted.

Notes

1   Cited in Xiao Jiansheng, *Chinese History Revisited*, Hong Kong: New Century Press, 2009, pp. 377–382.
2   Cited in Chen Duxiu, "Christianity and the Chinese," *New Youth* magazine, Vol. 7, No. 3, July 1, 1921, available at http://bbs.tianya.cn/post-no01-54440-1.shtml
3   For a discussion of the rise of Christianity in contemporary China and its potential impact on political changes, see, for example, Jinghao Zhou, "The role of Chinese Christianity in the process of China's democratization," *American Journal of Chinese Studies*, Vol. 13, No. 1, April 2006, pp. 117–136; Daniel H. Bays, ed., *Christianity in China: From the Eighteenth Century to the Present*, Stanford, CA: Stanford University Press, 1999, pp. 307–353; Joseph Tse-Hei Lee, "Christianity in contemporary China, an update," *Journal of Church & State*, Vol. 49, Issue 2, April 2007, pp. 277–304, http://heinonline.org/HOL/LandingPage?handle=hein.journals/jchs49&div=22& id=&page=; Lian Xi, *Redeemed by Fire: The Rise of Popular Christianity in Modern China*, New Haven, CT: Yale University Press, 2010; D.C. Schak, "Protestantism in China: A dilemma for the party-state," *Journal of Current Chinese Affairs*, Vol. 30, No. 2, 2011, pp. 71–106; Ian Johnson, *The Souls of China: The Return of Religion after Mao*, New York: Pantheon Books, 2017; Jinghao Zhou, *Chinese vs. Western Perspectives: Understanding Contemporary China*, Lanham, MD: Lexington Books, 2014, pp. 147–162; Hong Qu, "Religious policy in the People's Republic of China: an alternative perspective," *Journal of Contemporary China*, Vol. 20, Issue 70, 2011, pp. 440–441, www.tandfonline.com/doi/abs/10.1080/10670564.2011.565176?journalCode=cjcc20
4   See "Xi Jinping attends national conference on religious work and gives important speech," *People's Daily*, April 24, 2016, http://cq.people.com.cn/n2/2016/0424/c365403-28208895.html. For a discussion of Xi's views on religion, see André Laliberté, "The politicization of religion by the CCP: a selective retrieval," *Asiatische Studien-Études Asiatiques*, Vol. 69, No. 1, 2015, pp. 185–211, www.degruyter.com/abstract/j/asia.2015.69.issue-1/asia-2015-0010/asia-2015-0010.xml
5   "State Administration for Religious Affairs Administration head Wang Zuo'an: four contradictions between the enemies and us within the religious arena are worth particular attention," Guancha.cn (Beijing), August 9, 2016, www.guancha.cn/politics/

2016_08_09_370576.shtml. See also "Foreign powers warned to stay out of religion," *Sunday Examiner* (Hong Kong), August 31, 2018, http://sundayex.catholic.org.hk/print/5805

6 "China commands that even retired officials shun religion," Reuters, February 5, 2016, http://uk.reuters.com/article/uk-china-religion-idUKKCN0VE0BP

7 See Wang Zuo'an, "Emphasis must be put on politics in doing well work on religion," *Seeking Truth*, July 17, 2017, http://cpc.people.com.cn/n1/2017/0717/c64102-29410197.html

8 Cited in "Beijing tightens control on religious beliefs," Ucanews.com (Hong Kong), February 8, 2016, www.ucanews.com/news/beijing-tightens-control-on-religious-beliefs/75159

9 For a discussion of why Catholics are not as effective in recruiting converts as Christians, see, for example, Caroline Kitchener, "Catholics have a messaging problem in China," *The Atlantic*, February 9, 2018, www.theatlantic.com/international/archive/2018/02/catholic-vatican-china/552800/

10 For a discussion of Zhou Enlai's views on Christianity, see, for example, Chen Ling, "New testimony of Zhou Enlai's talks on Christianity in 1950," *History Pedagogy*, No. 6, 2016, www.doc88.com/p-8856319893844.html. See also, Liu Jianping, "Zhou Enlai's recognition of the question of Christianity and its practice in the New China," *Party Archives*, No. 3, 2010, www.cnki.com.cn/Article/CJFDTotal-DANG201003016.htm

11 For a discussion of Catholic bishops and priests languishing in Chinese jail, see, for example, Marco Tosatti, "Chinese priests and bishops 'forgotten' in jail," www.lastampa.it, January 14, 2012, www.lastampa.it/2012/01/14/vaticaninsider/eng/world-news/chinese-priests-and-bishops-forgotten-in-jail-TfxbyzX1mfLIymz18fNVOK/pagina.html. See also Tom Philipps, "Catholic bishop dies in China after 14 years in prison," *The Telegraph*, February 6, 2015, www.telegraph.co.uk/news/worldnews/asia/china/11396106/Catholic-bishop-dies-in-China-after-14-years-in-prison.html

12 For a discussion of the party and government departments handling Christianity, see, for example, Liaw Jiann-feng, "On the Communist Party's religious policies and management," zhanwang yu tansuo ("Prospects and Exploration"; Taipei), Vol. 8, No 12, 2010, pp. 61–62, www.mjib.gov.tw/FileUploads/eBooks/aaa3aa0e77e54082afcde6af5c6eab73/Section_file/50bf185abbe44094b6bc786ee6608973.pdf. See also "Communist Party takes control of religious affairs," CSW.org.uk, March 22, 2018, www.csw.org.uk/2018/03/22/press/3885/article.htm. Also notable is Shaotang Tso, "The relationship between state and church within Chinese Christianity: a research in neo-institutionalism," Master's thesis, National Chingchi University, Taipei, July 2004, p. 49, https://nccuir.lib.nccu.edu.tw/bitstream/140.119/33734/7/26001207.pdf

13 Ibid.

14 For a study of the work of the TSPM and the CCC, see, for example, Hsiung Zi-jian, "The organization and activities of the China Christian Three-selves Patriotic Movement Committee and the China Christian Council," *Mainland China Studies*, Taipei, Vol. 40, Issue 12, 1997, pp. 52–66, https://nccuir.lib.nccu.edu.tw/bitstream/140.119/26745/1/123.pdf

15 Cited in Philip Puellala, "Exclusive: China–Vatican deal on bishops ready for signing – source," Reuters, February 2, 2018, www.reuters.com/article/us-pope-china-exclusive/exclusive-china-vatican-deal-on-bishops-ready-for-signing-source-idUSKBN1FL67U. See also Jason Horowitz and Ian Johnson, "China and Vatican reach deal on appointment of bishops," *New York Times*, September 22, 2018, www.nytimes.com/2018/09/22/world/asia/china-vatican-bishops.html

16 Cited in "Cardinal Zen: Vatican–China deal weakens the Church," Catholicnewsagency.com, March 8, 2018, www.catholicnewsagency.com/news/cardinal-zen-vatican-china-proposal-weakens-the-church-94708

17 Cited in Wang Zuo'an, "The total number of believers in our country's five main religions exceed 100 million," *People's Daily*, March 9, 2011, http://news.sohu.com/20110309/n279737050.shtml. See also Gui Hua, "How come we can tackle cults but

we cannot lay our hands on house churches," Guanchazhe Net, May 14, 2015, www.globalview.cn/html/societies/info_3148.html

18 Cited in Eleanor Albert, "Christianity in China," Council on Foreign Affairs, May 7, 2015, www.cfr.org/backgrounder/christianity-china

19 Cited in Tom Phillips, "China on course to become 'world's most Christian nation' within 15 years," *The Telegraph* (London), April 19, 2014, www.telegraph.co.uk/news/worldnews/asia/China/10776023/China-on-course-to-become-worlds-most-Christian-nation-within-15-years.html

20 Cited in Antonia Blumbert, "China on track to become world's largest Christian country by 2025, experts say," *Huffington Post*, April 22, 2014, www.huffingtonpost.com/2014/04/22/china-largest-christian-country_n_5191910.html

21 For a discussion of why the CCP is so afraid of organized protestors or oppositionists, see, for example, Lily Kuo, "The only thing China's communist party fears is organized protest – no matter the topic," Qz.com, January 27, 2014, https://qz.com/170874/the-only-thing-chinas-communist-party-fears-is-organized-protest-no-matter-the-topic/

22 Cited in Li Xiaobai, "Strange phenomena: the past, the present and the future," Beijing Shouwang Church website, September 26, 2012 https://t3.shwchurch.org/2012/09/26d/%E5%BC%82%E8%B1%A1%EF%BC%9A%E8%BF%87%E5%8E%BB%E3%80%81%E7%8E%B0%E5%9C%A8%E4%B8%8E%E6%9C%AA%E6%9D%A5/#

23 For a discussion of how the Falun Gong appeared to pose a threat to the party, see, for example, James Tong, "Anatomy of regime repression in China: timing, enforcement institutions, and target selection in banning the Falungong, July 1999," *Asian Survey*, Vol. 42, No. 6, November/December 2002. See also Julia Ching, "The Falun Gong: religious and political implications," *American Asian Review*, Vol. 19, No. 4, Winter 2001, pp. 1–18.

24 For a discussion of the government policy of restricting the establishment of cross-county or cross-provincial church organizations, see, for example, "Our reaffirmation of the standpoint of house churches," Early Rain Reformed Church (Chengdu), August 31, 2015, https://asiafriendfinder.com/p/blog.cgi?site=ffz&month=8&oid=21699033_36661&action=change_month&od=chinesefriendfinders&year=2015

25 For a discussion of the significance of the China Gospel Fellowship, see, for example, Robert P. Menzies, "The future of the Church in China: why China's house churches will prevail," Pneumareview.com, February 21, 2017, http://pneumareview.com/the-future-of-the-church-in-china-why-chinas-house-churches-will-prevail/2/

26 See Karrie J. Koesel, "The rise of a Chinese house church: the organizational weapon," *China Quarterly*, Vol. 215, September 2013, pp. 572–589.

27 For a discussion of Xi Jinping's views on security, see example, Chen Zhuqin and Hu Pan, "Xi Jinping raises for the first time views on mega-national security, and systematically raises '11 types of security,'" *Eastern Morning Post* (Shanghai), April 16, 2014, http://henan.people.com.cn/n/2014/0416/c351638-21004943.html

28 Cited in Gong Xuezeng, "Deng Xiaoping and the establishment of socialist religious theories with Chinese characteristics," Zhongguo minzu bao (China Nationalities Paper), February 10, 2016, http://fo.ifeng.com/a/20160210/41549857_0.shtml

29 Cited in Matt Spetalnick and Jeremy Pelofsky, "Bush focuses on religious freedom in Beijing," Reuters, August 10, 2008 www.washingtonpost.com/wp-dyn/content/article/2008/08/09/AR2008080900762_pf.html

30 Cited in Calum MacLeod, "In China, Michelle Obama calls for universal rights," *USA Today*, March 21, 2014, www.usatoday.com/story/news/world/2014/03/21/michelle-beijing-china-visit/6685835/

31 Cited in "Demolition of churches in Zhejiang and religious freedom in the Mainland: Ying Fuk-tsang says the incidents have seriously shocked the churches," *Christian Times*, June 4, 2014, http://christiantimes.org.hk/Common/Reader/News/ShowNews.jsp?Nid=83673&Pid=5&Version=0&Cid=220

32 Cited in Wang Xiaoshi: "In trying to 'bring down China,' the U.S. is brandishing three weapons," *Global Times*, December 25, 2014, http://opinion.huanqiu.com/cul ture/2014-12/5291682.html

33 Cited in Wang Anwei, "Chinese lawyer released after televised confession; he has helped to defend the rights of churches," *New York Times*, Chinese edition, March 25, 2016, https://cn.nytimes.com/china/20160325/c25china/

34 For a discussion of the views of Zhang Kai, see, for example, "Lawyer Zhang Kai's speech at the Trinity College in the U.S.," WeChat account of Zhang Kai, February 26, 2016, http://mp.weixin.qq.com/s?__biz=MjM5MDYwMzYzMw==&mid=406033695&idx= 4&sn=fed6c7ae60402959b0f48c29df0ea8f9&scene=5&srcid=0226sAXFLxXVCHCm ENNoopYg#rd

35 For a discussion of Beijing authorities putting pressure on Hong Kong's Christian churches, see, for example, Ray Kwong, "China expands crackdown on Christianity to Hong Kong," *Hong Kong Economic Journal*, September 1, 2015, www.ejinsight.com/ 20150901-china-expands-crackdown-christianity-hong-kong/

36 See, for example, the account of Hong Kong-based divinity school dean Ying Fuk-tsang's account of meeting Chinese officials in the Central Liaison Office: Ying Fuk-tsang, "I got into the Central Liaison Office …," Thestandnews.com (Hong Kong), February 2, 2016, www.thestandnews.com/politics/%E6%88%91%E9%80%B2%E5% 85%A5%E4%BA%86%E4%B8%AD%E8%81%AF%E8%BE%A6/

37 Cited in "The political and social repercussions of the spread of Christianity in the villages," Beijing Xiu Yuan Economic and Social Research Foundation, Beijing, August 2, 2014, www.xiuyuan.org/yjbgshow.asp?id=81. For a brief look at the Xiu Yuan or Longway Foundation, see "A brief introduction of the Xiu Yuan Founda-tion," Xiu Yuan Foundation, Beijing, n.d., www.xiuyuan.org/gywm.asp?id=1

38 "The political and social repercussions of the spread of Christianity in the villages."

39 Ibid.

40 Ibid. See also Dong Leiming and Yang Hua, "The spread of Western religion in China's villages," Guancha Net, June 9, 2014, www.guancha.cn/DongLeiMing/ 2014_06_09_235967.shtml

41 Author's interview with a senior member of a house church in Guangdong, January 2017.

42 Cited in Wang Hongfang, "Investigation into the state of female Christian groups in the villages – using N Village in Zhejiang as sample," *Guangli Xuejia* (*China Manage-ment Magazine*), Beijing, October 2012, pp. 383–384. http://d.wanfangdata.com.cn/ Periodical/glxj201219316

43 Cited in "Jiang Zemin on the United Front: on religious work," Central United Front Work Department website, February 26, 2014, www.rmzxb.com.cn/c/2014-02-26/ 297938.shtml

44 Ibid.

45 See Jiang Zemin, "Maintain the stability and continuity of the party's policy on reli-gion," in *Selected Articles on Religious Work in the New Era*, Beijing: Religion and Cul-ture Press, 1995, p. 210. See also "Jiang Zemin invites leaders of various religious groups for a seminar at Zhongnanhai on January 30, 1991," *People's Daily*, January 30, 1991, http://cpc.people.com.cn/GB/64162/64165/76621/76653/5290615.html

46 See Jiang Zemin, "We must perform well in work toward religions," in *Selected Articles on United Front Work in the New Era (Sequel)*, Beijing: Central Party School Press, 1997, pp. 287–288.

47 Cited in Si Tianke, "Relevant legal basis for the fact that house gatherings of Chris-tians need not be registered," Si Tianke's blog, August 31, 2007, http://blog.sina.com. cn/s/blog_a4f3fc110101j0sa.html

48 For a discussion of how Hu Jintao's experience in Tibet contributed to his rise, see, for example, Willy Wo-Lap Lam, *Chinese Politics in the Hu Jintao Era*, London: Routledge, 2006, pp. 8–10.

49 Cited in "Major work priorities for the state administration of religious affairs in 2011," www.sara.gov.cn, January 24, 2011, www.sara.gov.cn/xwzx/xwjj/7090.htm

50 Cited in "Hu Jintao on the United Front," China.com.cn, December 20, 2015, www.china.com.cn/guoqing/zhuanti/2015-12/30/content_37422083_7.htm

51 See "Hu Jintao's report to the 17th Party Congress," Xinhua News Agency, October 24, 2017, http://news.sina.com.cn/c/2007-10-24/205814157282.shtml

52 Cited in "Hu Jintao stresses at the second collective study session of the Politburo that the party's objectives in religious work must be fully implemented," Xinhua News Agency, December 19, 2007, www.gov.cn/ldhd/2007-12/19/content_838664.htm

53 "Develop the positive functions of people's organizations and religion," *People's Daily*, May 4, 2008, http://theory.people.com.cn/BIG5/68294/120979/120980/7191036. html. See also "Hu Jintao: correctly recognize and handle the relationship between the general public who are believers and non-believers, and the relationship among the masses who believe in different religions," Central United Front Work Department website, February 26, 2014, www.rmzxb.com.cn/c/2014-02-26/298104.shtml

54 See "Persecution under 'cultural security' – an interview with Minister Hong Yujian on the 'demolition of crosses in Wenzhou,'" Chinaaid.net, April 25, 2014, www.chinaaid. net/2014/04/blog-post_25.html. For a study of Xi's overall policy toward Christianity, see Willy Lam, "Vatican agreement latest front in Xi's widening religious clampdown," *China Brief*, Jamestown Foundation, October 10, 2018, https://jamestown.org/p rogram/vatican-agreement-latest-front-in-xis-widening-religious-clampdown/

55 See Zhong Mingjiu, "The level [of importance] of the Central Conference on Religion expected to be raised," *Ming Pao* (Hong Kong), April 22, 2016, http://premium. mingpao.com/cfm/Content_News.cfm?Channel=ca&Path=202007428446/caf1.cfm

56 Cited in "National conference on religion work opens in Beijing," Xinhua News Agency, April 25, 2016, http://news.xinhuanet.com/politics/2016-04/25/c_ 128929212.htm; See also "The party authorities' objectives on Tibetan Buddhism: unity in politics, respect [regarding issues of] beliefs," United Front Work Department, August 27, 2015, http://xm.ifeng.com/fojiao/dongtai/xiamen_2015_08/27/ 4284340_0.shtml

57 See "Xi Jinping discusses Buddhism in Paris: Buddhism plays a big role in the cultural renaissance of China," Phoenix Television, March 30, 2014, http://sd.ifeng.com/chi nese/yinxiangqilu/detail_2014_03/30/2055524_0.shtml

58 Cited in "Former head of SARA: we must guide members of the faithful to understand clearly 'whether God or the law is more powerful,'" *Guangming Daily* Net, June 16, 2015, www.chinesetoday.com/big/article/1011305

59 "Central United Front work meeting: positively provide guidance to the mutual accommodation of religion and socialist society; necessarily uphold the direction of sinicization," Xinhua News Agency, May 20, 2015, http://bbs1.people.com.cn/post/ 2/1/2/148468352.html

60 Ibid.

61 Cited in "Uphold the direction of sinicization – positively provide guidance to the mutual accommodate of religion and socialism," *Zhejiang Daily*, July 6, 2015, http:// zjnews.zjol.com.cn/system/2015/07/06/020725157.shtml

62 Author's telephone and WeChat interview with a Shandong-based pastor, October 2017.

63 Cited in "Head of Administration on Religious Affairs: resolutely counter efforts by foreign countries to infiltrate China by using Christianity," China News Service, December 25, 2014, http://news.china.com/domestic/945/20141225/19146617.html

64 Ibid.

65 Cited in "International conference on 'The Path of the Sinicization of Christianity' opens in Beijing," Chinareligion.cn, November 23, 2015, www.chinareligion.cn/ya owen/2015-11-23/3032.html

66 Ibid.

67 For a discussion of the contributions of Christian missionaries and scholars to the Tang and Qing courts, see, for example, Willy Lam, *Chinese Politics in the Era of Xi Jinping*, London: Routledge, 2015, pp. 271–273.

68 See Guo Baosheng, "The sinicization of Christianity means turning Christianity into [something] Communist and socialist," Radio Free Asia, November 24, 2015 www. rfa.org/mandarin/yataibaodao/shehui/ck-11242015095751.html?from=groupmessa ge&isappinstalled=0

69 Cited in Zhuo Xinping, "Christianity and China's modernization," Konrad Adenauer Stiftung Forum paper (n.d.), www.kas.de/wf/doc/kas_6824-1522-1-30.pdf?051011091504

70 Cited in "National conference on religion work opens in Beijing," Xinhua News Agency, April 25, 2016, http://news.xinhuanet.com/politics/2016-04/25/c_ 128929212.htm

71 Cited in "SARA head: enthusiastically provide guidance to ensure the compatibility of religion and socialist society," Gov.cn, May 13, 2015, http://big5.gov.cn/gate/big5/ www.gov.cn/xinwen/2015-05/13/content_2861036.htm

72 Cited in Guo Baosheng, "The goal of the 'five penetrations' and 'five transformations' is to thoroughly refigure and control Christianity," Chinaaid.net, September 3, 2015, www.chinaaid.net/2015/09/blog-post_89.html. See also "Editorial, from 'three alterations and one demolition' to 'five penetrations and five transformations': the goal of remolding the church is obvious," *Christian Times* (Hong Kong), August 28, 2015, http://christiantimes.org.hk/Common/Reader/News/ShowNews.jsp?Nid=90885& Pid=2&Version=1461&Cid=942&Charset=big5_hkscs

73 There has been a long tradition of Chinese politicians and intellectuals attacking Christians as anti-scientific or even morally evil. The best example is the "Anti-Christian Movement" of 1922–1927. Leading theoreticians and scholars sympathetic to the Communist cause, including Communist founders Chen Duxiu and Li Dazhao, issued a statement in 1922 decrying the "evil damages of religion." "Religion and human beings cannot coexist," they added. See Yang Tianhong, *Christianity and Republic-Period Intellectuals: A Study of the Anti-Christian Movement of 1922–1927*, renminchubanshe (People's Press), 2005.

74 Cited in Lan Xifeng, "Wang Zuo'an: the sinicization of Christianity is the necessary condition for it to go on a path that is commensurate with socialist society," *Zhongguo Minzu Bao* (China Nationalities Paper), August 12, 2014, http://blog.sina.com.cn/s/ blog_9da15c960102uzj4.html

75 See John Sudworth, "Why many Christians in China have turned to underground churches," BBC News, 26 March 2016, www.bbc.com/news/world-asia-china-35900242

76 That the police (together with the PAP) have become the major enforcer of Beijing's policy toward Christians is evidenced by the many reports in the international media about law-enforcement officials wrecking churches or beating up believers. See, for example Katie Mansfield, "Christian church destroyed as Chinese police drag worshippers into street and beat them," Express.co.uk, June 11, 2017, www.express.co. uk/news/world/814645/china-church-religion-crackdown-shuangmiao-henan; staff reporter, "Police raid 'underground' church in China during Mass," *Catholic Herald*, April 28, 2017, www.catholicherald.co.uk/news/2017/04/28/police-raid-under ground-church-in-china-during-mass/. Since 2016, the police have been putting up surveillance video equipment in churches across China. See, for example, Guo Baosheng, "Is it true that installing surveillance equipment in churches is due to 'fighting terrorism'?" Chinaaid. net, March 28, 2017, www.chinaaid.net/2017/03/ blog-post_57.html

77 For a study of the background of the dynamics between official and house churches, see, for example, Jacqueline E. Wenger, "Official vs. underground Protestant churches in China: challenges for reconciliation and social influence," *Review of Religious Research*, Vol. 46, No. 2, Dec. 2004, pp. 169–182.

78 Cited in "Communique of the Fourth Plenary Session of the 18th Central Committee of CCP," China.org.cn, December 2, 2014, www.china.org.cn/china/fourth_plena

ry_session/2014-12/02/content_34208801.htm. See also Zachary Keck, "Fourth Plenum: rule of law with Chinese characteristics," *The Diplomat*, October 20, 2014. http://thediplomat.com/2014/10/4th-plenum-rule-of-law-with-chinese-characteristics/

79 "National conference on religious work for 2015 opens in Beijing," China News Service, December 26, 2014, www.chinanews.com/gn/2014/12-26/6916354.shtml

80 Ibid.

81 "Former head of SARA: We must guide members of the faithful." See also Ye Xiaowen, "Develop the positive role of religion in promoting social harmony," *Study Times* (Beijing), December 26, 2006, www.china.com.cn/xxsb/txt/2006-12/26/con tent_7561750.htm

82 For a discussion of the "legal suppression" of Christianity, see, for example, Katie Mansfield, "China launches 'Religious Winter' in bid to destroy Christianity in fierce crackdown," *Sunday Express* (London), September 30, 2016, www.express.co.uk/ news/world/715834/China-Christians-launches-religious-winter-bid-destroy-Christia nity. See also "As China plans another crackdown to suppress religion, Christianity continues to grow," Lifesitenews.com, September 29, 2016, www.lifesitenews.com/ news/as-china-plans-another-crackdown-to-suppress-religion-christianity-continue

83 Cited in "Order 686 of the State Council of the People's Republic of China," Gov. cn, September 7, 2017, www.gov.cn/zhengce/content/2017-09/07/content_ 5223282.htm?from=timeline. See also "China Church further squeezed by revised regulations," Ucanews.com, February 8, 2018, www.ucanews.com/news/china -church-further-squeezed-by-revised-regulations/81469

84 For a discussion of the impact of the new law on foreign NGOs, see, for example, Nectar Gan, "Why foreign NGOs are struggling with new Chinese law," *South China Morning Post*, June 13, 2017, www.scmp.com/news/china/policies-politics/article/ 2097923/why-foreign-ngos-are-struggling-new-chinese-law

85 For a discussion of relations between Hong Kong Christian groups and their coun- terparts in the mainland, see, for example, Javier C. Hernandez and Crystal Tse, "Hong Kong Christian groups feel new scrutiny from mainland," *New York Times*, August 26, 2015, www.nytimes.com/2015/08/27/world/asia/hong-kong-christia n-groups-feel-new-scrutiny-from-mainland.html

86 See "China detains Zhejiang Christians amid cross removal dispute," BBC News, August 5, 2015, www.bbc.com/news/world-asia-china-33783463. See also Yu Xuejun, "The greedy lifestyle of a 'frugal pastor,'" Jinhua News Net (Zhejiang), August 5, 2015, www.jhnews.com.cn/2015/0804/526063.shtml

87 Cited in "Pastor Yang Hua of the Huo Shi Church in Guizhou is accused of 'leaking state secrets,'" Radio Free Asia, December 27, 2016, www.rfa.org/mandarin/yataiba odao/shehui/ql1-12272016100936.html

88 Cited in "Jiang Zemin on the United Front."

89 For a discussion of the career of Jiang Zemin and his exposure to the West, see, for example, Willy Wo-Lap Lam, *The Era of Jiang Zemin*, Singapore and New York: Prentice Hall, 2006, pp. 11–85.

90 For a discussion of the factors behind religious persecution in Zhejiang, see, for example, Zhang Yan, "Almost 1,000 crosses were destroyed in Zhejiang within two years: China may further restrict the Christian Church," *New York Times*, Chinese Edition, May 23, 2016, https://cn.nytimes.com/china/20160523/c23chinacross/zh-ha nt/; Lie Huo, "Reflections on the demolition of crosses in Wenzhou," *Christian Times* (Hong Kong), July 29, 2014, http://christiantimes.org.hk/Common/Reader/News/ ShowNews.jsp?Nid=84576&Pid=6&Version=0&Cid=150. For a discussion of the full or partial destruction of seminal churches in Zhejiang, see, for example, "Zhejiang: list and pictures of 64 demolished Christian churches," Asianews.it, May 21, 2014, www.asianews.it/news-en/Zhejiang:-list-and-pictures-of-64-demolished-Christian-chur ches-31135.html

91 For a discussion of the significance of the tearing down of the Sanjiang Church, see for example, Carrie Gracie, "China's city of churches brought to heel," BBC News, May

4, 2014, www.bbc.com/news/blogs-china-blog-27279762; "China begins demolition of 'oversized' church," *The Guardian*, April 28, 2014, www.theguardian.com/world/2014/apr/28/china-demolition-oversized-church-sanjiang

92 For a discussion of Zhejiang officials' initial support for the construction of the San-jiang Church, see Wu Nan, "Local officials face discipline for allowing construction of Sanjiang Church in Wenzhou," *South China Morning Post*, April 30, 2014, www.scmp.com/news/china/article/1500819/local-officials-accused-deliberately-hindering-demolition-sanjiang-church

93 Cited in "*Zhejiang Daily* on the tearing down of church buildings: backed by foreign support, there are people who smear 'the three transformations and one demotion,'" *Zhejiang Daily*, August 23, 2014, www.guancha.cn/FaZhi/2014_08_23_259606.shtml

94 Cited in "The deputy director of the Nanjing Union Theological Seminary blasted the demolition of the Sanjiang Church as a case of 'crude trampling on human rights,'" Gospelherald.com, April 29, 2014, http://chinese.gospelherald.com/articles/23971/20140429/%E9%87%91%E9%99%B5%E5%89%AF%E9%99%A2%E9%95%B7%E8%AD%B4%E5%BC%B7%E6%8B%86%E4%B8%89%E6%B1%9F%E6%95%99%E5%A0%82%E6%98%AF-%E7%B2%97%E6%9A%B4%E8%B8%90%E8%B8%8F%E4%BA%BA%E6%AC%8A.htm

95 Cited in "Hong Kong: love and persistence in the storm of the demolition of crosses in Zhejiang," *Kingdom Revival Times* (Hong Kong), September 11, 2015, www.krt.com.hk/modules/news/article.php?storyid=12877

96 For a discussion of the intransigence of Zhejiang officials, see Dan Southerland, "Zhejiang's Christians are resisting a campaign against church crosses," Radio Free Asia, August 11, 2015, www.rfa.org/english/commentaries/east-asia-beat/china-churches-08112015122240.html

97 For a discussion of Xi Jinping's personal views on the Christian Church, see, for example, Yu Jie, "Why does Xi Jinping persecute the Christian Church?" *Christian Times*, September 7, 2015, http://christiantimes.org.hk/Common/Reader/News/ShowNews.jsp?Nid=91024&Pid=6&Version=0&Cid=150

98 The official China General Social Survey of 2009 said there were 1,425,984 Christians in Zhejiang, or 2.62 percent of the population. Cited in Xinhua Wang, "Explaining Christianity in China: why a foreign religion has taken root in unfertile ground," Master's thesis, Department of Sociology, Baylor University, 2014. https://web.archive.org/web/20150925123928/https://baylor-ir.tdl.org/baylor-ir/bitstream/handle/2104/9326/WANG-THESIS-2015.pdf?sequence=1. Given the fast growth of the Christian population in the 21st century, the figure could be close to 2 million

99 For a discussion of the significance of Wenzhou as a center for the dissemination of Christianity, see, for example, Cao Yaxue, "Interviews with pastors in Wenzhou on the suppression and reconstruction of Christianity," Voice of America, November 26, 2015, http://m.voachinese.com/a/caoyaxue-interview-wenzhou-church-20151126/3075268.html. See also Nanlai Cao, *Constructing China's Jerusalem: Christians, Power and Place in the City of Wenzhou*, Stanford, CA: Stanford University Press, 2010.

100 For a discussion of the influence of "Christian entrepreneurs" in Wenzhou and other cities, see, for example, Nanlai Cao, "Christian entrepreneurs and the post-Mao state: an ethnographic account of church–state relations in China's economic transition," *Sociology of Religion*, Vol. 68, No. 1, Spring 2007, pp. 45–66. See also David Volodzko, "The boss Christians of Wenzhou," *The Diplomat*, March 6, 2015, http://thediplomat.com/2015/03/the-boss-christians-of-wenzhou/

101 For a discussion of Xia Baolong's role in religious persecution in Zhejiang, see, for example, "A single instruction from the party secretary leads to the demolition of crosses by the Zhejiang government," Aboluowang.com, March 1, 2014, http://hk.aboluowang.com/2014/0301/376089.html#sthash.OK7sDjDu.dpbs. See also "Demolition of crosses in Zhejiang has resulted in large-scale confrontation between police and citizens," Voice of America, June 13, 2014, www.voachinese.com/a/zhejiang-violent-20140613/1936121.html

102 "Notice regarding the three-year 'three transformation and one demolition' action by the Zhejiang People's Government," March 13, 2013, General Office of the Zhejiang Government, www.zj.gov.cn/art/2013/3/13/art_13012_77021.html

103 Cited in Zheng Zijian, "The fermentation of the incident of Zhejiang crosses: experts say the authorities are worried about the excessive fast growth of Christianity," HK01. com (Hong Kong), February 27, 2016, www.hk01.com/%E5%85%A9%E5%B2%B8/ 9246/-01%E5%B0%88%E8%A8%AA-%E6%B5%99%E6%B1%9F-%E6%8B%86%E5% 8D%81%E5%AD%97%E6%9E%B6-%E7%99%BC%E9%85%B5-%E5%B0%88%E5%AE %B6%E6%8C%87%E5%AE%98%E6%96%B9%E6%86%82%E5%9F%BA%E7%9D% A3%E6%95%99%E7%99%BC%E5%B1%95%E9%81%8E%E5%BF%AB

104 Cited in Liang Song'en, "*Yazhou Zhoukan* reports that 'Zhejiang Christians are no longer silent lambs,'" Chinese.gospelherald.com, September 6, 2015, https://chinese.gospelherald. com/articles/25400/20150912/%E4%BA%9E%E6%B4%B2%E9%80%B1%E5%88%8A-% E5%A0%B1%E5%B0%8E-%E6%B5%99%E6%B1%9F%E5%9F%BA%E7%9D%A3%E5% BE%92-%E4%B8%8D%E5%86%8D%E6%98%AF%E6%B2%89%E9%BB%98%E7%9A% 84%E7%BE%94%E7%BE%8A.htm

105 Cited in "The Zhejiang government's comments on the demolition of religious and illegal premises: 2.3 percent of illegal structures belong to the Christian Church," *Qianjiang Daily* (Zhejiang), August 20, 2014, http://news.china.com/domestic/945/ 20140820/18722747.html

106 See "Members of the Standing Committee of the Zhejiang Provincial Party Committee take the initiative to talk to religious figures: 'the Wenzhou experience' will be implemented across the province," *Zhejiang Daily*, June 9, 2015, http://zjnews.zjol. com.cn/system/2015/06/09/020689877.shtml

107 Cited in Wei Dedong, "Open letters by the Christian and Catholic Churches on the demolition of crosses reflect the severe relationship between the government and the church in the region," *Gospel Times*, July 15, 2015, www.gospeltimes.cn/news/36690/% E9%AD%8F%E5%BE%B7%E4%B8%9C%EF%BC%9A%E6%B5%99%E6%B1%9F%E5% 9F%BA%E7%9D%A3%E6%95%99%E4%BC%9A%E3%80%81%E5%A4%A9%E4%B8% BB%E6%95%99%E4%BC%9A%E5%85%B3%E4%BA%8E%E6%8B%86%E5%8D%81% E5%AD%97%E6%9E%B6%E7%9A%84%E5%85%AC%E5%BC%80%E4%BF%A1% E5%8F%8D%E6%98%A0%E5%BD%93%E5%9C%B0%E6%94%BF%E6%95%99%E5% 85%B3%E7%B3%BB%E4%B8%A5%E5%B3%

108 See "China arrests Pastor Guo Yuese who opposes the demolition of crosses," Voice of America, February 1, 2016, www.voachinese.com/a/china-detain-pastor-20160129/ 3169440.html. For a discussion of the persecution of Pastor Gu, see Ying Fuk-tsang, "Pastor Gu Yuese in the midst of the storm of the demolition of crosses," *The Initium* (Hong Kong), February 3, 2016. https://theinitium.com/article/20160203-opinio n-yingfuktsang-cross/

109 See "Christians in Zhejiang broaden their struggle [against the authorities] as the demolition of crosses is stepped up," Thestandnews.com (Hong Kong), August 28, 2015, https://thestandnews.com/china/%E6%B5%99%E6%B1%9F%E5%9F% BA%E7%9D%A3%E5%BE%92%E5%A4%A7%E6%8A%97%E7%88%AD-%E6%8B% 86%E5%8D%81%E5%AD%97%E6%9E%B6%E9%A2%A8%E6%9A%B4%E5%8D%87% E7%B4%9A/

110 For a discussion of the installation of surveillance cameras in churches, see, for example, Thomas Williams, "China installs surveillance cameras in churches to spy on Christians," Breitbart.com, April 4, 2017, www.breitbart.com/national-security/2017/ 04/04/china-installs-surveillance-cameras-in-churches-to-spy-on-christians/. See also Alice Yan, "In 'China's Jerusalem', 'anti-terror cameras' the new cross for churches to bear," *South China Morning Post*, April 3, 2017, www.scmp.com/news/china/poli cies-politics/article/2084169/chinas-jerusalem-anti-terror-cameras-new-cross-churches

111 Author's interview in February 2017 in Shenzhen with an active member of the underground church in Wenzhou.

112 See Cao Yaxue, "Interviews with pastors."

113 Cited in Men De, "Two reflections on Pastor Wang Yi's weibo talk," Gospelherald. com, April 10, 2014, www.gospelherald.com.hk/news/edi-1362/%E6%9B%BC%E5% BE%B7%EF%BC%9A%E5%B0%8D%E7%8E%8B%E6%80%A1%E7%89%A7%E5% B8%AB%E5%BE%AE%E5%8D%9A%E8%A8%80%E8%AB%96%E7%9A%84%E5% 85%A9%E9%BB%9E%E5%8F%8D%E6%80%9D

114 Author's interview with theology lecturer, Hong Kong, May 2017. Also see Sudworth, "Why many Christians in China have turned to underground churches."

115 See Vivienne Zeng, "Chinese Christians make crosses at home as church crosses are removed by government," Hong Kong Free Press, July 27, 2015, www.hongkongfp. com/2015/07/27/zhejiang-christians-make-crosses-at-home-as-church-crosses-are-rem oved-by-govt/

116 Cited in Ying Fuk-tsang, "Commentary on the National Conference on Religion," Christiantimes.org.hk, April 24, 2016, http://christiantimes.org.hk/Common/Reader/ News/ShowNews.jsp?Nid=94012&Pid=6&Version=0&Cid=150&Charset=big5_hkscs

117 Cited in "Chinese priests ordered to put up signs banning children from churches," Catholic News Service, February 9, 2018, www.catholicherald.co.uk/news/2018/02/ 09/chinese-priests-ordered-to-put-up-signs-banning-children-from-churches/. See also "China tightens control on churches, enforces law against teaching Christianity to children," Gospelherald.com, September 15, 2017, www.gospelherald.com/articles/71384/ 20170915/china-tightens-control-churches-enforces-law-against-teaching-christianity-children.htmv

118 Cited in Charlie Campbell, "China's leader Xi Jinping reminds party members to be 'unyielding Marxist atheists,'" *Time*, April 25, 2016, http://time.com/4306179/china -religion-freedom-xi-jinping-muslim-christian-xinjiang-buddhist-tibet/

119 "Churches in Guangdong and Xinjiang have been hammered and several tens of people arrested," Radio Free Asia, July 12, 2016, www.rfa.org/cantonese/news/reli gion-07122016095540.html?encoding=simplified

120 Ibid.

121 Cited in *Report on Religious Freedom in Mainland China (2016)*, Hong Kong: China Human Rights Lawyers Concern Group, 2016, p. 42.

122 For a discussion of the plight of Shouwang Church, see, for example, "Church members of persecuted Beijing's Shouwang Church administratively detained," Chinaaid.org, October 30, 2015, www.chinaaid.org/2015/10/church-members-of-perse cuted-beijings.html. See also "Items to report on celebrations on July 16, 2017 by the Beijing Shouwang Church," Beijing Shouwang Church, July 15, 2017, https://t3. shwchurch.org/2017/07/15/%E5%8C%97%E4%BA%AC%E5%AE%88%E6%9C%9B %E6%95%99%E4%BC%9A%E4%B8%BB%E6%97%A5%E6%8A%A5%E5%91%8A% E4%BA%8B%E9%A1%B9%EF%BC%882017%E5%B9%B47%E6%9C%8816%E6% 97%A5%EF%BC%89/

123 Cited in "China's pre-Christmas church crackdown raises alarm," BBC News, December 18, 2018, www.bbc.com/news/world-asia-china-46588650. See also "100 members of the Chengdu Early Rain Church arrested; some were forced to sign pledges to stop attending church functions," *Ming Pao*, December 11, 2018, http://premium.mingpao. com/cfm/Content_News.cfm?Channel=ca&Path=101107867113/caa1.cfm

124 For a discussion of "cults" as defined by the party, see, for example, "Our country has specifically identified 14 cult organizations including the Shouters," *Youth Times* (Beijing), June 3, 2014, http://news.sina.com.cn/c/2014-06-03/011730279732.shtml. See also Murong Xuecun, "China's clampdown on 'evil cults,'" *Time*, June 17, 2014, www. nytimes.com/2014/06/18/opinion/murong-chinas-clampdown-on-evil-cults.html?_r=0

125 Cited in Liu Jianping, "Zhou Enlai's understanding of and practice regarding the issue of Chinese Christianity at the beginning of the establishment of the new China," *The Party's Archives* (Beijing), Vol. 135, Issue 3, 2010, pp. 46–51, http://dangshi.people. com.cn/GB/138903/138906/11587983.html

126 For Wu's role in setting up the TSPM, see, for example, Duan Yi, "The pioneer of the sinicization of Christianity: on the founder of the TSPM crusade Mr Wu

Yaozong," *China Nationalities Paper*, July 10, 2015, www.gospeltimes.cn/index.php/p ortal/article/index/id/29329. For a discussion of the views of Wu Yaozong, see, for example, "Wu Yaozong's son: Wu Yaozong, the founder of China's Three-Self Patriotic Church, is a 'tragic figure,'" Radio Free Asia, February 17, 2014, www. chinaaid.org/2014/02/wu-yaozongs-son-wu-yaozong-founder-of.html

127   Cited in "The present condition of the mainland Chinese church: the TSPM and house churches," Pu Shi Institute for Social Science (Beijing), October 10, 2010, www.pacilution.com/ShowArticle.asp?ArticleID=2634. See also Wang Weifan, "The pattern and pilgrimage of Chinese theology," *The Chinese Theological Review*, 1990, pp. 26–44.

128   For a discussion of the career of the early "rightist" Christians such as Jia Yumin and Ni Tuosheng, see, for example, "Wang Yi: Christian rightists in 1957," Quora.com, June 17, 2014, www.quora.com/profile/Simon-Lee-22/Hermons-World/%E7%8E% 8B%E6%80%A1%EF%BC%9A1957%E5%B9%B4%E7%9A%84%E5%9F%BA%E7% 9D%A3%E5%BE%92%E5%8F%B3%E6%B4%BE%E5%88%86%E5%AD%90%E4%BB% AC. See also Joseph T.H. Lee, "Watchman Nee and the Little Flock Movement in Maoist China," *Church History*, Vol. 74, Issue 1, March 2005, pp. 68–96.

129   Ibid.

130   For an assessment of Ding Guangxun, see Chen Zhuqin, "100th birthday of Ding Guangxun: he silently endured the stigma of 'heresy' and is resolute in loving the country and the church," *The Paper* (Shanghai), November 2, 2015, http://m.thepap er.cn/newsDetail_forward_1390914. For an official view of the contributions of official Christian leader Ding Guangxun, see, for example, "Symposium commemorates late Chinese Christian leader," Xinhua News Agency, September 22, 2015, http:// news.xinhuanet.com/english/2015-09/22/c_134649432.htm

131   For a discussion of the significance of Wang Mingdao as an advocate of free Christianity that is independent of state interference, see, for example, Hing Hung Otto Lui, "Development of Chinese church leaders – a study of the relational leadership in contemporary Chinese churches," Ph.D. thesis, Fuller Theological Seminary, July 2011. See also Xing Tsang-fu, "60th year anniversary of the arrest of Wang Mingdao and the publication of 'We – for the sake of faith,'" Chinaaid.net, November 8, 2015, www.chinaaid.net/2015/08/60.html

132   Most of Wang's better-known sayings come from his most famous article, *Women shi weili xinyang* ("We – for the sake of faith"), which is contained in *Selected Works of Wang Mingdao*, Chinese Christian Life Web (n.d.), http://cclw.net/other/wangminda o/wmd9/htm/chapter03.html. For an English version of "We – for the sake of faith," see the translation by Frank W. Price, Missionary Research Library, New York, *Occasional Bulletin*, Vol 7., No. 3, March 15, 1956.

133   For a discussion of how Buddhism has enjoyed the patronage of the CCP, see, for example, Elizabeth Bond, "China: the patron of global Buddhism?" worldpolicy.org, April 19, 2012, https://worldpolicy.org/2012/04/19/china-the-patron-of-global-bud dhism/. See also Echo Huang, "Officially, China's Communist Party believes in atheism, but it makes an exception for two religions," Qz.com, February 28, 2017, https://qz.com/920779/officially-chinas-communist-party-believes-in-atheism -but-it-makes-an-exception-for-two-religions/

134   For a discussion of Xi Jinping's status as "leader for life," see, for example, Jeremy Wallace, "Is Xi Jinping now a 'leader for life,' like Mao? Here's why this is dangerous." *Washington Post*, February 27, 2018, www.washingtonpost.com/news/monkey-cage/ wp/2018/02/27/is-xi-jinping-now-a-leader-for-life-like-mao-heres-why-this-is-danger ous/?utm_term=.e00a30696607

135   Author's phone and WeChat interview with a pastor in an underground church in central Henan Province, April 2017.

136   Author's interview with a senior member of a house church in Zhejiang Province, November 2017.

137 Cited in Tom Phillips, "Chinese preacher 'grateful' to be jailed amid 'anti-church' campaign," *The Telegraph*, October 13, 2014, www.telegraph.co.uk/news/world news/asia/china/11158630/Chinese-preacher-grateful-to-be-jailed-amid-anti-church-campaign.html. For a discussion of the message of Huang Yizi, see also Carey Lodge, "China: pastor released from 'black jail' after opposing cross demolitions," *Christian Today*, February 9, 2016, www.christiantoday.com/article/china-pastor-released-from -black-jail-after-opposing-cross-demolitions/79129.htm

138 See *Selected Works of Wang Mingdao*.

139 "Pastors in seventeen cities sign petition: 'We – for the sake of faith: a petition to the National People's Congress on the conflict between state and church,'" Boxun.com, May 13, 2011, www.peacehall.com/news/gb/china/2011/05/201105130242.shtml. See also "No response to the petition of pastors: the situation of Shouwang Church has become more dangerous," Radio Free Asia, May 30, 2011, www.rfa.org/mandarin/zhuanlan/xinlingzhilyu/zhongguozongjiaopohaibaogao/m0527mind-05302011134956.html

140 See "A conference on the forced demolition of Christian churches: speakers say this incident has severely shocked the church," *Christian Times* (Hong Kong), June 6, 2014, http://blog.sina.com.cn/s/blog_c57bc5020101pzmo.html

141 See "The deputy director of the Nanjing Union Theological Seminary."

142 Cited in "Re-announcement of Chinese house churches on the relationship between the government and the church (Beijing Manifesto)," Boxun News, October 19, 2015, www.boxun.com/cgi-bin/news/gb_display/print_versiOn.cgi?art=/gb/china/2015/10&link=201510190801.shtml

143 See Yang Jun, "A church that has been thrust into the public sphere," Chinaaid.net, August 17, 2015, www.chinaaid.net/2015/08/blog-post_80.html

144 See "Editorial: churches must avoid becoming politicized," *Global Times*, April 26, 2011, http://opinion.huanqiu.com/1152/2011-04/1652371.html

145 Author's interview with Professor Xing in Hong Kong, December 2018.

146 Cited in "Chinese Christian rights lawyers group is established," *Epoch Times*, January 21, 2006, www.epochtimes.com/gb/6/1/21/n1197817.htm. For a discussion of the relationship between human rights lawyers and the church, see Xing Tsang-fu, "China's rights defense movement and the Christian faith," Chinaaid.net, May 12, 2015, www.chinaaid.net/2015/05/blog-post_90.html. See also Southerland, "Zhejiang's Christians."

147 For a discussion of Zhang's views, see, for example, "Lawyer Zhang Kai: the relationship between the government and the church has reached an extremely nervous juncture," *The Initium* (Hong Kong), August 27, 2015, https://theinitium.com/article/20150827-china-church-cross-lawyer/

148 See "Human rights lawyer Zhang Kai was arrested; his lawyer colleagues ask the authorities for his release," Voice of America, August 29, 2015, http://blog.sina.com.cn/s/blog_5f54b3d10102wl6y.html. See also Chris Buckley, "Lawyer who advised churches in China faces secretive detention," *New York Times*, September 1, 2015, www.nytimes.com/2015/09/02/world/asia/china-lawyer-churches-zhang-kai.html?mcubz=1

149 Ibid.

150 Cited in Wang Xinyi, "Professor Liu Peng announces citizens' suggested draft for a 'Law on Religion,'" *Christian Times*, August 15, 2013 www.christiantimes.cn/news/11937/%E5%88%98%E6%BE%8E%E6%95%99%E6%8E%88%E5%85%AC%E5%B8%83%E4%B8%AD%E5%9B%BD%E3%80%8A%E5%AE%97%E6%95%99%E6%B3%95%E3%80%8B%EF%BC%88%E8%8D%89%E6%A1%88%EF%BC%89%E5%85%AC%E6%B0%91%E5%BB%BA%E8%AE%AE%E7%A8%BF%E8%A6%81%E7%82%B9

151 Cited in Yu Jianrong, "A study of the legalization of Christian house churches," Aisixiang.com, December 18, 2013, www.aisixiang.com/data/70584.html

152 See Ying Fuk-tsang, "Intellectuals and the Chinese Church," *Zhanwang Zhonghua Journal* (Hong Kong), No.12, February 2001, pp. 22–25, www.godoor.net/text/history/zhjh16.htm

153 For a discussion of the Christian faith of intellectuals during the Republican period, see Yang Tianhong, *Christianity and Intellectuals in the Republican Period*, Beijing: Renmin Press, 2005. See also Shi Jinghuan and Wang Lixin, *Christian Education and the Chinese Intellectual*, Fuzhou: Fujian Education Press, 1998.

154 For a discussion of Lin Zhao as a devoted Christian, see Ren Bumei, "Li Zhao as a Christian," Chinaaid.net, May 1, 2017, www.chinaaid.net/2017/05/blog-post_70.html. See also Yuan Zhiming, "Remembering Lin Zhao, the Christian victim of the Cultural Revolution," *Gospel Herald*, May 2, 2013, www.gospelherald.com.hk/news/edi-1288/%E9%81%A0%E5%BF%97%E6%98%8E%EF%BC%9A%E8%BF%BD%E6%86%B6%E6%96%87%E9%9D%A9%E5%9F%BA%E7%9D%A3%E5%BE%92%E5%8F%97%E5%AE%B3%E8%80%85%E6%9E%97%E6%98%AD

155 For a study of the doctrines of Yuan Zhiming and Zhang Boli, see, for example, Tobias Brandner, "Trying to make sense of history: Chinese Christian traditions of countercultural belief and their theological and political interpretation of past and present history," in Francis Khek Gee Lim, *Christianity in Contemporary China: Sociocultural Perspectives*, London: Routledge, 2013, pp. 78–90.

156 Cited in Yu Jie, "Why does Xi Jinping persecute Christians?" *Christian Times* (Hong Kong), September 7, 2015, http://christiantimes.org.hk/Common/Reader/News/ShowNews.jsp?Nid=91024&Pid=1&Version=0&Cid=145&Charset=big5_hkscs

157 Cited in Fredrik Fällman, "Public faith? Five voices of Chinese Christian thought," in *Contemporary Chinese Thought*, Vol. 47, 2016, Issue 4, January 20, 2017, pp. 223–234, www.tandfonline.com/doi/abs/10.1080/10971467.2015.1262610?needAccess=true

158 Ibid.

159 See Wei Dedong, "The open letters on demolished crosses [published by] the Christian and Catholic churches in Zhejjiang reflect the severe relations between the government and the church in this province," *Gospel Times*, July 15, 2015, www.gospeltimes.cn/index.php/portal/article/index/id/29374

160 Cited in Li Xiangping, "Socialization and China's religion – the changes of faith in the past 30 years," Pacilution.com [Beijing], December 22, 2011, www.pacilution.com/ShowArticle.asp?ArticleID=3228

161 Author's interview with a Shanghai-based pastor in June 2017.

162 Cited in Carey Lodge, "A top Chinese intellectual converts to Christianity," Christiantoday.com, November 11, 2015 www.christiantoday.com/article/top.chinese.intellectual.converts.to.christianity/70277.htm

163 Cited in Eleanor Albert, "Christianity in China," Council on Foreign Affairs, New York, May 7, 2015, www.cfr.org/backgrounder/christianity-china

164 Cited in Wang Xinyi, "Conference on religion and rule of law is again held in Beijing," *Christian Times*, November 28, 2015, www.christiantimes.cn/news/19720/2015%E5%AE%97%E6%95%99%E4%B8%8E%E6%B3%95%E6%B2%BB%E7%A0%94%E8%AE%A8%E4%BC%9A%E5%8C%97%E4%BA%AC%E5%86%8D%E5%BA%A6%E4%B8%BE%E8%A1%8C-%E5%AE%97%E6%95%99%E5%9C%BA%E6%89%80%E4%B8%BB%E4%BD%93%E4%B8%8E%E7%95%8C%E9%99%90%E6%88%90%E5%85%B3%E6%B3%A8%E8%AF%9D%E9%A2%98

165 See Carsten T. Vala, "Protestant Christianity and civil society in authoritarian China: the impact of official churches and unregistered 'urban churches' on civil society development in the 2000s," *China Perspectives*, Issue 3, 2012, pp. 43–52. http://search.proquest.com.easyaccess1.lib.cuhk.edu.hk/docview/1496063144/F671ED7E214C47EDPQ/22?accountid=10371

166 Cited in Li Fan, "The impact of Christianity on Chinese politics," *Background & Analysis*, Vol. 20, The World and China Institute, December 4, 2008, www.gongfa.com/html/gongfazhuanti/xianzhengzhuanxing/20081203/139.html

167 Cited in Tom Phillips and Harriet Sherwood, "China accused of trying to 'co-opt and emasculate' Christianity," *The Guardian*, November 17, 2015, www.theguardian.com/world/2015/nov/17/china-accused-emasculate-christianity-secret-conference-communist-party

168 Cited in Wang Ce, "The forceful demolition of crosses will ignite China's 'Revolution of the Crosses,'" Boxun.com, August 19, 2015, www.boxun.com/news/gb/p ubvp/2015/08/201508190624.shtml#.Vo0oqKNunsY

169 Cited in Guo Baosheng, "Explaining the movement to sinicize Christianity," *China Strategic Analysis*, China Strategic Analysis Center Inc., January 16, 2017, http://zha nlve.org/?p=215

5

HOW THE CHINA–U.S. COLD WAR OPENS UP OPPORTUNITIES FOR THE CIVIL SOCIETY

Introduction: the new Sino–U.S. Cold War has exacerbated contradictions within China and provided a window of opportunity for the civil society

Well before American Vice-President Mike Pence declared the moral equivalent of a Cold War on China in a late-2018 speech at a Washington think tank, it had become apparent that the PRC and the United States were locked in a bitter struggle for supremacy. The trade dispute that began to wreak havoc on bilateral ties in the spring that year was but one manifestation of an all-out confrontation between the status quo superpower and a quasi-superpower that wants to rewrite the rules of the game in matters ranging from global finance to geopolitical contention. The Donald Trump administration has accused China of not only piling up astronomical trade surpluses, but also stealing intellectual property rights; forcing PRC-based American multinationals to freely yield their intellectual property rights (IPR) to Chinese counterparts; espionage activities such as hacking into government systems; building bases on South China Sea isles whose sovereignty is in dispute; bullying Taiwan; and stifling the rights of dissidents and ethnic minorities. The hawkish administration of President Xi Jinping is also alleged to have mounted a "comprehensive and coordinated campaign" to influence American politics through dubious lobbying tactics. "Beijing is employing a whole-of-government approach, using political, economic and military tools, as well as propaganda, to advance its influence and benefit its interests in the United States," Pence argued. A November 2018 study by 32 senior American Sinologists also concluded that "China is intervening [in the U.S.] more resourcefully and forcefully across a wider range of sectors than Russia."[1] Secretary of State Mike Pompeo even vowed to:

> oppose [China] at every turn. … Whether that's a risk through the stealing of intellectual property or trade rules that are unfair or activity in the South

China Sea or their continued expansion in space and their efforts to develop their military, each of those actions has been met with a strong and vigorous response from the [U.S.] and we'll continue to do so.[2]

Even worse for Beijing is the fact that, as the CCP administration has vastly expanded its global clout through generous overseas foreign direct investment via the Belt and Road Initiative (BRI), American allies and quasi-allies, especially the U.K., France, Germany, Japan, South Korea, Australia, New Zealand and India, are wary of the rise of a crypto-superpower that does not seem to follow international law and global norms. Even smaller EU countries that are relatively dependent on Chinese investment have joined the U.S. alliance in exposing Chinese-originated espionage and influence peddling. After a well-documented exposure of how Beijing has sought to buy influence in Australian politics through hefty donations to politicians, the CCP's CUFWD is shown to be doing similar things in New Zealand, Germany and France.[3] Accusations of spying by Chinese companies and agents have also been made by countries including Norway, Poland and Lithuania.[4] A late-2018 poll conducted by Pew Research Center demonstrated that, when it comes to global leadership, most countries preferred the U.S. over China by a wide margin. A survey of citizens in 25 countries showed 63 percent favored the U.S., and only 19 per cent supported China. Corresponding figures for Asian countries were 73 percent in favor of the U.S., and 12 percent for China.[5]

As the following sections show, the China–U.S. confrontation has exposed chinks in the armour of the "China model." President Xi, who changed the PRC Constitution in March 2018 to enable himself to rule for life, is seen as incapable of handling the multifaceted challenges posed by the U.S. and its allies. Instead of trying to mend age-old problems in the political and economic system by deepening reforms, Xi has steered the ship of state on an ultra-conservative course – and toward the restitution of Maoist norms such as *ziligengsheng* ("self-reliance"). Many of Trump's criticisms of Beijing's economic policies, however, precisely target Xi's abandonment of Deng Xiaoping's open-door policy and the strongman princeling's re-embracing of the Maoist ethos of tight party control over the economy. The fact that most Chinese are beneficiaries of four decades of Deng's reforms means that Xi cannot put the blame for Washington's apparent "anti-China containment policy" on so-called American neo-imperialism. Indeed, a sizeable number of liberal intellectuals are convinced that Trump's anti-CCP salvoes could help nudge the country back to Deng's tradition of economic liberalization and the partial adoption of global political and foreign-policy norms.

The monumental crisis facing the Xi administration, however, could result in ample opportunities for intellectuals, dissidents, rights attorneys, underground church personnel and civil-society crusaders to lay into the current administration for forsaking Deng's relatively tolerant economic and political platforms – and even to clamor for thorough-going political reforms. This chapter looks at various theories about the drastic decline or even demise of authoritarian regimes for reasons including (a) factional rivalry when the leader in power is seen as cleaving to outdated, ultra-conservative ideals; (b) gross governmental mismanagement coupled with economic decline; and (c) greater readiness on the part of liberal party members and the intelligentsia to speak out. In light of the fact that Xi, who is also general secretary of the party and chairman of its Central Military Commission, has beefed up what critics call an Orwellian police state, few observers expect that the CCP will implode in the foreseeable future. However, hundreds of professors, jurists and church campaigners were bold enough to speak out in 2018 and early 2019 in support of political liberalization. And fissures in the body politic exposed by the China–U.S. Cold War has thrown into sharp relief the increasingly ferocious battle between the civil society and the party on how to shape the country's future.

The China model – and the Xi administration – challenged during the clash between Western liberal capitalist values and Beijing's hard authoritarianism

Pushback against the phenomenon of "authoritarianism going global"

Beijing bids to overtake the United States and become the world's biggest power by the 2040s: the BRI and the global marketing of the China model

It is no secret that President Xi's super-ambitious goal for the 21st century is to attain superpower status by the 2040s. This is the objective of the Chinese Dream (announced in late 2012) and that of "a new era of socialism with Chinese characteristics," which was enunciated at the 19th CCP Congress five years later. Apart from economic prowess and military strength, Xi is confident that what he calls "the Chinese wisdom" will have gained widespread recognition and even approbation around the world before the middle of the 21st century.[6] As the Chinese way of doing things – or what is usually known as the China model – consists of a hard-authoritarian state riding roughshod over intellectuals and the civil society, it is of critical importance whether Beijing's aggressive marketing of the China model will work. If the majority of nations, including members of the traditional Western liberal alliance, find nothing wrong with conducting business with a Leninist state, the morale of dissenters and civil-society supporters in China will nosedive – and their chances of getting moral and financial support from overseas could be diminished.

Much has been written about President Xi's no-holds-barred global projection of hard and soft power. What has been termed the world's most aggressive and expensive overseas propaganda exercise (the Chinese term is *dawaijiao*, or "making propaganda worldwide") is keenly felt by ordinary folks in regions ranging from the U.S. to Africa.[7] The propaganda function of the 525 Confucius Institutes has been thoroughly debated. Much less covered but equally intriguing is the fact that Chinese multinationals – whether state-owned enterprises (SOEs) or putatively private firms – are working hand in glove with the party in making generous donations to academic institutions in the U.S. and EU, in addition to building schools and sports facilities in the developing world.[8]

Short of attaining world dominance, Beijing is obsessed with becoming the final arbiter of political and economic developments in its backyard, the Asia-Pacific region. Geopolitically, the CCP leadership seems confident of tackling the "anti-China containment policy" spearheaded by the U.S. via the "island chain" mechanism. Through providing economic largesse such as hefty imports, Beijing's has improved overall relations with South Korea and at least economic ties with Australia and New Zealand. The CCP has excellent relations with Thailand and particularly the "pro-Chinese" regime of mercurial Philippine President Rodrigo Duterte.[9] Thanks to support from such client states as Laos and Cambodia, Beijing has succeeded in preventing the Association of Southeast Asian Nations (ASEAN) from collectively raising protests against its occupation of disputed islets in the South China Sea.[10] At the moment, most of China's neighbors are undertaking the delicate balancing act of depending on China for economic benefits while continuing to rely on American defense to prevent the PRC from becoming the region's sole hegemon. Beijing seems convinced, however, that momentum is going its way in the battle eventually to win hearts and minds in the Asia-Pacific region.

It is no secret that, as the pioneer of the "China model of development," which Beijing believes is more suitable for developing countries in Asia, Africa and Latin America, China wants to modify aspects of Western-determined global norms that it deems prejudicial to countries that do not share liberal capitalistic values. Take, for example, the financial world order mainly inaugurated by the U.S. in the early 1950s. Starting with the Hu Jintao era, Beijing has complained about the lack of representation of developing countries in the World Bank and the International Monetary Fund (IMF). Beijing has successfully boosted its voting rights in the IMF. In 2015, Beijing set up the Asian Infrastructure Investment Bank, which is supposed to offer competition to the World Bank and the Asia Development Bank as a lender for the developing world. Despite U.S. opposition, a number of American allies, including the U.K., France, Germany, Australia and Canada, have become members.[11] Moreover, Beijing wants to challenge "U.S. dollar hegemony" by vastly expanding the use of the renminbi as a currency for global commercial transactions.[12]

President Xi is also gunning for the fast-paced advancement of science and technology, which he regards as another successful attribute of the China model. The Chinese government announced in 2015 a surprisingly ambitious "Made in China 2025" strategy. The game plan envisages Chinese technology in areas such as ICT, artificial intelligence (AI), robotics, big data and DNA engineering overtaking that of advanced countries such as Germany, Japan and the U.S. by 2025. As with the rest of the economy, state investment is critical. The Ministry of Industry and Information Technology would, in the incubation period, provide 30–50 million yuan in funding to more than 100 projects in 25 industries. Undertakings in core technologies will get more than 100 million yuan. A substantial portion of the breakthroughs in these technologies by both SOEs and private firms are being used to buttress China's extremely sophisticated police-state apparatus.[13] And, to the extent that Western tech giants are also contributing to the building of this 24-hour, all-digital surveillance system, perhaps the most sinister aspect of the China model is its being to some extent accepted as "the new normal" by Western multinationals.[14]

Nothing better illustrates the success – and problems – of China's projection of both hard and soft power than the BRI. Although the BRI has economic and military implications, it is also a spectacular ideological narrative telling the world, especially the Western alliance that is responsible for laying the groundwork of the world order since World War II, that the Chinese brand is on the rise. Since 2013, its year of initiation, the PRC has bankrolled infrastructure and related projects in close to 80 countries. The National Development Reform Commission of the central government estimated in late 2017 that, in the next five years, Beijing would be spending from $120 billion to $130 billion on these megaprojects annually. Together with investments made by partner countries, more than US$1 trillion worth of funds have been earmarked for projects including railways, bridges, ports and container terminals, telecommunications, oil depots and pipelines, as well as technological zones and research facilities.[15] Apart from bonding with developing countries in regions such as Central Asia, ASEAN and Africa, the BRI has also afforded invaluable opportunities for China to secure naval ports as well as full-scale military bases in countries ranging from Pakistan and Sri Lanka to Djibouti. This is despite Beijing's putative foreign-policy principle of not building overseas military outposts.[16]

The China model seems to be gaining the upper hand to the extent that non-democratic countries doing business with the PRC – and benefitting from its loans – seem to prefer Chinese values and ways of doing things to Western standards. Annually, some 50,000 Africans go to colleges and graduate schools in China. According to a late-2018 report by the human rights watchdog Freedom House, Chinese officials have held training sessions on new media or information management with representatives from 36 countries.[17] For some observers, this illustrates what Xi has always called Beijing's commitment to building a "community of common destiny" or "community of shared destiny for mankind." There are also accolades saying that Xi is about to attain the goal of *datong* ("great harmony and common prosperity" among the nations) once advocated by Confucius. Indeed, in an August 2018 speech marking the fifth anniversary of the inauguration of the BRI, Xi cited the age-old Chinese *tianxiaguan* ("worldview") of *hexiewanbang* ("using harmony to unite 10,000 countries,") which, the president added, would facilitate China attaining the "commanding height of the international moral high ground."[18]

In his article "Authoritarianism goes global," Sinologist Andrew Nathan noted the considerable success with which the CCP has exported the China model overseas. "By demonstrating that advanced modernization can be combined with authoritarian rule, the Chinese regime has given new hope to authoritarian rulers elsewhere in the world," Nathan wrote. According to the China expert, Beijing was "playing a key role in a circle of authoritarian states that pick up techniques of rule from one another." Beijing also tried to "shape international institutions to make them 'regime-type-neutral' instead of weighted in favor of democracy," he added.[19] The Xi administration's apparent success in projecting soft power overseas will also render dissident and civil-society groups in its heavily policed country more isolated than ever.

Pushback from the U.S.-led Western alliance

President Donald Trump's muscular military and trade policy against China has amounted to a momentous pushback against Beijing's global power play. The military aspects of the intensification of a so-called "anti-China containment policy" actually began with Trump's predecessor President Barack Obama. It was Obama who said explicitly that, "we must not allow China to write the rules of the game."[20] Although Obama was sometimes characterized as adopting a "soft" foreign policy against authoritarian states ranging from China to Syria, he was the mastermind of the "pivot to Asia" strategy. The "policy rebalance" not only meant stationing more U.S. military hardware on American bases in the Asia-Pacific region, but also deepening defense-alliance relationships with a host of countries, including Japan, South Korea, Vietnam, India, Australia and New Zealand. Washington also negotiated with Canberra the right to station 2,500 troops in the northwestern Australian port of Darwin.[21]

Soon after taking office, Trump presided over a huge increase in military expenditure. He began to refer to the Asia-Pacific region as the Indo-Pacific region, thus emphasizing the role of India – and to some extent Japan, Australia and Vietnam – in reining in the geopolitical ambitions of China. The concept of the Quad – a so-called "coalition of countries with democratic values" that ropes in the U.S., India, Japan and Australia – has been revived to highlight the struggle between a U.S.-led ideological system and the China model.[22] And, although Trump seems to belittle the value of NATO, he has called upon European allies to counter Beijing's effort to turn the South China Sea into a Chinese lake. Not only naval vessels from nearby Australia, but also warships from France and the U.K. have taken part in "freedom of navigation patrols" near Chinese-fortified islets in the South China Sea whose sovereignty is disputed by several ASEAN members.[23] The Trump administration has particularly incurred the ire of Xi by selling arms to Taiwan and allowing U.S. defense companies to manufacture weapons on the island. Trump also began the "custom" of having U.S. aircraft battle carrier groups sail down the Taiwan Strait with increasing frequency.[24] Although U.S. allies have yet to join Washington in playing the "Taiwan card," the Xi leadership is at pains to respond effectively to Trump's series of geopolitical challenges.

Equally significantly, the U.S. has started to directly challenge the BRI. In July 2018, U.S. Secretary of State Pompeo unveiled what some analysts call an "Indo-Pacific business initiative" by announcing US$113-million-worth of U.S. investment in new technology, energy and infrastructure projects in different emerging

Asian countries. Many government officials and academics have compared this miniscule sum with the billions of dollars that Beijing has lavished on BRI initiatives.[25] However, Pompeo highlighted the difference between the U.S. and the Chinese approaches. Pompeo said Washington wanted a "free and open" Asia not dominated by any one country, an apparent reference to China's growing economic clout. "Like so many of our Asian allies and friends, our country fought for its own independence from an empire that expected deference," Pompeo said. "We thus have never and will never seek domination in the Indo-Pacific, and we will oppose any country that does." Pompeo's senior adviser Brian Hook said the new U.S. initiative was "not a strategy to counter" the BRI, and he criticized the latter as "a made in China, made for China initiative."[26]

Although the Western alliance – in addition to Japan and South Korea – does not seem to have the wherewithal to match the astronomical sums Beijing has spent on the BRI, it has laid bare the glaring problems of Xi's apparent imperial overreach. First of all, infrastructure building has become a vehicle for "Chinese-style neo-imperialism." According to an open letter written by 27 EU ambassadors in Beijing, 89 percent of BRI projects are controlled by SOE conglomerates, rather than carried out in partnership with local stakeholders. The senior diplomats lamented the fact that the BRI "runs counter to the EU agenda for liberalizing trade and pushes the balance of power in favor of subsidized Chinese companies."[27]

Then, there are widespread complaints against how Beijing has sought to gain control over smaller states who are the apparent beneficiaries of the PRC's BRI-related largesse. A host of developing countries ranging from Sri Lanka to Djibouti have accused Beijing of waging "debt trap diplomacy." Sri Lanka, which has borrowed heavily from the Chinese government to build its Hambantoto port, has been forced to allow a key SOE, the China Merchants Port Holdings, to run the facility for 99 years.[28] According to the Center for Global Development, eight developing economies run the risk of owing China astronomical sums in return for loans to develop infrastructure: Pakistan, Laos, Mongolia, Kyrgyzstan, Tajikistan, Djibouti, Maldives and Montenegro. Take, for example, Pakistan, the long-term ally of China. It owes China US$6.33 billion, and Beijing has pledged more than US$40 billion for the anticipated China–Pakistan Economic Corridor. The Pakistanis are now rethinking the loans. Djibouti, a former French colony in northeastern Africa with a GDP of a mere US$1.73 billion, owes China US$1.2 billion. Not unlike Sri Lanka, Djibouti has to host a massive naval port for the PRC.[29]

Ding Xueliang of the Hong Kong University of Science and Technology noted that, "more and more government departments and nonofficial organizations in the entire world are adopting measures to counter China's 'expansionism and influence.'" Professor Ding added that these units were alerted to Beijing's "threatening as well as assertive and aggressive acts overseas."[30] Kong Dan, a "princeling" in the ruling Communist Party and former chairman of state-owned conglomerate Citic Group, said the Sino-U.S. trade war was ultimately about "paths" – namely, a clash between Washington's market-led liberal democracy and Beijing's state-led authoritarian model. "For them [the U.S.], if they don't contain us now, our

development is set to threaten them," he said in a speech at an academic conference in September 2018. "So they are attacking our path, since our model of
development is seen as a serious threat to them."[31]

The China–U.S. trade war as a reflection of the U.S.–China struggle for supremacy – and the showdown between the China model and liberal Western capitalist values

On the surface, the 2018 and 2019 trade war between China and the U.S. – which
has been called the largest-scale trade skirmish in modern economic history – was
about dollars and cents. On a deeper level, President Donald Trump was not shy
about the fact that the battle represented a wholesale and all-out attack on the
Chinese political, economic and ideological system.[32] A key target is Xi's departure
from the open-door and fair-trade proposals of the Great Architect of Reform
Deng Xiaoping. Trump repeatedly protested that trade between the countries had
been "very unfair, for a very long time." Trump added: "These tariffs are essential
to preventing further unfair transfers of American technology and intellectual
property to China, which will protect American jobs." While addressing a rally in
West Virginia in August, Trump laid bare his aim of preventing China from
becoming a full-fledged superpower. "When I came [to office] we were heading in
a certain direction that was going to allow China to be bigger than us in a very
short period of time," Trump said. "That's not going to happen anymore."[33] What
is also new is that pretty much all of America's allies in Europe, Asia and Australia
have swiftly joined American efforts to "contain" China.

The gist of Washington's malcontent is the increasingly heavy party-state involvement in areas including (a) Beijing's overall control of both SOE conglomerates
as well as private giants that enjoy the backing of members of the "red aristocracy";
(b) subsidizing the high-tech sector, as manifested in the Made in China 2025
campaign; (c) ensuring that breakthroughs in Chinese technology will advance the
capability of the PLA; and (d) subsidizing the export sector, including both low-
and high-end industries located particularly along the southeast coast. As stated by
the Office of the U.S. Trade Representative's Report to Congress filed in early
2018, China's goal was using party-backed industrial policy to dominate high
technology and the world economy. "Their common, overriding aim is to replace
foreign technology with Chinese technology in the China market through any
means possible so as to ready Chinese companies for dominating international
markets," the report said. It accused Beijing of pursuing "a wide array of industrial
policies in 2017 that seek to limit market access for imported goods, foreign man-
ufacturers and foreign services suppliers," while offering substantial aid to domestic
firms.[34] Equally significant is that advances in the ICT field – such as Huawei's
dramatic development of 5G technology – could elevate the PLA's capacity in
areas ranging from cyberwarfare to ferreting out state and high-tech secrets from
enemy states. The 5G technology could revolutionize military communications
and help speed up command-and-control operations.[35]

On the one hand, Trump and the bipartisan U.S. leadership are battering the "anti-Western" and "party in control of everything" ethos of the China model. On the other hand, Trump is making use of the trade war to ensure that China – the U.S.'s only strategic competitor in the world – can never win in a battle of dominance with the U.S. "The whole of American society appears to have reached a consensus on a new approach to dealing with China," said well-known commentator Deng Yuwen, a former senior editor at the Central Party School. "For the first time in 40 years, the U.S. now sees China as a rival nation to be contained and beaten," Deng added.[36] As China State Information Centre chief economist Zhu Baoliang said, "the substance of the trade war is the showdown between two country's systems, institutions and ideology." Zhu cited as examples American dissatisfaction with SOE reform (which is constrained by Xi's insistence on the party's control over the economy) and sloppy protection of IPR. Yet the Western nations are also repulsed by Xi's super-nationalistic, "brandish-the-sword" worldview, the objective of which is to stoke the flames of nationalism and to bolster China's hard and soft power globally.[37]

The first indication that Trump was not just interested in cutting the humongous trade deficit with the PRC was the April 16 announcement that Chinese Internet giant ZTE would be barred for seven years from procuring American components such as computer chips and software systems. Trump seemed to be targeting the entire Chinese high-tech sector, which is committed to Beijing's vaunted Made in China 2025 goal.[38] At the same time, the Federal Communications Commission banned government funds from being spent on products made by PRC companies such as Huawei and ZTE that were deemed to be a "risk to U.S. national security."[39] Several influential American legislators such as Senator Marco Rubio issued statements that accused Chinese tech firms of "hijacking U.S. technology … to prepare for 'cyber battles of the future.'"[40]

Yet the most devastating strike against a PRC tech giant was the battle against Huawei, perhaps China's most successful multinational. On December 1, 2018, Sabrina Meng Wanzhou, Huawei's CFO and daughter of founder Ren Zhengfei, was detained by Canadian authorities upon Washington's request that Meng be extradited to the U.S. to face charges including selling equipment to Iran. Trump announced an unprecedentedly tough series of measures to prevent American companies from working with Huawei, particularly in relation to 5G technology. As of early 2019, countries including the U.K., France, Germany, Italy, Belgium, the Netherlands, Canada, Australia, Japan and India have announced either an end to using Huawei's 5G technology or at least vastly diminished business ties with the PRC giant.[41] In the wake of the arrest in January 2019 of Wang Weijing, a senior executive with Huawei Poland (and a former Poland-based Chinese diplomat), on espionage charges, Warsaw asked the EU and NATO to work on a joint position whether to ban Huawei from their markets.[42]

Yet another piece of evidence that Washington and its allies have taken up a joint stance to thwart PRC technology is that various governments have joined Washington in preventing Chinese giants from acquiring tech firms in a number of countries. Paris and Berlin took new measures in 2018 to restrict PRC companies from buying tech firms in France and Germany. The French and German governments have also lobbied the EU to consider legislation barring Chinese behemoths such as Huawei from acquiring technological companies throughout Europe.[43]

The U.S. and its allies are also zeroing in on perhaps the most egregious aspect of the China model: Beijing's systematic deprivation of the human rights of its citizens. Although Trump was not that much interested in issues of civil liberties, China's atrocious treatment of dissidents, including rights lawyers, has been widely criticized by members of the U.S. Congress. Secretary of State Pompeo surprised many observers by denouncing Beijing's "awful abuses" of locking up as many as 1 million Uighurs in so-called "re-education camps."[44] In the West, Chancellor Angela Merkel campaigned vigorously for the release of Liu Xia, the wife of deceased Nobel prize winner Liu Xiaobo. Liu was eventually set free in July 2018. During her 2018 visit to China, Merkel also visited Li Wenzu, the wife of veteran rights attorney Wang Quanzhang. Wang was held incommunicado from his relatives from mid-2015 to late-2018, when he was put through a secret trial for alleged "incitement to subvert state power." Even UK Foreign Secretary Jeremy Hunt met Li Wenzhu and other human rights activists while on a trip to Beijing in July 2018 that was largely focused on winning Chinese business deals.[45]

The increasingly tough challenges facing the selling of the China model

The hard edges of China's global soft power projection were put under the microscope in a June 2018 White House document entitled "How China's economic aggression threatens the technologies and intellectual property of the United States and the world." The 35-page statement, attributed to White House trade adviser Peter Navarro, accused the Chinese party-and-state apparatus of using spies, hackers, SOEs, front companies, as well as ethnic Chinese scholars and students resident in the U.S., to "threaten the technologies and intellectual property of the United States and the world." The paper asserted that the PLA and state-security units had dispatched personnel (including scholars and students) numbering in the tens of thousands to the U.S. and other countries so as to "access the crown jewels of American technology and intellectual property."[46]

Along with numerous reports in the Western media about PRC efforts to buy cultural and political influence in the U.S., the EU and Australia, the White House document testified to growing global awareness of the increasingly self-aggrandizing aspects of Chinese soft power projection: namely, gathering intelligence and pilfering IPR so as to expedite China's transition to a superpower, coupled with the use of corruption and other dubious means to influence the perception of China among elites in the West. The result has been an unprecedented pushback from Western nations – and a significant downgrade of the assessment of the China model in Northern America, the EU, Australasia, as well as among liberal sociopolitical groupings across Asia.[47]

In theory, intelligence gathering should be distinguished from soft power projection, which is often defined as the practice of amplifying and spreading the attractive aspects of a country's cultural quintessence to the rest of the world. In practice, this is not always the case. Well-known Sinologist David Shambaugh estimates that the party-state apparatus spends about US$10 billion annually on soft power projection.[48] This raft of initiatives and projects include many activities that sometimes fall outside the traditional rubric of the promotion of a country's culture overseas. Consider the following instances: Beijing sending or facilitating the passage of some 300,000 students and scholars to study or do research in the U.S.; state-security personnel recruiting some of these students/scholars as "nonconventional gatherers" of intelligence; copious donations by PRC multinational corporations to influential politicians and universities in the West; obtaining the IPR of Western tech firms through illegal means; buying supplements in popular Western newspapers and magazines; vastly expanding the foreign-language services of PRC state television and news agencies; stopping "anti-Chinese" books and videos from being published overseas; buying off – or intimidating – professors and opinion-leaders who are deemed "China bashers."[49]

The U.S. and Australia have been at the forefront of the pushback against these practices. From early 2016, the Trump White House has accused Chinese multinationals – especially high-tech firms – of stealing IPR belonging to U.S. tech companies. Since late 2017, however, Washington has also begun to address potential threats to American national security from groups such as PRC students and businesspeople. In a Congressional testimony in February 2018, FBI Director Christopher Wray said his agency believed that a portion of PRC students and scholars in the U.S. could be functioning as spies. He characterized naivete in American universities about the intelligence risk of Chinese "nontraditional collectors [of intelligence], especially in the academic setting" as widespread, adding that the PRC favored a "whole-of-society" approach to espionage.[50] Concerns about student spies and the relatively tight supervision of PRC students exercised by Chinese missions in the U.S. have led the White House to consider curtailing the number of visas offered to PRC students specializing in the sciences, technology, engineering and mathematics.[51]

The spotlight has also been shone on donations made by PRC- or U.S.-based businesses and organizations associated with the CUFWD, which supervises the country's soft power projection as well as overseas influence peddling. In January 2018, the University of Texas at Austin refused a donation from the China United States Exchange Foundation (CUSEF). CUSEF is headed by Tung Chee-hwa, former chief executive of Hong Kong and current vice-chairman of the Chinese People's Political Consultative Conference (CPPCC), a top United Front organ.[52] Moreover, a bipartisan group of 26 members of Congress has asked Secretary of Education Betsy DeVos to investigate whether IT giant Huawei Corporation illegally obtained IPR through its donations to a host of American universities.[53]

Canberra has also taken extraordinary measures to curb PRC lobbying – and Beijing's soft power projection in general – since the 2015 release of a documentary on Chinese influence peddling in Australia. The much-watched video was produced by the Fairfax media group with the help of the Australian Security Intelligence Organization. It exposed how PRC-born business moguls sought to influence Australian politics by making hefty donations to politicians from major parties. These businessmen, who in many cases had become naturalized Australian citizens, also supported pro-Beijing Chinese newspapers and the research of PRC-friendly academics.[54] The Fairfax report did not put an end to Beijing's efforts to shape Australian discourse on China. In June 2018, officials from the Chinese consulate in Sydney tried unsuccessfully to kill a news feature aired by popular news magazine *60 Minutes*. The segment reported on PRC attempts to build a dual-use port on Vanuatu through loans that would be difficult for Vanuatu to repay.[55]

Canberra has struck back ferociously. On June 28, 2018, the Australian government passed a National Security Legislation Amendment (Espionage and Foreign Interference) Bill, which places tough restrictions on the activities of foreign agents – including companies, government institutions and individuals – that would threaten Australian national security through donations, espionage and other forms of undue foreign interference. The law was passed despite the fact that the PRC remains Australia's largest trading partner, and the Chinese government has responded by slow-walking visa applications for senior Australian ministers wishing to visit the PRC.[56]

What has perhaps most alienated Western countries is the readiness with which PRC authorities have openly violated international law by dispatching their state security agents to harass – or even kidnap – both foreign and PRC-born critics of the CCP. In early 2018, the home of New Zealand academic Anne-Marie Brady was broken into, and some of her possessions were stolen, including cell phones and computers. An authority on China's United Front and propaganda departments, Brady published a monograph in 2017 on how Beijing is using soft power to influence foreign governments and silence its critics.[57] The harassment of Brady followed in the wake of the 2015 kidnapping in Pattaya, Thailand, of Hong Kong-based publisher Gui Minhai, a PRC-born Swedish citizen, by agents from PRC security services. After his release from a Chinese jail in late 2017, police repeatedly prevented PRC-based Swedish diplomats from helping Gui leave the country.[58]

A recent report by the New York-based Council on Foreign Policy pointed out that, although China's image has improved in developing countries, the effectiveness of "China's soft power campaign is limited by the dissonance between the image that China aspires to project and the country's actions." After all, aspects of Chinese culture frequently cited by Xi Jinping – a combination of Confucian norms and the "core values of socialism with Chinese characteristics" – do not jibe well with the allegedly criminal activities perpetrated by PRC diplomats and state security agents posted abroad.[59] And this in turn has emboldened domestic critics of the Xi regime – including intellectuals, lawyers and other social activists – to expose the glaring aberrations committed by party authorities.

Amazing number of liberal Chinese intellectuals who agree that the China–U.S. trade confrontation has shown up ingrained imperfections of the China model

Views of intellectuals who think Beijing has overplayed its hand in seeking virtual hegemonism

Given the Xi regime's tight control over intellectuals and the media, one would have thought that the propaganda machinery would have been chockablock with condemnation of Trump's "conspiracy" against China. However, it is testimony to the problematic nature of Xi's pugilistic global hard and soft power projection that an unexpected strain of thought emerged in early 2018 among intellectual and media circles. A popular way of thinking is that China's bellicose, muscle-flexing foreign policy has resulted in a head-on collision with the U.S. which the Chinese cannot win. According to Jia Qingguo, a professor of international relations at Peking University who has the reputation of a pragmatist, "China should adopt a lower profile in dealing with international issues." He said at a mid-2018 forum in the capital that Beijing should not "create this atmosphere that we're about to supplant the American model," said the English-speaking Jia, who is also an adviser to the government.[60]

Even the chief editor of the *Global Times* wrote in his blog that, "our country has indeed in the recent past adopted some high-sounding rhetoric." "This has boosted the concern of the U.S. and the West about China's rise," said the boss of the CCP mouthpiece known for its hawkish views. "It's essential to make some adjustments." "The public will understand necessary compromises [with the West]," he added.[61] In an editorial on August 1, *Global Times* went so far as to say, "we should under all circumstances refrain from actively challenging the U.S. or to show the U.S. how strong we are." The paper added that, although China must retaliate when bullied by the U.S., the leadership should refrain from "excessive retaliation." Most importantly, *Global Times* asked the authorities to "consider the possibility that the U.S. would continue to be the world's premier innovative center, and that it will for a long period and in many aspects remain ahead of China."[62]

These unusual developments have mirrored long-standing concerns among liberal scholars that, owing to its urge to fulfill the "Chinese dream" of becoming a superpower by 2049 or earlier, Beijing's projection of hard and soft power may suffer from what Renmin University America expert Shi Yinhong characterized as "strategic overdraft." Pointing to China's ultra-ambitious agendas in the economic, diplomatic and military fields, Shi indicated that the CCP leadership must "prevent excessive expansionism, which will result in 'strategic overdraft.'"[63] In a similar vein, Nankai University's international relations scholar Liu Feng has introduced the term "strategic adventurism" (*zhanlue maojin*) to describe Beijing's global gambit. "A country on the rise should guard against the problem of 'strategic adventurism,' meaning staging in different areas excessively fast-paced and agitated challenges to the big country in control," he argued.[64]

A number of political scientists have advocated re-hoisting the Deng Xiaoping banner of "taking a low profile and never taking the lead" in foreign affairs – which is the opposite of the pugnacious nationalism favored by President Xi. For Wu Qiang, a former politics lecturer at Tsinghua University, "a number of technocrats and professionals are dissatisfied with the fact that ideological concerns such as nationalism have hijacked China's economic and foreign policy." He added that the recent clash with the U.S. had strengthened the view that China should return to the "keep a low profile" foreign policy mantra laid down by Deng Xiaoping – and that China should work with global norms and not circumvent or challenge them.[65]

Liberal intellectuals lay into Xi's statecraft and praise elements of Western and American values

Yet it has fallen on the shoulders of one of China's highest-profile liberal social scientists, Peking University economist Zhang Weiying, to lay into the China model that President Xi has put forward as an alternative to the U.S.-dominated "global norms." Zhang said China's rapid growth in past decades stemmed not from the "China model" but from a "universal model" that relied on marketization, entrepreneurship and three centuries of accumulating technology in the West, as in the success stories of other developed economies. Professor Zhang argued that promoting the China model would mislead the world into adopting a hostile attitude toward China.

> In the eyes of Westerners, the so-called "China model" is equal to "state capitalism," which is incompatible with fair trade and world peace, and therefore must be contained. ... Blindly emphasizing the "China model" would lead us onto a path of strengthening state-owned enterprises, expansion of state power and overly relying on industrial policy, which would lead to a reversal of reform progress, wasting previous reform efforts, and the eventual stagnation of economic growth.[66]

Individual intellectuals have become bolder in critiquing the major statecraft of Xi: a return to Mao-style dictatorship and an end to most of the market-oriented reforms introduced by Deng Xiaoping. Some radical thinkers even hinted that Trump's salvoes against the China model – especially the party-state's control of enterprises and the dearth of a level playing field for SOEs, private enterprises and foreign firms – were on target and should be favorably reviewed by the Xi administration.

In July 2018, a Tsinghua University law professor, Xu Zhangrun, surprised the Beijing intelligentsia – and observers outside China – by penning an article that was highly pejorative about Xi. Without naming the paramount leader, he blamed the putative "eternal core of the party" for turning back the clock on both political and economic reforms. Most intellectuals, he wrote, were struck by the feeling that, "while reform has gone on for 40 years, we're back overnight to the *ancien régime*." Xu, a famous liberal, said intellectuals were dismayed by "the full-scale return of totalitarian politics." Xu zeroed in on ingrained political and economic problems that had deteriorated under Xi. He cited "aristocratic privileges" accorded senior officials, either serving or retired, including how their spouses and children could take advantage of their political positions to make huge profits. At the same time, the phenomenon of "SOEs making advancements and private firms making a retreat" is being exacerbated. Xu called upon Xi to observe fixed tenures – and to focus on economic construction instead of Cultural Revolution-style ideological movements to boost cadres' loyalty to himself. Finally, in view of China's long experience of "using the open-door policy to bring about domestic reform," he urged Beijing not to endanger ties with "the Western world led by the U.S.," but to continue to adopt universal norms.[67]

Rebel scholars who dared challenge Xi include a politics professor at the Central Party School, Cai Xia. Even before the trade dispute with the U.S. started in earnest in March 2018, Cai cast not-so-subtle aspersions at Xi by saying: "More and more people in and outside China are puzzled by his words and deeds." "What does he want to do; where does he want to bring China to?" she asked. Claiming that Xi suffers from "cognitive disorder," Cai said: "Owing to his immense powers and the fact that China faces severe political, economic and social crises … his cognitive disorder has boosted the risk of a major revolution such as the French Revolution happening in China."[68]

A key reason why progressive intellectuals dared to criticize Xi was his apparent failure to handle the multiple challenges posed by Trump. He Jiangbing, a senior financial research scholar, noted in a mid-2018 essay that China lacked the where-withal to parry the threats of Trump. He pointed out that the Xi administration had failed to make a dent in long-standing problems including over-leveraging, the housing bubble and, more recently, the depreciation of the renminbi. Unless Xi were to use market-oriented reforms to fix these and similar economic problems, China just lacked the means to hit back at American challenges. "Now you [the Chinese government is] bent on challenging the U.S., yet the bubble economy cannot sustain" the cuts and thrusts of a trade war, he wrote. "If you are bent on hurling yourself at the steel pin of Trump, then go ahead. But for many people, it's like eggs being pelt at a boulder, or even worse, bubbles knocking themselves at a steel needle."[69]

Zi Zhongyun, a veteran expert in international affairs who once served as an interpreter for Mao Zedong, was even more forthright in criticizing the China model. She asserted that, if China accepted the demands of the U.S., the Chinese economy would improve greatly – and that the issue of special privileges and monopolies granted to people with political connections would be put to an end. Zi agreed with Washington that the services sector should be opened much wider, because American-style services were much better developed. "If American-style hospitals flourished in China, China's blood-sucking medical model would be banished," she wrote. "If American-style education took root in China, Chinese students need not go abroad to enjoy advanced pedagogical concepts." She also expressed the hope that, once Western-style financial services can freely set up shop in China, the renminbi will soon be internationalized. Other benefits included lower interest rates for private enterprises and the possibilities that non-state-dominated industries might develop and that a consumer society would come into being. Zi, however, did not think that Beijing would accept the conditions laid down by Washington. She added that most of China's economic woes could be attributed to monopolization of resources by the privileged classes, "and this is why the Chinese government would never accept America's terms."[70]

In testimony before the Senate in early 2019, the commander of U.S. Indo-Pacific Operations, Admiral Philip Davison, said China represented the "greatest long-term strategic threat to a free and open Indo-Pacific and to the United States." Warning that the U.S.–China geopolitical rivalry in the Pacific was actually more far-reaching than most pundits believe, Davidson argued that, "those who believe this is reflective of an intensifying competition between an established power in the United States and a rising power in China are not seeing the whole picture." "Rather, I believe we are facing something even more serious: a fundamental divergence in values that leads to two incompatible visions of the future," he said.[71] The problem for the Xi administration is that more and more Zi-like intellectuals are gravitating toward the American vision – and they are bold enough to say so out loud.

Conclusion: how can intellectuals and civil-society activists speed up political change?

Despite the zeal with which Xi Jinping is turning back the clock on reform, what Deng Xiaoping calls the *daqihou* ("macro climate") seems to be militating against Xi's anachronistic infatuation with Maoism. The two pillars of CCP legitimacy are under threat. As we have discussed, the Xi administration's hard and soft power projection is meeting with unprecedented challenges; this has handicapped Xi's ability to stoke the flames of nationalism, which consists in projecting awesome images of China soon displacing the U.S. as the world's sole superpower. The other pillar of legitimacy – economic development and improvement in the living standards of ordinary Chinese – is also facing tough tests.

Several examples suffice to illustrate the malaise that is eating away at the PRC's economic viability. Despite apparent efforts to restructure the economy, Beijing is still relying heavily on government injections by different levels of government and SOE conglomerates into sectors such as infrastructure and housing so as to generate economic growth. Yet total social debt has mushroomed to close to 300 percent of GDP. The value of real estate, estimated in 2017 at US$42.7 trillion, was almost four times the GDP of 2016 – and the bursting of the property bubble could have a disastrous nationwide impact. Most Chinese have borrowed profusely to pay for mortgages, and this has affected the expansion of consumer spending, which has been touted as a powerful new locomotive of growth. Indeed, household debt doubled from 29.6 percent of GDP at 16 trillion yuan in 2012 to 44.3 percent of GDP at 33 trillion yuan in 2017.[72] Whereas most countries have stopped quantitative easing, Beijing had, by mid-2018, boosted the money supply to minimize the impact of the trade war. The first action of the People's Bank of China (PBoC) in 2019 was to further reduce the reserve requirement ratio by 1 percent, a move that would augment liquidity by 1.5 trillion yuan. In addition to the PBoC, the Finance Ministry and the National Development Reform Commission were instructed to further cut taxes and to come up with expansionary industrial policies.[73] However, so many companies are on the brink of bankruptcy that additional borrowings from banks are mostly being used to pay interest rates on loans. President Xi is also worried about unemployment spiking owing to domestic and foreign-owned factories moving their productions to Southeast Asia because of both American tariffs and China's rising production costs. His much-ballyhooed move to invigorate the high-tech sectors has met with rebuffs and even boycotts by the U.S. and its allies.[74]

It is also not a coincidence that, as the two pillars of legitimacy – economic growth and nationalistic glory – are facing problems, the Xi administration is devoting unprecedented resources to buttressing an AI-enabled police-state apparatus to quell dissent and minimize the number of "mass incidents," a euphemism for protests and disturbances. The following sections will show that, although intellectuals and NGOs are going through a prolonged winter, opportunities for these reformers and pacesetters are opening up owing to the Xi administration's loss of support within the party as a result of its perceived failure to counter Washington's "anti-China containment policy." Few members of the civil society believe that the regime will collapse in the near term of, say, five to ten years, yet they seem confident of at least being able to promote positive, forward-looking ideas among the public, thus sowing the seed for Beijing's eventual embrace of universal norms such as rule of law and respect for civil liberties.

Whether – and when – the CCP will collapse, and its implications for the civil society

Minxin Pei, a veteran Sinologist who has done substantial research on the transition of authoritarian regimes, thinks that a cataclysmic change involving the possible demise of the CCP as the sole ruling force in China could come earlier than many people reckon. "Evidence from contemporary China and insights from history and social science suggest that the possibility of a transition from authoritarianism in China in the not-too-distant future (perhaps within the next decade and half) is much greater than many think," he wrote in a 2016 paper.[75] Pei's views are shared by China experts including David Shambaugh, who was bitterly criticized by the Chinese media after publishing an article in 2015 called "The coming Chinese crack-up." "The endgame of Chinese communist rule has now begun, I believe, and it has progressed further than many think," wrote Shambaugh. The Sinologist cited phenomena such as the ossified ideology of the party, compliance feigned by the rank and file, massive corruption, increasing repression of the civil society and emigration by the elite to the West.[76]

Professor Pei has identified the following four "main symptoms of decay" in the Chinese polity: the atrophy of its ideology, the erosion of its performance [particularly in economic development], endemic official corruption, and an intensifying power struggle and growing dissension among elites over their survival strategy. Pei also noted that, although the possibility of regime collapse resulting from military confrontation with the U.S. over issues such as Taiwan is not high, a new version of the Cold War could hasten the CCP's collapse. "The costs of such a strategic conflict between China and the United States, however, including the unavoidable curtailment of the two countries' commercial ties, would inevitably accelerate the CCP's decline," he wrote. "Although regime breakdowns are impossible to predict, they are far more likely to occur in autocracies in an advanced stage of regime decay than in those in better shape."[77] The fact that Xi was subjected to attacks from within the party for failing to handle Trump's fusillades has demonstrated that internal bickering among factions has intensified despite the continuation of Xi's personality cult.

He Qinglian, a former dissident social scientist now resident in the U.S., argues that the CCP regime will, at least in the foreseeable future, continue to decay without an obvious breakdown. He, who has written widely on China's economy and corruption, indicated in a series of articles in the mid-2010s that the simultaneous concurrence of four criteria was necessary for the CCP's collapse: "a domestic governing crisis [a coup, or a financial crisis], a complete breakdown of relations between the government and the people, continual violent resistant movements, and foreign invasion." She added:

> For now, a foreign enemy is but a fictional idea; the chance of a coup is slim; a financial crisis exists only at local government levels and is manageable; and small-scale resistant movements, despite their frequent occurrence, are not enough to shake the CCP regime.

She called this condition *kui'erbubeng* ("decaying [just] short of collapse").[78]

It is, of course, difficult to predict for how long this state of decay might last. It should be noted that the economic situation in China has deteriorated markedly since He's articles were published a few years ago. For example, the financial crisis that "exists only at local government levels and is manageable" has spread to the rest of the economy. Although He argued that a "foreign enemy" had yet to materialize, the multidimensional challenges that Donald Trump has posed to China have plunged the two countries into a ferocious new Cold War. In any event, the civil society could function as a catalyst for the strengthening of pro-reformist forces in China. Both Pei and He make reference to the role of rival or nongovernmental institutions in Chinese society. Pei noted that, particularly if China were to go through a transition to a reform-oriented regime, "the relative independence and robustness of key social institutions such as the church, business groups, professional organizations, and labor unions" would be major factors for change. The Sinologist added that civil-society groups would be more effective in promoting sociopolitical change if they had tighter links among themselves – and if they could put together a national network.[79]

He Qinglian had a comparatively low opinion of ordinary Chinese citizens' preference for democratic change. She pointed to the large number of people – 150 million "environmental refugees" and beneficiaries of social welfare, fresh college graduates and pensioners – who survive on government handouts. "For these groups of people, democracy is a dream, but their livelihood is very real," she said. But He argued that, based on Internet surveys, at least 200,000 Chinese "do have certain understanding of democracy and are willing to take personal action [to strive for democratization]."[80] Short of going to jail, intellectuals and NGO combatants are doing all they can to expand the numbers of democracy-loving Chinese – and to educate them about how to incrementally effectuate changes in the system.

Escalation of internecine bickering within the CCP: the backlash against Xi Jinping in 2018

Despite Chairman Mao's famous remarks about the existence of "mountain strongholds" or cliques within the party – "it would be very strange if there were no factions in the party" – it has been a long-standing trait of the CCP to maintain a façade of unity.[81] Fissures within the ranks have only been revealed to the outside world during crises such as the student demonstrations of 1989 and the Cold War-like confrontation between the U.S. and China. For a period of about six weeks in mid-2018, it was clear that forces within the party – helped by the intelligentsia – had mounted a challenge to Xi's authority. The pretext was the Xi leadership's failure to effectively retaliate against Trump's tariffs, as well as Washington's efforts to thwart China's high-tech program and to launch a "witch-hunt" against U.S.-based Chinese "spies." Xi's critics also doubled down on the supreme leader's abrogation of term limits for the state presidency in March 2018, which could in theory render Xi "Emperor for Life."[82]

At least a moratorium was imposed on the relentless personality cult that has been built around Xi since the 19th Party Congress, which conferred upon the 65-year-old dictator Maoist titles such as "illustrious core of the leadership," the highest commander of the military" and the *renmin lingluren* ("pathfinder for the people"). In early July, various cities mothballed portraits and display photos of Xi. The Shaanxi Academy of Social Sciences suddenly ended its research into "The Great Wisdom of Liangjiahe," a reference to Xi's innovative ideas and exploits while serving as a student in the Liangjiahe Village during the Cultural Revolution. Most inexplicably, Xinhua News Agency, on July 11, ran an article criticizing Hua Guofeng – Mao's designated successor who was in power for only two years – for cultivating a cult of personality. This was seen as an indirect way of slamming Xi, whose personality cult had rivalled that of Chairman Mao. In a rare departure from routine, there was no reporting about Xi on the front page of the *People's Daily* on July 9 – and similarly for three days in June.[83]

It is a well-established custom within the party that, whenever the No. 1 needs extra support, he would mastermind a ritualistic *biaotai* or public declaration of fealty among central and regional leaders in both the civilian and military sectors. In July 2018, NPC Chairman Li Zhanshu, a long-standing Xi confidant, coined a new slogan to eulogize the "eternal core" of the party leadership. Li, also a member of the Politburo Standing Committee (PBSC), urged all cadres and party members to do their utmost to "ensure that party central authorities with comrade Xi Jinping as their core will have the power to *yichuidingyin* ['call the final shots'] and to *dingyuyizun* ['settle differences with utmost authority']." After NPC boss Li raised the banner relating to *yichuidingyin* and *dingyuyizun*, most provincial or mayoral leaders felt uncomfortable about playing the *biaotai* game. Even well-known sycophants of Xi's such as the party secretaries of Tianjin and Beijing, namely Li Hongzhong and Cai Qi, have not said anything to burnish Xi's authority. The only exception was Jiangxi Party Secretary Liu Qi, who vowed to uphold Xi's authority to *yichuidingyin* and *dingyuyizun*. Liu's *biaotai*, however, came after a five-day visit to Jiangxi by Li Zhanshu.[84] Xi also failed to secure public protestations of fealty from members of the top brass.[85]

Although, soon after coming to power at the 18th Party Congress, Xi arrogated to himself the chairmanship of the Central Financial and Economic Commission and the Central Commission for Comprehensively Deepening Reforms, the supreme leader seems to lack the professional knowledge and expertise to function as economic czar. There have been widespread reports about Xi clashing with his principal economics adviser, Vice-Premier Liu He, about how to deal with the Americans. White House chief economist Larry Kudlow claimed while speaking at a conference in the U.S. that the super-nationalistic and hawkish Xi was preventing doves such as Liu He and other State Council bureaucrats from engaging in give-and-take with the Americans. "I think Xi is holding the game up," Kudlow said. "I think Liu He and others would like to move but haven't."[86] Other top officials in charge of the economy, notably Premier Li Keqiang, have long been known as free-market advocates.[87]

There seemed to be no authority forceful enough to stop internecine bickering among State Council departments handling the economy. Both Hong Kong and Western media have reported on open warfare among State Council officials on ways and means to resuscitate the economy, including how to lend a hand to enterprises that may fall victim to the trade war.[88] A bone of contention is whether monetary and fiscal policies should be further loosened to avert an economic slowdown. On July 13, Xu Zhong, the director of the Research Bureau of the PBoC, published an article slamming the Finance Ministry for its apparent "dearth of effective fiscal policies" to help sectors hurt by the ongoing Sino-U.S. dispute. Xu even complained that the Finance Ministry had "low transparency," and that it was "behaving like a hoodlum."[89] Such open warfare among departments or officials, which is rare in the tradition of the party-state apparatus, could only be symptomatic of Xi's much-weakened authority.

It is, however, not easy to identify Xi's opponents within the party. After all, the paramount leader still has undisputed control of the army and the police. A good reason why the conservatives won over the liberals in the June 4 crisis of 1989 was that Deng had the full support of the PLA. Yet there is a common denominator that has pulled together anti-Xi forces in the party – the fifth-generation princeling's betrayal of Deng Xiaoping's reforms: Xi's over-concentration of powers in his own hands runs against Deng's insistence on collective leadership; Xi's emphasis on the party's tight control of key aspects of the economy has provided an excuse for the Trump administration to "punish" China; and Xi's renunciation of Deng's "keep a low profile" foreign-policy dictum has not only resulted in the country's "strategic overdraft" but provided corroboration of the "China threat" theory – that Beijing is out to wrest world leadership from the hands of the U.S.-led Western alliance.

The most potent anti-Xi bloc within the CCP's top echelons consisted of the descendants of Deng and allied leaders who masterminded the reform programs in late 1978; they were frustrated by Xi's rejection of Deng-style reforms and his apparent re-embracing of Maoism. Leading this group were the offspring of Deng Xiaoping and former-President Liu Shaoqi, who were notable victims of the Cultural Revolution. Take, for example, an internal speech given by Deng Pufang, Deng's eldest son, in September 2018. Referring to the past 40 years of reform, Deng said that, although reforms begun by his father had met with attacks and difficulties, "the pace of historical progress won't stop." "We must bite our teeth and never retrogress," he said. "The reforms won't be shaken in a hundred years."[90] Princelings who do not see eye to eye with Xi have underscored the imperative of drawing the right lessons from the Cultural Revolution: this seemed an indirect casting of aspersions on Xi's resuscitation of Maoist norms. For example, General Liu Yuan said, at a ceremony marking the contributions of his father Liu Shaoqi, that, "our generation has personally gone through the Cultural Revolution – and it must never, never again happen." "We must never commit such a mistake again," he added.[91] Other critics of Xi included the two sons of the late party General Secretary Hu Yaobang, a liberal icon whose death on April 15, 1989 ignited the student demonstrations. Both Hu Deping and Hu Dehua were disappointed that their reform-related suggestions made to Xi in 2013 were jettisoned by the dictatorial Xi.[92]

Although, so far, resentment against the Maoist turn in Xi's policies has been evinced by intellectuals and "rightist" princelings, other victims of the paramount leader's crypto-Maoist economic measures have also become vocal. The most vociferous protests have come from private firms, who feel that they are being squeezed by the exacerbation of the policy of *guojinmintui*, or "state-owned enterprises making advances while private firms are beating a retreat." It is understandable that, at a time when China's economy is threatened by what Beijing perceives to be unfair treatment by the U.S., General Secretary Xi might want to go back to his Maoist roots and sing the praises of autarky. During an August trip to northeastern Heilongjiang Province, Xi re-hoisted the famous Maoist flag of *ziligengsheng*, or self-reliance, which was a much-used slogan during the Cultural Revolution. The clause *ziligengsheng* appeared twice in Xi's 2019 New Year's message to the nation. While inspecting factories in the northeastern province, Xi reiterated that SOEs should be "made stronger, better and bigger." "Any ideas or views that cast doubt or aspersions on SOEs are wrong," he said.[93]

Xi's apparent reinstatement of at least some aspects of Maoist economics has coincided with widespread speculation that private enterprises will be put under tighter party control – and that the more successful ones might even be forced to sell stocks and shares to SOEs. Former entrepreneur Wu Xiaoping even went so far as to say that, "private firms have finished their historical mission." According to the *Shanghai Security News*, 46 private companies listed on the Shanghai Stock Market sold their shares – and, in more than half of these cases, their controlling stake – to SOEs in the first half of 2018.[94]

Despite their awareness that President Xi is no friend of either market forces or the private sector, businesspeople and liberal economists demonstrated unusual boldness in defending the fruit of 40 years of reform. These anti-Xi views were aired during a mid-September meeting of the China Economy Forum of 50, a progressive think tank whose founders included Xi protégé Liu He. Duan Yongji, president of Stone Group, one of China's earliest private enterprises, said at the conclave that, "non-state firms have played the role of the savior of the country." "Yet we have only been given titles and emblems, but not provisions and ammunition," Duan added, in apparent reference to the fact that private firms were taxed heavily while being discriminated against when applying for loans from state-controlled banks. Veteran economist Wu Jinglian, perhaps China's best-known advocate of a free market, noted at the meeting that the fate of reform depended on the development of the non-state sector. He argued that, in the past 40 years, China's economy had done best "when we are committed to the market and the rule of law."[95] Even Hu Deping, a long-time supporter of the market economy, felt duty-bound to support private enterprises. He warned against a repetition of the erroneous experiment in the 1950s of *gongsiheying*, or "joint management by state and private companies." "Some non-state firms are being forced to go down the road of *gongsiheying*," he said in September 2018. "It will be terrible if this [erroneous idea] were to become a trend."[96]

Contributions of intellectuals and the civil society

As discussed earlier, it was a group of public intellectuals who first dared, in mid-2018, to challenge Xi's quasi-Maoist governance philosophy – and his inability to fend off Trump's attack on China's statist economy. These not-so-subtle critiques of a socialist despot who had just annulled constitutional term limits became a catalyst for other anti-Xi elements among princelings, cadres and the intelligentsia to express their support for a liberalized economy and, to some extent, a liberalized political system. Although some of the first batch of intellectuals who lambasted Xi in June and July 2018 were penalized by party censors, fully 100 avant-garde thinkers, academics, commentators and NGO activists unveiled, on December 30, 2018, a public statement called "100 Chinese public intellectuals publish their thoughts on forty years of 'reform and the open door.'" The petition contained the forward-looking intelligentsia's bold call for "building up the nation based on human rights." As Shandong-based senior journalist Chen Baocheng noted, "if there is no freedom of speech and thought, reform will be totally meaningless." Or, as lawyer and former judge Chen Tianyong proclaimed, "Reform should be beneficial to the protection of private property and free-market economics. Reform must boost the freedom of citizens"[97] (see Chapter 2.)

As the conclusion of this book, we explore further avenues whereby dissidents, liberal intellectuals, members of house churches, rights attorneys, labor organizers and other NGO pace-setters can take advantage of the difficulties encountered by Xi and his crypto-Maoists so as to nudge the ship of state toward reforms more in line with the requirements of international standards.

A new renaissance? Spreading the word about global norms

If He Qinglian is right about the fact that, potentially, 200,000 Chinese are willing to do something to advance the prospects of democracy, the actions and writings of intellectuals, rights attorneys, house church supporters and civil-society groups recorded throughout this book provide examples aplenty of how they have broadened the horizons of ordinary citizens.

Occupying the front line are a very limited number of dissidents who still dare to tilt against the windmill – at least when they are out of prison. One example is Hu Jia, winner of the Sakharov Prize in 2008 who was jailed from 2009 to 2011. In an interview, Hu said he was willing to be the "tankman" – a reference to the fearless man who blocked the approach of tanks on Tiananmen Square on June 4, 1989. What Hu meant was that, even though he was under tight police surveillance, he would stay upfront and voice his opposition without restraint. Hu said that, for many years, activists working for less sensitive political causes such as AIDS/gender, the environment and labor had told him that he had given them opportunities. "I have enlarged their space and made their crusades seem less provocative because I'm engaged in the most sensitive issues," Hu said. "I am willing to be a forerunner in the battle field, and I have offered invisible protection for them."[98]

Many intellectuals want to revive the gist of *minguo*, or Republican Period (1911–1949) culture, which benefitted from China's first-ever "renaissance" during the May Fourth Movement of 1919. Although the slogan of the May Fourth Movement was the introduction of Mr. Cai ("science") and Mr. De ("democracy") from the West, these norms are also in line with the celebration of freedom of opinion and expression already evident in the Period of the Spring and Autumn (approximately 771–476 BCE) in ancient China. Veteran commentator Zi Zhongyun described how the *qimong* ("enlightenment") of the Republican Period has been followed by another "stage of benightedness," which was marked by "the unity of politics and religion [Communist ideology], and where political leaders become ideological teachers." Zi has given new impetus and urgency to the goals of the intellectuals, including celebrating independence of thinking and popularizing global norms. "Intellectuals must liberate themselves, fight to have an independent personality and integrity, and minimize their dependence on … 'open-minded emperors,'" Zi said. "They should diligently engage the public and propagate global values: human rights, rule of law, freedom, democracy and constitutional governance."[99]

Church leaders such as Wang Yi, the pastor of Chengdu's Early Rain Reformed Church, are willing to go to jail to demonstrate that, as citizens of the modern world, the Chinese should be able to choose what to believe in. A former lawyer, Wang also believes in consolidating and strengthening a community of civil-society enthusiasts so as to force the party-state apparatus to observe limitations to its powers – and to allow citizens to enjoy rights enshrined in the Constitution (see Chapter 4). A generation of legal scholars and rights attorneys who have defended dissidents and Falun Gong practitioners have taught the Chinese that they have an inalienable right to freedom of thought, expression, assembly and participation in government. Lawyers such as Zhu Jiuhu have also highlighted the inviolability of private property – as well as the rights of private entrepreneurs to ensure that their businesses will not be expropriated by the powers that be. Apart from mainstream values, NGOs focusing on citizens who live on the fringes of society have also opened the minds of ordinary Chinese regarding tolerance of diversity in society. A member of at least a dozen-odd feminist and LGBT-oriented groups in southern and eastern China told this author that, "we focus on community education instead of outright confrontation [with the authorities] in this harsh climate." The issue of gender equality and LGBT rights used to be taboo in Chinese society; now it is at least acceptable to talk about, for example, the rights of women to use legal means to protect themselves against sexual harassment.[100]

Fostering "an organized state of disorganization"

Xia Yeliang, a former Peking University economics professor who is now living in Washington, DC, coined the term "an organized state of disorganization" to describe how, despite being splintered – and under 24-hour surveillance – civil-society leaders and participants might yet play a critical role when the time for political change is ripe. Xia indicated that it was well-nigh impossible for any forces to organize an opposition party either within China or abroad. "Currently the civil society in China is unorganized," Xia said.

> Yet through the media and through different kinds of real-life interactions and appeals to people's conscience, a large group of civil-society activists – and politicized citizens aware of the importance of civil rights – could be formed to clamor for action when opportunities arise.[101]

Xia argued that, although it was difficult to organize on a national scale, a slow but sure accumulation of public sphere-expanding actions by individuals and NGOs in different cities and provinces could produce big changes.[102] For Li Fan, different kinds of NGOs and civic-minded groups are still growing, despite the government crackdown. The party's unprecedented control over the Internet notwithstanding, the net has enabled "these groups to exist in accordance with the principle of 'organizing without [formal] organizations.'" Li, who became known for his study of local-level elections in Chinese villages, said the state of "disorganized organization" would remain a long-term characteristic of civil-society units. He noted that the growing number of social organizations outside the party's control had found a way of preserving their strength despite the unprecedented crackdown.[103]

The peculiar behavior of a good number of dissident intellectuals serves to illustrate the principle of a "state of organization while being disorganized." Owing to face-recognition and other AI software – plus the deployment of seemingly ubiquitous police and neighborhood-committee "vigilantes" – the nation's radical intellectuals are on a tight leash. However, at least politically conscious scholars living in big cities can meet periodically for lunches and dinners. [It would, however, be difficult for dissidents from neighboring cities to meet together on a periodical basis.] Similarly, intellectuals can organize trips to sweep the graves of noted victims of the Cultural Revolution or the June 4, 1989 massacre. This is despite the fact that they would be watched all the way by police – and that some intellectuals might be roughed up by law-enforcement officers or by triad members paid for by public security departments. Such gatherings, plus close connections through the net, have fanned the fire of resistance.[104]

Although joint activities performed by intellectuals might seem haphazard, they could none the less exert collective pressure on the authorities. On the occasion of the death and sea burial of Nobel Prize winner Liu Xiaobo in July 2017, a few dozen dissidents managed to travel to Shenyang, where the Peace Prize laureate had been incarcerated, to express collective condemnation of a case of the authorities denying medical treatment to a seriously ill patient. Those who could not reach Shenyang did a good job coordinating interviews with the Hong Kong and foreign media, thus ensuring that the CCP authorities would face rounds of condemnation from the global media.[105]

The other occasion was the plethora of articles written by senior academics and commentators asserting that Trump was in many ways right when he pinpointed aspects of the economy that had been excessively controlled by the party-state authorities. At the height of the Sino-U.S. confrontation over trade, some 1,000 alumni of Tsinghua University lodged a public protest over views expressed by Hu Angang, a well-known professor at the School of Public Policy and Management of Tsinghua University. In articles and speeches, Hu, a specialist in the national capacity of nations, has since 2013 claimed that China had already surpassed the U.S. in terms of economy, technology, as well as other measurements of national strength. Hu also alleged that the China model was vastly superior to the American political and economic systems. The protestors claimed that Hu should be sacked by the university.[106]

As discussed above, the Xi administration has taken hard-line measures not seen since the Cultural Revolution to break the back of house churches – even well-established ones with deep roots in the cities. Large urban churches such as Shou-wang and Zion in Beijing have more than a thousand members each, and they had been meeting every week since the late 2000s. By 2017 and 2018, however, police had closed down their regular venues. A member of the Zion Church based in Beijing told this author that the police had successfully stymied organized activities by this congregation of 1,500. "Police have personally warned old and new believers that coming to our gatherings would mean 'trouble,'" he said. The interviewee said Zion had earlier rented an office in a building for the regular congregations. "We were told by police the lease was no longer valid and there are police outside the building at all hours," he said.[107]

Yet the Zion church and other similarly placed underground congregations could well adopt the strategy of "organizing without formal organizations." The Zion church decided to break up its congregation by dividing it into 40 or 50 groups. "These groups meet separately away from churches or easy-to-identify premises, most often in large parks or forests in the suburbs," said the Zion activist. "And they don't necessarily congregate." As a whole or individually, group members receive weekly recorded messages from their pastors through social media. "And while it may be no longer possible for the pastors to personally communicate with us, the mere fact that these subgroups have not been broken up by police is a manifestation of solidarity and demonstration of our faith," he added.[108]

In mid-2018, some 116 pastors from house churches around the country issued a public petition protesting the new Regulations on the Administration of Religious Affairs, which came into effect in February that year. "Christian churches across China have suffered from varying degrees of persecution, contempt, and misunderstanding from government departments … including various administrative measures that attempt to alter and distort the Christian faith," said the petition. "Some of these violent actions are unprecedented since the end of the Cultural Revolution."[109] The flame of faith, despite flickering, has been held up for all to see.

Intervention via "atomized actions"

Intellectuals, dissidents and NGO participants have also sought to impact society through staging small-scale or "atomized" actions. In her recent book, *Mobilization with the Masses*, Toronto University political scientist Diana Fu argues that, in an authoritarian state, individuals or civil-society participants could take different types of individualized, well-tailored, and sharply focused actions that could avoid head-on confrontation with the police; this would avoid mass imprisonment or even the total obliteration of entire civic-minded groupings. One method identified by Fu is "disguised collective action," which encourages civil-society groups to exercise "strategic adaptations" by organizing atomized actions of protest instead of collective and large-scale activities or movements. The repertoire of atomized actions includes "verbally threatening state officials; contacting journalists with their grievances; staging sit-ins at government offices; holding flash demonstrations; and, in extreme cases, threatening to commit suicide in a public space." Although many atomized actions – of which petitions could be one example – merely deal with individual grievances, others could help foster a collective consciousness that might have the potential to mushroom into a social movement. "By bringing participants face-to-face with similarly disadvantaged individuals, organizations construct a collective identity as citizens of a polity that has denied them their legal rights," Fu wrote.[110]

Typical atomized actions include the protests lodged at subway stations by members of a tiny group of women's rights activists subsequently known as the "Feminist Five." Li Maize (also known as Li Tingting) was a lone activist who was first involved in a small-scale protest against domestic violence. She and four other women were arrested by the police in March 2017 for planning to distribute leaflets in Beijing, Guangzhou and Hangzhou about sexual harassment in China's packed public transport system. Their arrest made them well known not only in China, but also overseas. And awareness about women's rights nurtured by the Feminist Five could be behind the partial success of the #MeToo movement in different locations and institutions across the nation.[111]

Non-group-based, apparently spur-of-the-moment actions could also take place during a drama or in a concert hall. What happened during a performance of Ibsen's *Enemy of the People* at Beijing's Grand Theatre had a sizeable impact on China's netizens. The play was performed in German by the Schaubühne Theatre in September 2018. The work centered on efforts by the crusader Dr. Stockmann to expose the scandal of water pollution at the baths of a German town. Toward the second half of the performance, Dr. Stockmann, a central character in the drama, suddenly turned the theatre hall into some kind of townhall meeting. During an exchange with the audience, which was conducted in English and Chinese, actors asked whether audience members supported Dr. Stockmann. Soon, the topic turned to issues of censorship and freedom of expression. The leaders of the Grand Theatre were so nervous that they implored the German team not to reenact the Q&A with the audience again. Moreover, the scheduled show in Nanjing was cancelled.[112] Something unexpected happened during a Shanghai performance of the French musical *Les Misérables* at about the same time. After the performance was over, several dozen spectators stayed put in the famed Shanghai Cultural Square Theatre. As though by prior arrangement, they stood up and sang the English version of "Do you hear the people sing?" A video of the incident had a wide circulation on the Internet before the sensors removed it. Said a netizen, "Yes we don't have power to change reality. But we can at least sing a song to express our deeply felt emotions and aspirations."[113]

Although *gongren tuanti*, or labor-related NGOs – most of which are based in relatively liberal southern provinces such as Guangdong – have not been reported as widely abroad as other sectors, they have displayed tremendous originality and ingenuity in adapting to the harsh climate. After the mass clampdown on *gongren tuanti* in late 2015, labor activists decided to *huazhengweiling*, or operate as individuals and not as organizations. Consider the case of a Guangdong-based labor activist whose organization was crushed in 2015. "Now we function as individual counsellors or consultants to our former clients in the factories," he said. "We give advice to workers on topics such as their legal and welfare rights in our homes, in cafes or wherever we can find a safe venue that can contain a dozen or so people."[114] Other labor organizers have established "society-run non-enterprise units," which mainly offer non-sensitive services such as psychological counselling and rehabilitation after workplace injuries. "We are taking up mostly individual cases rather than factory-wide issues," said a Shenzhen-based labor organizer. "Individual cases can percolate gradually to larger groups in the labor community."[115]

The Jasic Factory labor unrest in 2018 showed that activists can be mobilized quickly to put pressure on the party-state as what was originally an atomized action morphs into a sizeable social movement. The Jasic incident took place in May when veteran worker representative Yu Juncong criticized the factory's welfare standards in a Weibo post. He was fired immediately. Things swiftly got out of hand in mid-July, when two other would-be unionists in Jasic, Liu Penghua and Mi Jiuping, were beaten up by triad society members for allegedly "stirring up trouble." Liu and Mi led 20-odd workers to the local police station demanding the right to set up a union. They also started holding demonstrations at the factory with the support of more colleagues. On July 27, some 25 workers were arrested by local police for "picking quarrels and making trouble." A few days later, however, a few hundred students from Peking University and Renmin University in Beijing, as well as Zhongshan University in Guangdong, converged on the scene to show solidarity with the workers. Moreover, several thousand students from 16 universities in different cities initiated an Internet petition supporting the right of workers to unionize. Although the Jasic authorities showed signs of a compromise by declaring their intention to allow workers to establish private unions, a few dozen Beijing students who claimed to be "fervent Marx followers" continued to stay in Shenzhen. The police waited until August 24 to detain the students and to forcibly send them back to Beijing. Moreover, the parents of the student leaders were given severe warnings about how to better rein in their children.[116] Although labor unionism was effectively suppressed in Jasic, it would be held up as an example of how a small-scale action could be transformed into an internationally reported incident involving "asymmetrical warfare" between a handful of determined, socially conscious groups and the quasi-police state.

A budding network against Xi's reinstatement of the "neo-totalitarian state"

By early 2019, more evidence had emerged that President Xi was moving China from hard authoritarianism to what Sinologist David Shambaugh calls the "neo-totalitarian state," namely a return to the Maoist era of near-total control of thought enabled by a world-class police-state apparatus.[117] The repression is also intensifying owing to the CCP administration's repeated failure to resolve long-standing socioeconomic ills, which have ranged from fake food and beverages to sky-high medical and surgery costs. The political scene has become characterized by what He Qinglian calls "a complete breakdown of relations between the government and the people," which she has listed as a condition for regime collapse.

Although intellectuals, dissidents and NGO pioneers are as yet unable to pose a challenge to Xi's AI-assisted police-state apparatus, there are indications that what the CCP fears most – cross-provincial protests that could flare up into a ferocious nationwide rebellion – might happen sooner than many would think.

Take, for example, the series of demonstrations by demobilized soldiers across China in the spring and summer of 2018. Groups ranging from several hundred to a few thousand held sit-ins outside government buildings in several cities including Zhenjiang in Jiangsu Province, Yantai in Shandong, Luohe and Luoyang in Henan Province and Chengdu and Zhongjiang County in Sichuan Province. Retired soldiers demanded better livelihood supplements and medical benefits, and younger servicemen who had worked in the PLA for relatively short periods wanted better job placements and welfare payouts. Many of these flare-ups were also in response to reports that demonstrators or their relatives had been roughed up by the police and even thugs. Most alarming for the authorities was that demobilized soldiers had built up a quasi-national network, with groups in each city communicating with each other using social media. Thus, demonstrators in most of the cities cited above hailed from like-minded groups from a number of different provinces.[118] The administration's pitiful problem-solving skills were demonstrated by the fact that similar protests had flared up in 2016 and 2017. The 2016 rally outside the PLA headquarters in Beijing was the first time that the nation's powerful generals were unable to prevent disorder from breaking out right on their doorstep.[119]

The year 2018 also witnessed other cross-country protests of varying magnitudes. In July, tens of thousands of mostly middle-class Chinese held gatherings in several cities after the collapse of some 800 so-called peer-to-peer lending platforms earlier in the year. The victims had been promised high interest rates for deposits in quasi-Ponzi-scheme operations, which also sold a rich array of "wealth management products." About 8,000 of these so-called "financial refugees" from 30 provinces planned to hold a demonstration outside the China Banking Regulatory Commission in downtown Beijing in early August. Yet the authorities mobilized thousands of police and the quasi-military PAP to block the protestors: some were beaten up, and all of them were forcibly removed from the site of the demonstration. Protests in other cities were also harshly suppressed. At least three victims of these large-scale fraud schemes committed suicide in September. Their bodies were forcibly taken away by the police and quickly cremated. Grieving relatives were prevented from talking to foreign reporters. In yet another indication of the fast deterioration of the CCP's governing ability, the first wave of collapse of peer-to-peer lenders had taken place in early 2016, when 80 such companies went bust.[120]

Then there was the massive scandal involving the sale of improperly manufactured health vaccines made by the private company Changchun Changsheng

Biotechnology in Jilin Province. Such faulty vaccines against rabies, diphtheria, whooping cough and tetanus had been administered to hundreds of thousands of children. In July, a few dozen parents managed to hold a brief protest outside the State Health and Family Planning Commission. But demonstrations in both Beijing and the cities were suppressed thanks to heavy-handed police intervention. The demonstrators were particularly agitated by the fact that instances of faulty vaccines had occurred repeatedly in the previous decade.[121] Some also remembered an equally heart-wrenching scandal in 2008, when hundreds of thousands of children developed kidney stones and other diseases after consuming milk powder and other milk products laced with melamine. As with other instances of social malaise, it took the authority of the No. 1 official, Xi Jinping, to speed up investigations and to mete out heavy penalties to vice-ministerial-level officials charged with oversight of health products.[122]

These and other social scandals have inspired intervention by NGO activists as well as rights lawyers. Zhao Lianhai, whose son was a victim of contaminated milk in 2008, became China's best-known crusader against fake and faulty medicine when he organized a group of parents to protest against government inaction. He was sentenced in 2010 to two and a half years in jail for "disturbing social order." Zhao said in July 2018 that he was working on a comprehensive database of children affected by tainted vaccines. "We are going to submit it to the State Health and Family Planning Commission, providing them with this information from the parents, and then hope that they will help us," Zhao said.[123] Two lawyers – Tang Jingling and Yu Wensheng – who represented parents in vaccine scandals in the years 2006–2009, are still in jail for alleged "subversion of state power." Yet perhaps the most brilliant protest was masterminded by nationally famous rights lawyer Zhang Kai. An article he wrote in late July 2018 about the vaccine disaster, called "We are all in the same boat," was posted on Weibo for 17 hours before it was removed by the censors. So many readers not only read the article, but also made use of the "tipping function" of Weibo that Zhang collected 1.4 million renminbi. He vowed to use the money to set up a fund for compensating the victims of the faulty vaccines.[124]

It may be true that, for the foreseeable future, members of the civil society might lack the means of thwarting the "neo-totalitarianism" that Xi is evidently building. Yet, as Shambaugh noted, the Orwellian machinations of the CCP can only succeed if there is at least acquiescence from the people. The ultimate question of the longevity of a near-totalitarian regime, writes the Sinologist, is "would society stand for it?" Shambaugh had this to say about the dire state–society relationship in China:

> With 700 million citizens connected to the Internet and social media such as WeChat, would they stand to have their communications cut off and shut down? Millions of Chinese now have passports – might they just leave the country under such circumstances? Would citizens go back to monitoring each other or tolerating secret police among them? One does not know the answers to these questions until the time comes – but it is no longer 1989 in China.[125]

Benefitting from the relative, but as yet very limited, liberalization of freedom of expression in the wake of the Trump challenge, Peking University sociologist Zheng Yefu raised a stir with an article in early 2019 calling upon the CCP to call it quits from Chinese politics. In view of the disastrous failure of political reform in recent decades, wrote Zheng, "the only thing that CCP leaders can do – which could be [worth being] recorded in history books – is to lead the party to fade out of the historical stage" with minimal social shocks. Zheng was careful to note that people who have lived under the yoke of the CCP deserve some responsibility for the morass. "The nature of rulers is determined by the kind of citizens who are being ruled," he said. The sociologist noted, however, that it would be futile to expect the rulers to voluntarily give up power. "If we do not make calls [for change], do not put pressure [on the authorities], then we should not, and do not deserve to have the end of this authoritarian political system," he contended.[126] The most useful contribution of intellectuals, rights attorneys, church campaigners and NGO activists may be to convince the general populace that it is in their best interest to say "no" to China's fast-deteriorating political system, and, should cataclysmic eruptions occur owing to domestic- or foreign-policy crises, give support to the forces of liberalization and change.

Notes

1   Cited in David Brunnstrom and Matt Spetalnick, "Pence accuses China of 'malign' campaign to undermine Trump," Reuters, October 4, 2018, www.reuters.com/a rticle/us-usa-china-pence/pence-accuses-china-of-malign-campaign-to-undermine-trump-idUSKCN1ME209. See also Kate O'Keeffe, "Scholars warn of Chinese influence operations in U.S.," Wall Street Journal, November 28, 2018, www.wsj.com/articles/scholars-warn-of-chinese-influence-operations-in-u-s-1543449490

2   See Robert Delaney, "Pompeo promises US will meet China's strategies with 'strong and vigorous response,'" South China Morning Post, October 27, 2018, www.scmp.com/news/china/diplomacy/article/2170463/mike-pompeo-promises-us-will-meet-chinas-strategies-strong-and

3   Cited in Tara Patel, "French are target of widespread spying by Chinese, Figaro says," Bloomberg, October 23, 2018, www.bloomberg.com/news/articles/2018-10-23/french-are-target-of-widespread-spying-by-chinese-figaro-says. See also Rob Schmit, "Australia and New Zealand are ground zero for Chinese influence," October 2, 2018, www.npr.org/2018/10/02/627249909/australia-and-new-zealand-are-ground-zero-for-chinese-influence. For a discussion of the work of the Chinese United Front in promoting the country's influence overseas, see, for example, "China's overseas United Front work: background and implications for the U.S.," U.S.–China Economic and Security Review Commission, August 24, 2018, www.uscc.gov/Research/china%E2%80%99s-overseas-united-front-work-background-and-implications-united-states

4   For a discussion of alleged PRC espionage activities in Lithuania, see, for example, "Intelligence warns of China's increasingly aggressive spying in Lithuania," The Baltic Times, February 5, 2019, www.baltictimes.com/intelligence_warns_of_china_s_increa singly_aggressive_spying_in_lithuania/. See also "Chinese intelligence hacked Norwegian software firm Visma to steal client secrets, investigators say," Reuters, February 7, 2019, www.scmp.com/news/world/europe/article/2185218/chinese-intelligen ce-hacked-norwegian-software-firm-visma-steal

5 Cited in Pew Research Center, "Most prefer that U.S., not China, be the world's leading power," October 1, 2018, www.pewglobal.org/2018/10/01/most-prefer-tha t-u-s-not-china-be-the-worlds-leading-power/

6 For a discussion of Xi's "China's wisdom and blueprint," see Dong Genhong, "On the basic characteristics of China's wisdom," *Study Times* (Beijing), November 8, 2017, http://theory.people.com.cn/n1/2017/1108/c40531-29633586.html. See also Li Junru, "China's wisdom and the China blueprint," *Beijing Daily*, September 18, 2017, www.china.com.cn/opinion/theory/2017-09/18/content_41604978.htm

7 For an official view of how the new media can be used in the service of *dawaixuan*, see, for example, "The new situation of the new media serving the purpose of a multi-dimensional *dawaixuan*," Anhuinews.com (Anhui), August 13, 2018, http://fbh. anhuinews.com/system/2018/08/13/007937097.shtml

8 See Jackson Kwok, "Confucius Institutes and the challenge of academic freedom," Lowy Institute, May 11, 1018, www.lowyinstitute.org/the-interpreter/con fucius-institutes-and-challenge-academic-freedom. For a discussion of the overseas propaganda activities of the CCP, see, for example, Anne-Marie Brady, "'The new (old) model': the CCP propaganda system under Jiang, Hu and Xi," in Willy Lam, ed., *Routledge Handbook of the Chinese Communist Party*, London: Routledge, 2018, pp. 165–180.

9 For a discussion of Duterte's China policy, see, for example, Richard Javad Heydarian, "Duterte to China: 'If you want, just make us a province,'" *Asia Times*, February 22, 2018, https://nationalinterest.org/blog/the-buzz/duterte-china-if-you-want-just-ma ke-us-province-24599

10 See, for example, Manuel Mogato, "ASEAN communique stalls amid disagreement on South China Sea stance," Reuters, August 5, 2018, www.reuters.com/article/us-a sean-philippines/asean-communique-stalls-amid-disagreement-on-south-china-sea-sta nce-idUSKBN1AL05R

11 For a discussion of the division between the U.S. and Western Europe on the issue of joining the AIIB, see, for example, Nicholas Watt, Paul Lewis and Tania Branigan, "U.S. anger at Britain joining Chinese-led investment bank AIIB," *The Guardian*, March 13, 2015, www.theguardian.com/us-news/2015/mar/13/white-house-pointe dly-asks-uk-to-use-its-voice-as-part-of-chinese-led-bank

12 Some of the loans Beijing has made to developing countries are denominated in the Chinese currency. There are even reports Beijing wants to set the example of buying petroleum in renminbi, not dollars, which has been the only world-recognized trans- action currency for oil and gas. See David Dollar and Samantha Gross, "China's cur- rency displacing the dollar in global oil trade? Don't count on it," Brookings Institution, April 19, 2018, www.brookings.edu/blog/order-from-chaos/2018/04/19/ chinas-currency-displacing-the-dollar-in-global-oil-trade-dont-count-on-it/

13 For an assessment of the Made in China 2025 program, see, for example, Jost Wüb- beke, Mirjam Meissner and Max J. Zenglein, "Made in China 2025: the making of a high-tech superpower and consequences for industrial countries," Mercator Institute for China Studies, Berlin, No. 2, December 2016, www.merics.org/sites/default/files/ 2017-09/MPOC_No.2_MadeinChina2025.pdf. See also "Ministry releases Made in China funding plan," *China Daily*, October 12, 2017, www.chinadaily.com.cn/busi ness/2017-10/12/content_33165546.htm

14 For a study of how the Chinese police-state system has been partly built by technology provided by Western countries, see, for example, Racqueal Legerwood, "U.S. firms' sales to China's police: sales may not break the law – but are they defensible?" Human Rights Watch, August 6, 2018, www.hrw.org/news/2018/08/06/us-firms-sales-china s-police. See also Joel Gehrke, "Marco Rubio: Google, other US companies are aiding Chinese surveillance," *Washington Examiner*, July 26, 2018, www.washingtonexaminer. com/policy/defense-national-security/marco-rubio-google-other-us-companies-are-a iding-chinese-surveillance

15   See Victoria Craw, "China's Belt and Road Initiative could redraw the map on global trade," News.com.au, July 23, 2017, www.news.com.au/finance/economy/world-economy/chinas-belt-and-road-initiative-could-redraw-the-map-on-global-trade/news-story/eb752b6332e24ea219e36d0f16742463. See also Jonathan Hillman, "How big is China's Belt and Road?" CSIS.org, April 3, 2018, www.csis.org/analysis/how-big-chinas-belt-and-road

16   For a discussion of China's growing military bases, including those along the BRI, see, for example, David Tweed and Adrian Leung, "China is making a bold military power play," Bloomberg, March 7, 2018, www.bloomberg.com/graphics/2018-china-navy-bases/

17   See Victoria Breeze and Nathan Moore, "China has overtaken the U.S. and U.K. as the top destination for anglophone African students," Qz.china.com, June 30, 2017, https://qz.com/africa/1017926/china-has-overtaken-the-us-and-uk-as-the-top-destination-for-anglophone-african-students/. See also "The rise of digital authoritarianism: freedom on the net 2018," Freedom House, New York, October 2018, https://freedomhouse.org/sites/default/files/FOTN_2018_Final%20Booklet_11_1_2018.pdf

18   For a study of the concept of "community of common destiny," see, for example, Denghua Zhang, "The concept of 'community of common destiny' in China's diplomacy: meaning, motives and implications," *Asia and the Pacific Policy Studies*, April 16, 2018, https://onlinelibrary.wiley.com/doi/full/10.1002/app5.231. For an explication of Xi's *datong* concept, see, for example, Xinhua News Agency commentator, "The commonality of the world, the world as a family: on how to put together a community of common destiny for mankind," Xinhua News Agency, January 15, 2017, www.xinhuanet.com//politics/2017-01/15/c_1120313455.htm. See also Willy Lam, "Xi reasserts control over PRC politics as trade war deepens," *China Brief*, Jamestown Foundation, September 19, 2018, https://jamestown.org/program/xi-reasserts-control-over-prc-politics-as-trade-war-deepens/

19   Cited in Andrew Nathan, "China's challenge," in Larry Diamond, Marc F. Plattner and Christopher Walker, eds., *Authoritarianism Goes Global*, Baltimore, MD: Johns Hopkins University Press, 2016, pp. 34–37.

20   Cited in Shannon Tiezzi, "The state of the union: Obama's challenge to China," *The Diplomat*, January 22, 2015, https://thediplomat.com/2015/01/the-state-of-the-union-obamas-challenge-to-china/

21   For a Chinese view on the escalation of defense relations between the U.S. and a host of Asian countries, see Yao Jianing, "Watch out: US pushes forward 'Indo-Pacific strategy' to contain China," China Military Online, August 14, 2018, http://eng.chinamil.com.cn/view/2018-08/14/content_9252085.htm. See also "Chinese media mocks Australia, Japan, India, Vietnam alliance," *Asia Times*, June 7, 2017, www.atimes.com/article/beijing-mocks-australia-japan-india-vietnam-alliance/

22   For a discussion of the significance of the "Quad," see, for example, Ankit Panda, "US, Japan, India, and Australia hold senior official-level quadrilateral meeting in Singapore," *The Diplomat*, June 30, 2018, https://thediplomat.com/2018/06/us-japan-india-and-australia-hold-senior-official-level-quadrilateral-meeting-in-singapore/. See also "Australia, U.S., India and Japan in talks to establish Belt and Road alternative: report," Reuters, February 19, 2018, www.reuters.com/article/us-china-beltandroad-quad/australia-u-s-india-and-japan-in-talks-to-establish-belt-and-road-alternative-report-idUSKCN1G20WG

23   See Nicola Smith, "UK sends 'strongest of signals' on free navigation in South China Sea," *The Telegraph*, June 3, 2018, www.telegraph.co.uk/news/2018/06/03/uk-sends-strongest-signals-free-navigation-south-china-sea/

24   For a discussion of Trump's "Taiwan card," see, for example, Phil Stewart and Idrees Ali, "Exclusive: U.S. weighs new warship passage through Taiwan Strait," Reuters, October 20, 2018, www.reuters.com/article/us-usa-china-taiwan-exclusive/exclusive-u-s-weighs-new-warship-passage-through-taiwan-strait-idUSKCN1MU04F

25   Cited in "Pompeo announces $113 million in new US initiatives in 'Indo-Pacific'," CNBC.com, July 30, www.cnbc.com/2018/07/30/pompeo-to-announce-initiatives-focusing-on-digital-economy-energy-an.html

26   See Lesley Wroughton and David Brunnstrom, "Wary of China's rise, Pompeo announced U.S. initiatives in emerging Asia," Reuters, July 30, 2018, www.reuters.com/article/us-usa-trade/wary-of-chinas-rise-pompeo-announces-us-initiatives-in-emerging-asia-idUSKBN1KK0V5. See also, "BRI a made in China, made for China initiative: US official," Press Trust of India, July 30, 2018, https://economictimes.indiatimes.com/news/international/world-news/bri-a-made-in-china-made-for-china-initiative-us-official/articleshow/65195619.cms

27   See "EU ambassadors band together against Silk Road," Handelsblatt.com, April 17, 2018, https://global.handelsblatt.com/politics/eu-ambassadors-beijing-china-silk-road-912258

28   For a discussion of "debt trap diplomacy" in the case in Sri Lanka, see, for example, Erin Cook, "South Pacific waking to China's 'debt-trap' diplomacy," *Asia Times*, September 7, 2018, www.atimes.com/article/south-pacific-waking-to-chinas-debt-trap-diplomacy/

29   For a discussion of Djibouti and other countries falling victim to the "debt trap policy," see, for example, Tim Fernholz, "Eight countries in danger of falling into China's 'debt trap'," Quarz.com, March 8, 2018 https://qz.com/1223768/china-debt-trap-these-eight-countries-are-in-danger-of-debt-overloads-from-chinas-belt-and-road-plans/

30   See Ding Xueliang, "The frequent counterattack against China by foreign countries is not an act of impulse," *Financial Times*, Chinese edition, April 24, 2018, http://tjapi.xinhuaapp.com/News/NewsDetail?id=346195&appId=317&projectId=51&from=timeline&isappinstalled=0

31   Cited in Frank Tang, "As trade war rages on, China looks inward to keep economy rolling," *South China Morning Post*, October 1, 2018, www.scmp.com/economy/china-economy/article/2166425/trade-war-rages-beijing-looks-inward-keep-economy-rolling

32   For a discussion of the multidimensional nature of the China–U.S. confrontation, see, for example, "Hong Kong scholar: even if the trade war is resolved, America's containment policy still exists," *Ming Pao* (Hong Kong), November 11, 2018, http://premium.mingpao.com/cfm/Content_News.cfm?Channel=ca&Path=33702443681/cab2.cfm

33   See Ana Swanson, "U.S. and China expand trade war as Beijing matches Trump's tariffs," *New York Times*, June 15, 2018, www.nytimes.com/2018/06/15/us/politics/us-china-tariffs-trade.html

34   Cited in Toluse Olorunnipa, "Trump says China no longer on quick path to be bigger than U.S.," Bloomberg, August 22, 2018, www.bloomberg.com/news/articles/2018-08-22/trump-says-china-no-longer-on-quick-path-to-be-bigger-than-u-s. See also *2017 Report to Congress On China's WTO Compliance*, United States Trade Representative Office, January 2018, https://ustr.gov/sites/default/files/files/Press/Reports/China%202017%20WTO%20Report.pdf/

35   For a discussion of the military use of 5G technology, see "Why 5G, a battleground for the U.S. and China, is also a fight for military supremacy," *South China Morning Post*, January 31, 2019, www.scmp.com/news/china/military/article/2184493/why-5g-battleground-us-and-china-also-fight-military-supremacy

36   See Deng Yuwen, "The U.S. sees the trade war as a tactic to contain China. So does Beijing," *South China Morning Post*, July 4, 2018, www.scmp.com/comment/insight-opinion/united-states/article/2153587/us-sees-trade-war-tactic-contain-china-so-does

37   See Shen Yan, "Expert: we must prevent the China–U.S. trade war from exacerbating deep-seated contradictions piling up in China," Cn.Reuters.com, July 4, 2018, https://cn.reuters.com/article/expert-interview-china-conflicts-0704-we-idCNKBS1JU0GX

38   Cited in "Is the battle over computer chips a harbinger for 'economic cold war'?" BBC, Chinese edition, April 24, 2018, www.bbc.com/zhongwen/trad/business-43858521

39 Cited in Robert Delaney, "Donald Trump to hit US$50 billion of Chinese imports with 25 per cent tariffs and restrict investment in US hi-tech industries," *South China Morning Post*, May 30, 2018, www.scmp.com/news/china/policies-politics/article/2148346/donald-trump-unveil-curbs-chinese-tech-investment-us

40 Cited in Joel Gehrke, "Marco Rubio: China tries hijacking US tech for 'cyber battles of the future,'" *Washington Examiner*, April 17, 2018, www.washingtonexaminer.com/policy/defense-national-security/marco-rubio-china-tries-hijacking-us-tech-for-cyber-battles-of-the-future. See also Todd Shields, "Huawei and ZTE targeted while security ban advances at U.S. FCC," Bloomberg, April 17, 2018, www.bloomberg.com/news/articles/2018-04-17/huawei-zte-targeted-as-security-ban-advances-at-u-s-fcc

41 For a discussion of the implications of the detention of Sabrina Meng, see, for example, Bob Bryan, "Chinese tech giant Huawei's CFO proves Trump's trade war is 'escalating to a new level,'" Businessinsider.com, December 6, 2018, www.businessinsider.com/us-china-trade-war-huawei-cfo-arrest-sabrina-wanzhou-trump-tariffs-2018-12. See also Robin Emmott, "U.S. warns European allies not to use Chinese gear for 5G networks," Reuters, February 6, 2019, www.reuters.com/article/us-usa-china-huawei-tech-eu/u-s-warns-european-allies-not-to-use-chinese-gear-for-5g-networks-idUSKCN1PU1TG

42 Cited in "Poland calls for 'joint' EU–Nato stance on Huawei after spying arrest," Reuters, January 13, 2019, www.theguardian.com/world/2019/jan/12/huawei-sacks-chinese-worker-accused-of-spying-in-poland-wang-weijing

43 For a discussion of tighter control over Chinese firms' acquisition of Western European tech companies, see, for example, Zhang Danhong, "Exit the dragon? Chinese investment in Germany," Deutsche Welle, February 5, 2018, www.dw.com/en/exit-the-dragon-chinese-investment-in-germany/a-42457712. See also, "Macron wants limits on Chinese investments, takeovers in Europe's strategic industries," Reuters, July 23, 2018, www.scmp.com/business/companies/article/2099613/macron-wants-limits-chinese-investments-takeovers-europes

44 Cited in "Pompeo denounces China's treatment of Uyghur, Christian minorities," AFP, September 22, 2018, www.rferl.org/a/china-muslim-uyghur-christians-pompeo-assails-treatment/29503526.html

45 See "In China, Angela Merkel meets wife of detained human rights lawyer," Radio Free Asia, May 25, 2018, www.rfa.org/english/news/china/merkel-lawyers-05252018134454.html. See also, "UK foreign secretary met human rights figures on China visit," AFP, July 31, 2018, www.dailymail.co.uk/wires/afp/article-6010271/UK-foreign-secretary-met-human-rights-figures-China-visit.html

46 Cited in "How China's economic aggression threatens the technologies and intellectual property of the United States and the world," White House Office of Trade and Manufacturing Policy, The White House, June 18, 2018, www.whitehouse.gov/wp-content/uploads/2018/06/FINAL-China-Technology-Report-6.18.18-PDF.pdf

47 For a discussion of the diminishing returns for China's soft power push, see, for example, Willy Lam, "Hard edges of China's soft power projection meeting increasing resistance," *China Brief*, Jamestown Foundation, July 10, 2018, https://jamestown.org/program/hard-edges-of-chinas-soft-power-projection-meeting-increasing-resistance/

48 Cited in Jeffrey Gil, "Has Beijing abandoned its soft power strategy?" *Asia Times*, March 3, 2018, www.atimes.com/beijing-abandoned-soft-power-strategy/

49 For a discussion of China's soft power projection, see, for example, Editorial, "Soft power is about influence not control," *South China Morning Post*, July 31, 2017, www.scmp.com/comment/insight-opinion/article/2104686/soft-power-about-influence-not-control. See also Joseph S. Nye, "China's soft and sharp power," Project Syndicate, January 4, 2018, www.project-syndicate.org/commentary/china-soft-and-sharp-power-by-joseph-s--nye-2018-01?barrier=accesspaylog

50 Cited in Betsy Woodruff and Julia Arciga, "FBI director's shock claim: Chinese students are a potential threat," *The Daily Beast*, February 13, 2018 www.thedailybeast.com/fbi-directors-shock-claim-chinese-students-are-a-potential-threat; The Associated

Press, "FBI chief says Chinese operatives have infiltrated scores of 'naive' US universities," February 14, 2018, www.scmp.com/news/world/united-states-canada/a rticle/2133274/fbi-chief-says-chinese-operatives-have-infiltrated

51 See Elizabeth Redden, "U.S. to limit visa length for some Chinese students," Insidehighered.com, May 30, 2018, www.insidehighered.com/quicktakes/2018/05/30/us-limit-visa-length-some-chinese-students

52 See Josh Rogan, "University rejects Chinese Communist Party-linked influence efforts on campus," *Washington Post*, January 14, 2018, www.washingtonpost.com/opinions/globa l-opinions/university-rejects-chinese-communist-party-linked-influence-efforts-on-camp us/2018/01/14/c454b54e-f7de-11e7-beb6-c8d48830c54d_story.html?utm_term=. ebdcb9d3098a. See also, "A state university in the U.S. rejects donation from foundation founded by Tung Chee-hwa," Radio Free Asia, January 19, 2018, www.rfa.org/manda rin/Xinwen/6-01192018122612.html

53 Cited in Hai Yan, "Congress asks for investigation of research cooperation efforts between Huawei and American universities," Voice of America, Chinese edition, June 20, 2018, www.voachinese.com/a/news-congress-asks-to-investigate-huawei-resea rch-programs-in-us-20180620/4446947.html

54 For a discussion of Australia's effort to stop Chinese infiltration and espionage, see, for example, Nick McKenzie, Chris Uhlmann, Richard Baker and Daniel Flitton, "ASIO warns parties that taking China cash could compromise Australia," *Sydney Morning Herald*, June 6, 2017, www.smh.com.au/national/asio-warns-parties-that-taking-china -cash-could-compromise-australia-20170602-gwjc8t.html. See also Abc.net.au, "ASIO warns parties that taking China cash could compromise Australia," June 5, 2017, www.abc.net.au/news/2017-06-05/asio-china-spy-raid/8589094

55 See Tara Francis Chan, "How China tried to shut down Australian media coverage of its debt-trap diplomacy in the Pacific," Businessinsider.com, Jun. 21, 2018, www.busi nessinsider.com/how-china-censors-media-it-disagrees-with-australia-2018-6; Radio Free Asia, "Chinese embassy tries to stop Australian media from exposing Chinese actions in the South Pacific," June 20, 2018, www.rfa.org/cantonese/news/australia -media-06202018084509.html

56 Cited in "Overhaul for foreign interference laws in bipartisan deal," *Sydney Morning Herald*, June 7, 2018, www.smh.com.au/politics/federal/overhaul-for-foreign-interfer ence-laws-in-bipartisan-deal-20180607-p4zk29.html

57 For a discussion of Chinese state agents allegedly trying to intimate Professor Brady, see, for example, Phil Pennington, "Professor blames break-in on Chinese spies," Radio New Zealand, February 16, 2018, www.radionz.co.nz/news/national/350589/profes sor-blames-break-in-on-chinese-spies. See also Charlotte Graham-McLay, "Fingers point to China after break-ins target New Zealand professor," *New York Times*, September 21, 2018, www.nytimes.com/2018/09/21/world/asia/new-zealand-break-ins-a cademic.html?smprod=nytcore-ipad&smid=nytcore-ipad-share

58 See Wang Yun, "Gui Minhai is again led away by police in full sight of Swedish diplomats," Radio Free Asia, January 22, 2018, www.rfa.org/mandarin/yataibaodao/ renquanfazhi/wy-01222018125931.html. See also Fred Hiatt, "Why is China afraid of this man?" *Washington Post*, July 29, 2018, www.washingtonpost.com/opinions/ global-opinions/china-is-trying-to-muzzle-gui-minhai-these-poems-tell-his-story/2018/ 07/29/c75b18dc-91bc-11e8-b769-e3fff17f0689_story.html?utm_term=.d945b9b1c341

59 Cited in Eleanor Swift, "China's big bet on soft power," Council on Foreign Relations, February 9, 2018, www.cfr.org/badckgrounder/chinas-big-bet-soft-power

60 Cited in Chris Buckley, "As China's woes mount, Xi Jinping faces rare rebuke at home," *New York Times*, July 31, 2018, www.nytimes.com/2018/07/31/world/asia/ xi-jinping-internal-dissent.html

61 Cited in Willy Lam, "West concerned by Xi Jinping's aggressive tactics," Asianews.it, May 10, 2018, www.asianews.it/news-en/West-concerned-by-Xi-Jinpings-aggressi ve-tactics-43849.html

62 Cited in "Editorial: will China and the U.S. confront each other strategically and affect the next generation?" *Global Times*, August 1, 2018, http://opinion.huanqiu.com/editorial/2018-08/12618314.html

63 See Shi Yinhong, "China must guard against strategic overdraft," Phoenix Television, October 4, 2016, www.360doc.com/content/16/1004/12/6150202_595692619.shtml. See also Cai Yongjia, "Professor Shi Yinhong: the risk of China's 'strategic overdraft' has increased," *Lianhe Zaobao* (Singapore), September 21, 2016, www.zaobao.com/znews/greater-china/story20160921-668655

64 Cited in Liu Feng, "Strategic overdraft – an analysis of a concept," *Theoretical Research*, June 16, 2017, www.sohu.com/a/149461660_618422

65 Cited in "Scholar says article by the State Assets Supervision and Administration Commission reflects a division of views within the top leadership," I-Cable News, Hong Kong, April 23, 2018, http://cablenews.i-Cable.com/ci/videopage/news/525757/%E5%8D%B3%E6%99%82%E6%96%B0%E8%81%9E/%E5%9C%8B%E8%B3%87%E5%A7%94%E5%A0%B1%E5%91%8A%E6%89%B9%E4%B8%AD%E8%88%88%E6%87%89%E5%B0%8D%E6%84%9A%E8%A0%A2%E8%A2%AB%E5%8B%95

66 Cited in Nectar Gan, "Economist Zhang Weiying slams 'China model' that 'inevitably leads to confrontation with the West,'" *South China Morning Post*, October 26, 2018, www.scmp.com/news/china/politics/article/2170447/economist-slams-china-model-inevitably-leads-confrontation-west#comments

67 For a discussion of the Xu Zhangrun phenomenon, see, for example, Lily Kuo, "Cracks appear in 'invincible' Xi Jinping's authority over China," *The Guardian*, August 4, 2018, https://www.theguardian.com/world/2018/aug/04/cracks-appear-in-invincible-xi-jinpings-authority-over-china. See also, "Chinese commentators take aim at Xi Jinping's unlimited presidency, lack of reform," Radio Free Asia, August 1, 2018, https://www.rfa.org/english/news/china/commentators-08012018114312.html

68 There were widespread reports that Cai was forced to recant her anti-Xi remarks. See "Cai Xia: his cognitive disorder and the risk for a big revolution hitting China," 2newcenturynet.blogspot, March 20, 2018, http://2newcenturynet.blogspot.com/2018/03/blog-post_249.html. For a discussion of Beijing's efforts to muzzle the views of Cai Xia and other Central Party School academics, see, for example, Nectar Gan, "China's President Xi Jinping warns Communist Party schools against 'Western capitalist' values," *South China Morning Post*, May 1, 2018, www.scmp.com/news/china/policies-politics/article/1940396/chinas-president-xi-jinping-warns-communist-party

69 Cited in Jia Ao, "Financial scholar: China's 'Minsky moment' has quietly arrived," Radio Free Asia, June 26, 2018. www.rfa.org/mandarin/yataibaodao/jingmao/hc-06262018104354.html. See also He Jiangbing, "Cracks have appeared in the Chinese bubble; Xi Jinping is not sure what to do," Boxun.com, July 4, 2018, www.boxun.com/news/gb/pubvp/2018/07/201807040957.shtml

70 See Zi Zhongyun, "Peace before the storm: the China–U.S. trade war will usher in the ultimate contention," China50plus.com, June 18, 2018, www.china50plus.com/%E8%B5%84%E4%B8%AD%E7%AD%A0%EF%BD%9C%E6%9A%B4%E9%A3%8E%E9%9B%A8%E5%89%8D%E7%9A%84%E5%AE%81%E9%9D%99%EF%BC%8C%E4%B8%AD%E7%BE%8E%E8%B4%B8%E6%98%93%E6%88%98%E5%8D%B3%E5%B0%86%E8%BF%8E%E6%9D%A5%E7%BB%88/?from=timeline&isappinstalled=0

71 Cited in Tyler Durden, "China is the 'greatest long-term strategic threat' to US, top Pacific commander tells Congress," Zerohedge.com, February 13, 2019, www.zerohedge.com/news/2019-02-13/china-greatest-long-term-strategic-threat-us-top-pacific-commander-tells-congress

72 For a discussion of the size of China's total social debt, see, for example, Martin Wolf, "China's debt threat: time to rein in the lending boom," *Financial Times*, July 25, 2018, www.ft.com/content/0c7ecae2-8cfb-11e8-bb8f-a6a2f7bca546. See also, "China tops the world in gross real estate value," *GBTimes* (Beijing), September 5, 2017, https://gbtimes.com/china-tops-world-gross-real-estate-value. See also Evelyn Cheng, "China central bank chief raises new worry in China: mortgage-driven household

debt," CNBC.com, October 23, 2017, www.cnbc.com/2017/10/23/china-central-ba nk-chief-new-worry-household-debt.html

73 For a discussion of the rationale behind Beijing boosting liquidity, see, for example, Kevin Yao and Fan Cheng, "China July new loans stronger than expected; money supply picks up," Reuters, August 13, 2018, www.reuters.com/article/us-china -economy-loans/china-july-new-loans-stronger-than-expected-money-supply-picks-up- idUSKBN1KY1C8. See also "China prepares for testing 2019 by freeing up US$210 billion in latest move to boost ailing economy," *South China Morning Post*, January 4, 2019, www.scmp.com/economy/china-economy/article/2180758/china-prepa res-testing-2019-freeing-us210-billion-latest-move. For a discussion of the efficacy of such moves, see, for example, He Jiangbing, "China needs structural reforms in both domestic and foreign policies," *Apple Daily*, January 21, 2019 https://hk.news. appledaily.com/local/daily/article/20190121/20595648

74 For a discussion of China's job losses due to the trade war, see, for example, He Huifeng, "Chinese firms start to cut jobs and move overseas as US trade war and rising costs start to bite," September 21, 2018, www.scmp.com/economy/china-economy/a rticle/2165000/chinese-firms-start-cut-jobs-and-move-overseas-us-trade-war

75 Cited in Minxin Pei, "Transition in China? More likely than you think," *Journal of Democracy*, Vol. 27, No. 4, October 2016, pp. 5–19.

76 See David Shambaugh, "The coming Chinese crack-up," *Wall Street Journal*, March 6, 2015, www.wsj.com/articles/the-coming-chinese-crack-up-1425659198

77 Minxin Pei, "Transition in China?" See also Minxin Pei, "China is losing the new cold war," *Project Syndicate*, September 5, 2018, www.project-syndicate.org/commenta ry/china-cold-war-us-competition-by-minxin-pei-2018-09?barrier=accesspaylog

78 See "Why a *duanyashi* ['precipitous'] collapse will not take place in China," Heqinglian net, June 27, 2017, http://heqinglian.net/2017/06/27/china-future/; www.voachi nese.com/a/china-enco-20170626/3917204.html

79 Minxin Pei, "Transition in China?" Author's email communication with Pei in August 2018.

80 Cited in He Qinglian, "China future: 'decaying without collapse,' which lies between 'strength' and 'collapse,'" VOA Chinese, May 13, 2015, www.voachinese.com/a/ heqinglian-20150312/2678502.html

81 Cited in Li Jing, "Netizens give new interpretations to Chairman Mao's 60 famous aphorisms," *People's Daily Online*, October 9, 2009, http://cpc.people.com.cn/GB/ 64093/64103/10164381.html

82 For a discussion of the possible attacks on Xi in mid-2018, see, for example, Willy Lam, "Xi's grip loosens amid trade war policy paralysis," *China Brief*, Jamestown Foundation, August 1, 2018, https://jamestown.org/program/xis-grip-on-author ity-loosens-amid-trade-war-policy-paralysis/

83 Cited in Xu Bo, "The undercurrents are making waves: who has stopped the Xi Jinping personality cult?" Voice of America, July 16, 2018, www.voachinese.com/a/ voaweishi-20180716-io-china-xi-personal-worship-comes-to-a-stoop/4484613.html; "Xinhua article attacking Hua Guofeng for conducting a personality cult has been excised," Radio Free Asia, July 12, 2018, www.rfa.org/mandarin/yataibaodao/ zhengzhi/ql1-07122018102402.html. See also Sun Jiaye, "Does Xi Jinping fear a coup while taking a trip abroad," *Ming Pao*, July 16, 2018, http://premium.mingpao. com/cfm/Content_News.cfm?Channel=ca&Path=67403591442/caq1_er.cfm

84 See, "Li Zhanshu has called for [giving Xi] the power to be the final arbiter, but few people have seconded Li," Radio French International Chinese Service, July 24, 2018, http://cn.rfi.fr/%E4%B8%AD%E5%9B%BD/20180724-%E6%A0%97%E6% 88%98%E4%B9%A6%E5%A4%A7%E5%96%8A%E5%AE%9A%E4%BA%8E%E4%B8% 80%E5%B0%8A-%E6%9A%82%E6%97%B6%E6%B2%A1%E5%87%A0%E4%BA% BA%E8%B7%9F%E8%BF%9B. See also Zong Wi, "Liu Qi chairs meeting of the Standing Committee of the Jiangxi Communist Party and plans economic work for

the second half of the year," *Jiangxi Daily*, July 24, 2018, http://jx.ifeng.com/a/20180724/6748252_0.shtml

85   In mid-August 2018, Xi called a meeting of the PLA top brass on the subject of "party construction within the army." The commander-in-chief called upon military officers to "uphold the party's absolute leadership over the army." Although Xi seemed to be asking top generals to rally around him as the unchallenged leader of the country's military and police forces, there was a surprising lack of senior generals joining the *biaotai* ("show your allegiance") ritual. PLA officers who went on the record seconding Xi's speech included, for example, Deputy Political Commissar of the Southern Theatre Command Bai Lu, Deputy Secretary of the PLA Commission for Disciplinary Inspection Yang Chengxi and the political commissar of an unspecified division of the Rockets Forces, Zhang Youxiang. These officers could not be called members of the top brass. See, "Xi Jinping takes part in the CMC's Conference on Party Construction and gives major speech," Xinhua News Agency, August 20, 2018, www.xinhuanet.com/mil/2018-08/20/c_129935640.htm. See also, "Firm up the army spirit by following the party; open up the new situation of strengthening the army and revitalizing the army: Xi Jinping's important talk at the CMC Conference on Party Construction has elicited strong reaction from the entire army and People's Armed Police," CCTV, August 23, 2018, http://tv.cctv.com/2018/08/23/VIDEtiVVMArj3S08Pptgiqtl180823.shtml

86   Cited in Robert Delaney, "Xi Jinping 'doesn't intend to follow through' on trade war talks and local Chinese officials are 'like mafioso dons,' says top Donald Trump adviser Larry Kudlow," *South China Morning Post*, July 19, 2018, www.scmp.com/news/china/article/2155890/xi-jinping-doesnt-intend-follow-through-trade-war-talks-says-top-donald. Also see Lin Feng, "Kudlow: the responsibility for the U.S. and China failing to reach a trade agreement lies with Xi Jinping," Voice of America, Chinese edition, July 19, 2018, www.voachinese.com/a/kudlow-2018-7-18/4488387.html#https%3A%2F%2Fwww.voachinese.com%2Fa%2Fkudlow-2018-7-18%2F4488387.html

87   For a discussion about possible divergence between the views of Liu He and Xi Jinping, see, for example, Lam, "Xi reasserts control." See also Frank Tang, "Xi Jinping's top economic adviser Liu He meets pro-market liberals as debate over China's future direction rages," *South China Morning Post*, September 17, 2018, www.scmp.com/economy/china-economy/article/2164534/xi-jinpings-top-economic-adviser-liu-he-meets-pro-market. For a discussion of the policy differences between Xi and Premier Li Keqiang, see, for example, Duncan DeAeth, "Trouble may be brewing for China's leaders at the CCP Beidaihe Summit," *Taiwan News*, August 1, 2018, www.taiwannews.com.tw/en/news/3496725

88   For a discussion of policy clashes within the Xi administration, see, for example, Elias Glenn, "China's policy debate deepens as trade war threatens economy," Reuters, July 18, 2018, www.scmp.com/news/china/article/2155890/xi-jinping-doesnt-intend-follow-through-trade-war-talks-says-top-donald. See also "Politics watch: China's Finance Ministry and Central Bank clash as economy worsens," Sinoinsider.com, July 18, 2018, https://sinoinsider.com/2018/07/politics-watch-chinas-finance-ministry-and-central-bank-clash-as-economy-worsens/; "Dissent surfaces as China begins to question if it's ready for trade war with U.S.," Bloomberg, June 26, 2018, www.japantimes.co.jp/news/2018/06/26/business/dissent-surfaces-china-begins-question-ready-trade-war-u-s/#.WzGv6tIzZRY

89   Cited in "The PBoC suddenly complains about lack of enthusiasm on the part of the Finance Ministry: what are the signals being emitted?" Finance.sina.com.cn, July 16, 2018, http://finance.sina.com.cn/china/2018-07-16/doc-ihfkffak2720011.shtml; See also Xu Zhong, "There's a big role for fiscal policy under current conditions," Wallstreetcn.com, July 13, 2018, https://wallstreetcn.com/articles/3359944

90   Cited in "The internal speech of Deng Pufang, the son of Deng Xiaoping, is revealed at a sensitive movement," DWNews.com (Beijing), October 23, 2018. http://news.dwnews.com/china/news/2018-10-23/60092785.html

91   Cited in Liu Yuan, "One should not trip over the same boulder twice: we should never make the mistake of the Cultural Revolution," *Hong Kong Economic Times*, August 20, 2018, https://china.hket.com/article/2141848/%E4%B8%80%E5%A1%8A%E7%9F%B3%E4%B8%8D%E8%83%BD%E7%B5%86%E5%85%A9%E6%AC%A1%20%E5%8A%89%E5%B0%91%E5%A5%87%E5%AD%90%EF%BC%9A%E5%8B%BF%E5%86%8D%E7%8A%AF%E6%96%87%E9%9D%A9%E9%8C%AF

92   For a discussion of Xi's much-worsened relationship with Hu Deping, see, for example, Gao Xin, "Blackening out Deng Pufang and bitterly criticizing Hu Deping: Xi Jinping masterminds counter-attack toward the 'rightist wing' of the princelings," Radio Free Asia, November 5, 2018, www.rfa.org/mandarin/zhuanlan/yehuazhongnanhai/gx-11052018154534.html. See also Edward Wong and Jonathan Ansfield, "Many urge next leader of China to liberalize," *New York Times*, October 21, 2012, www.nytimes.com/2012/10/22/world/asia/many-urge-chinas-next-leader-to-enact-reform.html

93   See Nectar Gan, "Xi says it's wrong to 'bad mouth' China's state firms … but country needs private sector as well," *South China Morning Post*, September 28, 2018, www.scmp.com/news/china/politics/article/2166108/xi-jinping-reassures-chinas-state-owned-enterprises-and-private. For a discussion of Xi's obsession with the Maoist philosophy of *ziligengsheng*, see, for example, "What's uppermost in Xi Jinping's mind as seen from his New Year address," Xinhua News Agency, January 1, 2019, www.xinhuanet.com/politics/xxjxs/2019-01/01/c_1123933810.htm

94   Cited in "Forty-six private firms listed on the Shanghai market have sold controlling stakes to state companies," JRJ.com, September 27, 2018 https://baijiahao.baidu.com/s?id=1612713127175242335&wfr=spider&for=pc. See also Yuan Li, "Private firms have made modern China, are they being forced to beat a retreat?" *New York Times*, Chinese edition, October 8, 2018, https://cn.nytimes.com/business/20181008/china-economy-private-enterprise/

95   Cited in "Stone Group President Duan Yongji: private firms are given titles and insignia, but not provisions and ammunition," Guancha.cn, September 17, 2018, www.guancha.cn/economy/2018_09_17_472343.shtml. See also "China Economy Forum of 50 conference: Liu He shows up, Wu Jinglian and others make speeches," Finance.sina.com, September 16, 2018, http://finance.sina.com.cn/zt_d/50ren20th/

96   Cited in "The son of Hu Yaobang wrote article to warn against the return of joint ventures between the public and private sectors," Radio Free Asia, September 28, 2018, www.rfa.org/cantonese/news/policy-09282018074341.html

97   Cited in An Delie, "More than 100 Chinese public intellectuals cry out for reform," Radio French International, December 30, 2018, http://cn.rfi.fr/%E4%B8%AD%E5%9B%BD/20181230-%E5%8E%86%E5%8F%B2%E5%85%B3%E5%A4%B4-%E4%B8%AD%E5%9B%BD%E7%99%BE%E4%BD%99%E5%85%AC%E5%85%B1%E7%9F%A5%E8%AF%86%E5%88%86%E5%AD%90%E4%B8%BA%E6%94%B9%E9%9D%A9%E5%A5%8B%E8%BA%AB%E5%91%90%E5%96%8A

98   Author's telephone and WeChat interview with Beijing-based Hu Jia, August 2018.

99   Cited in Zi Zhongxun, "Why do we need another emancipation?" Sohu.com, August 21, 2015, http://cul.sohu.com/20150821/n419462453.shtml. For a discussion of pro-democracy values spread during the Republican Period, see, for example, Edmund S.K. Fung, *In Search of Chinese Democracy: Civil Opposition in Nationalist China, 1929–1949*, Cambridge, MA: Cambridge University Press, 2000.

100 Author's interview with an LGBT activist in Guangzhou, September 2018.

101 Cited in "Xia Yeliang: the future of China depends on the civil society," Radio Free Asia, February 22, 2013, www.rfa.org/mandarin/yataibaodao/zhengzhi/ck1-02222013095620.html

102 Author's interview with Xia Yeliang, Washington, DC, October 2017.

103 Cited in Li Fan, "Retrogression: an analysis of the current 'late-stage totalitarianism' in China," *China Strategic Analysis*, No. 1, October 2016, http://zhanlve.org/?p=87

104 Based on author's interviews with dissidents in Beijing and those who have recently fled to the West. Overseas human rights watchdogs have demanded that dissidents in

China have the right to pay respects at the graveyards of victims of the June 4 massacre. See, for example, "Citizens have the right to hold memorial ceremonies for heroes of the June 4 massacre," Civil Rights and Livelihood Watch (U.S.), Msguancha.com, May 21, 2018, www.msguancha.com/a/lanmu2/2018/0521/17495.html

105 For a discussion of how dissidents felt about the death and burial of Liu Xiaobo, see, for example, Javier C. Hernandez, "In China, despair for cause of democracy after Nobel laureate's death," *New York Times*, July 20, 2017, www.nytimes.com/2017/07/20/world/asia/liu-xiaobo-nobel-peace-prize-china-democracy.html

106 Cited in "Hu Angang criticized as 'singing the praises of emperors' as one thousand people sign a petition for his dismissal from Tsinghua University," BBC Chinese Service, August 3, 2018, www.bbc.com/zhongwen/simp/chinese-news-45058201

107 Author's interview with a member of the Zion Church of Beijing, September 2018.

108 Ibid. See also, "China bans Zion, Beijing's biggest house church," Christianitytoday.com, September 10, 2018, www.christianitytoday.com/news/2018/september/china-bans-zion-beijing-house-church-surveillance-ezra-jin.html

109 Cited in "A joint statement by pastors: a declaration for the sake of the Christian faith (2nd edition, 116 pastors)," Early Rain Covenant Church Facebook, September 1, 2018, www.facebook.com/earlyraincovenantchurch/posts/279629072763966?__tn__=K-R

110 Cited in Diana Fu, *Mobilization with the Masses: Control and Contention in China*, Cambridge: Cambridge University Press, pp. 106–124. See also Diana Fu, "Disguised collective action in China," *Comparative Political Studies*, 2016, pp. 1–29, DOI: 10.1177/0010414015626437

111 For a discussion of the strategies of the feminists, see, for example, Diana Fu, "Why is Beijing afraid of Chinese feminists?" *Washington Post*, July 27, 2017, www.washingtonpost.com/news/monkey-cage/wp/2017/07/27/why-is-beijing-afraid-of-chinese-feminists/?utm_term=.4bc6ebdac213

112 Cited in "China cancels Ibsen's 'An Enemy of the People' amid ever-widening censorship," Radio Free Asia, September 13, 2018, www.rfa.org/english/news/china/censorship-09132018124920.html. See also Didi Tang, "China brings down the curtain on Ibsen play," *Sunday Times*, September 13, 2018, www.thetimes.co.uk/article/china-brings-down-the-curtain-on-ibsen-play-kf76gkgtc

113 Cited in "Audience who watch *Les Misérables* in Shanghai stays behind to chant 'Do you hear the people sing?'" *Hong Kong Economic Times*, September 26, 2018, https://china.hket.com/article/2168544/%E6%BB%AC%E6%BC%94%E3%80%8C%E5%AD%A4%E6%98%9F%E6%B7%9A%E3%80%8D%20%E8%A7%80%E7%9C%BE%E6%95%A3%E5%A0%B4%E4%B8%8D%E8%B5%B0%E5%90%88%E5%94%B1Do%20You%20Hear%20the%20People%20Sing%EF%BC%9F%EF%BC%88%E6%9C%89%E7%89%87%EF%BC%89

114 Author's interview with Guangdong-based labor organizer, August 2018.

115 Author's interview with Shenzhen-based labor activist, September 2018.

116 For a discussion of the Jasic labor incident, see, for example, Jenny Chan, "Shenzhen Jasic Technology: the birth of a worker–student coalition in China?" *Hong Kong Free Press*, September 1, 2018, www.hongkongfp.com/2018/09/01/shenzhen-jasic-technology-birth-worker-student-coalition-china/; "Riot police in China's Shenzhen detain 50 labor activists in dawn raid," Radio Free Asia, August 24, 2018, www.rfa.org/english/news/china/riot-police-in-chinas-shenzhen-detain-50-labor-activists-08242018114510.html; "Police have detained more than 50 people in effort to put an end to the labor movement in Jasic," *Ming Pao*, August 26, 2018, http://premium.mingpao.com/cfm/Content_News.cfm?Channel=ca&Path=33701979421/caa1.cfm

117 Cited in David Shambaugh, *China's Future*, Cambridge, MA: Polity Press, 2016, pp. 129–130.

118 For a discussion of the plight of the demobilized soldiers, see, for example, Chris Buckley, "Marching across China, army veterans join ranks of protesters," *New York Times*, June 25, 2018, www.nytimes.com/2018/06/25/world/asia/china-veterans-protests.html. See also "Veterans protest in Zhenjiang, Jiangsu Province, constituting a

grave resettlement problem for the Chinese government," BBC Chinese Service, June 27, 2018, www.bbc.com/zhongwen/simp/chinese-news-44614192

119 See Philip Wen and Ben Blanchard, "Chinese military veterans stage protests in central Beijing over pensions," Reuters, February 23, 2017, www.reuters.com/article/us-china-military/chinese-military-veterans-stage-protests-in-central-beijing-over-p ensions- idUSKBN1620G5

120 See, for example, Yujing Liu, "Investors left to rue losses as fraudulent Chinese P2P lenders collapse in tighter regulatory environment," *South China Morning Post*, July 19, 2018, www.scmp.com/business/companies/article/2155357/investors-left-rue-losses-fraudulent-chinese-p2p-lenders-collapse

121 See Ben Westcott and Yong Xiong, "Rare two-day protest over China vaccine scandal reveals public anger," CNN, July 31, 2018, https://edition.cnn.com/2018/07/31/asia/vaccine-protest-scandal-china-intl/index.html

122 Cited in Bill Chappell, "Chinese company's flawed vaccines draw anger and a criminal inquiry," NPR.org, July 23, 2018, www.npr.org/2018/07/23/631509868/chinese-companys-flawed-vaccines-draw-anger-and-a-criminal-inquiry

123 See "Chinese parents of vaccine victims protest, call for new law," Radio Free Asia, July 30, 2018, www.rfa.org/english/news/china/vaccine-scandal-07302018170458.html

124 See Zhang Kai, "My article 'We are all in the same boat' was tipped 1.4 million yuan in 17 hours," Renminbao.com, July 28, 2018, www.renminbao.com/rmb/articles/2018/7/28/67664.html. See also "Lawyer Zhang Kai: all in the same boat," *The Initium* (Hong Kong), September 28, 2018, https://theinitium.com/article/20180728-mainland-vaccine-zhangkai-1/

125 Shambaugh, *China's Future*, pp. 130–131.

126 Cited in An Delie, "Peking University professor Zheng Yefu urges the CCP to fade away with dignity," Radio France International, January 8, 2019, http://trad.cn.rfi.fr/%E4%B8%AD%E5%9C%8B/20190108-%E5%8C%97%E5%A4%A7%E6%95%99%E6%8E%88%E9%84%AD%E4%B9%9F%E5%A4%AB%E4%BF%83%E4%B8%AD%E5%85%B1%E9%AB%94%E9%9D%A2%E9%80%80%E5%A0%B4%E4%B8%94%E6%89%B9%E8%A9%95%E8%AE%80%E6%9B%B8%E4%BA%BA%E9%80%86%E4%BE%86%E9%A0%86%E5%8F%97%E4%BB%A4%E4%BA%BA%E5%88%AE%E7%9B%AE

INDEX